D0758839

COGNITION
and the
SYMBOLIC PROCESSES
Volume 2

Edited by

Walter B. Weimer
David S. Palermo
THE PENNSYLVANIA STATE UNIVERSITY

LAWRENCE ERLBAUM ASSOCIATES, PUBLISHERS

1982   Hillsdale, New Jersey

Lawrence Erlbaum Associates, Inc., Publishers
365 Broadway
Hillsdale, New Jersey 07642

Library of Congress Cataloging in Publication Data

Weimer, Walter B.
  Cognition and the symbolic processes.

  V. 2 has title: Cognition and symbolic processes.
  V. 2 is based on the second Pennsylvania State Univer-
sity of Conference on Cognition and the Symbolic Pro-
cesses held May 16–19, 1977.
  Includes bibliographies and index.
  1. Cognition.   2. Symbolism (Psychology)   I. Palermo,
David Stuart, 1929–   joint author.   II. Title.
BF311.W374   153.4   74-13834
ISBN 0-470-92550-7 (v.1)   AACR2
ISBN 0-89859-143-0 (v.2)

Printed in the United States of America

Both the editors and contributors to this volume were saddened to hear that our friend James J. Gibson passed away in December, 1979. Jimmy had an infectious sense of humor that complimented the clarity and originality of his intellect, and his constant smile and the twinkle in his eyes were present throughout our conference. We wish that he could have been present at many more such gatherings, but since that cannot be so the editors wish to dedicate this volume to the intellectual and personal memory of Jimmy Gibson.

Contents

Preface

This volume results from the second Pennsylvania State University Conference on Cognition and the Symbolic Processes held at Penn State's Conference
Center, May 16–19, 1977. Like the first conference, emphasis was directed
toward both current issues in theoretical and cognitive psychology and new
directions for fruitful theory and research. The general format took the form of a
major (or, better, focal) paper on a topic (generally, what is the relevance of area
X to current theory and research?), followed by critical commentary from a
discussant, and then a general discussion involving conference participants and
members of the audience. The major concern of all contributors is with the
construction of a psychology of the higher mental processes through the evaluation of and improvement upon past efforts, as well as the exploration of related
areas or disciplines for relevant new ideas. The contributors to this volume share
in common the rejection of not only behavioristic and associationistic approaches
but also the sensory information-processing model that earlier dominated and (by
weight of numbers of adherents and publications) indeed still dominates cognitive psychology. Beyond that, there is considerable divergence of opinion expressed in the pages that follow. Perhaps the most frequently debated issue
concerns the nature and adequacy of the Gibsonian approach to perception and its
relevance to cognition: The participants tend to polarize readily into defense and
elaboration of Gibson's ideas or into criticism and rejection of one or more
Gibsonian tenets. Although unintended, that result is not undesirable—the issues
in the debate are sharpened and clarified in the process.

Some other unintended occurrences must be acknowledged at the outset.
Although the chapters of this volume result from the conference, most were
presented in rough-draft form. The chapter by Proffitt and Halwes (Chap. 14, not

presented at the conference) is included because it relates to the work of Hayek (and, to a lesser extent, Gibson). James J. Gibson himself, although present at the conference, is not represented by a chapter. The major reasons for this are, first, that Gibson presented a chapter from his then in-press book, *An Ecological Approach to Visual Perception,* and it would be redundant to reprint it here; second is the extreme length of the discussion chapter (Chap. 10) on Gibson's views prepared by Shaw, Turvey, and Mace. Following the old saw that the best laid plans of mice and conference organizers often go astray, several originally scheduled participants were unable (at the last minute, of course) to attend. This forced John Macnamara, originally a discussant, to present a major paper (Chap. 4) with no discussant. Our press gangs recruited James E. Martin to present the essentials of his recent research to fill the remainder of that conference session, and his chapter (Chap. 6) likewise has no discussant in the volume. Weimer contributed an earlier unpublished paper to the conference notebooks, chiefly to provide material for discussion in the event that preliminary copies of other papers were delayed or unavailable. That paper was not intended for publication here, but Pribram, instead of contributing a substantive area chapter, delivered a summary of the conference that discussed Weimer's paper. Thus rather than reference it elsewhere, Weimer's paper (originally intended as a successor to the historical theme article, "Psycholinguistics and Plato's Paradoxes of the *Meno*") has become Chapter 16. Mortimer Mishkin commented upon Pribram at the conference, arguing that Pribram's incorporation of holographic modeling of brain function results in an account that is not constructive enough. Unfortunately, when faced with the task of constructing a new and independent chapter, Mishkin decided that his work load did not permit the effort, with the result that his views are not included in the volume.

The conference was made possible through the support of the Pennsylvania State University, the College of Liberal Arts, the Institute for Arts and Humanistic Studies, the Department of Psychology, and Lawrence Erlbaum Associates. As in the past, royalties from the sale of this volume will partially fund future conferences. The editors would like to thank Doris MacKenzie and W. L. Wadlington for aid in taping and partially transcribing the proceedings.

Walter B. Weimer
David S. Palermo

1 Observational Perspective and Descriptive Level in Perceiving and Acting

Carol A. Fowler
Dartmouth College and Haskins Laboratories
and
Michael T. Turvey
University of Connecticut and Haskins Laboratories

The perspective that an observer takes on a system sets limits on his or her possibility for understanding its workings, and hence the individual's explanations of them. Investigations of these limits, typically with reference to the scientist as observer (e.g., Fodor, 1975; Kauffman, 1976; Medawar, 1974; Pattee, 1970; Polanyi, 1968; Putnam, 1973; Wimsatt, 1976), suggest that they have to do in part with the perceptual systems or other measuring devices at an observer's disposal. In addition, and crucially, the limits on explanation and understanding relate to the tiered character of the systems that the observer studies (Pattee, 1970; Polanyi, 1968). Understanding and explanation are possible only if the measuring devices intercept appropriate levels of a system's organization.

Of course, scientists are only special cases among the larger class of observers, and many of the philosophers' concerns with respect to observational perspective and understanding apply to any observer—scientist or not. Beyond the realm of scientific observation, the following are particularly applicable: The nature of observational information extracted from an object is contingent upon perspective; perspective constrains understanding and explanation; and it does so partly because of the tiered nature of the observed world. These all have implications for the way in which the character of a scientist's selected investigatory problem must dictate how it is to be investigated.

The development within cognitive psychology of an ecological attitude toward investigation and theory may be ascribed in substantial part to a set of concerns similar to those just noted, but in primary reference to observers who are the perceiver/actor subjects of investigation. In particular, concerns of this type occupy a central location in the theory of direct perception (Gibson, 1966, 1977;

1

Mace, 1977) and in the developing and complementary theory of action (Fitch & Turvey, 1978; Fowler & Turvey, 1978; Turvey, 1977; Turvey, Shaw, & Mace, 1978).

Out aim is to examine these concerns with observational perspective and explanation and to underscore their significance for understanding the informational and practical relationship of an individual to his or her environment. We first consider the scientist/observer and then, by analogy, the perceiver and actor.[1]

SCIENTIFIC PERSPECTIVES

A Necessary Compatibility in Grain-Size of Theoretical Explicanda and of the Observed Events Generated in Their Investigation

A scientist begins an experimental investigation with a problem requiring solution or explanation. A general constraint on his or her investigatory procedures is that they yield events similar in grain-size to those events referenced in a statement of the problem itself.

The observed grain-size of event sets limits on what actual types of things an observer will be able to recognize as types. But understanding and, hence, explaining a system's workings in relation to some scientific problem depends on types that are relevant to the workings being detected. The types that *are* relevant tend to be compatible with or similar in grain to the to-be-explained aspects of the system (cf. Putnam, 1973). Consider by way of example the problem of discovering the strategies adopted by skilled players of chess relative to novices. And consider a game of chess itself as observed by a physicist and by a psychologist in their professional capacities. In theory, from their separate, special perspectives on the game, the observers can supply exhaustive descriptions of the goings-on of the game of chess, but the descriptions will differ in the grain of the events to which their different vocabularies refer. Hence the two observers provide different answers to the question of what is going on in the game. The descriptions differ also in the generality of their referents. The things and processes to which the physicist refers are referenced in descriptions of any physical event; but psychologist's descriptive vocabulary generalizes at most to other events in which subjects of psychological study are involved.

More important, however—and following from this difference in generality—the categories essential to a psychologist's explanation of a game of chess and of the strategies of its players are not concepts for a physicist. For example, there is no physical distinction between ruleful moves in chess and moves that are not ruleful. Hence from the physicist's perspective, there is no entity called "ruleful move in chess." Nor is there a physically motivated definition of the concept of strategy. Thus from his or her perspective the physicist can describe a chess game and can understand or explain its physical events but is unable to understand or explain its psychological aspects, including the strategies of its players.

As noted, the reason that physical terms and their referents lack type correspondence with psychological terms and referents has to do with differences in their generality. Physical law characterizes everything that is. In contrast, biological law characterizes only living things and psychological law, only some living things. Like the subset of all moves of chessmen, called "ruleful moves in chess," the subset of everything that is, called "living things," lacks physical specification. However, it is a natural subset: It includes all and only those physical systems that reliably maintain themselves in certain types of functional organizations. These persisting organizations are such that the fine-grained components of the system work reliably as collectives to engender coherent molar functions, including reproduction of individuals and evolution of the species. As noted, biological systems restrict themselves to the fine-grained functioning allowed under physical law that is concomitantly coarse-grained functioning of a particular (biological) type. For Pattee (1970,1973), biological systems are as they are because they embody an organized set of restrictions or *constraints* on their physical functioning. The restrictions exclude all but a (biologically) principled subset of physical possibilities and thereby create a domain of coherent molar functioning that we recognize as biological in nature.

Evidently, then, a principled reduction in the physically determined power of a system can create a new domain of entities. In the case of biological systems, the embodied constraints on physical functioning add a new level of functioning in the system. That is, a biological system is tiered in having, at once, a physical domain of parts and processes and another domain composed of coarser-grained events that is fashioned from it.

The notion that a set of restrictions can create new functional possibilities seems paradoxical. However, the *loss* in power is in the number of sequences of physical states that may be realized, whereas the gain is in the new significance attached to those sequences that do occur. A smaller number of possible sequences at a fine grain of observation is exchanged for a larger (up from zero) number of possible events at a coarser grain of observation.

Human language also exemplifies this point. The rules of a grammar constitute a set of organized restrictions on word order. Without a grammar, no particular ordering of words has significance, and the concept of "sentence" (among others) is absent in the language. Somewhat paradoxically, the imposition of restrictions on word order provides the language user with a class of possible actions and a concept that is available in the absence of those restrictions: The language user can produce sentences, which are coherent molar units of the language.

Returning to the issue of explanation in reference to observational perspective, the nature of the dependency between the two is fairly evident. The sets of principles regulating what goes on at different levels of a system are not the same; in fact, the principles of a more abstract or coarse-grained level are a set of restrictions *on* the possiblities allowed by principles governing events of a finer grain. Because of this, a statement of the abstract principles cannot be given in the language of the finer-grained level. That is, they are irreducible to a finer-grained descriptive level. As Pattee noted (1971):

> The necessity for alternative description comes about because physical laws at the microscopic dynamical level are assumed to be complete. That is, the laws of motion predict the behavior of the system completely insofar as it is deterministic, so that additional constraints at this detailed level are incompatible with these laws. Equations of constraint are always simplifications of the detailed dynamics which express some additional regularity of the collective system, and therefore these equations cannot be at the same level of description as the laws of motion [p. 45].

If a problem concerns the molar events of a system, an investigator can only discover a solution to it by making observations from a vantage point sufficiently distanced from the microscopic detail of the system to make salient its molar functional organization and the constraints that give rise to it.

An experimental problem restricts observational perspective in a second way as well. Not only the grain but also the character of a problem promotes a special inspectional partitioning of the system under study into component parts and processes. Although many partitionings are abstractly possible, not all partitionings enable explanation or solution to a problem. We briefly consider this point next.

Observational Perspectives as Special Partitionings on an Event Chosen in Relation to a Problem Under Investigation

Speaking about the observational perspectives that a biologist may take on an organism, Kauffman (1976) makes the following claims. First, an organism may be seen to be doing indefinitely many things. What an observer takes it to be doing dictates how he or she will partition it descriptively into component parts and processes. Different adequate descriptions of what the organism is doing lead to different partitionings, and there are indefinitely many adequate decompositions of an organism. Second, according to Kauffman, the parts and processes of one partitioning must be compatible with, but need not be deducible from or translatable into, the parts and processes of another.

Thus, depending on the observer's purpose in making observations (say, depending on whether the interest is in an animal's intake and digestion of food or in its self-reproducing capacities), he or she differently decomposes it into component parts. What will constitute a significant collective of parts and processes for the purposes of one investigation need not constitute a significant collective for the purposes of the other. Hence the partitionings need not be the same; nor do they need to differ only hierarchically (i.e., in the grain of events observed). They are constrained only to be compatible—that is, not to imply anything about the properties of the organism that contradict the implications of any other adequate decomposition. But this compatibility constraint is too weak to ensure transitivity of explanation across partitionings (cf. Putnam, 1973). Hence an inappropriate partitioning may preclude solution of a problem.

Two implications of these aspects of observational perspective for theories of perceiving and acting are as follows. First, theories of perceiving and acting are theories *about* observers as well as being theories devised by observers. The constraints on understanding imposed by observational perspective apply to the subjects of psychological investigation as well as to their investigators. Thus a subject detects, and acts in reference to, a principled subset of everything that is. The principles delimiting the subset define his or her needs-to-know and intents, and they set limits on what can be a significant event for that subject.

A second implication has to do with the theorist. An adequate explanation of psychological events demands that a theorist's observational perspective mimic that of the perceiver/actor. Only if it does will his or her descriptions reference just those aspects of world events that have significance for the perceiver/actor's life.

We turn now to consider these implications for perceivers and for perceptual theorists.

PERCEPTUAL PERSPECTIVES ON AN ENVIRONMENT

We begin by making clear the character of the analogy or even the identity that we wish to establish. First, in a schema for perception, the perceiver rather than the scientist is the observer. Second, as Shaw and Bransford (1977) point out, perceivers "perceptually mine the world for information on a need-to-know basis [p. 4]." We take the various needs-to-know of a perceiver as analogous to a scientist's investigatory problems. As we suggest, the character of these species-specific or personal attitudes of "looking for" are reflected both in permanent restrictions on an individual's perspective on events and on that person's temporary perceptual attunements to special properties of ongoing events. The permanent restrictions are like the investigator's "paradigms" (Kuhn, 1970); they define the range of things that an animal will need to know. The specialized perspectives of different species, of different individuals, and of the same individual under different circumstances are distinguished somewhat in the grain of observed events, but primarily they are distinguished in respect to the partitionings of the material environment that constitute significant collectives for them. Third, we compare an animal's obtaining information that it needs to know with a scientist's *understanding* of a system in respect to the problem that he or she is investigating. (Explanation in science presupposes some measure of *understanding*. Understanding has to do with detecting or recognizing a prob-

Term 1 *distal stimulus* physical descriptors: size shape distance	Term 2 *proximal stimulus* wavelength & intensities of light rays	Term 3 *percept* physical descriptors of distal stimulus as they have meaning for perceiver

FIG. 1.1. A schema for perception in which the referents of the proximal stimulus descriptors are fine grained relative to those of the descriptors of the distal stimulus and percept.

lem's solution in the workings of a system; explanations are statements intended to promote understanding by someone else.)

A fairly typical schema for perception is given in Fig. 1.1. It depicts the event of perceiving as involving three essential terms: The first is the distal stimulus—described, for example, as a familiar object of some particular size, shape, and distance from the perceiver; the second is the proximal stimulus—variously described as the converging rays of light at the perceiver's eye, a retinal mosaic of points, a retinal image, or perhaps an aggregate of features; the third term is the percept itself, which may represent the size, shape, distance, and, in addition, the identity of the distal stimulus as an object with meaning for the perceiver.

The distal stimulus is characterized in terms of the properties of an object that are extracted by the perceiver. As a component of the world (rather than as a stimulus for a perceiver), an object might be assigned other descriptors with more microscopic referents. But the coarse-grained descriptors better characterize the stimulus for the perceiver and thus provide a more or less psychological or observer-related description of the object.

In contrast to this is the theorist's description of the proximal stimulus. The proximal stimulus is the perceiver's only personally extrinsic source of information about the properties of the distal stimulus. Yet a conventional claim is that the proximal stimulus is equivocal and fails to specify those properties. As Gibson (1966) pointed out, the foregoing characterization of the proximal stimulus is based on a physical rather than a psychological description of reflected light. It is observer-neutral. As such, the referents of its description are often equated with those of a description of radiant light—they are the wavelengths and intensities of individual light rays. This grain of description fails to capture an important categorical distinction between ambient (reflected) and radiant light—precisely, that one (ambient) but not the other (radiant) has been structured by its contact with the material environment and thereby makes reference to it. Since the level of the theorist's description of the light (and, by hypothesis, of the perceiver's perspective on the light) is fine grained relative to the structure of the environment, it obscures that structure rather than revealing it (cf. Putnam, 1973). This implies a lack of type correspondence between the psychological properties of the distal stimulus and the described physical (or psychophysical) properties of the proximal stimulus, so that the latter cannot specify the former. In particular, the proximal stimulus will lack appropriate richness of types to represent the range of types of object properties that perceivers detect.[2]

Given the difference in grain between the components of the distal and proximal stimuli, the transduction from one to the other is considered destructive of the psychological properties of objects. It follows that perceptual processing itself must be *constructive,* because perception is of the psychological properties, and in itself, the proximal stimulus does not enable detection of them.

Gibson's (e.g., 1950, 1966, 1977) contribution to the theory of perception has been to modify the schema given in Fig. 1.1. His modifications are twofold and relate to the two issues concerning perspective (grain, partitioning) considered in the introductory section. Both modifications adjust the perceiver's supposed perspective on the reflected light, and the second also alters perspective on the material environment. Thus, the first adjustment is in the grain of structure in the light that is held to constitute the proximal stimulus for a perceiver. The second is a partitioning of the environment into sets of properties ("affordances") that collectively have significance for the animal. Concomitant with this, the light's structure is partitioned into just those invariants that specify affordances to a sensitive observer.

In short, Gibson recognized that theorists had adopted inconsistent perspectives on the three terms of the perceptual schema given in Fig. 1.1 (see Turvey & Shaw, 1979). The perspectives on the distal stimulus and on the percept revealed a coarse-grained structure, whereas the closer-to perspective on the proximal stimulus revealed its microscopic properties. As noted, if the schema depicted in Fig. 1.1 were an accurate reflection of the perceiver's perspectives on the environment and on the proximal stimulus, then his or her perceptual processing would necessarily be constructive. However, the inconsistent characterization of the distal and proximal stimuli may be on the part of the perceptual theorist; it may not signify either an incapacity of reflected light to carry information about world properties or an inconsistency in the perspectives of a perceiver on the material environment and ambient light. Were there a detectable grain of structure in the proximal stimulus compatible with (and due to) that of the affordances of the environment for some perceiver, then perception of affordances might be direct.

Figure 1.2 incorporates Gibson's proposed change in the description of the proximal stimulus into the perceptual schema of Fig. 1.1. According to the new schema, the perceiver adopts an observational perspective on the proximal stimulus that best fits the need to detect certain world properties. From that perspective, structure compatible in grain (and owing) to that of significant environmental properties is revealed. Concomitantly, the categories in the revealed structure correspond to object property-types. Hence perception need not involve constructing perceptual correlates of significant event properties; it may only involve their detection.

Clearly, adopting this distanced perspective on reflected light is not a matter of choice for a perceiver; radiant light, which lacks macroscopic structure, provides no information to a visual system. Evidently, perceivers are primarily sensitive to higher-order variables of stimulation, and this must be because perceivers constitute a particular kind of perspective on the world. By virtue of that, they intercept only observer-related rather than observer-neutral versions of reflected light—that is, only levels of structure of reflected light sufficiently coarse-grained to serve their particular perceptual needs.

The foregoing discussion has concerned the notion that perceivers' perspective on the light to their eyes must be sufficiently abstracted from its microscopic detail to make salient its significant environment-imposed structure. The grain of ambient-light structure to which perceivers are sensitive is presumed to be compatible with that of the world events in which they participate.

However, considerations of the grain of significant events are insufficiently constraining of perceivers' possible perspectives on the world in relation to their needs to know. Any arbitrary set of coarse-grained events will not provide a perceiver with information that he or she needs. In addition, individual perceivers may be constrained to intercept just those partitionings of environmental properties into collectives that are significant to their individual lives (cf. Runeson's [1977] notion of ''smart'' perceptual devices).

Gibson's concept of affordance captures this second type of constraint on observational perspectives. An affordance is a set of properties of an environment that as a collective has significance for a particular (species of) animal. Which properties of a world cohere must be different for different species of animals with their different needs-to-know. And they may differ also for different members of a species as a function of their different lifetime experiences.

In relation to Kauffman's (1976) discussion of a scientist's selective partitioning of a subject of study into different collectives, we can say the following by way of analogy. The surfaces and media that constitute the earth are infinitely structured. The world offers indefinitely many ways in which it may be par-

Term 1	Term 2	Term 3
distal stimulus	*proximal stimulus*	*percept*
affordances	affordance-specific invariants	affordances

FIG. 1.2. A schema for perception in which the referents of the descriptors of the three terms in the schema are compatible in grain and kind.

titioned into superordinate categories of parts and processes. Different (species of) animals with different life-styles or a given individual on different occasions tends to detect different partitionings. The different partitionings of the world's constituents by the species or individual must be compatible, but they need not be deducible from, nor translatable into, one another.

Consider the following example. A sneaker for a person is an instance of a category of things called "footwear." It is an instance of that category because *some* of its properties are values along a set of dimensions that are essential to a thing's being footwear. It is foot-sized and -shaped; it offers a buffer between a foot and the ground (here, one of rubber); and it can be secured to the foot (here, by a shoelaced canvas covering over the instep). This cluster of properties of a sneaker specifies its membership in a class that also includes shoes, sandals, and boots.

This cluster of properties does not exhaust the invariant properties of a sneaker. Another property is that sneakers are dark inside because the canvas covering prevents light from accessing the sneaker's interior. This property is not essential to a thing's being footwear (consider a sandal, for instance). When a person recognizes a sneaker to be footwear, he has detected as a significant collective one of an indefinite set of partitionings of the sneaker. A different species of animal may detect a different set of partitionings. For the mouse that stores its supplies in a sneaker, the sneaker belongs to a class of things that might be called "storage places," and its essential properties are perhaps that it be mouse-sized, enclosed, and dark inside. This cluster of a sneaker's properties renders it an instance of a class of things that excludes sandals and includes holes in the wall.

In short, the environment for a given animal is species-characteristic, and thus it is not that captured by a physical, observer-neutral, "objective" description. But it is not a subjective environment either (cf. Gibson, 1977). The environment for any given animal is real; it is captured by an animal-referential physical description and is a special selection among the indefinitely many partitionings of properties that the world offers. (Morever, just as the different species may be sensitive to different partitionings of world components, so may different intra-specifics or even the same individual on different occasions. For example, the subset of a book's invariant properties that constitute a significant collective may differ for an individual in search of something to throw and for the same or a different individual looking for an evening's relaxation.)

Thus an animal's needs to know, including both its permanent and temporary needs, may dictate the perspective that it adopts at once on the proximal and on the distal stimuli. The perspective intercepts a limited amount of detail in the observed system, and it selects which collectives of components in the system the perceiver will detect as collectives. We turn now to consider the analogous case of the actor.

EFFECTIVE PERSPECTIVES ON THE BODY AND ON THE ENVIRONMENT

Activities look to be guided by intentions more or less in the way that scientists' investigations are guided by their choice of a problem. If the intentions of an actor are indeed analogous to scientists' problems, then they constrain his or her manner of self-regulation in the ways that the scientists' problem limits the investigatory procedures that can realize their aims of understanding and explanation. As we have said, there are at least two general ways in which scientific problems constrain investigatory procedure and observational perspective. First, to yield useful information, the procedures have to provide observations compatible in grain with those giving rise to the problem. And second, the problem dictates the partitioning of the object of study into component parts and processes.

By analogy, we can say that an intention, like a scientific problem, has a grain in that its statement refers to outcomes or occurrences in the world that are only detectable as coherent occurrences at some levels of description of the actor and the environment. (Just as "ruleful move in chess" is not a category on a physical level of description of a chess game, neither is any given coherent activity a category given a too-fine perspective on the actor's body and its environment.) In order for an actor to realize his or her intentions in the media of body and the environment, the actor should have to adopt a regulatory perspective on them that matches the grain of those intentions.

Likewise by analogy, the *character* of an intention, like the character of a scientific problem, selects a particular partitioning of its object into component parts and processes that collectively will being about an intended outcome.

We can illustrate these points by considering two schemata for action analogous to those for perception examined earlier. The two schemata represent a contrast in the action literature, and they differ in just the way that the perceptual schemata given earlier contrast. One suggests that actors adopt a regulatory perspective on their bodies that is fine grained relative to the grain of their intentions, whereas the other suggests that the grains of regulatory perspective and of the intentions are compatible. The actor-as-observer analogy that we develop is just one of several arguments in favor of the second view.

Term 1	Term 2	Term 3
intentional act	*self-instructions*	*intention*
physical descriptors:	commands to	physical descriptors
displacement	individual	of movements
velocity	muscles	with meaning for
acceleration		the animal

FIG. 1.3. A schema for action in which the referents of the actor's self-instructions are fine grained relative to the grain of the intended act itself and hence of the referents of the actor's intention.

Term 1	Term 2	Term 3
intentional act	*self-instructions*	*intention*
effectivity	coordinative	effectivity
	structures	

FIG. 1.4. A schema for action in which the referents of the actor's self-instructions are compatible in grain and kind with those of the intended act and of the intention.

In both schemata, there are three terms. (But they are not analogous in every case to the three perceptual terms of Fig. 1.1 and 1.2.) The first term is the intentional act itself. In Fig. 1.3, the intentional act is given a set of kinematic descriptors including the displacement and velocity of the limbs, for example. In Fig. 1.4, the intentional act is described as a goal-directed activity (an "effectivity," according to Turvey, Shaw, & Mace, 1978).

The middle term of the schemata is the actor's set of self-instructions. Here the two views differ quite significantly—one (Fig. 1.3) proposing that an actor adopts a level of self-instruction that is fine grained in relation to his or her perspective on the intended act itself; and the other (Fig. 1.4) proposing that the actor's perspectives on the three terms are compatible in grain and kind.

The last term of both schemata is the actor's intention. It is specified in Fig. 1.3 as a set of physical descriptors of some movements that have collective significance for the actor. In Fig. 1.4 the intention is described as the actor's effectivity.

Figuire 1.3 represents a theoretical orientation that has its origin in the 19th-century "keyboard" or "push-button" metaphor (see Bernstein, 1967; Luria, 1966). In that metaphor, movements are controlled via a cortical keyboard, the keys of which, when pressed, trigger commands to individual muscles. Hence a plan for action is a description of the body's movements in terms of the parameters of its constituent muscle contractions. Strictly speaking, this view has no modern counterpart, since current accounts of movement control recognize a role for sensory feedback in an action's regulation. However, it does have modern counterparts in respect to the close-to perspective on an actor's body that the theorist adopts and holds the actor's plan to adopt. An example is Schmidt's (1975) schema theory. Schmidt proposes that well-learned activities are controlled by a set of response specifications. As in the keyboard metaphor, these are detailed commands to individual muscles. For Schmidt, they are supplied in part by an abstract schema for movements of the appropriate type. But the schema is particularized via information about the "initial conditions" of the current movement (i.e., the "preresponse state of the muscular system and of the environment [p. 235]"). Thus, the response specifications supply all the details of the muscular contribution to the movement—at least over the period of time before feedback can be utilized.

The second theoretical orientation, given in Fig. 1.4, treats the actor's level of self-regulation as coarse rather than fine grained (e.g., Easton, 1972; Greene, 1972; Turvey, 1977). In this view, instead of commanding individual muscles, the actor regulates muscle systems called coordinative structures. (Coordinative structures are groups of muscles organized in such a way that collectively they produce a coherent molar action. See, e.g., Turvey, Shaw, & Mace, 1968; and Fowler, Rubin, Remez & Turvey, 1980; for a fuller description of them and for some examples. The role of these systems in many automatized activities including locomotion [see, e.g., Grillner, 1975] is well documented.)

Since all intentional acts are coordinated, it is patent that they are effected by coordinated muscular activity. Thus the disagreement between the two views depicted in Fig. 1.3 and 1.4 cannot be on the issue of whether or not coordinative structures underlie intentional actions. Rather, the views diverge fundamentally on the actor's supposed regulatory perspective on these systems. In the first view, the actor's perspective is fine grained relative to the muscle systems and thus is insensitive to them (again, more or less as a description of a chess game from a physical stance fails to capture its coarse-grained categories, or as a word-level description of an utterance misses out on the concept of sentence). In the second view, the actor's perspective is sufficiently more distanced that it is sensitive to constrained relationships among muscles—that is, to coordinative structures.

We favor the second view because, among other reasons, it fits the several notions that we have been developing: in particular, that types in a system or medium are only types at some levels of structure of the system; that type correspondence is only maintained *across* different media (here, across the different terms of the action schema) if the media can register the appropriate levels of structure; and that the *meanings* of these types for an observer (an actor or a theorist) are only available in the various media registering the types if the observer's perspective is sufficiently distanced for him or her to be sensitive to the appropriate levels of structure.

We show how the schema in Fig. 1.4 best fits these notions shortly, but first it may be worthwhile to establish that the manner of regulation that it proposes is in fact feasible for an actor. After all, it may be argued that individual muscles are indeed regulated in the course of acting and that someone or something has to be controlling them. If an actor addresses several muscles as a unit, how are the control parameters prescribed for the individual muscles? The answer seems to be that the coordinative structures are semiautonomous devices. A given coordinative structure is characterized by particular organized relationships among its component muscles; and these constraints provide many control parameters for the individual muscles. A loose analogy might be made between the actor's governance of coordinative structures and the act of driving a car. To turn a corner in an automobile, the driver has only to turn the steering wheel. The linkages among various of the car's components cause the vehicle to turn in the appropriate direction. In like fashion, the constrained relationships among muscles supply relatively fixed controls over the activities of the body. An actor may supply modulatory controls to it more or less as a driver can turn the steering wheel. But the individual need not be concerned with the fixed controls over aspects of an activity that he or she would never wish to alter; they take care of themselves. (See Fowler et al., 1980, and Turvey, Shaw, & Mace, 1978.)

But the schema in Fig. 1.4 is more than just feasible. Something approximating this schema more closely than the schema in Fig. 1.3 must represent the actual state of affairs for an actor. According to the schema in Fig. 1.3, the significance of an intended act for an actor is temporarily lost at a crucial point in its execution—in the translation from the intention (term 3) to its realization as a set of instructions to the musculature (term 2). That is, the translation is destructive just as is the translation from distal to proximal stimulus in Fig. 1.1. This proposal is implausible and, according to Bernstein (1967) among others (e.g., Fowler et al., 1980), unworkable as well.

Weiss (1941) seemed to recognize this flaw in schemata like that in Fig. 1.3 when he criticized investigators of motor skills for confining their studies to the physiology of activity. He believed that they would never uncover the principles explaining the animal's consistent restriction to the performance of coordinated acts. The reason those principles would remain obscure is that they are not the same as the principles of physiological functioning. The latter principles, as Weiss realized, fail to rule out many organismic states or activities that never occur. For example, absent from a physiological description of the nervous activity surrounding an animal's activity is the general concept of intentional coordinated act. Also missing are the concepts relating to the species-characteristic act-kinds that "intentional coordinated act" subsumes. These are the concepts that are significant to the actor, and they are only detectable from a more distant vantage point than that which reveals the individual's physiological functioning. The level of physioloical functioning lacks type correspondence with the level of intentional activity by the actor.

Recall that Pattee (e.g., 1970) ascribes the *biological* organism's persistent restriction to sequences of physical states with molar, biological significance to their incorporation of a grammar of constraint on their physical functioning. The constraints create a domain of molar functioning by enabling all and only a restricted set of sequences of physical states.

Weiss' argument is similar to this: Organisms consistently engage in acts—that is, in coordinated movements with some biological or psychological significance to them. The restriction to intentional coordinated acts implies that the principles needed to explain the activities of animals are not principles of physiological functioning but rather are a grammar of restrictions *on* that functioning.

The constraints of concern to Weiss are the fixed constraints that persist throughout the lifetime of an animal. Presumably they arise in the special fit between animal and environment by virtue of the animal's species membership. These restrictions ensure that *activity* will occur and that unorganized convulsions will not.

We may view the temporary "intentions" that animals work to achieve in a similar way. They may add constraints that select among the possible activities of the animal. The actor's body provides the means by which his or her intentions are realized, and those intentions select the manner of regulation both by choosing the grain of component of the body that is regulated and by selecting the partitioning of these components into functional collectives.

Two related considerations suggest that the actor's self-regulatory perspective is coarse grained. One has already been considered. For any animal, the environment consists of coarse-grained components and events. And the course of events to which an intention refers is also macroscopic. If the animal's self-regulations are to be sensitive to these macroscopic events, then they must be macroscopic in focus as well. Thus, for example, if an actor wishes to jack up an automobile in order to change the tire, the environmental components involved and the intended activity are large-scale. The intention calls for the actor to pump the jack handle up and down alternately. To do this, the activities of the two arms have to be coordinated with respect to the jack handle. It would not be particularly useful for the actor to regulate the activities of both arms independently (or components of both arms). For one thing, as already noted, the *sense* of the act would be lost at this fine-grained level of control. In addition, however, that strategy, even if possible, would be inefficient. Since the arms will consistently work together as a unit during the activity of pumping, the efficient strategy is to organize the musculature to create a functional system (coordinative structure) encompassing both arms. Once that system is established, the actor has only to address it as a whole rather than its parts individually.

Another way to view this is to recognize that according to the schema of Fig. 1.4, actors adopt a strategy not unlike that of linguistic theorists writing a grammar of some language. For linguists, that strategy is at once to *simplify* the description of the language and to *express its orderliness* by separating its regular, invariant properties from properties that are idiosyncratic to particular components. Thus, abstracted from the rules of the language are linguistic universals. And removed from the lexicon are any properties of words that are predictable by the general rules of the language. The proposal depicted in Fig. 1.4 is that an actor likewise at once *simplifies* the regulation of the body *and* maintains a sensitivity to the significance of his or her intended act by abstracting from a detailed description of the body's activity those aspects of self-organization that will be invariant throughout the act. These organizational aspects give the act its molar structure just as the universals of language (at one level) and the rules of a particular language (at another) give a spoken utterance its molar structure.

In day-to-day circumstances, actors never regulate their bodies at a level below this abstract one, just as speaker/hearers never interact outside the laboratory with the language system below the level at which it is meaningful. Regulation of activity would be infeasible if it failed to take advantage of the constrained relationship among muscles that enable coordinated activities. It would be infeasible not only by virtue of being inefficient but also because it would imply that actors regulate their bodies at a level at which the significance of the activity is lost.

We suspect, then, that by referring to environmental events having a certain grain, the intention selects the grain of the components of the actor's body that he or she must regulate to get the job done. In addition, the *character* of the intention must select a partitioning of the body into component systems. Some activities—walking, for example—are effected by coordinating the activities of the four limbs. The four limbs together constitute a system whose function is locomotion. The activity of jacking up a car, on the other hand, involves a different partitioning of the body into systems. Here the two arms constitute a single system whose organization differs somewhat from the organization of the arms in walking, where they swing 180 degrees out of phase. Also in contrast to walking, the legs act as fixed supports in jacking; they are differently organized with respect to arm movements in the two act-types.

Thus the *type* of act that an intention calls for dictates, to a large extent, the way that the muscles and segments of the body will be partitioned into subsystems. In every case, the subsystems will be organized with respect to some macroscopic function that has some significance for the actor, but the particular significance will differ according to the partitioning.

CONCLUSIONS: ON AVOIDING A DISCONTINUITY OF DESCRIPTORS

The larger theme that we have pursued in this chapter concerns the need to maintain a compatibility among descriptor sets. Thus, we sought to make the case that in describing the environment, the light reflected from the environment, and perception of the environment, the descriptors chosen for each domain should not be different in number, in grain size, in degree of variety, or in type. And we sought to make the identical case for the descriptor sets of the domains relevant to action. Let us now, in concluding, highlight what we take to be the significance of the compatible or commensurate descriptor theme for a general theory of perception and action.

It is, perhaps, self-evident that where a scientist ascribes incompatible descriptor sets to what he or she takes to be the end points of a process (such as the proximal stimulus and the percept in perception, or the intention and the muscular instructions in action), the task is thereby defined: Discover the steps or, more generally, the means by which the terminal descriptor set is *derived* from the initial descriptor set. But when a scientist assumes a commensurability of descriptor sets, then the task cannot be that just defined. In contrast, first and foremost, the scientist's task is to discover the compatible vocabularies for describing the different domains over the phenomenon (perception or action) is defined.

Our arguments have been intended to rationalize and schematize the form of the latter task. We see these arguments as dissuasive of a number of markedly unattractive hypotheses about the relation between animal-as-epistemic-agent and environment that are fostered by the assumption of inequitable descriptors. Here, by way of summary, we underscore the contrast between some of these hypotheses of the inequitable descriptors view and corresponding hypotheses of the commensurate descriptors view with three examples.

Consider the task of perceptual theory as captured by the following quote from Koffka (1935) in reference to a commonplace description of the light to an eye:

> And that raises at once the problem: how the enormous richness and variety of our visual behavorial environment can be aroused by such a mere mosaic of light and shade and colour. I think, when formulated in these terms, the problem must appear thrilling by the very paradox which it seems to involve. How can such rich effects arise out of such poor causes, for clearly the dimensions of our environmental field are far more numerous that those of the mosaic of stimulation [p. 75].

The paradox that Koffka identifies promotes a most unattractive state of affairs—namely, skepticism about the claim that an animal can know its environment. In the view expressed, what an animal knows is a matter of the reconstructive facility of its nervous system, and reconstructions from insufficient data must be subject to error, even about the possible existence of objects (cf. Shaw, Turvey, & Mace, Chap. 10, this volume). But from the arguments made in this chapter, this paradox should not be taken as a fact of reality, but rather as the consequence of an inappropriate description of the light as reflected from an environment. In this particular case, to reverse the traditional assumption of discontinuity in descriptors is to ward off skepticism about the epistemic relation between an animal and its environment.

Consider now the case of human conversation. Typically, a speaker means something by what he or she says. However, on the inequitable descriptors assumption, that meaning is lost in the mechanical embodiment of the message; meaning is absent in the acoustic signal generated by the speaker's vocal activity, and the recovery of meaning is thereby designated as the responsibility of the listener's brain (cf. MacKay, 1969). This story poses two unattractive hypotheses: that the meaning intended by the speaker disappears at some point in the communicative process, and that there is a point in the listener's brain activity when the neural process concomitant to the received sound acquires meaning. But on the equitable descriptors assumption, the conundra as to how these translations can take place should not be taken as real. Rather, we suppose that they are only apparent and are due to inappropriate descriptions of the media (neural process, sound waves) over which conversation is defined. The sought-after descriptor sets preserve meaning over the different media; they do not destroy it at one stage and reincarnate it at another.

As a final example, let us consider the relating of perception and action. Suppose that we were interested in the problem of an animal pursuing its prey. The terrain in which such activity takes place is cluttered with objects, and the terrain itself is uneven. The chasing predator must leap obstacles and brinks in the terrain, and we might ask how it knows when to leap and how much force to apply to leap a given object or crevice optimally—that is, to leap a sufficient but not excessive height using sufficient but not excessive amounts of force. Assuming inequitable descriptors, we would claim that the descriptors on the perception side and those on the action side are quite different. The perception descriptors must be correlates of the visible properties of the environment (such as its height and distance from the predator), whereas the action descriptors might be time to initiate the leap and the force of extensor thrust. Given these two descriptor sets (or something like them), we should, as scientists, ask how the perception descriptors are *translated* into the required action descriptors. But if we avoid the assumption of inequitable descriptors, we suppose that the perception descriptors and action descriptors are not distinct: The information made available to the animal-as-perceiver should directly provide the information required by the animal-as-actor. Thus, a description of the optical flow concomitant to a moving animal ought to specify when the animal should initiate its leap and how much force it should apply. Lee's (1974, 1976) analyses of the optical information available to a moving observer suggests strongly that it does.

CHAPTER NOTES

[1]The issues we consider do not exhaust those that are critical to understanding the nature of observation by scientists or by observers in general. Another important set of issues has to do with the introduction of error into an observational enterprise. These issues are considered by Shaw, Turvey, and Mace, (Chap. 10, this volume).

[2]This conclusion seems unavoidable when the light is given a fine-grained description. But it is surprising given such classical problems of perception as the constancies of shape, size, and distance. The puzzle of shape constancy, for example, is that perceivers see a distal object—a chair, say—as having the same shape when viewed from many different perspectives even though the perspectives may offer vastly different proximal stimuli to the perceiver. But given a fine-grained description of the light, *this* should not be a problem for a perceiver. Rather, the problem is just the reverse of this. In a fine-grained description of the light, the categories or types are *few* in number, and each includes large numbers of instances. Instances of a type are not significantly different from one another. Thus the problem of shape perception for a perceiver ought to be that all shapes look alike, not that the same shape looks different from different perspectives.

The grammatical constraints that a more abstract perspective acknowledges *create* categories and hence create more significant differences among instances (cf. Medawar, 1974).

ACKNOWLEDGMENTS:

This work was supported by NIH Grant HD01994 and NSF Grant NS13617 to Haskins Laboratories.

REFERENCES

Bernstein, N. *The coordination and regulation of movements.* London: Pergamon Press, 1967.

Easton, T. On the normal use of reflexes. *American Scientist,* 1972, *60,* 591–599.

Fitch, H. & Turvey, M. T. On the control of activity: Some remarks from an ecological point of view. In D. Landers & R. W. Christina (Eds.), *Psychology of behavior and sports.* Urbana, Ill.: Human Kinetics, 1978.

Fodor, J. *The language of thought.* New York: Cromwell, 1975.

Fowler, C. A., Rubin, P., Remez, R., & Turvey, M. T. Implications for speech production of a general theory of action. In B. Butterworth (Ed.), *Language production.* New York: Academic Press, 1980.

Fowler, C. A. & Turvey, M. T. Skill acquisition: An event approach with special reference to searching for the optimum of a function of several variables. In G. Stelmach (Ed.), *Information processing in motor control and learning.* New York: Academic Press, 1978.

Gibson, J. J. *The perception of the visual world.* Boston: Houghton Mifflin, 1950.

Gibson, J. J. *The senses considered as perceptual systems.* Boston: Houghton Mifflin, 1966.

Gibson, J. J. The theory of affordances. In R. Shaw & J. Bransford (Eds.), *Perceiving, acting, and knowing.* Hillsdale, N.J.: Lawrence Erlbaum Associates, 1977.

Greene, P. Problems of organization of motor systems. In R. Rosen & F. Snell (Eds.), *Progress in theoretical biology* (Vol. 2). New York: Academic Press, 1972.

Grillner, S. Locomotion in vertebrates. *Physiological Reviews,* 1975, *55,* 247–304.

Kauffman, S. Articulation of parts explanation in biology and the rational search for them. In M. Grene & E. Mendelsohn (Eds.), *Topics in the philosophy of biology.* Dordecht, Holland: Reidel, 1976.

Koffka, K. *Principles of gestalt psychology.* New York: Harcourt Brace, 1935.

Kuhn, T. *The structure of scientific revolutions.* Chicago: University of Chicago Press, 1970.

Lee, D. Visual information during locomotion. In R. B. MacLeod & H. Pick (Eds.), *Perception: Essays in honor of James J. Gibson.* Ithaca, N. Y.: Cornell University Press, 1974.

Lee, D. A theory of visual control of braking based on information about time-to-collision. *Perception,* 1976, *5,* 437–459.

Luria, A. *Higher cortical functions in man.* New York: Basic Books, 1966.

Mace, W. James J. Gibson's strategy for perceiving: Ask not what's inside your head, but what your head's inside of. In R. Shaw & J. Bransford (Eds.), *Perceiving, acting, and knowing: Toward and ecological psychology.* Hillsdale, N.J.: Lawrence Erlbaum Associates, 1977.

MacKay, D. M. *Information, mechanism, and meaning.* Boston: MIT Press, 1969.

Medawar, P. A geometrical model of reduction and emergence. In F. Ayala & T. Dobzhansky (Eds.), *Studies in the philosophy of biology.* Los Angeles: University of California Press, 1974.

Pattee, H. H. The problem of biological hierarchy. In C. H. Waddington (Ed.), *Toward a theoretical biology, 3.* Chicago, Aldine, 1970.

Pattee, H. H. The recognition of description and function in chemical reaction networks. In R. Buvet & C. Ponnamperuma (Eds.), *Chemical evolution and the origin of life.* Amsterdam: North Holland Publishing, 1971.

Pattee, H. H. The physical basis and origin of hierarchical control. In H. H. Pattee (Ed.), *Hierarchy theory: The challenge of complex systems.* New York: Braziller, 1973.

Polanyi, M. Life's irreducible structure. *Science,* 1968, *160,* 1308–1312.

Putnam, H. Reductionism and the nature of psychology. *Cognition,* 1973, *2,* 131–146.

Runeson, S. On the possibility of "smart" perceptual mechanisms. *Scandinavian Journal of Psychology,* 1977, *18,* 172–179.

Schmidt, R. A schema theory of discrete motor skill learning. *Psychological Review,* 1975, *82,* 225–260.

Shaw, R. & Bransford, J. Introduction. In R. Shaw & J. Bransford (Eds.) *Perceiving, acting, and knowing: Toward an ecological psychology.* Hillsdale, N.J.: Lawrence Erlbaum Associates, 1977.

Turvey, M. T. Preliminaries to a theory of action with reference to vision. In R. Shaw & J. Bransford (Eds.), *Perceiving, acting, and knowing: Toward an ecological psychology.* Hillsdale, N.J.: Lawrence Erlbaum Associates, 1977.

Turvey, M. T., & Shaw, R. The primacy of perceiving: An ecological reformulation of perception as a point of departure for understanding memory. In L.-G. Nillson (Ed.), *Perspectives on memory research: Essays in honor of Uppsala University's 500th Anniversary.* Hillsdale, N.J.: Lawrence Erlbaum Associates, 1979.

Turvey, M. T., Shaw, R., & Mace, W. Issues in the theory of action: Degrees of freedom, coordinative structures and coalitions. In J. Requin (Ed.), *Attention and performance VII.* Hillsdale, N.J.: Lawrence Erlbaum Associates, 1978.

Weiss, P. Self-differentiation of the basic pattern of coordination. *Comparative Psychology Monograph,* 1941, *17,* 21–96.

Wimsatt, W. Reductionism, levels of organization, and the mind-body problem. In G. Globus, G. Maxwell, & I. Savodnik (Eds.), *Consciousness and the brain: A scientific and philosophical inquiry.* New York: Plenum Press, 1976.

2

The Need for Complementarity in Models of Cognitive Behavior: A Response to Fowler and Turvey

H. H. Pattee
Department of Systems Science
State University of New York at Binghamton

The principal themes Fowler and Turvey have presented in their chapter are: (1) the need for commensurability of observed events and the representation of these events, and (2) the need for compatibility of representation of intentions and representation of the corresponding actions. The observer's differing perspectives and intentions in differing situations are assumed to lead to multiple representations and classifications of events, often forming hierarchical layers of resolution or function and ordered levels of coordination and constraint; but Fowler and Turvey stress the need for *compatibility* of these representations as the overriding constraint. The authors support this view with commonsense functional arguments of simplicity and efficiency. Why do we need more detail in our descriptions of events than we need to respond appropriately to events? Why should intentions be represented in more or less detail than the actions to be controlled? Why should the description of the ends not always be compatible with the description of the means?

This sounds like a reasonable argument from the functional or metaphorical perspective, but as Fowler and Turvey point out, other partitionings of our experience are possible; and I argue that *incompatible* representations also play an essential role in our models and explanations. What does it mean to explain a "coordinative structure," which Fowler and Turvey invoke to achieve compatibility between goals and actions? One part of the explanation is to describe the function; but surely another necessary part of our explanation is to show a structure that will actually execute the functional activity. These two modes of descriptions will generally not be compatible. For example, the keyboard of a calculator has key labels that are function descriptions, but to explain what the function means or how it is executed in detail requires a new description that is

21

not compatible with the simplicity of function labels. Fowler and Turvey are correct in emphasizing the need for such macrofunctional control and for the coordinative microstructures that autonomously execute the functions, but I differ with them on how these different modes of description are epistemologically related, and on whether one can claim an explanation of cognitive behavior only by compatible sets of descriptions.

I outline my arguments at three levels—at the level of physics, where I explain in what sense description of laws and description of rules (constraints, measurements, or controls) are incompatible; at the level of biology, where I show in what respect description of structure and description of function are incompatible; and at the level of epistemology, where I argue that description of intentions (mind) and description of action (body) are incompatible. These examples are illustrations of a generalized complementarity principle asserting that explanation or understanding requires the articulation of two formally incompatible representations or modes of description.[1] How do these ideas apply to the area of cognitive psychology? I am not opposing the ecological attitude elaborated by Fowler and Turvey, nor am I supporting it in opposition to the information/ processing approaches. I am claiming that these are two complementary modes of description that have not yet been completely articulated and, more fundamentally, have not been recognized as essentially complementary, in the sense that any explanation of cognitive behavior will require both modes of description.

COMPLEMENTARITY IN PHYSICAL DESCRIPTIONS

Among the principles of physics, there is no explicit recognition of the need for the concept of control; and even constraints are not considered fundamental. Neither fundamental particles nor stars nor galaxies are controlled or constrained. When a physicist uses the concept of constraint, it is either as a boundary condition or as a practical alternative representation of the structures that interact with the variables of primary interest. However, there is one fundamental exception, the "measuring device," which is a form of control constraint, but one that physicists avoid like psychologists avoid the homunculus, and for very much the same reason; namely, both devices raise more questions than they answer. Like E. B. White's Golux, they are not "mere devices." Cognition and volition are unavoidable aspects of measuring devices and homunculi.

Control constraints arose in the context of design and engineering, where there is always a cognitive organism or homunculus lurking in the background. This is Michael Polanyi's primary criticism of Laplacean reductionism, which asserts total predictability or determinism when total information of initial conditions is supplied. But this total information requries perfect measuring devices, which in turn implies perfect control constraints and, hence, perfect design.

Although this line of argument may have been convincing to scholastics as a proof of the existence of God, it is not much help to psychologists in explaining how we walk and talk.

The basic distinction that must be made is between *laws* of nature and *rules* of constraints. One cannot usefully apply the concept of control to laws nor to all types of constraints. The same is true for information. Informational and control constraints must be describable in terms of alternative states that are not dynamically related. That is, they must change in time but not change as a function of rates, as do the laws of nature. Such constraints are nonintegrable or nonholonomic, and their behaviors can be said to execute a control rule.[2]

I agree that the commonsense engineering concepts of control are useful for modeling many aspects of life where evolution has replaced the cognitive design activity—or, of you wish, where evolution is the design—but the engineering concepts are not enough to explain cognitive control. The basic distinction between laws and rules can be made by these incompatible sets of criteria: laws are *inexorable, incorporeal,* and *universal*; rules are *arbitrary, structure-dependent,* and *local.* In other words, we cannot alter or evade laws of nature, whereas we can redesign or eliminate a rule; laws do not need a device or structure to execute them, whereas rules can only be executed by specific physical structures that we call control constraints; and finally, laws hold at all times and all places in the universe, whereas rules hold only where and when there is a physical structure to execute them.

Since laws are inexorable and universal, no physical structures can exist without laws; nor can structures, however complex, evade laws in any sense. Therefore all rules and their control constraints depend on laws. Futhermore, an "unconstrained degree of freedom" is not an "undetermined degree of freedom," for it must always follow the laws of nature. In fact, good biological as well as good engineering design makes the maximum use of natural (noninformational) constraints and laws of nature, so that the control information can be kept to a minimum. The laws are inescapable, and many natural constraints are there, anyway, like the surface of the earth; so we should expect that the evolution of coordinated structures has made full use of these laws of nature and natural constraints.

Nevertheless, our mode of description of natural laws is fundamentally incompatible with our mode of description of control or measurement, since control and measurement require a volitional coordination of events as distinct from the events themselves (i.e., the events as described by natural laws).

How do these views differ from Fowler and Turvey's? Why can we not say with them that laws and measurements are simply an example of the brain's "partitioning the world" in two ways that "must be compatible, but they need not be deducible from, nor translatable into, one another"? The problem is that our description of laws requires the concepts of rate-dependence, reversibility (time symmetry), continuity, and causality (determinism or the inexorable flow of events); whereas our description of measurements requires the concepts of rate-independence, irreversibility, discrete events, and acausality (natural selection or, at the highest cognitive levels, selection by free will). In other words, in order to predict or control events successfully, the brain of the physicist has been led to partition the world into *formally contradictory* languages. It is from the apparent inescapability of this situation that the principle of complementarity became acceptable, even though its appreciation still produces a profound cognitive dissonance.

COMPLEMENTARITY IN BIOLOGICAL STRUCTURE AND FUNCTION

One of the most elementary examples of this minimum control strategy that we mentioned earlier is found, as one might expect, at the molecular genetic level where natural selection of control began, so to speak. The enzyme molecule is the paradim case of a control constraint, where we see only some hundreds of bits of genetic information specifying a highly coordinated structure, with over 20,000 atomic degrees of freedom. This machine can recognize a specific type of molecule among thousands of similar types and speed up a particular dynamic reaction by a factor of 10^6 to 10^{12} persistently and reliably.[3] This incredible performance is not explained only by an information-processing model in which each degree of freedom is simulated in detail, like a computer program. I have no doubt that such a simulation could be done as a technical exercise, and it would be an impressive computational task for even the smallest enzyme and the largest computer. But very little would be learned about nature's design and control of enzymes. The point is that the cell's control strategy, which is what we want to explain, does not use this approach at all. The cell specifies only the information necessary to string together a few hundred amino acids. From then on, the noninformational constraints and the laws of nature do the rest. Without further instruction or control, this string folds into a three-dimensional machine that recognizes its unique substrate molecules and catalyzes a particular bond, repeating this process until it receives additional control signals or until it is poisoned or denatured. The enzyme's folding, recognizing, and catalyzing activities are not explainable only as information processing. They are "autonomous behavior patterns" that have been very efficiently "built in" by the sequence of its primary structure specified in the genetic description. All this is a consequence of natural selection over some 3 billion years of evolution.

Why are the descriptions of information processing in the genetic program incompatible with the description of the enzyme's catalytic action? The fundamental incompatibility between information and action is that the rules of symbol manipulation, like measurement, are inherently rate-independent, whereas the laws of action are inherently rate-dependent. The sequence of amino acids in an enzyme's primary structure is not influenced by the rate at which the DNA is read. On the other hand, the action of the enzyme is largely defined by its rate of activity. More generally, as we have said, all physical laws are expressible as functions of rates—that is, as derivatives of some variable with respect to time. Rules, on the other hand, depend on order or sequence but cannot be expressed as functions of rates. All linguistic operations and all computations, insofar as they are defined by rules, cannot be functions of the rate of reading, writing, or computing. What we mean by a statement or calculation cannot depend on how fast we speak or calculate. Structure–function complementarity arises from this incompatibility, since the structural basis of functional organization requires some informational constraints that are rate-independent, whereas the function depends to some extent on rate-dependent dynamics.

I must emphasize that the amount of measurement or information constraint is not relevant for the complementarity principle. The amount of information is therefore incommensurable with the amount of action it controls. This is because the description of information is in a language that is different from and incompatible with the language describing the action.[4] Fowler and Turvey's demand that the resolutions or grain-sizes of descriptor sets be commensurate is reasonable provided that descriptor sets are entirely in one informational mode. In this case, Ashby's (1956) law of requisite variety[5] will hold, precisely because of this compatiblity of descriptor sets or codes. Similarly, Fowler and Turvey's analogy of automobile steering linkages to a coordinated structure is sound provided one remains in a dynamical constraint mode of description. The incompatiblity I am speaking about would occur when describing *intentional* control policy and how this interacts with the *deterministic* dynamical activity of what is controlled. For example, the informational content of an ignition key is incommensurable with the degrees of freedom of the automobile that it starts. This is because the information in the key is determined by the number of people you do not wish to use your automobile (i.e., an intentional policy) and has virtually nothing to do with the complexities of the deterministic mechanisms of automobiles. This example also illustrates the complementarity principle in the following sense: It is obvious that an ignition key cannot be explained as nothing but a slotted brass object with bumps on its edge, no matter how detailed the structural description may be. Nor can the key be explained as nothing but an informational representation of a population of potential car thieves, no matter how accurate our statistics on stolen cars.

Returning to more elementary biological behavior, at the simplest level of biological control, we see that the DNA molecule cannot be explained as nothing but an ordinary chemical structure obeying the laws of quantum mechanics; nor can it be explained as nothing but a data structure that is fed into an information processor. At the other extreme of biological complexity, we cannot explain a newborn mammal finding a nipple as nothing but a physical structure finding an optimum binding site, nor can we explain the action as nothing but information-processing control of all the degrees of freedom. The relative amounts of involvement of informational control and of noninformational constraints and laws are irrelevant, as I have said. That is because the problem of control does not reside within either of these two modes of description, but rather in *how these two modes are related to our cognitive models.* To explain cognitive control, we must first more fully appreciate the complementary relation between laws of nature and rules of control constraints. I endeavor to explain more generally why these alternative modes of representation are formally incompatible.

THE EPISTEMOLOGICAL BASIS OF COMPLEMENTARITY

The classical idea that we can explain control in cognitive systems without complementary modes of description verges on a self-contradiction, or at least a conceptual paradox. Complementarity may be viewed as a recognition of the paradox. It has its roots in the subject-object dualism and in the basic paradox of determinism and free will. When psychologists say they have explained some event, they usually have in mind the classical physics paradigm of an inexorable law or mechanistic regularity that, given some initial conditions, drastically reduces the uncertainty and the vast number of alternative possibilities for future events. This reduction in possibilities is what prediction means. Before we had the physics paradigm of inexorable laws and mechanisms, people imagined mythical explanations that often invoked godlike (or humanlike) decisions, which nevertheless had the same purpose as a law—namely, that of reducing the apparent number of alternative possibilities for future events. In other words, a key criterion for any explanation is a reduction in the set of alternative possibilities. This is, of course, the same condition that is required of a control process. To naively ask for an explanation of control is, therefore, something like asking for an explanation of an explanation or the prediction of a prediction. The apparent regress disappears only if we recognize control and explanation as two incompatible levels of description. When we do not make the meaning of these levels clear, we often find ourselves invoking some form of homunculus whenever we become frustrated by the classical paradigm's infinite regress, or by the circularity of ecological closure.

When we are describing totally artificial control systems, we simply evade the issue by cutting off the explanation at an arbitrary level. Thus we teach students about feedback control using the example of the thermostat, but fail to ask who sets the thermostat, or who constructed the thermostat, or who designed the thermostat, and so on. In fact, the concept of control is effectively eliminated by this "explanation," which leaves only a deterministic mechanism to work by itself.

Information-processing approaches to cognition and control that use only one mode of representation fail for exactly this reason. There is no doubt that computer simulation can mimic one level of certain types of relatively simple behavior, but there always emerges a higher level where all this classical, artificial mechanism—however complex—simply fails to have any meaning as an explanation of cognitive or intentional control. This is not the same problem as whether or not the computer program and hardware is anything like the brain's program and hardware. Even if the computer were homomorphic to the brain, the problem of explanation of control remains. In fact, even if the neurophysiologist could construct a working brain out of living neurons, the problem I am talking about would still be there. The problem of explicit single-level models of cognition is that the *mechanism* of the model destroys the *significance* of what we are trying to understand, very much like explanation destroys the humor in the joke or the image in the metaphor.[6]

COMPLEMENTARITY IN COGNITIVE PSYCHOLOGY

Physicists and psychologists have been intellectually buck-passing the mind-body problem for over 50 years. Psychologists have more or less uncritically accepted paradigms of physics for their models of experiment and reductionistic theories, and physicists have more or less uncritically invoked cognition, volition, and consciousness to interpret the laws of nature. In one of his earliest formulations of the idea of complementarity, Bohr (1934) concluded that this concept "bears a deep-going analogy to the general difficulty in the formulation of human ideas, inherent in the distinction between subject and object" [p. 91]; and since that time, there have been few discussions of the problem of measurement or of the meaning of quantum explanation that have not tacitly or explicitly invoked the mind of the observer as an irreducible element.[7] It is not likely, then, that new experiments on the brain or simulations on computers will suddenly reduce the mind to physics! On the other hand, if psychology restricts itself to the mimicry of activities that do not involve concepts of cognition, volition, or consciousness, it will truly become the science of the artificial.

What alternatives are there? The idea that I would promote is that psychologists make the difficult effort to assimilate the basic concept of complementarity as an epistemological principle. It is by no means a clear and distinct concept, but it is rich and suggestive. The complementarity principle does not promote resolutions of the central binary oppositions of psychology—mind and body, structure and process, subject and object, determinism and free will, laws and controls, etc. On the contrary, as we have seen, the principle of complementarity requires simultaneous use of descriptive modes that are formally incompatible. Instead of trying to resolve apparent contradictions, the strategy is to accept them as an irreducible aspect of reality. This is not yet an intuitively acceptable strategy for most scientists. There is a real cognitive dissonance for most of us if we are told that a single event is both particle and wave, or both structure and process, or both mind and matter. Complementarity is not to be confused with tolerance of different views. It is not a resolution of a contradiction, as if you were to agree that we are simply "looking at the problem from different perspectives," like the blind men and the elephant. Rather, it is a sharpening of the paradox. Both modes of description, though formally incompatible, must be a part of the theory, and truth is discovered by studying the interplay of the opposites.

As I tried to explain briefly in the preceding sections, the concepts required for physical description are complementary to the concepts required for cognitive control description in just this sense. Similarly, the concept of material DNA as a physical molecule obeying quantum mechanical laws is complementary to the concept of semantic DNA as a message obeying a coherent set of syntactical rules. There seems to be no possibility or compatibility of these two modes. The problem is to adapt our thinking to this complementarity instead of spending so much effort trying to resolve or avoid it. Furthermore there is not the slightest bit of evidence that in all the experiments and theories of psychology, there is any convergence toward resolution of any of these fundamental binary oppositions. One can even argue that the confusion is worse than ever.[8]

Therefore, just as I have argued (Pattee, 1972b) that physicists might consider how cognition might enter the measurement process, I would also suggest that it would be a good strategy if psychologists came to grips with complementarity as a serious epistemological framework for their theories and their interpretation of experiments.

Like it or not, we are faced with the fundamental epistemological problem that pervades long-standing unresolved questions in philosophy, physics, biology, and psychology. Perhaps it sounds presumptuous to raise such profound issues, which have been argued for centuries without resolution; but then again, we have assimilated new physical concepts and new facts of life; and in any case, I believe that progress in our enterprise of understanding the brain is going to require some deeper theoretical framework than classical mechanics and computers. We must appreciate the requirements for psychological explanation itself beyond the precise, counterfeit mimicry of cognition by computers on one hand and the obscure, mythical reality of the volitional homunculus on the other. The mind-body problem is not going to fade away.

CHAPTER NOTES

[1]The idea of complementarity is now most often ascribed to Bohr (1934) in the context of quantum theory, but the idea has many philosophical precursors—for example, Nicholas of Cusa's *coincidentum oppositorum*. A brief history of the complementarity principle can be found in Jammer (1974). Further discussion of my ideas on complementarity can be found in Pattee (1977, 1978).

[2]A discussion of these concepts can be found in Pattee (1972a, p. 248; and 1973, p. 41).

[3]It may be objected that the information in the structural gene for an enzyme is only a small fraction of the information necessary to read, translate, and synthesize the enzyme.

It is of course true that the DNA must also informationally specify the tRNA and ribosomal RNAs, as well as the synthetase enzymes and ribosomal proteins. Nevertheless, these structures are all syntactic; that is, they are the constraints that execute the rules of the coding language. They do not correspond to the instructions in that language that could be called the message. In other words, these syntactical constraints hold for *all* genetic messages that specify the structure of *all* proteins.

[4]For a psychologist's view of this incompatibility, see (1969) R. Gregory. Gregory points out that the essential difference between analog and digital representations "is not in their engineering, but rather that they represent logically different kinds of things. The distinction is between actual events in the world, which occur continuously, and symbolic representations of events, which are always discontinuous [p. 236]."

[5]In spite of a vocabulary that includes many mechanical and biological concepts, Ashby's (1956) descriptions remain tightly formulated in the informational mode (see Chap. 11). As in the case of general system theories, the data are always assumed to exist and to be cognitively recognized as data. The complementary questions of why the numbers are data (or why data are numbers) and why measurements of that type were made in the first place are never addressed.

[6]This is the characteristic problem of events that require complementarity for their representation. In quantum descriptions, the representation of the electron as a particle destroys formally, as well as conceptually, its interference properties as a wave, and vice versa. The complementarity of a physical *explanation* of the brain and an informational *control* model can be appreciated conceptually by picturing the ideals of classical explanation and control. An ideal physical explanation makes us feel that an event could only have happened the way it did (Wigner, 1964), whereas ideal cognitive control makes us feel that an event can only happen if we make a decision to make it happen. Laws of nature have been the classical paradigm of control. Classical physical laws completely determine events, so that the concept of control is either redundant or contradictory, whereas formal computation allows proofs only if physical laws are ignored or considered irrelevant. Einstein succinctly expressed this complementarity: "In so far as the propositions of mathematics are certain, they do not refer to reality, and in so far as they refer to reality, they are not certain." Cognitive behavior, since it inherently involves both "propositions" and "reality," will therefore require these complementary modes of explanation.

[7]A good discussion of physicist's dependency on psychological concepts is Jammer (1974), Chapter 4, on complementarity; and Chapter 11, on measurement.

[8]Newell (1973) says: "As I examine the fate of our [binary] oppositions . . . it seems to me that clarity is never achieved, matters simply become muddier and muddier. Thus, far from providing the rungs of a ladder by which psychology gradually climbs to clarity, this form of conceptual structure leads rather to an ever increasing pile of issues which we weary of or become diverted from but never really settle [p. 288]."

REFERENCES

Ashby, W. R. *An introduction to cybernetics.* New York: John Wiley, 1956.

Bohr, N. *Atomic theory and the description of nature.* Cambridge: Cambridge University Press, 1934.

Gregory, R. On how so little information controls so much behavior. In C. H. Waddington (Ed.), *Towards a theoretical biology* (Vol. 2). Edinburgh: Edinburgh University Press, 1969.

Jammer, M. *The philosophy of quantum mechanics.* New York: Wiley, 1974.

Newell, A. You can't play twenty questions with nature and win. In W. G. Chase (Ed.), *Visual information processing.* New York: Academic Press, 1973.

Pattee, H. Laws and constraints, symbols and languages. In C. H. Waddington (Ed.), *Towards a theoretical biology* (Vol. 4). Edinburgh: Edinburgh University Press, 1972. (a)

Pattee, H. H. Physical problems of decision-making constraints. *International Journal of Neuroscience,* 1972, *3,* 99–106. (b)

Pattee, H. Physical problems of the origin of natural controls. In A. Locker (Ed.), *Biogenesis, evolution, homeostasis.* Heidelberg: Springer-Verlag, 1973.

Pattee, H. Dynamic and linguistic modes of complex systems. *International Journal of General Systems,* 1977, *3,* 259.

Pattee, H. The complementarity principle in biological and social structures. *Journal of Social and Biological Structures,* 1978, *1,* 201.

Wigner, E. P. Events, laws of nature, and invariance principles. *Science,* 1964, *145,* 995.

3 Fowler–Turvey–Pattee Discussion

Macnamara: Are you implying that is is necessary to have two aspects, rate-dependent and rate-independent, and that the rate-independent system is analogous to the homunculus? Is this going to have to end up being an unanalyzable system? Must we state that it is the thing that makes our decisions?

Pattee: I think that the only strategy is to assume that it is a help unless proven otherwise. But the problem is, first of all, that every time you make a model that is predicted—whether rate-dependent or rate-independent—you still, at least from my point of view, always have an infinite regress or the free-will problem of volitional policies. Ultimately, there has got to be the last buck-passing, at which point we must say where the ultimate volitional act is. I have no idea. I think the brain of humankind is not likely to be modeled without some homunculus. Obviously, you can describe certain parts of its activity, but I think there is always an activity left.

Macnamara: Isn't it like the phenomenological distinction between intentional events and physical events? In fact, we continue to study perception, leaving such notions as "perceive," for example, as a rate-unanalyzed primitive. And that is the trouble with psychology—our primitives are immensely abstract, and we have to know them in our internal experience.

Pattee: All I propose is that useful modeling of psychology should include this complementary or dualistic mode.

Macnamara: You can't, in fact, build a model because you can never build a model of intention. If we ever have a computer or simulator, it is going to be the brain, and that is all it can ever model.

Pattee: A useful model of the brain at least recognizes that there are rate-independent models of analyzing. And I am not saying that those are unanalyzable, because one can make models of rate-independent precesses. Automation, if we think of it as simply a sequential machine, depends only on sequence, not on real-time rate. It can go slow or fast. But a bacterial spore can sit there for 10,000 years and do nothing. And the spore still contains all the information necessary to reproduce. So nature can make rate-independent models. The interesting problems, I think, that have not been faced are the transducer problems. The main problem is how do you transduce a rate-independent model like DNA into dynamics, because you are getting from a timeless system into the conscious and going back out again. This is the same problem in understanding and in reading symbols. Symbols are nontemporal, constructive. How do we read and write? Reading and writing take us from a dynamic system into a timeless system, and we want to get back out again. We want to write down something that is not in the physical time span and then read it and get the meaning of it. And these transductive operations are a transduction problem rather than a translation problem, and the problem involves the recognition of two complementary and distinct modes of description. They cannot be combined into one terminology because they have contradictory intensions.

Member of Audience: This is a question for Turvey and Fowler about skill acquisition, and that process being the model of the observer. One example given by Turvey indicated that in skill acquisition, there is more variation, independent variation over time. But in other areas, you find what may be the opposite practice; that is, there is some initial constraint, and the experimentation with small components of the skill becomes more constraining. Would you care to comment?

Turvey: In the example I gave of the characteristic feature of skill, any change in one of the two remote joints that I spoke of is countered by the direct change in the opposite direction from the other change, so that the variations in the upper arm and the lower arm are not independent of each other. That's the achievement that defines the skilled knowledge—these are no longer independent movements. But there is another way in which the term *constraint* is used. At the initial level of skill acquisition, we see that a person freezes out some of those configurational degrees of freedom that are later to be used—that is, are necessary later for the actual skilled performance. Initially, a person does behave, does look to be, quite rigid in his or her movements. I think that's an intentional (to borrow an "in" phrase at the moment) freezing of certain of the variables that are apt to be used. I think the reason they are frozen is that the person has to find a way to make them controllable degrees of freedom. As I initially confront any new task, I don't have to use individual movements vis-a-vis the task. I must marshal some control over them, and what this does is to convert those biokinetic free variables into controllable free variables. In highly skilled performances, if someone is using personal degrees of freedom fully, we say the individual has found a way of making them controllable degrees of freedom.

Member of Audience: Turvey mentioned the incompatibility of perception and action but then didn't say anything about it again. What is an example of how incompatible these categories would be? I have a case that I think would not count as an example, but I want to know whether it would (or wouldn't) and why. The example involves categorical perception and categorical production of speech sounds. Would this count as an incompatibility for the speaker? Is that not the kind of category you had in mind? I'm sure you had in mind one that has more to do with organization than with more abstract levels—is that the case?

Turvey: My own feeling is that the speech perception-speech production story may be the prime example of this kind of compatibility. I was motivated to look at theories of coordinated movement by my interest in how we could say that speech is perceived by reference to how we produce speech sounds and then raise the question of how we produce it. People would say that speech is produced by reference to how we hear it. Then I would say, how do you hear it? And I would get very much the same arguments, which I could see were invariant across these cases. So I remain interested in the speech production-speech perception confluence. But I was unable to see how we could understand that confluence without coming to terms with coordinated movement in the general case. Now switching to the general case, let me say what I think of this complementation story. Once I get the feeling for the right way of describing an actor (the right level of description), I will promote an orientation toward objects along the lines of Gibson, who argues that we have to worry about a description of the light in references to acting elements. We need to have a description of light in reference to a receptor, and eyeball, or an animal. I would ask the questions: What variables are relevant to activities, and how can I come to understand them all? For example, a significant variable relevant to the control of most of my activities is information about the time to contact—for example, in all kinds of skilled activities like hitting a ball or approaching a barrier that I must hurdle. I need information about time to contact, and there ought to be some way in which that is specified to me. I think that action structures that I am seeking to comprehend are designed in such fashion as to be compatible with the introjection (absorption) of that description, this is how I would approach the general problem of the confluence of perception and action.

I think the dualism that people have been bothered about for so long is the dualism between mind and body. I would like to argue that that is the wrong dualism: The dualism that is more pernicious than that is the one between animal and environment. We can't draw arbitrarily the animal-environment break. We can't logically separate animal from environment. Some of the puzzles we are getting into might be solvable if we step outside the biological device and say that our system is broader, that our system of interest is the animal-environment synergy. And some of these puzzles about how perceiving and acting fit together, or why we rejected that question about how they fit, are because of our traditional acceptance of a naive animal-environment dualism.

Fowler: I don't think there is anything magical about the facts of categorical production and categorical perception in speech. The information that is in the acoustic signal that I apparently hear categorically is there by virtue of my having moved my vocal tract in the proper way. That is, an airstream came out of my lungs and went through my moving vocal tract, and my moving vocal tract removed some of the frequencies that my vocal cords produced. The acoustic signal that comes into my ear was made vocal—so the information in the signal is about a moving vocal tract. So if speech is categorically produced, it is going to be categorically perceived. The information that I detect is information about what the speaker's mouth is doing. Now it's not surprising that that results in a kind of complementation. But in terms of what Turvey was talking about I think that the acoustic information only plays that complementary role in language acquisition or the acquisition of speech where a child is either imitating him- or herself or imitiating somebody else. Probably the process is more abstract for a well-experienced talker.

4 Meaning

John Macnamara
McGill University

This chapter works towards a theory of meaning for a simple kind of word, namely, sortal words for objects you could bump into, like *dog, cow,* and *wheelbarrow*. The ground on which we enter is embattled. No side has had a clear victory, though there have been some conclusive defeats. It is something of an adventure, then, to try again, and in the scope of a single chapter. I fear that all we shall achieve is a glimpse of what a satisfactory theory must be like. That glimpse suggests something rather different from any theory that has standing at the present time in psychology or philosophy.

The chapter begins with a critique of several theories of meaning that are widely accepted in psychology. This is followed by a critique of a few widely accepted philosophical theories. No attempt is made, however, to survey the philosophical literature. The reader should view this section more in the spirit of a foray made in the hope that it will yield a number of useful insights. After this come a set of criteria, or rather desiderata, for a theory of meaning. That will lead to a brief sketch of my own theory. The chapter concludes with an account of how children learn meanings. Though we will confine ourselves to names for things one could bump into, and though we will focus on hierarchically related names, I believe that the theory sketched here can be extended to other words.

PSYCHOLOGICAL THEORIES

The Traditional Theory: Abstraction

The most popular accounts of meaning and concept in psychology—which does not generally distinguish between the two—are all based on some form of abstraction. The traditional view of abstraction is that it is a singling out of some proper subset of features in the sensory array. For example, Walter Kintsch (1977, p. 484) defines "concept learning" as "learning to classify a set of objects into categories on the basis of relevant attributes." On page 386 we find that the "relevant attributes" are values on "stimulus dimensions." That is how we pass from individual to concept. The next citation, where *attributes* is still to be read, in the last analysis, as sensory attributes, refers to levels of concepts (Saltz, 1971):

> The concept of fruit is presumably an abstraction of the attributes that are shared by specific instances of fruit; one must abstract certain attributes that are common to both bananas and oranges, for example, to arrive at the more abstract concept of fruit. Note that of the total set of attributes that define a specific instance, such as banana, only a small subset are relevant to defining fruit. Not all fruit are crescent-shaped or have the consistency or taste of the banana [p. 37].

The core of Humean empiricism, from which the traditional psychological theory stems, is that the form of knowledge is the form of the sensory input. Associations among sensory traces aside, what we know are the impressions our senses receive from the environment. Modern psychology has emphasized that these traces are modified in various ways: For example, by the processes that create the perceptual constancies and by certain rules to which Gestalt psychologists drew attention. But none of these processes or rules change the basic language of sensory experience. Sensory and perceptual form, for example, can be expressed in a single medium. So from the standpoint of our present analysis such perceptual processes are irrelevant.

Consider now that *dog* and *animal* can be true of the same individual, Towser say. The only way the traditional psychological theory can handle this is by making a distinction in Towser phenomena. *Dog,* the theory claims, is true of him in virtue of one set of attributes; *animal* in virtue of another (though there may be overlap between the two sets, and indeed the animal set may be a proper subset of the dog one). That distinction we shall now see cannot be maintained.

A supporter of the distinction might argue that there are peculiarly canine features common to dogs but not to other animals. As a suitably subtle example of such a feature take a ratio of length to height of a head seen from the side. Let us suppose that we have calculated a mean value for this ratio and also a standard deviation so that we now have a typical canine head together with a measure of allowable variability. This, if one is kind enough to go along with the example, is a feature distinctive of dogs or perhaps it just gives us a probability that some creature is a dog. It is not entered in the meaning of *animal,* though it is entered in the meaning of *dog.* Now what might serve as a feature common to all animals? Not number of legs, since worms are legless animals. Not covering, since some animals have feathers or scales instead of hair. Such a feature cannot be color, or shape, or texture, or weight, since all these are variable. It cannot even be movement, since the movement of a bird, a dog, a fish, and a snake are very different. The trouble with the traditional theory is that there aren't any sensory or perceptual features that are common to all animals. This has the unfortunate consequence of making *animal* meaningless. And since parallel arguments would make *plant* and *furniture* meaningless, it should follow that *animal, plant,* and *furniture* mean the same, since they all mean nothing at all. Obviously, something has gone radically wrong, and that is precisely the attempt to maintain a distinction among sensory attributes between canine ones and animal ones.

Perhaps the traditional theorist would respond that whereas we have been looking for sets of attributes in Towser, he would have been looking for them in mental representations of *dog* and *animal*. This will not, I fear, serve the theorist's purpose. The basic reason is that the only type of representation he envisages is a sensory or a perceptual record. What we have just seen is that there cannot be a record of sensory features common to animals, because there aren't any such features.

Yet *dog* and *animal* differ in meaning. It follows that the difference cannot be attributed to sensory or perceptual processes of the type envisaged. It must be due to some other cognitive processes. It matters not for present purposes that we would never have coined two terms with different meanings if the only animals that existed were dogs.

That removes nothing from the interest of the fact that *dog* and *animal* are true of a single creature. The following illustration, inspired by Cassirer (1953), whose lead I follow here, will help to clarify what is going on.

Cassirer noted that mathematicians move from specific to generic expressions not by jettisoning symbols but by replacing them with ones of a higher order. Consider the formula for a straight line of slope .5: it is $y = .5x + c$. The formula for straight lines in general is not reached by omitting the .5 entirely. In the general formula the particular slope is replaced by a parameter that can vary over some range of values. It is $y = bx + c$, where b is the parameter. Applied to our purpose, it suggests that we form two abstract representations of the same thing, one more specific than the other. Just as $y = .5x + c$ and $y = bx + c$ can each represent a single line including its slope, "animal" can represent a single creature and leave out nothing in him that "dog" represents.

One of the lessons we should draw can also be illustrated by the mathematical example. The formula $y = bx + c$ does not represent a straight line in virtue of physical similarities between the formula and the line. Any such similarities that exist are accidental. Similarly the failure to find distinct sets of sensory attributes for dog and animal indicates that the meanings of these words are not representations of the creature in virtue of physical similarities between the meanings and the creature. In other words meanings are abstract with respect to the sensory array.

Fodor (1975) makes the same point with a different argument. He begins with the simple fact that a child must learn, in some sense, to classify the things he finds in the environment. Presumably he must try out various sortings of objects until he hits on "satisfactory" ones. Now either we visualize the process somewhat as predetermined mental photographs developing in the child's mind on contact with the environment, and that is not learning at all; or we visualize the child as playing a more active part and trying out the sortings. If the latter, the process is basically one of hypothesis formation and testing. But to form a hypothesis about experience and test it presupposes a medium other than experience in which to express the hypothesis and the results of the testing. Hence the need for a language of the mind that is abstract with respect to sensory experience.

Another argument for the same conclusion can be mounted on the fact that we can talk about the things we see, and so there is need for a connecting medium between speech and vision, one that is abstract with respect to both—see Miller and Johnson-Laird (1976).

Prototype Theory

A new line of research promises to improve our understanding of sensory tests for category membership. We must look at it because it sometimes gives rise to confusion between such tests and meaning. The research is aimed at prototypes of categories. In ordinary language a prototype is the original after which copies are fashioned, and that is very much the sense in which the term is mostly used by Rosch (1977) and her collaborators. There is another sense, now common in the psychological literature, that amounts to some type of average computed over category members.

The two senses, though distinct, are useful and well grounded in psychological research. Rosch has made particularly good use of hers in explaining how people judge one object as more typical of a category than another. For example, most people judge a robin to be a more typical bird than a penguin or a chicken. Moreover, if asked to imagine a bird or name one they are far more likely to imagine or name a robin than less typical ones. There is now a whole range of observations that show a robin to be more accessible under the description *bird* than penguins and chickens. Rosch argues that the reason is that children learn a word, like *bird,* as applied to the more typical exemplars; she and Anglin (1977) have published some evidence that they do. Children build their tests of category membership, the argument continues, on the perceptual data in the exemplars used to teach them. Little wonder, then, if the most typical exemplars fit the tests best. For example, if we suppose that the angle of inclination of a standing robin's body is taken by the child as a good index to the category *bird,* then penguins are more difficult to classify as birds because they stand completely upright.

The other tendency in the prototype literature presents the learner as averaging across instances and forming for himself a pattern or prototype that he has never seen. Rosch (1977) sometimes writes in that vein: "The most cognitively economical code for a category is, in fact, a concrete image of an average category member." Posner (1973) summarizes several studies that support the notion. He explains how he and his colleagues made several distinct patterns, and then prepared sets of random distortions of these patterns, one set for each pattern. They then presented the distorted patterns (not the basic patterns themselves) to learners and taught them to discriminate among the types. Then came a test period in which the learner saw for the first time the basic patterns and some new distortions as well as the original set on which he had learned. He was not told anything of the basic patterns. His job was once again to identify the pattern types. The interesting finding was that learners performed most accurately on the basic patterns. It was as though without seeing it, they had constructed the basic pattern of each type. In further studies they showed that learners also obtained some measure of the variability of each type. Experiments with similar results were conducted by Franks and Bransford (1971) on geometric shapes.

Central to this line of research is the belief that learning to recognize members of most categories involves learning to compute their similarity, along physical dimensions, to stored information. This seems eminently sensible and indeed inescapable since we all manage to assign objects to appropriate categories on the basis of observable physical properties. The extraordinary thing is how well children can do this after seeing one or two exemplars—see Miller's (1977) calculation that children learn about one word per waking hour up to the age of six.

The enormous value of prototypes must not lead us to mistake them for meanings. Posner certainly does, calling his prototypes "iconic concepts"—in my view a contradiction in terms. Posner, I take it, considers *meaning* and *concept* equivalent terms in the discussion of language. Rosch is generally more circumspect and uses the word *category* instead of *meaning*. But she does not distinguish between means for distinguishing category members and the mental representation of a category. Moreover, expressions like "semantic noun categories" sometimes escape her, in which "semantic" strongly suggests the confusion. However, little is to be gained from drawing up a schedule of errors; what is important is to avoid the confusion, or, if one insists on confounding things, to deal with the issues clearly.

Two further points about categories, both highly relevant to our present purpose: Prototypes seem suitable for discriminating among members of low level categories, e.g., among dogs, cats, and cows. They seem less suited to deal with superordinate ones, like animal. Rosch (1977) found that people take much longer to form images when instructed to imagine an animal, say, than a dog, and in a number of ways the difference between superordinate and subordinate levels revealed empirical differences. Rosch (1977) is quite willing to accept the idea that at the superordinate level images or prototypes will not serve in categorizing because at that level the "categories . . . possess few attributes common to members of the category." The situation is worse; they possess none. Indeed I have great difficulty, in the spirit of Berkeley, in conceiving how a single image of a chair can serve in the recognition of all chairs. Perhaps one should really speak of prototypes for individual types of chairs.

It is clear that a robin is a more typical bird than a chicken. This is probably because our perceptual tests for "birdiness" work better on robins than on chickens. Yet everyone allows that *a chicken is a bird*. They do not say, *a chicken is like a bird*. Implicitly they are saying that a chicken has all that anything needs to be a bird. Being a bird is not a matter of appearances. It makes no difference that chickens don't look much like the image we typically form for a bird.

The purpose of these observations is to show that what a child learns when he learns common names is more than a prototype. Rosch conceded that the meaning of *animal* cannot be an image. Neither can the meaning of *bird*. Prototypes may serve in perceptual tests, but they are not meaning.

Networks and Features

Information processing, so fascinated by language, has made several attempts to represent meaning. Quillian (1967, 1968, 1969) began with a theory of the form of word meanings that kept close to the model of dictionary definitions. His work has been adapted and supplemented by several other workers, e.g., Lindsay and Norman (1972, chapters 10 and 11), Smith, Shoben and Rips (1974), Anderson (1976).

Now we undoubtedly have much information that serves important psychological functions, but not everything that is relevant to the interpretation of a word or a sentence should be represented as the meaning of the word. The fact that fathers sometimes dote on their children is not part of the meaning of *father*. If it were it would be uninformative to tell some one that fathers sometimes dote on children; that would be true in virtue of the meaning of *father*.

The models run into serious trouble of this type. Take the network that expresses the meaning of *fascist* in Lindsay and Norman (1972, p. 425). It says *fascist* is ugly, cruel, short, radical and fat; and fascist is a person. Pass over niceties about use and mention and there remains the trouble that *fascist* means none of those things except, probably, person. It matters not that the stereotype of fascists may include cruel, ugly, radical and other such elements. In other words it is not a contradiction in terms to say that some fascist are not cruel; as it is a contradiction to say a bachelor is married. Moreover the model owes us an account of the meaning of *person*.

The argument extends to numerous theories that take meaning to be a set of semantic features. For example, several theories propose that "yellow" and "sings" are part of the meaning of *canary*. That would rule out the possibility of an albino canary. It would say that a plucked canary was not a canary at all. Such theories are equivalent to the network theories without the network of logical relations.

Much of the information that such theories seek to represent is really not part of the words meaning but what others call "collateral information." Later, when we have discussed the relation between meaning and truth we will define collateral information. In the meantime we can draw the distinction between it and meaning by asking whether or not some item of information is *necessarily* true of creatures that fall under a category name. If it is not, it is collateral and not part of meaning.

Definitions

One of the standard ways to decide whether or not someone knows the meaning of a word is to ask for a definition. In the Stanford Binet test of intelligence there is a vocabulary item that does just that, and many people take satisfactory answers to such questions as statements of meaning. Among the "correct" answers to the Stanford Binet request to say what an orange is are: "it's round"; "it's yellow"; "an orange is something to eat." It seems clear that what children do when asked what an orange is, is to answer one of two different questions: (1) how can you tell an orange from other things? (2) what does one normally want an orange for, or what does one normally do with one? Such translations are perfectly sensible, but the responses to them must not be taken as expressions of meaning. An orange would still be an orange even if the whole human race lost its taste for oranges; and an orange is an orange even when it's green. The theory now being discussed is generally not explicit, unlike some of the others. It must be mentioned here because it is very common; perhaps because it is implicit in the construction of dictionaries. Dictionaries, if I am right, answer the question of how to tell Xs from other things, and what to do with them. They also have a shot at the related concept; i.e., the set of necessary and sufficient conditions for belonging to the relevant category. Such statements must not be taken as meanings. If they were it would follow that anyone who did not know the definition of the concept, would not know the meaning of the word. For example, if H_2O specifies necessary and sufficient conditons for some stuff to be water, we don't want to say that no one knew the meaning of *water* before 1,800 A.D.

STOCKTAKING

Our critiques of psychological theories employed certain principles and it may help to make them explicit. We also reached negative conclusions about meaning and we will briefly list them.

Language picks out objects for consideration. The function of picking out objects we call reference. Language also describes objects and states of affairs. The function of describing, taking that term broadly, is a large part of what we intend by meaning. We are not directly aware of the form of meanings; we are aware of our words and of what they describe. Meaning has to be inferred on the basis of some skill. The skill we have been canvassing is commonsense judgment about the truth or falsehood of statements. For example, we all share the judgment (or intuition) that a *chicken is a bird.* From that we concluded that our judgment implies that a chicken has all that is necessary to be a bird. That in turn led to the conclusion that the meaning of *bird* cannot be an image of a typical bird. Because a chicken differs in obvious ways from a typical bird, such as a robin.

The whole argument is an exploration of that which is implicit in a common judgment. The judgment itself is a conclusion that a proposition is true. Judging true, then, is an important clue to underlying representation. Notice, however, that in judging *a chicken is a bird* we do not reveal that "bird" is part of the meaning of *chicken.* "Chicken" and "bird" might for example be related by some such logical connective as *implies* ($\supset$).

On the other hand if some feature really were a component of a word's meaning, that feature would be implied by predicating that word of some creature. For example, if "yellow" really were part of the meaning of *canary,* we would infer that if any creature is a canary, it must be yellow. The fact that commonsense does not rule out the possibility of an albino or of a plucked (not yellow) canary reveals that "yellow" is not part of the meaning of canary.

This method of arguing presupposes a close tie between meaning and belief in our judgments that a proposition is true or false. I think the argument is sound, though we shall see it challenged in the next section. Notice, however, that we have so far used our intuitions of truth to rule out theories of meaning, not to support them.

Our main negative conclusion was to reject traditional psychological empiricism, the doctrine that the form of knowledge is basically the form of the sensory input. Empiricism cannot satisfactorily handle the fact that a single creature is both dog and animal. In particular, abstraction as understood by traditional theorists does not work. Abstraction depends on our finding a distinction between those sensory attributes in virtue of which he is an animal as distinct from those in virtue of which he is a dog.

We concluded that meaning is not expressed in the form of an image, or of an average of sensory impressions, or indeed in the language of the sensory array.

PHILOSOPHICAL THEORIES

Most philosophical discussion of meaning has hinged one way or another on truth. That there is some connection between meaning and truth is not difficult to see. For example, if I ask you whether you think the following sentence true,

Mol an óige agus tiochfaid si[1]

you will say that depends on what it means. So truth depends on meaning. Does meaning depend on truth? Is truth the key to meaning? We will begin with a philosopher who answers no.

Putnam

Hilary Putnam (1975a, 1978) mounts a powerful argument against the view that the meanings people carry in their heads determine the truth or falsehood of sentences. He points out that most people do not know what determines whether something is gold, or water, or a dog. He is not talking about how we tell whether something is gold. The problem is that many do not know what gold is. What are necessary and sufficient conditions for something to be gold? Of course we have some idea: a precious metal, yellow in color, used in jewelry and dentistry. That serves well enough most of the time. We know, however, that other metals can look like gold and when some importance attaches to the matter we have recourse to an expert. He or she is supposed to be able to go beyond appearances and tell us for a fact whether some sample really is gold.

Why are the expert's tests considered better? Not merely because of his or her authority. Unlike an umpire who decides how a play is interpreted, whatever the facts, the expert is supposed to establish the facts. The reason the experts prevail is that their tests have a basis in science, and they can show that. On the assumption that the expert has discovered the nature of gold, he or she has the appropriate concept (leave aside their tests) and the layman does not.

How then, according to Putnam, do laymen manage to converse and reach mutual understanding if they do not know the concepts related to the words they use? (I am using concept solely to mean necessary and sufficient conditions for category membership. In that sense, if chemists have done their work well H_2O specifies the concept water.) Putnam's answer is that they manage to communicate because they share stereotypes; i.e., "standardized sets of beliefs." (Putnam, 1978, p. 115.) He also says that a stereotype is all that the layman has in his head: "this is the sole element of truth in the 'concept' theory." (Putnam, 1975b, p. 169.) The layman, however, may lack even the stereotype. Putnam says that he himself lacks the stereotypes for *elm* and *beech* and could not tell the trees apart. Even in the matter of stereotypes there is a "division of linguistic labor." Only the expert may know the full stereotype. The communal stereotype guarantees that reference will usually be correct. The community can allow the concept be whatever it turns out to be. That, for Putnam, is what science ultimately makes of it.

I have not given Putnam's case in its full force but I have said enough to show that it undermines some popular views of how meaning relates to truth. Since meaning in people's heads is stereotype, and since stereotypes may be false, one cannot go from truth to such meaning or from such meaning to truth. The strong part of Putnam's position is the argument that meaning does not normally provide necessary and sufficient conditions for category membership. Most people don't know such conditions for most common categories, and no one at all knows them for such ones as dog and cow. The weak part of his theory is the claim that meaning is stereotype. A stereotype is described as a standardized belief in the truth of some proposition. Now having four legs is part of the stereotype of dog. Yet people do not hesitate to call a creature a dog just because it lost a leg. Being yellow is part of the canary's stereotype. But people do not rule out the possibility of an albino canary. Being liquid is part of the stereotype of water, yet even young children are told that ice and snow are really water. There is little to be gained by appealing to a similarity metric. It seems inconceivable that any such metric could reveal enough similarities at the sensory level (the only relevant one) to warrant calling snow water. From these examples it follows that stereotypes will not explain our everyday use of names.

While keeping Putnam's observation that meaning (that people carry about in their heads) does not generally furnish necessary and sufficient conditions for category membership, we must reject the proposal that such meaning is merely stereotype. Since *concept* as I use it involves necessary and sufficient conditions for category membership, it follows that we must establish a distinction between the meaning people have, as competent speakers, and concept. In refusing to accept meaning as stereotype I am preparing to re-establish the link between meaning and truth. But first some other theories.

Verification/Falsification

Remember what we are looking for, a theory of the meanings people know for the names of physical objects; a theory that will handle such facts as that a dog is an animal. Because dog is not a category for which at present anyone can state necessary and sufficient conditions, it follows that the meaning of *dog* cannot be such conditions.

Can we, nevertheless, make a connection between meaning and truth? Suppose, for example, we wanted to be sure in general which things are dogs and which are not, a set of necessary and sufficient conditions is exactly what we need. That the meaning of a word (as generally known), does not supply.

Nonetheless, most of us believe that everything either is a dog or it is not. Nothing is in between. Implicitly we believe that necessary and sufficient conditions for being a dog exist. We just don't know them. We know where to look for them, in dogs.

Talk of necessary and sufficient conditions puts people in mind of Wittgenstein's analysis of the word *game* in his *Philosophical investigations*. He showed there do not seem to be necessary and sufficient conditions for something to be a game. The notion is vague. This seems right, but it does not follow that natural kind terms, like *dog,* are. In fact, common intuition is on the side that they are not vague.

In this connection, too, people mention fuzzy sets, i.e., sets in which membership is not a matter of all or none. They are prompted to do so by the observation that it is difficult to establish boundaries for species. Are wolves and foxes really distinct from dogs? Now vagueness can arise in at least two ways. The category might indeed be vague, as a fuzzy set is vague. But one's test for category membership might also be vague. For example, the birdwatcher peering at a little brown bird at the far side of the bush has little doubt about the distinctions among species. He has grave doubts about assigning this particular bird to one species. My own tests for whether or not something is water are vague, though serviceable. It does not follow that the category water is vague.

What happens is our sensory system gives us a useful first division of objects. The division is tested for its contribution to intelligibility. Adjustments are made. At one time seals and whales were treated as fish, but we were persuaded that it made more sense, because they were air-breathing milk-giving creatures, to place them with the mammals.

What has this to do with the layman's language? It is a backdrop to all his or her thinking and hence to his or her use of language. That is why the layman yields to the expert who says something is or is not gold. That is why we cease to call seals fish. Notice, too, that the layman and the expert's vocabulary overlap. *Gold* is both a layman's word and an expert's; the same word. Even more basic, the layman and expert are both human. And the expert's ideal of understanding is the layman's, though the layman may make less use of it.

All this is a preamble to a sympathetic analysis of theories that tie meaning and truth. We can see words like *dog* linked not to a set of necessary and sufficient conditions that people know, but to a set that they believe exists in those creatures they call dog. It may, of course, be necessary to extend *dog* to some creatures that are not now called *dog,* or to exclude some that now are. It is inconceivable, however, that terriers, spaniels, setters, poodles, and collies should be excluded, so central are they to our application of the name *dog.*

Before going on, a word of caution about terms that really are vague. Not only is *game* vague, but so is *tall.* Society does not establish precise points at which *tall* is applicable. Closely akin are *stream* and *puddle. Stream, brook,* and *river* are vague regions on the continuum that measures quantity of water. *Puddle, pond,* and *lake* are vague regions on the continuum that measures quantities of still water. *Mound, knoll, hill,* and *mountain* are vague regions on the continuum that measures quantities of earth raised above the plane. These are a different kind of term from *dog* and *cow,* and it is necessary to keep them distinct.

Michael Dummett (1978) has revitalized an approach to meaning that was made popular between the world wars by logical positivism. Although avoiding much of the empiricism of the logical positivists, he argues that the key to meaning is in our ability to verify or falsify statements. Since to verify or falsify is to establish a truth value for a statement, his approach depends on a connection between meaning, psychologically real meaning, and truth. Dummett does not, however, subscribe to the connection I have just sketched between meaning, ideal concepts and truth.

Dummett makes several valuable points that I think we should adopt. He insists that the speaker's grasp of meaning must be manifest in some "practical ability" (pp. 69 and 74). He demands, then, that a theory of meaning include an account of such an ability and of how it relates to the "understanding" of sentences. In addition the theory should explain how the meaning of a sentence is built from the meanings of its component words. Further, he distinguishes, with Frege, not only between sense and reference but also between these and force. *Force* denotes a range of intentional attitudes towards an utterance. It includes stating, questioning, commanding. Although there may be linguistic differences between statements, questions, and commands, a single sentence may also be employed with different forces. Story tellers use statement forms without intending their utterances to be taken as true.

Dummett's own choice of a practical ability to serve as the key to meaning seems unfortunate. He chooses the ability to verify or falsify a statement. (For utterances like commands he would, it seems, accept some other ability such as compliance, p. 73). To verify or to falsify is to establish a truth value. Meaning, on this account is the means employed for assigning a truth value.

Consider the child who is learning such words as *dog, cat* and *bird*. He hears his parents say such things as: *that is a cat; Freddie is a dog,* and *look at the bird*. The verificationist would have the child discover means for verifying his parents' statements. This seems odd. The child probably just accepts their word. It is easier to understand the verificationist approach when one thinks of the child's own efforts to use the words. He predicates them of various objects and watches his parents' reaction to see if he has used them correctly or not. Notice, however, that what the child is doing is neither verifying nor falsifying, as those terms are usually understood, but conforming to common usage. That must be so, since his parents do not have necessary and sufficient conditions for the application of *bird, dog* and *cat*.

The verificationist is aware of this and several moves are open to him that save his overall position. One is to present a new notion of truth. Another is to give up the idea that natural-kind terms have sharp boundaries. He may have independent reasons for coming to those conclusions. I do not propose to go into all the related issues. I prefer to see if a theory of meaning can be worked out with the conventional notions of truth and natural kinds. The theory I want would maintain a link between meaning and truth as truth has been understood in realist philosophy. Verificationism cannot provide that.

Truth Conditions

In the second chapter of her excellent book on semantics, Janet Fodor (1977) discusses a variety of theories that can broadly be characterized by the claim that meaning is a set of truth conditions. Truth conditions are not truth, nor verification. As their name suggests, they are conditions that determine the truth of an assertion. The general idea is this. *Freddie is a dog* is true if and only if the object picked out be Freddie satisfies certain conditions, C. The next move is to say that C specifies the meaning of *dog*. The theory can be stated in rather different ways. The most interesting version is that C specifies those properties that any creature under any circumstances must have if it is to be a dog. That is, C is a set of necessary and sufficient conditions for being a dog.

Janet Fodor's critique of this class of theories reveals their inadequacies and need not be repeated here. From our point of view the additional observation that needs to be made is that following Putnam to the extent we do, we realize that the meaning people have in their heads for *dog* cannot be necessary and sufficient conditions for being a dog. No one in fact knows such conditions. What is instructive for us is to note the existence and popularity of such theories. Dummett (1978) says they are the most popular theories of meaning at the present time. What is valuable in them is the determination to relate meaning and truth. What is weak in them is the confounding of meanings and necessary and sufficient conditions. In the terminology we have established, they wrongly confound meaning and concept.

Meaning and Use

The idea that meaning is use is associated with Wittgenstein, particularly in *Philosophical investigations*. I will not review Wittgenstein's main ideas on meaning—that is well done by Fodor (1977) for one. I want to make a single point suggested by the word *use*. In Wittgenstein's general theory the meaning of a word, say, *kettle,* is its use in some linguistic system. Besides the word there is the object, and it too has uses in the business of cooking. It ought to make sense to speak about the meaning of the object kettle. I think that this much is right, but on Wittgenstein's account the meaning of the word and the meaning of the object will be quite different.

In the theory that I will later adumbrate, I will suggest that objects, too, have meanings. In fact I will suggest that a word and the related objects have the same meaning. Our sensory experience is meaningful; we make sense of it. The notion of meaning is not foreign in the study of perception. Perception, in the world of information processing, is seen as an interpretative process. A percept is the sense we make of experience at one level. We also interpret percepts. The next level of interpretation I would like to call sense or meaning. We will see more of this. It is enough now to give warning that I will suggest that the meaning of the object kettle is the meaning of the word *kettle*. Of course, I am not suggesting that the object functions as a symbol in the way the word does. A word is a conventional symbol, and an object is usually not a symbol at all. That difference does not preclude their both accessing a common level of processing. Indeed the non-arbitrary nature of the objects' interpretation is exactly what is needed to guarantee that the arbitrary linguistic symbol is assigned a meaning that is constant to all members of a speech community.

The attraction of the view that word and object have the same meaning is that it suggests an explanation for how we can talk about the things we see. It indicates a path to follow if one wishes to explore one way in which words and objects are related.

DESIDERATA FOR A THEORY OF MEANING

One of the reasons for surveying psychological and philosophical theories of meaning was to find positive and negative criteria for a theory of meaning. The survey also provided an initial processing of the material. We will now go on to take stock of what we found. We will do so in the form of a list of guiding ideas, each followed by a brief comment on its justification and force.

Negative Conclusions

1. *We are not directly aware of meanings.*   This is commonly held in psychology. We adverted to it when we noted that meaning has to be inferred mainly on the basis of certain intuitions.

2. *Meaning is not given directly in sensory stimuli.*   This is a little different from the previous principle. We are not generally aware of sensory stimuli. Hence the need to separate a principle about awareness from one about sensation. Note however that percepts are in the language of sensation. Visual percepts involve color, shape, texture, and these are expressible in terms of sensory stimuli.

The principle derives from our analysis of widely held psychological theories of meaning. In rejecting them we rejected the notion that abstraction yields meaning. Abstraction is the singling out in attention of subsets of sensory features. Together with abstraction we reject the notion that meaning is a set of semantic features abstracted from the sensory array. We also rejected the view that meaning is an image of any sort, prototypical or other, or that it is an average computed over sets of sensory data.

3. *Meaning is not use.*   We did not refute the view that meaning is use as that is done in many books on semantics. Fodor (1977) is one such book.

Meaning and Truth

4. *Truth depends on meaning.*   This is taken as self evident. There is, however, a way of taking Putnam's position on stereotypes that would seem to

oppose it. If we take meaning, effectively, to be stereotype, then the truth of sentences will not depend on such meaning. We argued that stereotypes are not meanings.

5. *Truth value does not determine meaning.* This is based on Putnam's point, that most people do not know necessary and sufficient conditions for membership in most of the categories they have names for.

A similar line of argument shows that the means for correctly assigning truth value are not meaning. In particular means for assigning truth values can hardly be what the language learner is after.

6. *Truth value judgments provide a test of theories of meaning.* A theory of word meaning must not, without grave reasons, run foul of our commonsense judgments. Such reasons have not been given, so far as I know. In particular, if a theory claimed that being four-legged was part of the meaning of *dog,* then it would have to deny that a three-legged creature could be correctly called *dog* in the literal sense of the word.

Another obvious judgment we must respect is that if Rosy is a cow, necessarily it cannot be a cat. On the other hand if Rosy is a cow, it is also an animal. We noted that one can accept that without making "animal" part of the meaning of *cow*.

Distinctions

7. *Meaning is distinct from reference.* Informally, reference has to do with designating what one is talking about and meaning has to do with describing it. Modern logic began with a semantics that related language to objects that actually exist, their relations and properties. Such a semantics is called *extensional*. Modal logicians extend the semantics to objects in possible worlds and to their relations and properties. In such a semantics, called *intensional, dog* might refer to all possible dogs as well as to the actual ones. In fact *intension* is defined in terms of reference to objects in all possible worlds. Such reference is held in check, ideally, by a set of necessary and sufficient conditions associated with the terms. Hence modal logic makes a close connection between reference and what I call concept. Even in modal logic, however, a distinction is required between reference and meaning.

8. *Meaning is distinct from force.* *Force* denotes a speaker's intentional act in making an utterance as a whole. Frege distinguishes it from meaning and reference. The necessity of the distinction is widely, though not universally, accepted—see Janet Fodor (1977, chap. 2).

9. *Meaning and concept are distinct.* The reader will recall that I am using *concept* in a technical sense to signify necessary and sufficient conditions for category membership. I am also using *meaning* to denote something that ordi-

nary people have in their heads. Putnam forced on us the realization that meaning and concept, so defined, must be distinct. For example, if the concept of water really is specified by H_2O, that is not the meaning of *water*. The meaning of *water* did not change when people decided that water is H_2O. It would not change if we found out that it isn't H_2O.

10. *Meaning is distinct from partial concept.* I am here introducing the term partial concept to signify the understanding a person has of some object if that understanding is less than ideally adequate necessary and sufficient conditions for membership in the category the word names.

For example, we all have some understanding of the nature of dogs. It explains how they can bark, run about, digest food, and have puppies. Biologists know a great deal more. If they have specialized in dogs, they know all sorts of details about their digestive system, for example. They have a partial understanding of how it works. Of course some current biological beliefs may be wrong. I will use the word *partial concept* of such comprehension as a person has achieved.

I have not proved that meaning and partial concept must be distinct. The argument that proved meaning and concept distinct will not do. Several arguments will come up later, such as that meaning must be attainable without a scientific training, and meaning must be the same for all who use a word to communicate. These are sufficient to prove meaning and partial understanding distinct, but the arguments depend on principles yet to be laid down.

One argument can be made at present. People's theories are frequently erroneous, at least in some details. If we allowed a person's theory (understanding) of dogs to be the meaning of *dog* we could not explain how he might change his theory. For example, scientists once thought that all combustion involved a substance called phlogiston. One can imagine such a scientist believing that the explanation of a dog's muscular contractions involved phlogiston. It turns out that there is no such substance.

If that early biologist's meaning for *dog* was his theory of dogs, it would have included the notion of phlogiston. Being part of the meaning of *dog* (on this account of meaning) it would then be analytically true that dogs had phlogiston. But that is false. Therefore the theory that makes meaning equal to partial concept must be false. The argument runs parallel to that by which we argued that "four-legged" is not part of the meaning of *dog,* not a semantic feature.

11. *Meaning is distinct from collateral information.* Collateral information signifies information that is part neither of a word's meaning nor of the partial concept associated with it. The term is used in the philosophy of language.

Much of the information that psychologists place in semantic features is really collateral. That canaries are generally yellow is collateral information. That fascists tend to be cruel is too. Under that heading falls any information that one may glean about a class of objects that one would not tie by means of logical implication to the object. That may, for all I know, be most of my information about such a category as dogs.

Additional Desiderata

12. *Meaning is based on publicly observable events.*   We must not permit our rejection of empiricism to distract us from Wittgenstein's admonition that there is no p rivate language. What he intended to hammer home is the fact that English (and each natural language) is a public communication system. Children learn it from their parents on the basis of publicly observable objects and events. Meanings that are not tied to the publicly observable are non communicable; and therefore unlearnable. The point did not come up in previous discussion. It is made with sufficient clarity and force in the *Philosophical investigations.*

13. *Meaning is constant across all members of a speech community.*   This is perhaps the basis for the last point. It does not rule out ambiguity. It does not even demand that all members of a speech community know all meanings of an ambiguous term, such as *bank* (money, river). It claims, for example, that any member who knows those two meanings of *bank* enters the very same two meanings as anyone else who knows them. The principle does not rule out historical change of meaning. For example, in Old English *deor* meant animal, while its modern descendant, *deer,* means one species of animal. The introduction of *animal,* ultimately from Latin, dislodged the original meaning of *deer.* The principle just enunciated states that where such a change in meaning occurs, it must occur in a short time and it must not escape the attention of members of the speech community in which it is occurring. (It may not occur in a particular dialect.)

Meanings must be subject to a very strong constraint if communication is to be as successful as it generally seems to be. Of course partial concepts and collateral information will vary from speaker to speaker.

14. *Meanings exist in ordinary people's heads.*   This is merely to formalize a requirement that we have assumed all long. It implies that one can learn meanings without benefit of science. For the most part what science gives us is a partial concept. The distinction between meaning and partial concept helps to solve a problem in the philosophy of science. Do words change their meanings as science advances? Did *electron* mean something different to Maxwell from what it means to a modern physicist? And if so, are Maxwell's writings unintelligible today? The distinction between meaning and partial concept opens the way to a solution. Meaning remains constant although partial concepts change. Modern scientists can understand their predecessors.

15. *The skill that reveals grasp of meaning is categorizations.*   Dummett warned us that theories of meaning must be grounded in a practical ability. We

are dealing only with the meaning of category terms. Dummett's principle has some affinity with Wittgenstein's requirement that meaning should rest on the publicly observable. The appropriate ability to reveal grasp of meaning of the sort we are studying is successful categorization. A child gives good grounds for the belief that he knows the meaning of *dog* if he applies the word to all and only dogs.

Too much confidence should not be placed in our tests for grasp of a meaning. It is conceivable that a child might know the word *chopstick* and apply it only to chopsticks, and yet not have any idea of what a chopstick is for. Such a child lacks the central ingredient of the meaning of the word *chopstick*. On the other hand, a child who has a meaning may fail to reveal it for any of a number of reasons.

16. *The meaning of the word is the meaning of the object.*   This principle, which was introduced when we were discussing Wittgenstein, was employed implicitly in explaining the last principle. In using a nonverbal test for grasp of the meaning of *animal* with children who did not apply the word correctly, we were assuming that the adult meaning of the word and the meaning of the object is one and the same.

We cannot make the principle a strict criterion of a theory of meaning. What we can demand of such a theory is that it help to explain how we can talk about the things we perceive. Some words refer to them, but more than reference is involved. Some words describe objects. A general theory of cognitive psychology must explain how language relates to perception, both in the learning of words and in their use. Logically, the relation need not be identity of meaning. Such an identity would, however, greatly simplify psychology.

Besides the argument from simplicity there is another that is due to Ray Jackendoff (in a lecture given at McGill). I can point to the kettle and say, *that is what I boil water in,* and mean the very same as if I had said, *the kettle is what I boil water in.* In one sentence the listener supplies the appropriate meaning when he hears the word *kettle;* in the other he must supply the same meaning from an inspection of the environment. One might argue that on inspecting the environment the word *kettle* occurs to the listener and then he attains the meaning. But that is to forget that that cannot be how the child learned the meaning of *kettle* in the first place. When he first heard the word he had no other course than to determine what it meant by inspecting the object that it designated.

17. *A theory of meaning should specify a connection between meaning and our ability to assign objects to categories.*   There is broad agreement that the meaning of *dog* has some connection with the manner in which we distinguish dogs from other creatures. In principle 15 we used the connection, suggesting categorization as the skill that normally reveals grasp of meaning. At the same time we must distinguish dogs on the basis of sensory attributes, even though we

have rejected empiricism (which makes meaning a set of distinctive sensory features).

The discipline that studies how we distinguish in perception between categories is called pattern recognition. An adequate theory would tell us how sensory features are recognized and how they contribute to category assignment. We should not include such tests in meaning. There can be many ways to determine category membership; there can even be many equally valid ways: yet the meaning of the category is not many. For example one can sometimes determine which element some substance is by atomic weight or by electrical resistance. The meanings of the elements' names do not change with the discovery of new methods for deciding which elements are which. Sometimes the criteria for category decisions can be quite trivial. When I was a child one knew that if another child wore a ribbon it was a girl. Since then ribbon wearing has become much less common, yet one does not want to say for that reason that the meaning of *girl* has changed, even for me.

Nonetheless, there must be an intimate connection between meaning and concepts on the one hand and sensation and perception on the other. We do apply our words to the objects we see and feel, and any success in doing so presupposes a stable relationship between words and objects. It is therefore desirable that our theory explain how words, meaning, and concepts relate to our system of assigning objects to categories.

SKETCH OF THEORY OF MEANING

Our preparatory work is complete and we must now look for a theoretical entity that will satisfy the requirements we have just listed. I fear we will not find exactly what we want readymade, but many of the ingredients are in the late writings of Gottlob Frege. We begin with his treatment of thought.

For Frege (1918), a thought is "something for which the question of truth arises." A thought is ascribed a truth value. A thought is itself complex having as minimal components a reference to some object and a predicate. The reference picks out some object and the predicate bears the relation "true of" or "not true of" to that object. We must focus on the predicate.

Frege (1892) says that the predicate has "a reference" and that reference is a concept. In the *Grundgesetze* (vol. 1, sect. 3) we read that "a concept is a function whose value is always a truth-value." More simply, this means that the predicate itself is not part of the thought, but it designates a concept, which is. The sorts of concepts Frege had in mind were ones with "sharp boundaries"; that is a concept that would "unambiguously determine, as regards any object, whether or not it falls under the concept (whether or not the predicate is truly assertible of it)." (*Grundgesetze*, Vol. 1, sect. 56.)

In the essay "On sense and reference" he clearly distinguishes between sense and reference: "It is natural, now, to think of there being connected with a sign . . . besides that to which the sign refers, which may be called the reference of the sign, also what I would like to call the *sense* of the sign, wherein the mode of presentation is contained." It does not seem that Frege applied the distinction to predicates to differentiate between their sense and reference. In fact he held that thought and sense are identical. With John Perry (1979), though he was working on the problem of indexicals, I believe Frege ought to have distinguished between the sense of a predicate and its referent (a concept). And I believe that it is sense as so distinguished that we are after.

Meaning, then—for I shall use that term rather than Frege's *sense*—is distinct from concept. Since its main function is to guarantee that an expression denotes a concept I will call it a placeholder for a concept or, more briefly, a proconcept.

Incidentally, I believe I am well within the spirit of Frege's writing when I use concept, not of what people actually have in their heads (partial concept), but of an ideal set of necessary and sufficient conditions for category membership. The concept, in conjunction with the reference (to an object), determines the truth or falsehood of the thought in which it occurs; it has to do only secondarily with what people will assent to or affirm.

Proconcept is a neologism, I share the common antagonism to them and feel I must immediately justify its introduction and show it is not as unfamiliar as it sounds. To show it is not so strange I will relate it to a common usuage of the word *nature*. I will give several examples of such usage and then explain why the word *nature* will not do in its stead.

There is today, I am told, a new breed of poodle so tiny that it fits in a teacup—the adult of the breed! I have not seen it, but people who have report amazement that a mature dog should be so small. It jolts the stereotype. Why do people agree that it is a dog? I submit that what decides the matter is the fact that the teacup poodle was bred directly from poodles. In the layman's categorizing breeding is a winner. The reason is that parent and offspring are believed to share a nature. In fact, if you ask a layman why a dog has pups and not kittens, he is liable to tell you that it's a dog's nature to have pups.

The notion of nature is robust. It is undoubtedly part of the stereotype of dog that a dog has four legs. Yet if a dog loses a leg he does not for that cease to be a dog. The nature, dog, is not identified with surface phenomena, rather it serves to explain a variety of such phenomena. Similarly, a plucked canary remains a canary, at least for a while, though it is no longer yellow.

The layman's belief that water is a natural kind implicitly recognizes a common nature underlying a variety of phenomena. It seems likely that the idea starts off in connection with water in its liquid state. However, water can freeze and form ice and thaw and become liquid again; it can crystalize into snow and return to liquid again. All this is reflected in common speech where one tells a child, for example, *ice is really water*. The *really* there seems to warn him that, despite appearances, ice is water. The interchangeability of states indicates a common nature underlying all the states. And that nature is what explains, ultimately, why water is good to drink and good for plants.

Associated with differences between dog phenomena and cat phenomena in common belief is a difference in nature. The appeal to nature is an appeal to a fundamental explanation for the phenomena that are grouped together. Nature then is a commonsense explanatory construct. Before such a construct is invoked, the layman must recognize that a dog, for example, in all his manifestations is a single organism. The phenomena call for a single, though highly complex, explanation. *Nature,* in common speech, is a symbol for that largely unknown explanation.

Nature so used, has a close affinity to what I call proconcept. A proconcept is a symbol for a generally unknown concept; just as nature is a symbol for a generally unknown explanation. A concept is an ideal set of necessary and sufficient conditions for category membership. Now it is theoretically possible to have several sets of necessary and sufficient conditions for category membership. Both logic (Ajdukiewicz, 1969) and science, however, have always aimed at the set of such conditions that have the greatest explanatory power. That is, they value those necessary and sufficient conditions that contribute most to explanations of the phenomena associated with the category. In addition they value statements of such conditions in terms that show the greatest number of interconnections between the category to be defined and other categories that the theory dealt with. For example, a definition of measles in terms of a virus has greater explanatory power than a definition, however exact, in terms of spots on the skin The one in terms of virus helps to explain how the disease is communicated, the course of its development, and likely approaches to prevention. A definition in terms of spots would not help, directly, with any of this. Moreover, the definition in terms of virus relates measles to all other viral diseases. One in terms of spots would not.

By *proconcept* then, I mean a symbol for that concept that has maximum explanatory power. That is also what *nature,* in one of its uses, means. There are, however, two reasons for not taking *nature* as the technical term I need. (1) The term indicates primarily something in an object, whereas we need a term that indicates soemthing in the head. For meaning is in the head. (2) *Nature* is ambiguous. It can also mean, and this is the sense in which we have been using it, a symbol to indicate that internal organization. By using *proconcept* it is quite clear that only a symbol for something detailed is intended. The nature of gold involves a certain number of electrons; we do not want that number to be part of the meaning of the word *gold*. If we said that the meaning of *gold* was the nature of gold, there would be a danger that nature would be taken in the first sense and the number of electrons would be implicated. Better avoid that danger even at the cost of a neologism.

So far, to keep exposition simple, we concentrated on natural kind words, like *dog* and *water*. The theory extends naturally to names for artificial kinds, like *kettle* and *razor*.

The main difference between a natural kind word like *iron* and an artificial kind word like *kettle* is that the status of being iron does not depend on human intention and purposes. That of being a kettle does. A kettle is an object that is assigned to certain functions like boiling water; the metal of which it is made remains metal even if the kettle is melted down and is no longer a kettle. It follows that the concept "kettle" must represent the appropriate human intentions as its core. To know the meaning of *kettle* it is sufficient to know that there is a set of functions peculiar to kettles, because one has distinguished kettle shapes and kettle-related actions. The corresponding concept depends, ideally, on developments in cognitive psychology parallel to developments in biology that might yield the concept "dog."

The Individuation of Meanings

Meaning as proconcept might at first seem so vague as to be useless. After all I said that the meaning of *dog* is a placeholder for the concept "dog," which I don't know, and the meaning of *cat* is a placeholder for the concept "cat," which I don't know either. What supports the belief that the two meanings are different? What individuates them? I sound as though I claimed to know two chemical formulas and said the first was H_2O and the second was H_2O too. People would object that on that showing I seemed to know only one. Now it would be fatal to any theory of meaning if it failed to explain how the meaning of *dog* and *cat* might be different.

Two ways exist to differentiate meanings. One is intrinsic, the other extrinsic. For example, H_2O and $NaCl$ are different chemical formula. They differ in the elements they specify and in the ratios of one element to another. Extrinsic differentiation serves when intrinsic is not available. For example, I can specify two distinct ladies by the expressions, *Tom's* wife and *Harry's* wife, though I know nothing whatever of the ladies except their relations to Tom and Harry.

The meanings of *uncle* and *aunt* differ intrinsically. *Uncle* means "male sibling of parent;" *aunt* means "female sibling of parent." Each meaning is complex, of course, and designates a complex of concepts.

The meanings of *dog* and *cat* cannot be differentiated intrinsically, but they can be extrinsically. The extrinsic bases for differentiation are the phenomena. Dog phenomena and cat phenomena are sufficiently distinct to indicate two different categories, each with its own name. Because the categories are distinct, each calls for its own intrinsically distinct concept. Meaning is the link between the phenomena and the concept. But the phenomena are the bases for differences at the levels of meaning and concept.

The phenomena on their own will scarcely do the work required of them. The phenomena are in the environment while meanings (or their representations) are in the head. To keep meanings in the head distinct requires something in the head. It is convenient to appeal to the sensory tests that enable us to distinguish dogs from cats and to recognize which is which when we see one on its own.

What about the meaning of *animal*, though. We saw earlier that there are no sensory tests that distinguish animals from non animals, so we need some other principle of individuation. That is not far to seek, however. "Animal" is a superordinate category that embraces dogs, cats, cows, worms, etc. "Animal" is differentiated from "plant" by the set of subordinate categories. It is not necessary to know all the subordinate categories of any superordinate term, but it is necessary to know some; otherwise there would be no reason to call it superordinate.

I will not go further into the difficult problem of individuation.[2] In passing, thought, note that the above principles help to explain some of Eleanor Rosch's findings. Her subjects found difficulty in imagining creatures designated by superordinate terms like *animal, plant,* and *musical instrument.* They had little difficulty imagining a creature designated by subordinate terms, like *dog, rose,* and *guitar.* This is exactly what one would predict on the basis of the principles of individuation that have just been suggested for the two sorts of meanings.

Evaluating the Theory

It will not surprise anyone that the theory of meaning that has just been suggested satisfies the criteria we have drawn up. Nevertheless it will help to go through those criteria briefly, the better to grasp them and the theory of which they are the test.

The theory satisfies the first three negative criteria. We are not conscious of meanings as we have described them. They are not expressed in the language of the sensory array. They are not, for example, images. They are not the rules for the use of the words to which they are attached.

Meanings as proconcepts are distinct from all those theoretical entities from which they should be distinct. Meanings are not referents, concepts, partial concepts or collateral information. They are clearly distinct from the force attached to sentences. That is, a single sentence with a single meaning can be employed with different forces (or in different speech acts).

Meanings as proconcepts also satisfy the different positive criteria. Meanings rest squarely on publicly observable phenomena. Indeed the meanings of subordinate category words are individuated on the basis of differences among such phenomena. That is how they relate to our ability to categorize objects in the perceptual field. That is why skill in categorizing is a useful test of whether or not a person has grasped a meaning.

Because meanings rest on the publicly observable we begin to understand why they are the same for all members of a speech community. I am fully aware, however, that at this point the theory needs to be supplemented with some principles relating to sensory tests. The discipline that studies them is called pattern recognition. I do not intend to discuss it; I simply assume that some perceptual principles must explain why we see dogs as different from cats. The principles must be sharp enough to permit of quite delicate distinctions, yet not so sharp as to impose unhelpful distinctions. The sort of thing that has to be achieved can best be illustrated. Let us suppose that owing to differences in climate, dogs in the southern United States and in Canada were generally different, although all were called dogs. Otherwise, by the present theory, the meaning of *dog* would differ from southerners to Canadians. Clearly that would be undesirable. So if the theory is to show how it would avoid that, it needs theories of pattern recognition that are at present unavailable. On the other hand the theory does not, so far as I am aware, run foul of any principles of pattern recognition that are at present available. But ultimately that is not enough.

The theory relates meaning and truth in such a manner as to satisfy the relevant criteria. Truth is not in general a key to meaning as proconcept. It could only be such a key if we had knowledge of the relevant concept; and that we do not possess.

The link between meaning and truth is concept. A word like *dog* denotes a concept and it does so through its meaning. The concept is true of or false of the object that has been picked out by the subject of the sentence. That is the main way in which simple statements, such as *Freddie is a dog,* are true or false.

The link enables us to employ truth, not as the key to meaning but as a test of a theory of meaning. The test rules out theories that either do not link meaning to truth or that lead one to infer a sentence is true when one knows intuitively that it is false. A frequently given example of a theory that is ruled out is any that makes four-legged part of the meaning of *dog*.

Meaning as proconcept permits the claim that the meaning of the word is the meaning of the object in the sense indicated earlier. The child who sees dogs and succeeds in identifying them from cats and birds, attributes dog nature to dog phenomena. The nature thus hypothesized must be sufficient to exclude cat and bird phenomena but it must permit of that variability to which dogs give rise. The obvious problems in pattern recognition remain unsolved. The important point is that the nature so hypothesized is the physical correlate of the mental placeholder for the concept which actually specifies the nature of dogs. That mental placeholder can be formed before the child learns the word *dog*. And when he does learn the word, it is entered as the meaning of the word. The theory, then, indicates ways to explore the relation between perception and speech. In particular it suggests a method of explaining how we can speak about the things we perceive.

We thus see that meaning as proconcept satisfies all the requirements that we listed for a theory of meaning. I know of nothing else that does.

LEARNING MEANING

Before attempting an account of learning, one negative! Quine's quality space, the innate propensity to attend to some sensory qualities rather than others, though useful for other purposes, cannot be at the root of meaning. Indeed Quine would not wish it to be, inimical as he is to all talk of concepts and meaning. The qualities of which he speaks are sensory ones, and we have seen that meaning is not expressed in the language of sensation. I mention the point because I have frequently, in psychological discussion, heard appeal to Quine's quality space to account for meanings.

Two great principles of cognition are at work in the child as he learns meanings. One is the principle that every event has an adequate cause. Put psychologically, the principle expresses the belief that the world makes sense. For every event there is an adequate explanation. What exists objectively as a cause is represented in cognition by an explanation. Ultimately this all means that we expect the world to conform to our own principles of explanation. We do not need to go into the forms of explanation here. It is sufficient to note that the principle would give the child general specifications for concepts even when he could never hope to attain them in detail. That is what I meant, in describing concepts, by the expression "ideal explanation."

Another closely related principle of cognition is that differences in events are due to differences in underlying causes. The principle is at work in the psychologist's interpretation of chronometric studies. Differences between reaction times are attributed to differences between underlying processes. The principle guides the child's formation of meanings. Because cat phenomena are perceived as different from dog phenomena, they demand different explanations. They therefore demand different meanings to specify the appropriate explanations. Indeed, the meanings are individuated by the phenomena, or rather by the sensory tests that identify the phenomena.

Each object belongs in many kinds: Freddie is a pal and male as well as a dog and an animal. How does the child know which of such kinds his parents mean when they say *dog?* Leave aside the problem of how to detect a proper name. A partial answer to the present question is probably a constraint imposed by the child himself. He interprets all common names as applying to the lowest species, the most constrained set of phenomena, that he has identified. So if the child had distinguished animals, and among animals, dogs, he will at first take any name applied to a dog as appropriate for the lower level. That avoids confusion. If the child makes a mistake and takes *animal* as word for dog he will soon find, to his surprise, that his parents use it for cats and cows, and so he abandons it. That seems to be his initial strategy for handling hierarchically related terms.

The child learns the next highest term, *animal,* to refer to a group of living creatures that do not as a group fall under any lower level term. Having identified such creatures he may have the meaning "animal," but not as attached to the word, *animal.* Only later does he learn that *animal* can apply to individuals, i.e., in all situations in which he hears *animal* used of individuals for whom he already knows a lower level term. term.

That is how the child learns related names. I suspect the formation of the corresponding meanings takes the opposite direction. The child sets out with the broad observation that some creatures move about of their own accord and others do not. That prompts him to begin the formation of the meaning, "animal." Subsequently the child notices divisions among these creatures. That prompts him to form meanings related to different types of life—"dog," "cow," "horse," and so forth.

How does the child handle heterarchies, like *dog* and *pal*? *Pal* is a relational term, so the someone can be a pal of Tom's and not of Dick's. A dog is a dog to everyone. That distinction will provide a clue to the meaning of many terms. Often the discourse area will provide a clue. A single object can be both a penny and copper. *Penny* relates it to the monetary system; *copper* relates it to the system of minerals. A child who can follow the general drift of a conversation may find that helpful in learning such names. But I will go no further with this, as it leads away from the concerns that have been central so far.

CHAPTER NOTES

[1]Praise the young and they will improve.

[2]One problem in the individuation of meaning that may occur to readers of Nelson Goodman (1972) relates to mythological creatures like centaur and unicorn. The basis for the query is that since these creatures do not exist, one may scruple to allow that we have sensory tests that distinguish them. On the account of meaning that is being offered, absence of sensory tests would be an embarrassment. No sensory tests, no individuation of the meanings of subordinate terms, like *centaur* and *unicorn!* Goodman, however, shows that way out. Centaur and unicorn phenomena are quite distinct, whether as shown in pictures or in stories. They differ in appearance and behavior. To tell them apart we need sensory tests. So if one is otherwise disposed to accept meaning as proconcept, one need have no qualms occasioned by mythological beasts.

ACKNOWLEDGMENTS

This is Chapter 6 of a book, *Names for Things,* that is in preparation. It owes much to many people who read and commented on earlier versions: Ray Jackendoff, Steve and Judy Zucker, George Miller, Eric Wanner, and Jeremy Walker. I owe a special debt to two people. Anil Gupta read several versions and discussed the issues with me at length. Jerry Fodor wrote detailed, almost line-by-line comments on two earlier versions. Unfortunately, these people do not agree with everything I say.

REFERENCES

Ajdukiewicz, K. Three concepts of definition. In T. O. Olshewsky (Ed.) *Problem in the philosophy of language*. New York: Holt, Rinehart & Winston, 1969.

Anderson, J. R. *Language, memory and thought*. Hillsdale, N.J.: Lawrence Erlbaum, 1976.

Anglin, J. M. *Word, object and conceptual development*. New York: Norton, 1977.

Cassirer, E. *Substance and function*. New York: Dover, 1953.

Dummett, M. A. E. What is a theory of meaning? (11) In G. Evans & J. McDowell (Eds.). *Essays in semantics,* Oxford, Clarendon, 1978.

Fodor, J. A. *The language of thought.* New York; Crowell, 1975.

Fodor, J. D. *Semantics: Theories of meaning in generative grammar.* New York: Thomas Crowell, 1977.

Franks, J. J. & Bransford, J. D. Abstraction of visual patterns. *Journal of Experimental Psychology,* 1971, *90,* 65–75.

Frege, G. On sense and reference. First published in 1892—published in English translation in P. Geach & M. Black, *Philosophical writings of Gottlob Frege,* Oxford; Basil Blackwell, 1960.

Frege, G. *Grundgesetze der Arithmetik.* Jena, 1893, *1.* Partial translation in P. Geach & M. Black *Philosophical writings of Gottlob Frege* (2nd edition). Oxford: Basil Blackwell, 1960.

Frege, G. The thought. First published in 1918—published in translation in G. Iseminger (Ed.). *Logic and philosophy; selected readings.* New York: Appleton-Century Crofts, 1968.

Goodman, H. *Problems and projects.* New York: Bobbs-Merrill, 1972.

Kintsch, W. *Memory and cognition* (2nd edition). New York: Wiley, 1977.

Lindsay, P. H., & Norman, D. A. *Human information processing.* New York: Academic, 1972.

Miller, G. A. *Spontaneous apprentices.* New York: Seabury, 1977.

Miller, G. A. & Johnson-Laird, P. N. *Language and perception.* Cambridge, Mass.: Belnap, 1976.

Perry, J. The problem of the essential indexical. *Nous,* 1979, *13,* 3–22.

Posner, H. I. *Cognition: An introduction.* Glenview, Ill.: Scott, Foresman, 1973.

Putnam, H. The meaning of "meaning." In K. Gunderson (Ed.). *Language mind and knowledge.* Minnesota studies in the philosophy of science. Minneapolis: University of Minnesota Press, 1975a.

Putnam, H. Language and reality. Reprinted in H. Putnam, *Mind, language and reality.* Cambridge University Press, 1975b.

Putnam, H. *Meaning and the moral sciences.* London: Routledge & Kegan Paul, 1978.

Quillian, R. M. Word concepts: a theory and simulation of some basic semantic capabilities. *Behavioural Science,* 1967, *12,* 410–430.

Quillian, R. M. Semantic memory. In M. Minsky (Ed.). *Semantic information processing.* MIT Press, 1968.

Quillian, R. M. The teachable language comprehender: a simulation program and theory of language. *Communications of the ACH,* 1969, *12,* 459–476.

Rosch, E. H. Human categorization. In N. Warren (Ed.), *Advances in cross-cultural psychology.* London: Academic, 1977.

Saltz, E. *The cognitive basis of human learning.* Homewood, Ill.: Dorsey, 1971.

Smith, E. E., Shoben, E. J., & Rips, L. J. Structure and process in semantic memory: A featural model of semantic decisions. *Psychological Review,* 1974, *81,* 214–241.

Wittgenstein, L. *Philosophical investigations* (2nd edition). Oxford: Basil Blackwell, 1958.

5 Macnamara Discussion

Member of Audience: Jesperson wrote a book on negation that berated the logical grammarians of the 19th century for saying two negatives make a positive. "I ain't not going" is simply an emphatic way of saying, "I'm not going." It seems that the interpretation that you place upon "I refuse to entertain the notion" is simply an ignoring of an emphatic denial in the same way.

Macnamara: Suppose I say I do not mean an emphatic denial; I just say, "I refuse to, deny, entertain."

Member of Audience: Then, in fact, you have said something that refutes itself. But that's not an interpretation of ordinary language; it's a philosophical reconstruction of a self-refuting sentence.

Macnamara: If one produces some non-English translation into which we can translate English sentences, one will end up with that sort of contradiction. I'm not saying that there is nothing wrong with saying the English sentence. We all know what it means to say, "I never entertain the idea that John struck Mary, and I refuse to entertain it now."

Member of Audience: I want to discuss the notion of hierarchies of semantic markers as you described it. One need not start with a single node at the top. That structure can be very complex, and having a tree structure doesn't mean that one can only have one node at the top the way you do.

Macnamara: I know that, and I think it is irrelevant to the point I was making. The point was simply that a tree structure may, in fact, take different forms of domination and yet represent them all with the same structure. What redundancy rules are intended to do is, in fact, very like meaning postulates.

Member of Audience: The postulate form doesn't make any distinction between truth by virtue of logic or truth by virtue of fact. And semantic analysis does try to make that distinction.

Macnamara: Yes. But the logical structure is the same.

Member of Audience: I'm not sure. I think that is a question of whether a tree structure by definition has a formal apparatus that is capable of handling certain kinds of relationships. It doesn't imply, by definition, that one will have, say, color term under object name if one has one string of trees that has to do with color terms and another string of trees that has to do with other terms.

Macnamara: I agree, and my 1971 article argues that point. But the trouble is that I can reverse these relationships. It's to some extent arbitrary which dominates which, unless I have some very general, universal semantic tree from which I derive the semantic tree for this particular case. But that semantic tree will subsume all the terms in the English language.

Member of Audience: The case relations themselves don't spell out all that is involved in semantic interpretation. They are simply a necessary component. So I don't see how we get from the initial problem of the interpretation of markers all the way down to the bottom, to the conclusion that a semantical interpretation is impossible. Even if the problem is specifying cases, that doesn't mean that semantical interpretation is problematic.

Macnamara: I said there are two different problems. One is specifying the cases. The second concerns giving a proper definition of any case. I followed through one to show the contradiction. I think I could do the same for any other case and for any arbitrary definition that one can give. One further point, concerning negatives. It is sometimes claimed that negatives should be read as, "It is not the case that." But look at "John struck Mary." There is a problem of calling John an agent—semantically. But there is no problem with saying that John is the subject of the sentence, because that's not what is being denied. What is being denied is that someone struck Mary. That poses a problem with saying that John is an agent by any definition of the word *agent*. It is very hard to say a person is an agent when one just said he wasn't an agent.

Member of Audience: When one asserts that John is an agent, one is not necessarily making a statement about what John did or didn't do. We are saying that within the confines of the sentence, John is the agent of the verb, *struck*. And that doesn't mean that John struck Mary.

Macnamara: It surely does mean that if the sentence is intended as a statement of state of affairs rather than an example—that is, if it is used rather than mentioned. I am trying to describe the state of affairs or my representation of the state of affairs; and the representation (if we had a definition for agent, and if one allowed that John was supposed to be an agent) would be a problem when my representation says he didn't strike, because I've got to represent him as having struck.

Member of Audience: It seems to me that one glaring problem with the Katz and Fodor formulation was pointed out by Weinreich as one of combining the meanings of words to add up to a semantic interpretation, whereas one virtue of the case formulation was that there was at least a way to specify the qualitative differences in the relationships between certain classes of words.

Macnamara: Yes, that is an improvement.

Member of Audience: It seems to me that theorists who have gone the route of looking for abstract representations—semantic representations—using generally the case approach (and I would include Donald Norman's more recent formulations in this area), have been motivated by the finding that people do seem to paraphrase extensively when they recall sentences. It is almost as though there are things stored that are other than the actual words, and one can account for this in terms of interverbal associations, but that people have gone the more abstract route in an attempt to provide an alternative theory.

Macnamara: Theorists like Donald Norman replace a meaning postulate, which has the material implications sign, with something like "is a," which is not logically well defined and is not very clear. It depends on the system as to what it means. We tend to take it as an English expression, but it really isn't. It is not meant to be an English expression, but then we are not told exactly what it is or how it is defined. Nevertheless, we are told that such primitive terms are the meaning of ordinary English, but we are using our meaning system for ordinary English to interpret them and to make sure we get them right. And I am not sure that they are really better than the paraphrase. All such terms are doing is paraphrasing. I am not sure whether we are getting anywhere with this.

Member of Audience: It seems to me that your alternative would be interverbal associational structure. Is that what you . . .

Macnamara: Oh NO! There may be such things in psychology as associations, but I have never seen a good argument for them. It is clear that we must interpret sentences in some abstract representation or semantic space. This is because we can talk about the things that we see. I was talking to somebody at breakfast this morning, and I said that I have come to the belief that the function of the brain is to slow down light waves and turn them out as sound waves, because we can talk about the things that we see. Those two systems must come together somewhere. There are all sorts of structures in there, and there are all sorts of operations that traverse those structures that are called thinking. I don't know what they are, but associations will get you nowhere.

Member of Audience: I would like to return to the sentences with "entertain" and also provide a different indictment of orientations like Katz and Fodor's. I think the issue here involves the flexibility of the meanings of words, and if one allows for flexibility rather than the assumption of inflexibility, the apparent acceptability of the contradictory sentences is resolved. People's sentences make sense. If that utterance has to make sense, then it obligates the comprehender to move away from the modal notion of the terms involved.

Macnamara: There is no contradiction with such sentences as English sentences. The contradiction only arises when we substitute into that sentence or rather translate it into some semantic interpretation.

Member of Audience: Exactly. We must have some way for the meaning of "entertain" to be sensitive to context and, in these cases, take on something other than its modal or causal interpretation.

Macnamara: Well, I think that if you follow that approach, if you produce any definition clear enough to be stated, I can write it out in English and put it into that sentence and get a contradiction again.

Member of Audience: One cannot have a single fixed meaning or definition of the word, even though there is some core meaning.

Macnamara: Then I would write something like, "In no sense of the word do I entertain." I think that if you can be clear enough to state it, I can be clear enough to knock it down.

Pribram: "John struck Mary" already implies a contradiction, or else we wouldn't be talking about it. Language in sentences implies contradiction and allows conferences like this to take place.

Macnamara: The very fact that I say "John struck Mary" means that in some sense, I've got to be capable of thinking that John did not strike Mary.

Member of Audience: All such contradictions are built in, and there's nothing wrong with them.

Macnamara: Well, I don't think there's anything contradictory about saying "John struck Mary." I can confront someone by saying: "No, that is not true; John did not strike Mary." We have no logical contradiction, only a question about whether the event took place or not.

Turvey: I am confused. All these sentences clearly require a very abstract representation to permit us to appreciate them. You conclude by saying that there doesn't seem to be any representation that we could write, that there is nothing we can do in the sense of translating the sentence into some other form that would be sensible. So how about entertaining the proposition that language does not require a representational medium? Isn't that the way you are headed?

Macnamara: Yes, but I wouldn't care to entertain it myself.

Turvey: Then what are we going to say?

Macnamara: The problem is the extreme degree of abstraction. I think that there are very marked limits on psychology as an enterprise.

Turvey: There are limits on representation, too.

Macnamara: Yes. But I think that they are part of the limits on psychology; because otherwise, how could one explain such things as "John struck Mary" means the same as "John hit Mary" and somehow corresponds to an event if it actually took place. I can actually see that event with my eyes, and I must somehow hook that up with words. Now one problem that I didn't go into is that the events I am going to describe probably require something like a million semantic cases (at least a very, very large number). There are such expressions as "I heard Mary" and "I listened to Mary." "I heard Mary" doesn't present me as being very active; something is being done to me. But when I listen, although it's the same sort of physical process, I am now attending. "I looked at Mary" and "I saw Mary" are the same sort of thing. Now consider "I like idleness" and "I like mowing the lawn." One of Fillmore's cases is the thing acted upon, but how can we assign things to the same case if they are not acted upon in the same way? "John liked mowing the lawn"; "John loved listening to stories"; "John liked being read to"; "John liked reading the history of the 40-years war when sitting in the bath"; etc. They appear to be conceptually different, and yet they are clearly linguistic equivalents in some sense. All are objects of the sentence, direct objects of the main verb; and there is an equivalence class that linguists have captured. McCawley, who tries to equate anything less than surface structure with semantics, simply says that things like subject of the sentence and object of the sentence are both semantic and syntactic descriptions; and he says the proper semantic description is that these instances are arguments of the verb. So we have a verb like *strike,* which is a two-case verb, and we have two arguments. How do we know what will serve as an argument of the main verb? We find something that was the subject of the sentence. All he has done is rebaptize it and gain nothing. The whole enterprise of generative semantics got nowhere. We have a small number of linguistic cases, a small number of grammatical classes, a small number of grammatical structures; and these serve a huge number of purposes, depending on the lexical items that are put in.

Pattee: Is your conclusion that there is no adequate linguistic interpretation or representation of a linguistic statement? I would agree with that, and I have an example that is at the most primitive level—namely, the "Linguistic Description in DNA"—a form of statement that has no adequate interpretation except in the function of the enzyme that it produces. In general, there is no way adequately to take a linguistic statement and transform it into another linguistic statement that has anything dynamical about it. One can translate all one wants: DNA is translated into messenger RNA, but until we produce the actual transduction into the dynamics, we get nothing. To take the other extreme, the best example is interpreting a joke. There is nothing more futile than explaining a joke.

Shaw: When I hear someone say, "If we are going to have a linguistic representation, it is going to be in the world," it is not going to be in linguistics. It gets one back into the problems that Tarski and the semantic theory of truth try to handle. One must have some metacontext, and the metacontext of language is not just going to be another language.

Macnamara: That is exactly the opposite of what I am saying.

Shaw: You're saying there is going to be another language.?

Macnamara: Yes. Augustine in the Confessions began by saying that in order to learn a lesson, he had to know another language. Wittgenstein begins his *Philosophical Investigations* by saying, "What Augustine said is so clearly foolish that we don't have to consider it."

Shaw: Then you disagree with Pattee's point?

Macnamara: I also disagree with Wittgenstein. I think that I need a conception analogous to that of a physicist who sees a track in a cloud chamber. Physics needs a construct to explain this, and it theorizes that there is a particle that made the track. Now one says "Did you see the particle?" No, but there has got to be something like that to account for the observed behavior of the cloud chamber.

Likewise, in order to explain my performance, I need constructs like ideas and propositions. I am saying it is not very easy to get at those; those things are not physical events. Such psychological entities map onto physical events in a very, very abstract way.

Shaw: But not necessarily linguistically?

Macnamara: Not linguistically.

Shaw: I think you are hung up in Russell's Theory of Types, and I have the feeling that we have been here before.

Macnamara: We have been round and round, and everyone has been here before.

Shaw: Theorists try to avoid the reference problem by somehow defining the problems so that the Theory of Types is irrelevant (such as with constructable sets). What I am suggesting is that psychological constructable sets will not be linguistic sets of even a metalinguistic sort; otherwise, we have levels and have Theory of Types problems all over again.

Macnamara: That may be, but it may be that that is a limitation of psychology. Suppose we do have this abstract representation of space inside our head, onto which we map an interpretation of visual space and onto which we interpret sentences. In this manner, we bring sentences into correspondence (of some sort) with the physical world. Then understanding that process is a problem for psychology.

Shaw: But it is not necessarily a linguistic problem for psychology?

Macnamara: That is correct. Much more radically than Chomsky, who argued that there is an autonomy of speech and semantics, I claim that language and semantics are autonomous. The last chapter of *Syntactic Structures* claimed autonomy in a sense that one need not use semantic terms in the definition of linguistic functions as such. I am saying that you *can't* use them.

6 Presentationalism: Toward a Self-Reflexive Psychological Theory

James E. Martin
The Pennsylvania State University

> *No science can be more secure than the metaphysics which tacitly it presupposes.*
>
> A. N. Whitehead

PRIMACY OF PERSONS AND VALUES IN PSYCHOLOGICAL ANALYSIS

The first psychological fact is the fact of persons. Our phenomenological experience with persons defines the domain that it is the unique task of psychology to explain.[1] It is undeniable that persons exist and that they have some relation to nature as it is traditionally conceived by the natural sciences. Together, these facts make up the fundamental problem for theoretical psychology. This cosmological–metaphysical problem—that of understanding the character of persons and their relations to one another and to the physical and biological orders—provides the primary motivation for all nonapplied psychological inquiry.

The fundamental thesis of this chapter is that personhood is only defined in the context of considerations of value as expressed in ethics, logic, and epistemology. Moreover, the normative character of the system within which personhood has its proper meaning has been the major obstacle both to analyzing persons in terms of concepts of traditional natural science and to integrating personhood into that scientific world view—a world view in which all events are said to be explainable in terms of nonnormative, natural law. In this context, I develop a proposal for a psychological paradigm and a correlated metaphysic. By examining the epistemic background in which traditional science is carried out, I discover a vision of the whole that makes the scientific study of the person a coherent enterprise.

The conclusions reached here depend in large measure upon presuppositional analysis as a methodology for theoretical psychological inquiry. In this context, I have made what is, to the best of my knowledge, the first attempt to characterize the domain of persons in a way that is explicitly coherent with those presuppositions that tacitly ground psychological investigation. The result is an emerging view of persons as self-revealing foci of systematic and irreducible axiological constraints on structural domains.

The Ad Hominem Argument Against Classical Reductionism

Classical attempts at interpreting personhood in terms of the concepts of traditional science have inevitably resulted in self-contradiction. The structure of this self-contradiction is well known, but I do, nevertheless, sketch it briefly here.[2] Basically, the problem centers on the fact that understanding personhood in terms of the traditional scientific world view invariably involves conceptualizing the decisions governing judgment and action as finally grounded in something other than objectively good reasons. Personal events (including judgment and action) are understood as ultimately resulting from the structural character of the world as conceived from the classical viewpoint of the biological or physical sciences. Rational valuing (which appears, introspectively, to constrain and warrant decisions) is seen as epiphenomenal with respect to the explanation of those decisions. It is the reductionist view that rational valuing is "seen through," upon scientific analysis. The reductionist claims that an ultimate account of belief would refer to physical or biological law, not the realm of objective rational value. In traditional analysis, therefore, it is the realm of nonnormative law, not that of good reason, that determines belief.

The reductionist's self-contradiction becomes apparent when, in arguing for this position, he states that it is a position that *ought* to be believed; that is, the reductionist claims that there are *good* reasons that *require* us to see it as correct. Such a claim is a bit odd: Our reductionist has just told us that belief, in general, is solely determined by a matrix of value-free physical or biological causes. Now, a moment later, he or she insists that whatever the physical causes involved, rational value itself is an essential determinant of *his or her* belief in reductionism. Of course, reductionists say this because they believe the reductionist thesis. To believe any thesis is to believe that one's assent to it is required (and therefore partly determined) by objective rational value (by a context of good reasons). On the other hand, it is clear that the content of this belief contradicts what is presupposed in believing it. The content of the reductionist belief asserts that belief is only determined by nonnormative physical and biological law. Clearly, one cannot have it both ways. If classical reductionism is false, beliefs may, to a degree, be determined by a set of rational values. To that degree, it would be possible to say that we have warrant for our beliefs. We might, to an extent, be said to *know* the truth of our beliefs. If classical reductionism is true, one's belief in reductionism is not seen to be determined by objective rational value, and accordingly, one cannot say that one *knows* reductionism to be true.[3]

To repeat, the argument that belief is not constrained by the realm of (good) reason entails that the argument in question is, itself, not constrained by good reasons. Since its being grounded in good reasons is the *only* adequate warrant for a belief, the reductionist cannot know reductionism to be true, for if it were true, the context that constrains him to believe it would not be the realm of reason. In fact, it is clear that such a reductionism necessarily entails skepticism with respect to the possibility of knowing. Insofar as one's own beliefs are not understood to be determined by rational values, they cannot be believed to be true. The reductionist is, therefore, open to a kind of ad hominem attack.[4,5]

Initial Constraints on Psychological Theory

This self-contradiction occurs *only* because we naturally assume that an adequate understanding of human nature must be self-reflective. We assume (I think necessarily) that a theory that makes claims about persons in general is necessarily making a claim about the person proposing that theory. Consequently, it is a metatheoretical condition on learning theory that it explicate the learning theorist in the act of choosing his or her theory. If the learning theory analyzes choice in a way that denies that *this* choice is determined by rational values, the theory is inadequate.

Accordingly, an adequate account of learning must demonstrate that alleged judgments are partially dependent on a valid normative metatheoretical context that guides the psychological subject as he evaluates alternative hypotheses. Learning, after all, involves coming to a view of the world that is, with respect to the context of the learner, truer than the view he began with. Thus, far from eliminating value from psychology, an explanation of learning is *required* to see judgment as at least partially determined by *irreducible* and *objective* value. That is, it must be shown that the subject has made a particular judgment for reasons that are, at some level, objectively good. The psychologist is not required to argue the validity of either the empirical assumptions or the empirical conclusions of the psychological subject. However, if one is to account for genuine learning (including one's own), and avoid the ad hominem, one is required to affirm the valid nature of the subject's most fundamental metatheoretical assumptions, despite the subject's empirical assumptions and limitations.[6]

Moreover, insofar as one is seeking to learn truth, the assumption of the objective validity of the rational values that support (or determine) a given belief is one kind of cause of that belief. Therefore, beyond merely affirming the presence of efficacious reason as a cause of learning, the psychologist must come to see that the presupposition of objective validity, or efficacy, of reason is itself a cause of belief. When more fully explicated, this final presupposition will be shown to be the self-grounding basis for an explanation of belief or judgment.

In light of these constraints, we must reject a reductionist psychology because it can *never* address the inherently axiological-epistemic question of the *truth* of the beliefs whose acquisition we wish to explain. Since it is a defining characteristic of beliefs that the propositions believed are believed to be (at least relatively) *true,* the only way to show that (or to explain why) someone believes a proposition is to demonstrate that in the context of the person who believes it, the proposition in question *is,* to some extent, *objectively rationally warranted.* Since the reductionist is committed in principle to a characterization and account of belief in terms of nonnormative law, he or she is forever denied the possibility of either demonstrating the existence of, or giving an explanation for, belief.

In this context I propose to develop a theory of some of the learner's ultimate and a priori assumptions and presuppositions concerning the objective rational warrants for all judgments. The system resulting from such an unpacking forms the basis for both a definition and a causal explanation of judgment. Moreover, since it describes the presumptive context of its own being believed, it is a partial explanation of its being believed. Further, this system describes that presumptive context such that the theory of the presumptive context is seen to be valid in that presumptive context. Finally, the account explicates a view of the whole, including the knower, such that the presuppositions that guide knowers in the discovery of it are seen to be fundamentally appropriate to the to-be-known. I show that it is only in this way that the theory could *explain* the existence of genuine learning and avoid the sort of ad hominem objections considered earlier.

THE CHARACTER OF THE PRESUMPTIVE CONTEXT

The process of developing a theory about the mind's presuppositions is similar to that involved in the construction of any theory. Thus selection of a theory about presuppositions is necessarily constrained by a metatheory about those presuppositions—by a set of presuppositions about presuppositions.

The problem of inferring presuppositions is, in fact, exactly the problem faced by learning theorists. Suppose that a person gives evidence of having acquired some new knowledge. In order to understand this fact, the learning theorist must discover the subject's presuppositions, or the perspectival context of the subject's coming to model the world in this new way. Likewise, if we take the object of our investigation to be the learning theorist, our task is similar to his or her own. That is, we must discover those assumptions in terms of which the learning theorist uncovered the assumptions of the psychological subject. Insofar as we require a theory of the psychologist, it has become the goal of our investigation to define the methodology of presuppositional analysis. Since we, as psychologists, are the object of our own inquiry, our methodology is our subject matter.

Initial Comments on the Character of Presuppositional Analysis

At this juncture it may be instructive to introduce an example of an a priori presupposition. Consider a case from the history of philosophy and physics given to us by David Hume. One of the theses developed by Hume (1955) in his *Inquiry Concerning Human Understanding* was as follows: Hume claimed that all reasoning about, and knowledge of, matters of empirical fact depends on the assumption that the principle of causality obtains in the empirical world. He therefore concluded that the principle of causality could not be shown from experience to be operating in the world because such a demonstration, in that it would attempt to establish a matter of empirical fact, would necessarily presuppose the principle of causality.[7,8]

Now if Hume was correct in saying that all conclusions concerning matters of empirical fact depend upon inferences that assume that the events in the empirical world are causally related, then since persons *do* assume that they can make inferences about the world of contingent facts, we (following Kant, 1970) would be led to claim that the assumption of causality is part of the a priori framework in terms of which persons make judgments about the empirical world. That such an assumption would have an a priori character may be seen from the fact that inasmuch as it involves a claim about the structure of the empirical world, if Hume was correct the assumption could not be argued for, *or against,* unless it had already been made. In general, therefore, it is not possible to develop a conventional argument for the *validity* of a presupposition from within the domain that presupposition defines.

Nevertheless, we are not without guidance with respect to the *identification* of presuppositions. We may recognize presuppositions since arguments against them (from within the domains they define) are open to ad hominem attack, because those arguments already presuppose the presuppositions in question.

For example, it may be said to be a presupposition of inference about the empirical world that the past repeats itself. It is clear that all extrapolations from past experience (and their negations) depend on this presupposition. Moreover, if we were to observe a number of situations in the past in which the past did not repeat itself and if, on the basis of such past experience, we were to conclude that as a general rule, the past does not repeat itself, we would be open to the ad hominem. Our conclusion would be grounded in the very presupposition we were attempting to deny.

This chapter attempts to give a characterization of the final presuppositions of judgment. But such characterizations must, if true, presuppose precisely what they assert. In this context, the ad hominem is utilized against the denial of these characterizations by showing that these denials presuppose what they deny. Thus the *argumentum ad hominem* will be the key to identification of the ultimate presuppositions.[9]

A Deduction of Presentationalism

Let us proceed to a presuppositional analysis of judgment. I am concerned to discover those presuppositions that underlie all judgment. Certainly the presumptive contexts of judgments vary across intelligible domains. For example, the presuppositions in terms of which we confront the physical domain are different from those in terms of which we confront the musical domain. I am not interested in assumptions that vary from domain to domain. Rather, I discuss only those aspects of the presumptive context of judgment that can be argued to be universal. In so doing, I hope to explicate the final context, or perspective. This perspective is defined in terms of a set of ultimate assumptions about the intelligible world.[10]

Although there are a number of questions about the nature of judgments, at least one thing is certain. Judgments are arrived at through a process of evaluating alternatives. Alternative hypotheses are compared and ordered in terms of certain dimensions of value. That is, they are *evaluated* in terms of *good* reasons. The person on the street, the scientist in the lab, and your favorite TV detective all arrive at judgments by subjecting alternate possibilities to critical evaluation.

What does such an evaluation presuppose? First, it assumes a distinction between hypotheses and what they represent. The "thing as it is" is logically distinct from a "thing in experience," which in some sense represents the "thing as it is." From this distinction, we have the possibility that representations may be incorrect. On the other hand, an evaluation is coherent only if it is assumed that the to-be-represented "thing as it is" fully realizes the values that ultimately constrain the selection of hypotheses about it. Accordingly, the "thing as it is" is assumed to be subject to a priori constraints. It is not a "thing in itself" in the sense used to indicate an entity beyond or outside a priori categories.

In this way, one can locate the object of knowledge, the "thing as it is." It is distinct from our representations of it, and it is, in principle, knowable. In combination, these two conditions preserve and unite what is essential in both realism and idealism. The fundamental insight of modern realism has been that the object of knowledge contains an element of irreducible "otherness"—that it has a reality apart from its presentation to consciousness. This fact gives knowledge its value and makes it more than illusion. This insight is maintained in the distinction between the "thing in experience" and the "thing as it is." The basic claim of idealism, on the other hand, has been that there is a sense in which the object of knowledge is *not* fundamentally "other." This fact makes knowledge possible. In the present context, this insight is explicated by holding that the "thing as it is" is subject to the a priori axiological conditions on knowability; that is, the "thing as it is" is distinct from an unknowable "thing in itself." The epistemological position taken here (and assumed by the psychological subject) thus affirms what is central to both realism and idealism (see Urban, 1949).[11]

The goal of judgment is an appropriate or true understanding of the world. This activity presupposes that the to-be-known world is appropriate to the knowing activity of the knower. The selection of hypotheses in terms of rational values is only coherent if it is assumed that the system being represented is constrained by those values. In terms of such epistemic values, the to-be-known world is assumed to be the best of all possible worlds. The to-be-known world is assumed to be the complete expression of those rational values that govern the choice of hypotheses. A fully true understanding of that world would realize those values as fully as the world itself.

I do not mean that the rational epistemic values, as presently conceptualized, must be assumed to be exhaustive. Thus, I do not claim that the a priori constraints on the to-be-known world are exhausted by reason as presently understood. Reason is, at present, imperfectly explicated. We will not, therefore, be surprised if our present understanding of reason is criticized and deepened. However, note two qualifications of this admission: First, any criticism and deepening of our conception of reason will be grounded in reason itself and thus will involve assumptions concerning rational constraints on the object of inquiry. Second, to say that our explicit appreciation of reason might be deepened is *not* to say that the whole of reason, as presently available to us, might be fallacious. Such a claim is obviously open to ad hominem attack. We do have access to reason, and we must assume reality to be constrained by the reason that ultimately constrains our judgment.

These considerations entail that there is a deep sense in which the judge assumes the world to be *for* his or her rational judgment about it. In effect, the epistemological ideal which is assumed to constrain the to-be-known is precisely the satisfaction of the knower's epistemological valuing. Therefore, the world's being assumed to be for the knower as he or she is a rational knower of it involves the presupposition that *the world is for the rational knower in order that he or she may know it*. Finally, this can be unpacked only as the presupposition that the intelligible world is by definition a presentation for the rational knower. But such a presentation would be nothing less than a communication to the knower by other minds or persons (or protopersons).[12]

A domain is intelligible insofar as we can construct a coherent representation of it for ourselves. But a representation is just that—a *re*-presentation. It is a *re*-presentation of what is assumed to be a prior presentation, whose assumed intelligibility rests on the presupposition that it is defined for the knower in order that he or she may know it. The assumed intelligibility of the given, in the sense that existence is given, rests—if one will pardon the pun—on the fact that it is understood as being a gift (or present or presentation).

Intelligibility, like personhood, has an absolutely nonderivative and irreducible character. It is assumed to depend on value-guided intelligence, which is an aspect of personhood. The knowing person assumes, however tacitly, that he or she knows in the context of a world that is a community of persons (or protopersons). I have called the view that the intelligible domain is tacitly conceived by the knower to be the presentation of other minds *presentationalism*.

To summarize, the analysis includes three arguments. First, the criticism of putative knowledge presupposes an epistemically ideal world—a world defined in terms of rational values that govern the critical act and are only imperfectly realized in the knower's present understanding of the world. Second, an epistemically ideal world is nothing less than a world defined for the rational knower in order that he or she may know it—a world that therefore has the character of communication. Third, the full meaning of the assumed communicative character of the world can only be explicated as the presupposition of a personal, or protopersonal, world ground.

The Meaning of Representation

I have argued that our provisional understanding of the world must be representational. However, I do not wish to associate the presentationalist position with traditional epistemological representationalism. By representation, I do not mean that the defining relationship between ideas and their objects is thought to involve mere similarity. The defining relationship between ideas and their objects cannot be simply one of similarity. If it were, recognition of an object as a member of the class defined by a particular idea would require the recognition of some similarity between the object and that idea. However, since similarities are always recognized in terms of ideas, such a recognition of similarity would require a further idea. If the defining relationship between ideas and objects were one of similarity, we would require an infinite regress of further ideas to recognize such similarities.

Nor do I want to give the impression that knowing is construed as being indirect. That is, I do not claim that we only know *representations* of objects. Quite clearly, if we only knew representations of the world and not the world itself, we would be forever denied the possibility of evaluating the validity of our representations of the objective world. Furthermore, if our ideas were only similar to their objects, we would have no way of determining in which ways they would be similar to, or different from, their objects.

The view proposed here is that the knower receives directly from the world (or knows directly) a potential (i.e., a protopersonal focus of values) that, when fully realized, constitutes the character of the objective world. In this sense, an ideal understanding of the world would *become* the world to be understood. However, insofar as this potential (or protopersonal value) is not fully realized in our understanding, it is necessary to draw a distinction between the incompletely developed *idea* of an objective domain and the domain of objectivity itself. The incomplete idea—although it is, in this sense, becoming its object—is *not yet* its object. Accordingly, I speak of the object as having been represented in terms of imperfect ideas. The reader should bear in mind, however, that the defining relation between ideas and their objects is not thought to be similarity, but what obtains between entities in the process of becoming and the same entities in a fully developed state.[13]

Implications for the Study of Meaning

The claim that ideas develop in the way suggested here entails a new approach to psycholinguistic semantics. One feature of this approach is sketched next.

The fact that we know that we don't know everything there is to be known about a set of objects—for example, the set of tables—implies that our idea of the set of tables, or our meaning for the word *table,* is not exhausted by our present knowledge of tables. Moreover, we are aware of this fact; that is, we are aware that to identify the meaning of the word *table* with our present explicit concept of tables is an error.

Consider the philosopher who says, "I am investigating mind." What is the meaning of the word *mind?* It seems clear that the meaning of the word *mind* cannot be exhausted by a set of explicit concepts for the simple reason that in the course of investigation, our philosopher knows that his or her view of the nature of mind may radically change. One might, for example, begin as a materialist, in which case the meaning of *mind* would contain the concept *materiality.* However, as a result of investigation, one might change his or her opinions about materialism—in which case the meaning of *mind* might contain the concept *nonmateriality.* In this example, what our philosopher must mean when using the term *mind* is that structure that *will* emerge when he or she comes to know the *true character* of mind.

What the philosopher explicitly means when using the term *mind* is, in part, what he or she axiologically and *not* conceptually knows of mind. As argued above, the knower presupposes a direct knowledge of the epistemic value of the to-be-known world. This tacitly known value is increasingly realized in the progressive selection of theories about that world. Thus, structural knowledge of the world is assumed to possess validity to the degree that it realizes the values one knows directly, although tacitly. Such explicit constructions are *understood* to be provisional. What one *means* by a word invariably has reference to an ideal. This ideal is understood to involve a reality that fully manifests the values constraining the selection of ideas about it.

Toward a Primitive Metaphysic

We have come to the ultimate level of analysis. The knower conceives him- or herself to be a member of, to participate in, a community of presenting (or communicating) protopersons. This presupposition provides for the possibility of experience as we know it. Such community is the presupposed ground of intelligible structure. It is not possible to go further in the quest for the presuppositional underpinnings of experience. We may make explicit what such a community of persons involves, but we may not hope to find an assumed nonpersonal ground of that personal community.

We have considered that the intelligible world involves community inasmuch as the persons who present it are viewed as presenting the world to one another. Note that such community involves a kind of communion. That is, what makes presentations intelligible is that they are constructed in accordance with those values utilized by the knower in coming to know them. Therefore, it is possible to speak of a common ground of values that unites the presenter and the presentee. The same values constrain the constructive activities of the presenter and the representer. Value transcends the distinctions within the community and, in unifying the presenter and representer, provides for the possibility of intelligible communication.

This common ground of values entails an identification among communicating persons. By identification, I mean that the presenter and the presentee identify with each other in that each takes the other's values and point of view. In this way the presenter and the presentee constitute a personal community. Action by the presenter is thus necessary *for* the presentee. The presenter presents what he or she knows to the point of view or receiving self who does not know. The presentee, on the other hand, must somehow take the point of view of a presenting self who knows in order to understand what is being presented. By taking the perspective of the other, the knower achieves the point of view from which an understanding of the other is valued, and in terms of which his or her representations of the presentations of the other are to be evaluated. Such identification is involved in all communication. Moreover, it results from the communicators' participation in a common ground of value.

Identification is a condition on the possibility of learning. The a priori notions already unpacked amount to no more than the assumption that such an identification obtains as the basis for the intelligibility of any domain. At each level of analysis, identification is presupposed. The presentee assumes that at the most fundamental level, he or she is identifying with the values, contexts, and point of view of the presenter. In this framework the presentee attempts to apprehend the structure of the presenter's presentation.

Knowledge is thought to be possible because the presentation is assumed to be for the valuing presentee. The structural world is therefore assumed to be the joint product of a complementary giving activity of the presenter and a receiving (or taking) activity of the presentee. The consequence is that the presentee as well as the presenter is assumed to participate in the definition of the structural domain. The knower not only creates a representation of the intelligible world but also assumes him- or herself and the presented world to be defined in relation to one another. The presentee assumes that he or she knows the values in terms of which it was presented in the first place. It was, after all, presented *to* him or her.[14]

This move, one of the most radical, is at the same time one of the most important conclusions of this analysis. If the knower and the to-be-known are actually assumed to be defined in relation to each other, it becomes possible to give a natural and coherent answer to the question as to how we assume that knowledge is possible. We assume that we may inquire concerning the unknown simply because we assume that it is not *fully* unknown to us. In embodying the conditions that constrain its presentation to us, we have given the unknown an indelible character. We have given it its value for us and, accordingly, have given to ourselves the key by which we may come to unlock its riddles.

To understand fully the character of the solution that I am posing, it is necessary to see that the identification does not, in the deepest sense, result from anything that two more or less independent persons do. Rather, personhood is *defined* in the context of such identification. Thus, persons are distinct but *not* independently defined.

The events that psychology must describe are acts of persons in community. Note that independent persons are not the objects of psychological analysis. The reason for this is simply that as the notion has been developed, persons do not have existence independent of community. *Personhood* is both etymologically and scientifically a relational term. To grant independent existence to either the presenter or the presentee is to give a derived status to the other member of the pair. On the other hand, to grant independent existence to both is to reintroduce the epistemic problem at hand. Knowledge of the presenter by the presentee is *only* possible because they are not defined independently of each other. The presenter–presentee, knower–known, relationship is irreducible: Each is defined as being *for* the other. Therefore, neither member of the pair has an independent or a derived status.[15]

The knower assumes that he or she knows the presenter directly in the act of identifying with the presenter. What is assumed is a kind of personal (not structural) direct realism. It is assumed that protopersons, as foci of value, are known directly. At the same time, since the knower is identified with the protopersonal ground of the known (who is therefore defined in terms of the knower), what is assumed is an idealism.

THE NATURAL HISTORY OF IDEAS

There is more to be said about presumptive contexts than that they make judgment possible. They also provide the basis for a kind of intellectual growth. This section unpacks a general account of the development of ideas in terms of the presuppositions that ground judgment. Development of a true conception of reality requires an increasing self-consciousness with respect to those presuppositions. Consciousness can be shown to progress in three stages—from simplicity, to doubt, to an apprehension of the truth in self-consciousness. The final (or third) stage of self-consciousness must be achieved if we are to attain an adequate psychological theory. Therefore, the developmental process I sketch is an account of how one discovers, or learns, the true psychological theory. We achieve a learning theory that describes the process of its acquisition such that that acquisition is seen to be warranted. In this way we avoid the ad hominem argument leveled against reductionism.

A Historical Example

One essential insight of Kant's analysis of theoretical physical science was that the presuppositions of the investigator about a domain are central in the development of theoretical statements about that domain. Specifically, Kant held that a deductive theory concerning a domain would contain as first principles notions that were explicit statements of the assumptions in terms of which the domain had been tacitly viewed. That is, genuine theoretical work was said to involve, among other things, a postulation of those already tacitly held assumptions about the domain being studied.

For example, the law of inertia states that a physical body will continue in a given state of motion until acted upon by an outside force. It is clear that such a principle possesses a priori aspects. In particular, it involves the a priori assumption that the world is a causally organized system in which every change in state is caused. Galileo's achievement was to recognize as empirical the facts that motion is itself a state and that forces are causes. The law of inertia, therefore, contains both empirical and, as Kant suggested, a priori components.

No doubt, in some respects Kant's claim is fundamentally correct: Theories about a domain are typically compared and evaluated in relation to a set of more or less tacit, metatheoretical criteria. But such criteria amount to no more than prior assumptions about the domain in question: If it were not assumed that the domain under investigation possessed properties that corresponded to the metatheoretical criteria, it would be absurd to evaluate the relative truth of theories about that domain in terms of those criteria. Thus the metatheory embodies a set of prior assumptions about the object of inquiry. Accordingly, since statements about that object explicitly incorporate such prior assumptions, such statements will take on a necessary (noncontingent) character.

It is not necessary to go to modern science for examples that demonstrate the role of presuppositions in the development of thought. Any history of thought about a subject that exhibits some dialectical development can be shown to involve a progressive revelation of a set of presuppositions (Hegel, 1967). The culmination of such a history involves a bringing to consciousness of those metatheoretical presuppositions that have guided the progressive selection of the theories that make up that history. Insofar as those hitherto tacit criteria are brought to consciousness, they illuminate the prior historical development and, at the same time, define the goal of that development. That modern science develops toward theory grounded in that which is a priori simply indicates that it participates in the dialectical structure characteristic of human thought in general.

Stages in the Movement Toward Self-Consciousness

Note that understanding, insofar as it is grounded in the a priori, is grounded in what cannot be empirically supported. The kind of intelligibility we achieve through theoretical science, for example, is partially derived from a kind of self-consciousness. As noted, this movement toward self-consciousness is characterized as progressing through three stages.

The first stage is entirely lacking in self-consciousness. At this point the knower is not conscious of the distinction between the world and his or her representation of it. The knower is therefore not even conscious *that* he or she is representing the world. This stage is the lower bound of self-consciousness. Nevertheless, even judgments at this first stage involve an element of inference. Since they involve judgments, the simplest perceptions go beyond the wholly given. Precisely this fact ensures that the first stage is simultaneously genuinely mental and also that error is possible. The fact of error, brought to light through the experience of inconsistency, or incoherence, forces the knower to recognize the representational character of his or her thought and, thus, to enter the second stage.

The second stage (which passes through two moments) emerges as the knower becomes aware of the distinction between the world and his or her representations. One comes to know *that* one is representing the world. Nevertheless, in the first moment of the second stage, the knower remains unconscious of the axiologically based metatheoretical context that guides his or her representation of the world.

Movement from the first to the second stage results from the explicit discovery that it is possible to be in error and that judgments should therefore be understood as resulting in representations that are distinct from the objects they represent. It is understood that truth is a problem. An explicit distinction emerges between truth and error.

The distinction between our present conception of the world and the truth about the world entails the distinction between "the thing as it is" and "the thing in experience." The critical capacity that enables the knower to recognize that his or her explicit ideas do not realize the values that are assumed to constrain the intelligible world (that he or she does not apprehend the world as a coherent unity) entails the distinction between what the knower thinks and what is. Accordingly, the problem of truth only arises as the knower moves from the first to the second stage.

Examples of this second stage are found in the typical psychological subject, the scientist in the lab, or the person on the street, who are all confronting some domain of their experience in a more or less conventional way. At this stage, that domain is simply emerging for the observer. He or she is finding out about it. Insofar as the observer is conscious, the domain is wholly contingent in character.

The observer then discovers that it is impossible to synthesize the whole of this domain in a contingent fashion. Because a synthesis of the whole domain requires a priori notions, the observer cannot see the domain as fully realizing those values that constrain the developing vision of it until he or she becomes conscious of those a priori assumptions and postulates them. Because the observer cannot find a ground for the whole in the contingent realm, it becomes a real question whether or not the project—which the knower now suspects he or she cannot complete—could ever really have been begun.

The second moment of the second stage arises as the knower discovers a conception of the investigated domain that, to a degree, *begins* by explicitly realizing those values the knower had hoped to see in the world. To the extent that he or she is aware of presuppositions that acted as guides through the first moment of the second stage, the knower possesses material that can be postulated to be true a priori of the investigated domain. Thus, the knower will have made possible a postulate structure required for viewing phenomena as necessary (insofar as they are true a priori) and not merely contingent. Thus, the domain becomes intelligible for the knower because it explicitly manifests what he or she had all along assumed that it would. The knower becomes increasingly conscious of a ground that, from the point of view of the project chosen, he or she cannot doubt.[16]

The movement from the first to the second moment of the second stage of consciousness is characterized by a movement toward systematicity grounded in the introduction of postulates that are partially a priori. Understanding is increasingly seen to be grounded in principles that cannot be denied if intelligibility is to be retained. Theoretical understanding, as opposed to mere empirical generalization, is more and more developed. However, in the second moment, this movement is not fully explicit; that is, it is not yet clear to the knower that the epistemic development involved is a result of postulating metatheoretical presuppositions. The knower does not yet understand what he or she is doing.

Because it is not fully self-conscious, the second moment is not fully universal. This failure becomes apparent when an attempt is made toward universality. When the postulates adduced for the explanation of a particular domain (such as the postulates of physics) are taken as the key to the intelligibility of all domains, a reductionism necessarily ensues. The result of this reductionism is that we distort other intelligible domains. For example, the kind of necessity in terms of which physics is coherent is said to explicate fully the kind of intelligibility we discover in psychology. But such reductionism, since it imposes upon domains of intelligibility interpretations foreign to their subject matter, invariably misses or misconstrues important structural features of those domains. In the end it results in self-contradiction.

Such reductionism is only avoided by grounding the whole in a universal and, therefore, self-reflective set of presuppositions. Through the postulation of presuppositions about particular domains, the investigator has been able to move toward coherence *within* those domains. However, complete coherence requires the postulation of those presuppositions that are *universal* in judgment. Unless the investigator can ground presuppositional analysis per se, he or she must continue to view understanding as a mere, doubtful representation of the to-be-known world. The second stage of consciousness, which began by making doubt possible, is likely to end by seeming to make skepticism necessary. This problem is only resolved through the development of a third stage of consciousness.

The third stage emerges through more explicit understanding of difficulties raised by the first moment of the second stage and a consequent understanding of the role of presuppositions in the development of the second moment of the second stage. It is understood that a fully universal perspective must be defined in terms of presuppositions that ground *all* doubt, not just the doubts relevant to a particular domain of intelligibility. In line with the requirement for a set of universal presuppositions, it is understood that we require a set of presuppositions that characterize our discovery of them in such a way that they may be seen to be the valid ground of our discovery.

This condition will be achieved, in part, through dialectical historical accounts as I have just given. The assumptions explicated and postulated in the third stage of consciousness are precisely those that lead to the transcendence of previous stages. Accordingly, it is just *those* presuppositions that have guided consciousness toward self-consciousness. They lead to the discovery of themselves. They also characterize their discovery such that that discovery is seen to be valid. Their discovery will appear to be valid to anyone capable of reflecting upon the viewpoint they constitute (the viewpoint from which we doubt).

This viewpoint grounds the doubt that is already at work in the unconscious selection of representations characteristic of the first stage. The same viewpoint is explicitly active in the second stage of consciousness, which is *defined* in terms of the emergence of doubt. It is the same viewpoint, fully unpacked, that is finally seen to be grounded in indubitable presuppositions. Explication of those presuppositions is the movement into the third and final stage of consciousness.

The third stage of consciousness results from a presuppositional analysis of judgment in general. The knower is concerned to understand those presuppositions that ground inquiry into all intelligible domains. Because such presuppositions are universal, knowing reflects directly upon itself in their explication. At this point, the knower is becoming conscious of the presuppositions that underlie all judgments, including those in terms of which he or she now becomes conscious and postulates—the knower's final and universal presuppositions. (Note that the critical point of view is essentially that viewpoint taken by the presenter in presenting to the presentee. The perspective in terms of which the presenter's presentation is to be understood *must,* of course, be the point of view in terms of which the presentation was made to begin with.)

Psychology is at least partially responsible for this third-stage self-reflective enterprise. Psychology has a unique position among the sciences: Psychologists are required to explain the theoretical scientist as well as themselves in the act of explaining the scientist in his or her activities. Psychologists are also required to represent the perspective that governs the presuppositional analysis required for the dialectical understanding of any domain. But in so doing, it is clear that they are engaged in presuppositional analysis. Therefore, in constructing a representation of the perspective in terms of which presuppositional analysis has been done, we require that the representation also account for its own construction. This final level requires a fully self-reflective set of presuppositions. We seek a set of presuppositions that are discoverable in terms of themselves. When those assumptions are themselves postulated, we will have attained a genuinely theoretical psychology that at the same time will explain the activity of the psychologist discovering it.[17]

The last stage of self-reflectivity will enable us to provide a postulate structure that grounds the activity of theoretical science and other epistemic projects in a way analogous to the way theoretical science grounds the activity of empirical science. At the same time, the postulate structure will be seen to be self-reflective. That is, we aspire to a solution to the epistemic problem that does not in itself constitute a further problem. This solution not only grounds the possibility of science but (as it constitutes a basis for judgment in general) also provides for grounding all possible domains of experience. When fully explicated, we will have achieved the possibility of an apprehension of the whole in a self-conscious way.

Any contingent representation of the world may be doubted. Hence, it can never be said of such representations that we *know* (know that we know) them to be true. What cannot be doubted, however, is the universal context in terms of which we experience doubt. This context is, of course, the perspective from which we evaluate putative representations, including representations of this perspective. What is not doubtable is the reality of the presupposed epistemic ideal that creates and directs doubt. The final epistemic stage is achieved as the knower becomes conscious of, and postulates as true, the presuppositions underlying *all* doubt. He or she affirms that the real is the epistemic ideal, and conversely. In this way, the knower sees the known as manifesting what he or she has hitherto been unconsciously assuming that it would. The knower understands that the perspective that guides the evaluation of possible knowledge is, in some sense, identical to the objective protopersonal perspective that constrains the to-be-known. He or she becomes conscious of a ground of all experience that cannot be doubted.

This third and final stage is the perspective we seek to explicate in this chapter. The natural history of thought involves a dialectical movement of consciousness toward it: The history of thought progresses toward a fully self-conscious grasp of the whole. It is progress toward a perspective that has all along been the tacit guide of that historical process. From that perspective, the history of consciousness becomes intelligible as an explication of just that perspective.

We have seen that a psychological theory is required to explicate its acquisition such that its acquisition is understood to be valid.[18] Since psychological theory emerges at the third stage, this section has sketched the general character of the acquisition of psychological theory. Subsequent sections describe the final, or third, perspective in more detail. Having achieved such a description, we will be able to reconsider the development of that perspective in the context of the sort of dialectical process already outlined.

Learning as a Dialectical Process

The presentationalist position provides an alternative to the rationalist–empiricist controversy concerning the nature of learning. The rationalist view depends heavily on the tacit–explicit distinction. It is claimed by rationalists that knowledge is only possible in explicit form if it is there in some tacit form to begin with. The process of learning is viewed as an elicitation of tacit knowledge through a more or less unspecified interaction with the empirical world. On the other hand, empiricists have insisted that the learner is initially equipped with only general information–processing capacities. Beyond the influence of these, the structure of knowledge is said to be determined entirely by the structure of the world that one confronts.

Parallel to our refusal to accept wholeheartedly either realism against idealism or idealism against realism, we reject accepting either rationalism or empiricism against its alternative. In opposition to either, I propose what can be called a dialectical view of learning. On one hand, I of course agree with the rationalists—that we confront the world in terms of tacitly held presuppositions about that world. Clearly, knowing or learning would not be possible in the absence of such presuppositions. (In the face of a generally empiricist psychology, I have been at pains to emphasize this fact.) At the same time, the presuppositions that guide the knowing process are appropriate only to a world that is self-revealing—that is, a communication. This means that even though we conceive, with the rationalists, the knowing process to be guided by tacit understanding of the to-be-known domain, that tacit knowledge involves the presupposition that the to-be-known domain plays an active and structuring role in the learning process. With the empiricists, we must emphasize the importance of the environment in learning.

For the sake of expository simplicity, my account of presentationalism has perhaps suggested a rather static view of the presentation. It might have been inferred that I viewed the presented world as if it were simply an intelligible structure or object—its intelligibility resting entirely on the fact that it (as a finished product) is constrained by certain values. Such an understanding would not do justice to the rich possibilities inherent in presentationalism. On the contrary, presentationalism understands the learning process as inherently dialectical in nature—the learner being led through the three stages described earlier. It is only through dialectical interaction with a presenter that the presentee is led to recognize, in any intelligible domain, structures that realize his or her tacit valuing. The intelligible world is assumed to be self-revealing in the context of such a dialectical interaction. In the framework of presentationalism, the self-conscious competence of the presenter and the tacit knowledge of the presentee combine to produce, in the learner, the competence possessed by the presenter.

Traditional rationalism proposes an epistemic autonomy of the knower, whereas traditional empiricism proposes an epistemic autonomy of the known. In contrast, presentationalism sees learning as grounded in a self-revealing reason that is simultaneously the ground of the intelligible world and the knower's a priori appreciation of the world and that reason.[19]

THE ROLE OF PRESUPPOSITIONS IN PSYCHOLOGICAL DATA AND EXPLANATION

This section notes several ways in which presuppositions determine the character of data and explanation in the psychology of learning. First, the explanation for the learner's taking up a belief involves showing that he or she understands that belief to be warranted in a context of good reasons. It will be shown that this entails that the learner's judgments are grounded in a set of presuppositions. Second, the facts we intuitively take as psychological (in particular, facts concerning learning) are both specified and explained in terms of our presuppositions about persons and the world they confront. Third, we have seen that learning involves the learner's becoming explicitly conscious of the presuppositions which guide the learning process. Accordingly, the learner will be in the position of giving an explanation of his or her own learning if that learning is complete or results in self-consciousness.

Presuppositional Analysis and an Explanation of Judgment

We saw previously how an explanation of belief (or judgment) that asserts that belief is solely determined by a matrix of physical causes entails an essentially skeptical position. We must now give an account of the determinants of judgment or belief such that those determinants are seen to be rational warrants for belief. Moreover, in this context it is evident that presupposition of the objective validity of rational values is itself the final determinant of belief. Only insofar as I assume the validity of reason do I put confidence in the conclusions that reason warrants. Thus, an explanation of judgment will posit the judge's presupposition of the validity of rational values. This presupposition is what we are concerned with in this chapter.

Presuppositional Analysis and the Existence, Observation, and Explanation of Learning

I have argued that experience of, and therefore action in, the world involve the knower-actor in cosmological and metaphysical presuppositions and assumptions about the confronted world. Accordingly, we should expect these presuppositions and assumptions to inform and determine the subject matter of psychology from the beginning. This subject matter will become fully intelligible as the conditions necessary for it are uncovered and postulated as the a priori ground of all psychological phenomena.

In general, scientific theories are grounded in unified domains of phenomena. Any such domain first presents itself as a body of facts intuitively felt to be similar and interrelated. However, despite their apparent "givenness," the facts an investigator attempts to order are not defined independently of the conceptual framework that tacitly informs the investigator's observations. The empiricist claim that facts are simply there, independent of the manner in which they are taken, is false. The facts that comprise a domain of inquiry emerge in the context of the presuppositions and assumptions of investigators.

We seek a specification of the psychological domain in terms of a developing theoretical self-consciousness. In this context I suggest that the essential characteristic of psychological events is that they express personal foci of valuing. They are, therefore, defined in terms of the personal value they are intended to realize. Thus, concrete psychological events will be examples of success or failure, competence or incompetence, appropriateness or inappropriateness. The value that grounds personal activity creates a distinction between success and failure. When we see competence or incompetence in the world, we have evaluated some activity in relation to an axiological standard. Without such an ideal in mind, it is impossible to recognize either competence or incompetence.

In learning, the relevant ideal is defined by the epistemic presuppositions of the psychologist. To see the learner's judgment as competent or incompetent, we as psychologists must presuppose the objectivity of an epistemic ideal. Our perception of the relative truth (competence) or falsehood (incompetence) of a judgment depends upon *assuming* the validity of the ideal in terms of which the judgment may be understood to be either true or false.

Moreover, while the observation of learning requires the presupposition by the observer of axiological and epistemic constraints, the explanation of learning requires their *postulation*. Essential to any account that the learner has come to a competent grasp of a presented domain is the stipulation that the axiological constraints that guide the learner's judgment ground the domain he or she is confronting. Our explanation of learning centers on postulating the truth of the learner's presuppositions about the epistemic and axiological constraints on the to-be-known.

The theoretical account of learning is not grounded in the postulation of a priori notions that are separable from the data. By definition, learning involves the knower coming to realize values that are objectively in the to-be-known world. The very existence of learning, independent of its recognition or explanation, depends on the objectivity of axiological constraints on the to-be-known. What theoreticians must postulate in developing a learning theory is precisely that which is *necessarily present in every example of the phenomenon they intend to explain*. We explain learning by postulating what is necessary for the *existence* of learning—namely, that the world *is* constrained by values the learner tacitly assumes. Moreover, because they are the ground of all learning, these presuppositions could not be demonstrated or refuted through empirical experiment. Therefore it is necessary, in accordance with the model of theoretical development already sketched, to stipulate the a priori truth of these presuppositions.[20,21]

Learning as Presuppositional Analysis

If we see learning as the acquisition of a true understanding of some intelligible domain, we may expect it to result in the sort of development toward self-consciousness described earlier. In this view, learning that a proposition is true necessarily involves coming to know why it is true. To learn that a given proposition is true is to become aware of that matrix of good reasons that provide the warrant for asserting its truth.

Such an understanding will be grounded in the explication of an a priori perspective, approached as the learner moves toward the self-consciousness that I have characterized as the third epistemic stage. The knower, in developing self-consciousness, approaches the condition whereby it may be said that he or she knows a proposition x. This proposition would be a member of a set of propositions that describe a unified intelligible domain and that are brought into unified and coherent systematicity and necessity by virtue of their relationships to a set of a priori postulates.

Learning is not complete until the learner has achieved a fully explicit, self-conscious, warranted certainty of the truth. The learning of x requires the learner to become conscious of the self-grounding presuppositions in terms of which he or she judges x to be true. But, such an understanding will, at the same time, be an explanation as to *why* the learner holds x to be true. Thus, the learning of x requires a self-reflective account of the learning of x. At this point, it is the learner who can give the ultimate explanation of his or her own learning.[22]

THE QUEST FOR THE ABSOLUTE

We are in search of a kind of absolute—an absolute perspective that truly apprehends the whole of which it is a part. We will inquire into the assumptions underlying the possibility of criticism. We will, therefore, attempt to do no more than make explicit what we universally assume when we doubt. To the extent that we succeed, the adduced presuppositions will be beyond doubting. To doubt the objective truth of these presuppositions will be impossible, since the very act of doubting them requires utilizing them. They must, also therefore, be made the explicit grounds of a view that includes psychological events in the natural order.

I begin by showing that anything less than this would fail to approach those goals that psychologists have commonly set for themselves. This is not to say that the account of the absolute I subsequently present is beyond further elucidation. It is only to say that in the future, psychology must explicitly concern itself with the problem of absolute knowledge. Psychological theory is subject to constraints that *require* it to contain a proposal concerning the final or absolute context of the whole.

No doubt, some psychological inquiry can be pursued without explicit reference to these issues. However, any attempt to explicate the context of choice that governs judgment and action *must* include an account of the absolute assumptions and values that direct such choice. These assumptions and values must be arguably the ground in terms of which psychological phenomena emerge, as well as the context of the psychologist's discovery of them.

The following discussion focuses on epistemological aspects of the absolute. I consider the character of the epistemic values referred to earlier and show how the values that have already guided our inquiry and informed our methodology and argument determine an absolute epistemic ideal—a self-revealing and self-evident truth. Such an absolute truth, whatever else it might be, is a self-valuing conception of a unified whole.

The Necessity for an Absolute

The epistemic constraint whereby we presuppose that learning is possible is found in the assumption that we tacitly comprehend a coherent and systematic whole. Such knowledge is assumed to be both a priori and self-revealing. There are at least four reasons for thinking that we make such an assumption.

The Conceptual Relativity of Facts.   First, those assumptions that make judgments possible are assumptions about the whole of the domain under investigation. This follows from consideration of the conceptual relativity of facts. There can be no doubt that facts are defined in a conceptual context. Accordingly, any judgment about a matter of fact presupposes the conceptual context within which that judgment is made. The conceptual context involves assumptions *about* the domain within which the judged fact is alleged to have been discovered. Thus, a judgment about a matter of fact inevitably involves logically prior presuppositions and assumptions concerning a more global set of facts. Therefore, any judgment about a matter of fact in some domain is conditioned by a presupposition about the character of the relevant intelligible domain as a whole. Accordingly, the knower must always assume that he or she tacitly knows the whole. In order to assume that any particular judgment could be valid, the knower must first assume that he or she possesses a valid, if tacit, knowledge of the general character of the whole.

Moreover, note that knowledge of the whole necessarily includes knowledge by the knower *that* he or she actually knows the whole. That is, the knowledge of the whole required for any knowledge of the parts would be worthless if it were not *recognizable as* knowledge of the whole. Further, because of the conceptual relativity of facts, this recognition of the character of the whole must take place within a context. But since the only context of the whole is the whole, presuppositions about the whole must provide the context within which they are themselves known and known to be true. Knowledge of the whole is, therefore, self-revealing in the sense that it is the metatheoretical ground of apprehending itself. The ultimately self-evident character of knowledge of the whole is a necessary condition for the explication of true postulates about the whole.

The thesis that knowledge of parts is conditioned by knowledge of the whole entails the doctrine of *internal relations*. The doctrine of internal relations asserts that the character of any part is a function of its relation to the other parts of a given whole—that is, that the relationships among entities of a domain comprise the character of those entities. The opposing doctrine of *external relations* holds that the character of an individual part can be fully determined without reference to the relation between that part and the rest of the whole that includes that part. Clearly, to affirm the conceptual relativity of facts is to affirm the doctrine of internal relations. To hold that our judgments about the parts are conditioned by our assumptions about the whole entails that we assume that the true character of the entities that comprise a given domain is in the relationship among those entities. On the contrary, if we hold the doctrine of external relations, then the empiricist program is justifiable. We may look at the parts of a domain and infer their true character without any reference to their interrelationships.

The point of view taken in this chapter is that the truth about the parts of the whole is conditioned by the global axiological character of the whole. Precisely this fact led me to claim that final intelligibility is achieved as the investigator comes to postulate the necessary truth of his or her presuppositions about the whole. If the character of the whole did not condition the character of the parts, then knowledge of the whole would not constrain knowledge of the parts.

Insofar as we see the to-be-known as grounded in the a priori, we see the world as necessarily the way it is. Understanding, or explanation, requires that we discover good reasons for why things are the way they are. We must see how things are *necessarily* the way they are. Such a necessity derives from explicitly postulating a priori assumptions about the whole. Therefore, as we move toward full self-consciousness, as the presuppositions that inform our inquiry become explicit postulates, we expect to achieve a vision that is not only self-reflective but one in which the whole is seen to be subject to a systematic necessity.

Knowing Entails Certainty.   Second, if I claim to know something, it follows that I claim to *know that I know* whatever I claim to know. One thing I must claim to know when I claim to know something is just that I know that I know it. If I don't claim that I know that I know, then I cannot claim to know; at best, what I possess is right opinion. Since knowledge of any whole is a necessary ground for the possibility of correct judgments about the parts of that whole, such knowledge must be certain in the preceding sense. To know the whole is to *know* that we know it.

To claim any less leads directly to the skepticism of David Hume. Hume was unable to convince himself that he knew anything about the empirical world. This doubt did not result from the necessarily incomplete and provisional character of empirical judgments, but from the fact that Hume found it impossible to validate the presupposition of the causal character of the empirical world, which presupposition he assumed to ground all empirical judgments about that world. He found it impossible to validate a presupposition about the *whole* of the empirical world. Logically, what follows is skepticism, which, of course, is self-refuting.

Thus we are required to be dissatisfied with any characterization of final presuppositions about the whole in which those presuppositions are not absolutely certain. Anything less, as Hume has shown, would lead to an essentially skeptical position. The psychological subject, although only provisionally knowing particular empirical facts, must at some level know that he or she knows the character of the whole of any intelligible domain about which he or she makes judgments. The psychologist's task is to characterize that self-grounding knowing. Further, the psychologist's task is to characterize his or her *own* self-grounding knowing. A priori knowledge must be known to be true in the context of itself. Although we become aware of such principles through their operation in experience, the final a priori truth about the whole grounds both the experience that reveals it and the appreciation of itself as true.

The Methodology of Argument.   Third, that we assume a grasp of the whole may be seen by examining the methodology of theoretical criticism and development assumed in this essay. In every case, we understood criticism to be grounded in assumptions about the whole. Negative evaluation of a theory invariably involves seeing the theory in question to be in contradiction to what is tacitly or explicitly assumed about the domain in question. Positively, theories are said to develop in the direction of explicit postulation of those a priori assumptions. In either case, what is assumed to be known is the character of the whole. Further, since there exists no broader context, that global character is assumed to be knowable in its own context.

We have been seeking to characterize the universal critical context, what is universally presupposed when we doubt. We have seen that the most obvious invariant of the critical act is the fact of rational evaluation. In a particular epistemic context, arguments and theories are ordered in terms of their plausibility; alternatives are compared in relation to a rational epistemic ideal. This ideal is the source of critical doubt that guides the development of knowledge in a given epistemic domain. The act of evaluating a hypothesis amounts to a decision as to the degree of distinction between that hypothesis and the presupposed ideal. In effect, the ordering of hypotheses in terms of the degree to which they realize the ideal amounts to postulating the *truth* of that ideal. Although the explicit invocation of postulates does not begin until what I earlier called the second moment of the second stage, the simple evaluation of alternative hypotheses in terms of an epistemic ideal involves a prior implicit assumption of that ideal.

The assumed truth of the presupposed context grounds the methodological imperative to postulate presuppositions. Further, the methodological principle whereby we understand that it is required to postulate the presuppositions and assumptions that ground our inquiry is the positive complement to the use of the *argumentum ad hominem*. The latter invokes a proscription against contradicting one's presuppositions. But this proscription is warranted if and only if it is assumed that those presuppositions ought to be explicitly postulated to be true of the confronted domain. It is warranted if and only if we assume that the presuppositions of judgment are true, and that an adequate account of some domain involves stating what we know to be true about it. Therefore, critical evaluation rests in part on presupposition of an ideal and ultimate conception of the whole in question.

The Distinction Between Truth and Error.   Fourth, the final metatheory informs our primitive notions of truth and error. The judgments we can make in relation to a given domain are either true or false only if the argumentative presuppositions included in the metatheory are true. This final metatheory contains the universal presuppositions of every judgment. One is simply that it is possible to specify conditions under which any judgment is either true or false; that is, it is presupposed that if the contingent presuppositions of a judgment are true, then that judgment is either true or false. This is not to say that the presupposition that a judgment is true or false is necessarily true, but rather that it is possible to specify conditions under which such a judgment would be either true or false.

In effect, the metatheoretical ground of doubt, the context of good reasons, creates for the knower the distinction between truth and error by valuing truth above error. This is so because the distinction between truth and error is defined in terms of values realized by the object of knowledge. To doubt the ground of doubt that defines the distinction between truth and error would subject one to ad hominem attack because both this presupposition and its negation presuppose the presupposition in question. This context of good reasons is not only the ground of the eventual unfolding of intelligible domains but also that which cannot be denied without subjecting the denier to ad hominem attack.

In conclusion, we have seen that intelligibility requires the postulation of an absolutely certain presupposition about the whole. The presupposition we are concerned to discover is at once the already tacit ground of the possibility of knowledge and criticism and the ground of our knowing that presupposition truly.

The Character of the Absolute

I now turn to a description of the final presupposition about the whole—the presupposition that is the point of view that has been both the source and goal of our inquiry. In so doing, I hope to show in what context judgments and claims are determined. The result will given an account of the process of judgment such that the account will be appropriate not only for persons in general but for myself as well, in the activity of giving this account.

The Self-Evident Ground of Absolute Knowledge.   This subsection demonstrates a concrete self-evident presupposition that is the ground of judgment. Subsequent subsections show how this concrete self-evident epistemic presupposition, which is always present to us, determines the direction and development of our thought, meets the requirements for absolute knowledge already described, and is to be postulated as the ground of the completion of the three fundamental epistemic projects—knowledge of the knower, the known, and the whole that includes the knower and the known.

The reader has no doubt noticed that the argument constructed by David Hume with respect to the presupposition concerning causality is applicable to every epistemic presupposition. Thus, to argue the presupposition that the constraints on knowing are correlated with constraints on reality (to argue that reason is adequate to reality) would be to assume what one is attempting to demonstrate. The argument would be circular and would show nothing. In what sense could a presupposition be self-grounding? Where, then, can we begin? What, if anything, do we know *directly?*

What I know by direct intuition is that insofar as I would know, I must allow reason to determine my judgments. But I take this knowledge to be equivalent to the knowledge that reason is adequate to reality. That is, whenever I judge, I know directly that reason is adequate to reality. Adequate reason, or the reasonableness of the real, is the argumentative presupposition that defines the distinction between truth and error by valuing truth above error. The adequacy of reason is a universal presupposition in that it grounds the contemplation of all intelligible domains; it is a necessary cause of every case of knowledge. Moreover, every claim to know, whether true or not, argumentatively presupposes valid reason and involves the implicit claim to have been determined by such reason. Of course, it is impossible to prove the adequacy of reason since such a proof would presuppose precisely what is at stake. Nevertheless, to deny the adequacy of reason would be to utilize the true/false distinction that adequate reason defines. Moreover, such a denial entails that there could be no good reason for it. We could not take the denial of the adequacy of reason to be a case of knowledge.

Therefore, it is unnecessary, as well as impossible, to demonstrate the adequacy of reason. The efficacy of reason is presupposed as the ground of the distinction between true and false judgments. Reason always concerns questions and their answers; it concerns the "why." But about the adequacy of reason, there *is* no question, and therefore, it is not appropriate for reason to speak concerning it. Reason is *assumed* to be adequate. The ad hominem argument may be directed against those who claim to question the adequacy of reason. The argument shows that their question is merely verbal. At best, they are simply confused; at worst, they are consciously deceptive. In point of fact, the adequacy of reason is never seriously doubted.

But if so, we may inquire concerning the character of the distinction between affirming and denying the adequacy of reason. This distinction is defined by the ad hominem. It seems clear that the distinction does not involve *determining* the truth but *telling* the truth. I may apply the ad hominem to myself as a means of avoiding self-contradiction and consequent self-deception. The reader may apply the ad hominem to the author to avoid being deceived by the author's self-contradictions. The truth of the final epistemic presupposition is universally presupposed and thus never in question. What is in question is whether our theories will acknowledge it and, in this way, attain coherence.

The final epistemic presupposition, that reason is adequate, is not brought into question. It is not brought into question because to do so would be deceptive. To bring anything into question is to assume the adequacy of reason. The final presupposition is not determined to be true; it is simply known to be true. It is clear that only such direct knowing could be absolute, noncontingent knowing.

Although we may assume the presupposition concerning the adequacy of reason to be valid because we assume the adequacy of reason, there is no sense in which the adequacy of reason is either brought into question or warranted by this fact. The adequacy of reason is immediately, not mediately, known. It is the essential presupposition of every act of judgment and, as such, is essential to the true/false distinction that reason creates. In virtue of this presupposition, the formal, aesthetic, and other principles of reason are taken as having a relation to the world—reasoning can be *about* something. The presupposition of the adequacy of reason is also the first and fundamental presupposition of reasoning.[23]

The Problem of Knowing the Knower.   Let us begin by recapitulating some main features of the argument to this point. First, we have from the beginning sought a causal explanation of the process of judgment. Second, we have seen that such an account, intended to be appropriate for persons in general, is necessarily required to explain ourselves in the act of judging it to be true. The account should explain us in the act of learning it. Third, this condition of self-reflectivity requires us to reject the materialist reductionism typically proposed in the context of neo-Darwinian evolutionary theory. Having rejected a physicalist account, we found ourselves faced with the task of explicating the fundamental axiological metatheoretical assumptions that determine belief. These assumptions, or presuppositions, would be central elements in a causal explanation of judgment and knowing.

Psychological theory will be, among other things, a theory of the psychologist's metatheory. Psychologists are required to characterize their own metatheory, which governs their decisions as to how to depict their own metatheory, etc. This latter point reminds us of the self-reflectivity condition in terms of which we have already rejected reductionism. The condition that we explain our own theoretical activity entails more than a rejection of reductionism; it also prohibits us from supporting any theory that would deny the truth of the metatheory we assume and implicitly affirm when we argue the theory to be true. We cannot support a theory that, if it were true, would entail that we could not know that it were true, that it could not be true, or that it could be neither true nor false. Stated positively, we seek a theory that affirms the assumed grounds of our arguments for it. We seek a theory of judgment in terms of which what we presuppose and implicitly claim when we judge or argue the theory to be a true theory is true. We require a theory that, if true, can be coherently argued to be true.

We seek a theory of the knower that characterizes the metatheoretical context within which it is chosen such that the theory is valued above its competing alternatives by the metatheory as characterized. Failure to do so would open the theory to ad hominem attack. That is, if a theory that failed to meet the foregoing conditions were true, it could not be viewed as true in the context of the metatheory in terms of which it was evaluated. On the other hand, if it were chosen as true, then we would be sure that the tacit metatheory, in terms of which *we* had chosen it, could not be described by the theory. In this case, the theory would *be* false. In holding such a theory, the psychologist would be reduced to absurdity.

It is evident that the preceding requirement is an absolute metatheoretical condition on a theory of the ultimate context within which theories are chosen and argued. It is therefore part of the account of the perspective we wish to describe. Thus, in stating this condition on the sought theory, I have at the same time begun to describe the *content* of a theory about the most general metatheoretical context. I have begun to give a psychological theory. That is, we have found it to be an absolute metatheoretical constraint on our theory of the absolute metatheoretical constraints that it depict those constraints such that, in their context, the theory is valued and argued to be superior to competing alternatives. We are, therefore, required to characterize the metatheory such that it values the theory that characterizes the metatheory as valuing that theory, and so on.

In attempting to characterize the ultimate metatheory, we find that our theory of it is subject to certain constraints. But because the metatheory we seek is universal, we know that it constrains our selection of a theory about itself. Accordingly, *it is an absolute constraint on our theory of the metatheory that it stipulate that the metatheory constrain the theory in just those ways in which the theory is absolutely constrained.* Moreover, this latter constraint, as an absolute one, is *also* to be seen as a metatheoretical constraint on the theory. Therefore, according to this latter constraint, the metatheory is necessarily such as to impose this latter constraint on the theory.

Clearly, we are here confronted with an absolute constraint that results from the complete universality of the truth we are attempting to apprehend. We want to characterize the metatheory that grounds and is common to *every* act of knowing. We have been led to discover a constraint on our theory of the absolute that is just the constraint in terms of which it itself has been discovered. Thus, the foregoing condition is, according to its own rule, to be understood as a theoretical statement about the metatheory. It is known in its own context.

In effect, the constraint we have been considering is a version of the constraint that requires us to seek argumentative coherence. Negatively, if it did not constrain our theory of the knower, the theory might contain statements that would deny the presuppositions and implicit claims of those statements. Positively, this constraint requires the elucidation of constraints on judgment, including itself, that define the knower's most universal metatheory. Therefore, a condition on a psychological theory is that it be argumentatively coherent. But this implies that the metatheory in terms of which we are working values argumentative coherence.

I now show how the general condition that we seek argumentative coherence and avoid the ad hominem in psychological *and* nonpsychological realms depends on the fact that judgment is constrained by reason that is assumed to be adequate to the to-be-known. If explanation is achieved through argumentative coherence, and if the ad hominem is the negative argument we take most seriously, an account of the metatheoretical constraint in question will be central to an explanation not only of the arguments in this chapter but also of argument in general.

Every case of judgment involves the implicit claim that it has been determined by reason that is adequate to reality. I take it that it is the indubitable presupposition of adequate reason that grounds the condition that the knower, as well as ourselves, values argumentative coherence. Clearly, reason itself, and only reason, can require coherence between the presuppositions and claims of judgment.

So reason requires that the absolute constraints on a theory of the metatheory be incorporated into the theory of the metatheory. Moreover, as we have seen, the ultimate claims of reason are self-evidently true. Accordingly, we are required to constrain judgment such that it is consistent with the claims of reason. But as already shown, we do not on the basis of reason compare and evaluate claims of reason with respect to their negations. We only require that all judgments cohere with the self-evident claims of reason. This requirement is satisfied as we ground understanding in an explicit postulation of what is indubitable—namely, the self-evident validity of reason itself. Reason, then, is the source of the condition of argumentative coherence. The self-evident assumption that reason is adequate is sufficient to ground the requirement that all claims cohere with the indubitable claims of reason itself. It is reason, therefore, that requires that we acknowledge its own status as the final metatheoretical ground, because not only is reason the final epistemic constraint; it is also the condition that requires that the constraints on a theory of the metatheory be incorporated into the theory of the metatheory.

Thus the self-evident claims of reason have guided the course of our inquiry: They have grounded our own valuing of an argumentatively coherent view of psychology. They have led us to a conception of the knower in which the knower is conceived as being guided by reason and therefore as valuing argumentative coherence. They have, therefore, led us to a theory of learning that accounts for our acquisition of our own theory.

Reason, through the ad hominem, requires us to assent to its self-evident adequacy. Reason requires that we avoid self-deception in the denial of the adequacy of reason. The presupposition of the adequacy of reason requires us to postulate the absolute constraints on a theory of the final metatheory. Therefore, it is the presupposition of the adequacy of reason that, as the final metatheoretical constraint, requires us to see itself to be the metatheoretical ground of judgment and knowing.

The Problem of Knowing the Known.   Because reason is the perspective in terms of which knowledge is criticized, it is only by formulating such knowledge as is grounded in what reason assumes that knowledge can be beyond criticism. But the fundamental presupposition of reason is that reason is adequate to reality or that reality is reasonable. Accordingly, a coherent conception of the whole is only possible if I conceive the whole to be for being known by reason. I must postulate that the world is appropriate to my rational apprehension of it.

In so doing, I specify the character of the world such that learning becomes possible: I give a necessary component of an explanation of learning, or coming to know. I see every to-be-known domain as constrained by an axiological ground that determines that it is to-be-known. In so doing, I postulate what is indubitable, state a condition required for the explanation of coming to know, and state the fundamental axiom of a coherent understanding of the to-be-known world.

The Problem of Knowing the Whole.   Every act of knowing is grounded in what is finally an intuitively self-evident and, thus, unconditioned presupposition—that the act of apprehending the world is determined by reason that is adequate to that world. When this presupposition is examined, it involves a claim that both the knower and the known are under the constraint of reason. The rational value that determines the knower is defined in relation to the rational value that determines the known. Knowing, then, is understood to be grounded in a dual constraint on both the apprehending and the apprehended. An absolute account of the knower will involve a discursive explication of the intuitively self-evident fact that the knower is determined by reason. An absolute account of the known will involve a discursive explication of the intuitively self-evident presupposition that the known realizes rational value. An absolute account of the whole, which includes both the knower and the known, must face the fact that it is the *relation* between the axiological constraints on the knower and the known that is the central focus of the aforementioned intuitively apprehended, self-evident presupposition. It is this relation (reason itself) that defines the whole. In the final analysis, the presuppositions with which we are concerned are about this ground, which determines subjectivity and objectivity in relation to one another. Therefore, we must explicate the role of this self-evident relation as the ground of the whole from an epistemological perspective.

The world is for our knowing of it in a mediated way. On the other hand, *that* the world is for our knowing of it is *directly* present with us in every act of judgment. Although this final knowledge is explicated through experience, it is itself not determined to be true. As the subjective ground of experience, it determines all judgment.

Moreover, the nonderivative character of this presupposition is the key to our access to the world. If the final presupposition were not in some sense given, the world would not be knowable. If indeed the world is knowable, the first thing I must know about the world is that it is knowable and in what way it may be known.

Thus, the knower–known relation simultaneously involves an immediate taking of the world for being known and an immediate giving of the world for being known. The knower–known relation is the initial constitutive constraint upon (as well as the relation between) the knower and the known. It is also the point of tacit identification between the knower and the known of which I have spoken previously. It is not only a relation but also a point of union between the knower and the known.

The final presupposition claims that mind and reality are defined for one another in terms of reason. There is no mind without a reasonable reality to be apprehended by that mind. There is no reality except what is to be apprehended by a reasoning mind. Therefore, the whole *necessarily* contains a knower for whom the known is to-be-known. Further, as seen earlier, it is only because the assumed relation is self-evident that the knower is *actually* related to the known in the way the final presupposition asserts and, therefore, that the whole actually exists. Thus, the self-evident relation *necessarily* exists, because it defines and determines the whole. Therefore, the self-evident relation stipulated by the final presupposition is a ground of knowing, a ground of the known, and a ground of the whole that includes both.

Note that the self-evidence of the final presupposition entails that the presupposition is perceived from a perspective that, although not validating itself, claims for itself absolute and indubitable appropriateness. In directly apprehending the character of the relation between knower and known, the knower has self-evident access to the global character of the whole. The fact that he or she directly grasps a self-evident truth about the whole provides the knower with a single standpoint from which to contemplate not only the world but also the world as for being known, and his or her knowing it as for being known, and his or her knowing his or her knowing it as for being known, and so on. The perspective in terms of which the whole is apprehended is, thus, immediately although nondiscursively self-conscious. The knower knows the character of the whole and thus knows that he or she knows it, and so on.

The world's for-being-knownness requires a knower with direct access to the fact that the world is for being known. We see, therefore, that the fact that the world is for being known entails that the whole includes a knower whose judgment is governed by just the self-conscious perspective of which we have been speaking. Insofar as the final presupposition—that the world is for being known—is postulated, we postulate a whole that includes a nondiscursive but self-conscious reflection upon it. Thus we see our self-evident access to the final presupposition as determined by a constraint on the whole to which, in possessing the final perspective, we have direct access. But this means that the ground of the whole, assumed to determine the self-conscious knowing of it, is assumed to be self-revealing. The constraint on the to-be-known whole, which ensures that the whole is to-be-known, ensures that this constraint is itself known. It is a constraint on the whole that reveals itself to the knower.

Just as knowing the world involves a self-conscious grasp of the world, so grounding the world involves a self-revealing giving of the world. Moreover, from the perspective of the self-conscious knower, it becomes apparent that knowing the to-be-knownness of reality is a function of the fact that the to-be-knownness of reality is itself directly to-be-known. That is, the knower understands that self-conscious reflection on the whole is made possible by the self-revealing grounding, or presentation of the whole. In this way, the self-conscious knower understands him- or herself to be defined and constituted in relation to the self-revealing presentation of the world. He or she understands the self-conscious apprehension of the whole to be made possible by the self-revealing presenting ground of the whole.

As this juncture we recapitulate the way the nondiscursive self-consciousness develops toward discursive explicitness after its emergence from the simplicity of the first stage of consciousness. In the first moment of the second stage, described earlier, we find reason involved in the analysis of particular domains. Reason, in conjunction with presuppositions unique to those particular domains, governs judgments about those domains and, along with their specialized presuppositions, defines the distinction between truth and falsehood for each. In the second moment of the second stage, reason works to elucidate the presuppositions of specialized domains. From the third stage of conscious development, reason may elucidate itself as defining, at the most general level of analysis, the knower–known relation. In this way the knower becomes explicitly conscious of the knower–known relation. From this point of view, the knower may postulate the rational ground of the knower and the known: He or she may postulate the knower–known relation. Reason reflects directly upon itself and attains discursive self-consciousness. (Recall that reason requires coherence and therefore grounds the elucidation of presuppositions and grounds the invocation of the *argumentum ad hominem*.) In this final stage, the condition requiring coherence (reason) requires our recognition that it is the inner ground of our recognition of itself. Rather than contemplating the for-being-knownness of the world, the knower contemplates the fact that the for-being-knownness of the world is directly for being known, and that this fact, too, is directly for being known, and so on.

In this way the knower comes to see the whole that includes the knower–known relation as depending upon a self-revealing ground in relation to which the whole is coherent. This self-revealing ground of the whole is known explicitly as the knower attains the final stage of self-consciousness. In final self-consciousness, the knower becomes conscious of the self-revealing ground of the whole, the ground that determines his or her inner identity with that ground.

In achieving this final stage of thought, the knower perceives, first, his or her axiological identity with the ground of the whole and, second, the fact that this identity and his or her perception of it are dependent on that same ground. Accordingly, the ground of the whole is seen to be self-revealing to the knower who is part of the whole. It is only because of this immediate self-revelation by the ground of the whole to the knower that the knower can approach discursive understanding of the whole. Knowledge of the self-revealing character of the ground of the whole, though always present to the knower, is only explicated at the final stage of thought. Through his or her discursive self-consciousness, the knower attains explicit access to the self-revealing ground of the to-be-known.

In the act of dispelling my self-deceptive denial of my direct and self-evident access to the self-revealing ground of the whole, that final ground creates discursive self-consciousness in me by showing that my recognition of its self-evident and self-revealing character is grounded in its self-evident and self-revealing character. The ground of the whole, because it determines the whole, determines our coming to know the whole and to know itself, not only as the ground of the whole but also as the ground of our coming to appreciate itself as that ground.

The Identity of the Real and Ideal.   From the postulate that reason is adequate, it follows that there are axiological constraints on the whole; that is, the whole is reasonable. The epistemic ideality of the real and the reality of the epistemic ideal are, taken together, the indubitable grounds of doubt, or criticism. It is clear that these presuppositions are precisely what is explicated by the theory of the idea just introduced. The idea may be properly said to be becoming its object if and only if the epistemic real and the epistemic ideal are identified. Moreover, truth is the goal of thought just because of that identity.

The Distinction Between Truth and Error.   The axiological character of the critical act entails that judgment be intentionally defined. As we have seen, it is the axiological element in psychological phenomena in general that entails that psychological phenomena be seen to be either appropriate or inappropriate. The dimension of appropriateness/inappropriateness that is relevant for judgment is the dimension of truth/falsehood. The end of thought is truth. Truth is the realization of certain epistemic values. Judgments are either appropriate or inappropriate (true or false) because they are intended to realize the epistemic or critical values.

Accordingly, we see a connection between the presupposition that the object of knowledge is defined as the full realization of our epistemic values and the presupposition that, provided its contingent presuppositions are true, a judgment is either true or false. The former entails the latter, and conversely. The fact that thought aims at a realization of value in judgment requires that judgments be evaluated in terms of how well they succeed in the realization of the critical values—how true they are. On the other hand, the fact that a judgment is either true or false requires a value with respect to which the relative truth of that judgment is defined and evaluated.

Therefore the final self-evident presupposition that reason is adequate, the presupposition that the to-be-known world is the full realization of our epistemic values, and the presupposition of the existence of reason such that judgments may be either true or false are alternative characterizations of the self-grounding absolute.[24]

The Presentationalist Metaphysic.   Finally, that the rational values partially realized in the idea are fully realized or satisfied in its object entails an identity between the axiological ground of the idea and the axiological ground of the object. This identity is the common ground of valuing to which I referred in stating the presentationalist thesis. This identity of value entails that the object of knowledge is appropriate to the evaluative judgmental activity of the knower.

The thesis that the object of knowledge fully satisfies the values that guide the critical, judgmental activity is equivalent to the thesis that the object of knowledge is for being known. That the object of knowledge is for being known is, I have argued, equivalent to the object's being a presentation. It is equivalent to the object's being constrained by a focus of valuing that I have called protopersonal. In conclusion, the presentationalist thesis is, I think, demonstrably equivalent to the other characterizations of this absolute already considered.

Conclusions. That we value postulating our epistemic presuppositions entails that we presuppose a world that could be truly described only if we postulated our presuppositions including the presupposition in question. What is known at the level of the final presupposition is a ground of unity that transcends the distinctions among the various intelligible domains as well as the distinction between the knower and the known. We discover a protopersonal source with which we have all along been tacitly identified. In conscious apprehension of this source, we find ourselves identified with it. We discover, finally, a protopersonal ground of the whole that, in its relation to us, gives epistemic certainty and, therefore, knowledge.

What is known at this final stage is absolute; that is, what is discovered is the final presupposition. As the final presupposition, it is the ground of all doubting and all controversy. In this, of course, it is beyond controversy or doubt. Any mere representation of the world may be doubted. Hence, it can never be said of such representations that we *know*, or know that we know them to be true. What cannot be doubted is the very context in terms of which we experience doubt. This context is, of course, the perspective in terms of which we evaluate putative representations. But this perspective is none other than that of the ground of the to-be-known, the presenting other. When the knower becomes conscious of the objective nature of this point of view, when the knower postulates his or her own tacit subjective perspective to be simultaneously the ground of objectivity, the knower has knowledge that he or she cannot doubt.

We have seen that we must explicitly postulate presuppositions if we are to attain argumentative coherence. Therefore, in accordance with the requirement for coherence and the self-evident character of the final presupposition, I now postulate the absolute presupposition; that is, I postulate the reality of the self-evident, self-revealing, rational ground of the whole, which is, at the same time, the self-evident, self-revealing, rational ground of my apprehension of the whole. I postulate it to be an absolute, self-revealing, and self-evident truth. It is only in terms of the presupposition in question that such an act of postulation could be conceived to be valid. This final postulate could not have been arrived at by empirical induction. Without it, the whole project of discursive understanding must fail. I postulate what I postulate because of my presupposition of it. As I value its self-revelation, the absolute object and context of thought reveals itself to me and for me.

The absolute now apprehended is not only the metatheory about the whole, or the self-evident ground of knowing the whole, but also the ground of the whole, or the knower–known relationship; for the final presuppositions are about this final knower–known relationship. The absolute is, first, the ground of the presented world (which includes ourselves); second, the ground of our understanding of that world; third, the ground of our understanding of the ground of the presented world; and fourth, the ground of our understanding of the ground of our understanding. It reveals itself to us both from within and without. In recognizing this, we become self-conscious and postulate an indubitable ground of understanding, enter the third epistemic stage, and possess the key to an adequate psychology of learning.

PSYCHOLOGY AND ETHICS

I began this chapter by noting that the first psychological fact is the fact of persons. The experience of personal presence is not only a fact to be explained by psychology but also the fact presupposed in all psychological inquiry. This gives psychology its unique position among the sciences.

This section argues that the personal is intimately bound up with the ethical. It is argued that the presuppositions in terms of which we find persons' activities intelligible inform and are informed by ethical issues. Finally, in showing how the epistemic is associated with the ethical, we discover a link between knowing and acting. In this way we are able to point to the possibility of a unified psychological theory.

The Ethical Ground of Psychological Analysis

It should now be clear that the key to understanding any domain is to comprehend, first, why one wants to experience that domain to begin with. Such primitive motives toward a domain create the significance for us of that domain. Precisely these factors, as I have shown, act as a context and guide, usually unconscious, for our thinking about any area. Characteristically, we become conscious of those first motives toward, and assumptions about the significance of, some object as we approach the termination of our inquiry about it. Nevertheless, just those motives and that significance sustain and guide our coming to know the object.

This claim entails that it would be well to consider our primitive sense of the significance and value for us of psychological phenomena. If I am correct, such a primitive sense will guide our inquiries and will finally be explicitly expressed as the *result* of psychological investigation. Our proposals will be *valid* insofar as they express what is for us the primitive *value* of psychological phenomena.

The context in which the present investigation occurs is one in which persons are real and intrinsically valuable. The fundamental fact of the domain for this investigation has been the *phenomenological fact* that there are *persons*, not just responding bodies, who are present for me and whose value I recognize. Moreover, not only are other persons present for and valued by me, but I myself am also personally present for and valued by myself. The phenomenal domain within which persons (including ourselves) are present and possess intrinsic, and not merely instrumental, value is at some level absolutely universal. No matter what their professionally held metaphysical persuasions, the philosopher, the behaviorist psychologist, the nuclear physicist—all know and participate in this phenomenal domain when they are playing with their children, talking with old friends, communing with someone they love, and, undoubtedly, when seeking the truth.

A part of what these experiences have in common is that they involve identifying with some person. This entails entering into a sympathetic/empathetic relation with the person in question. In sympathy, the other's valuing is not conceived as distinct from the valuing of the knower. Sympathy is a sense of immediate identity with the other: The value shared with the other gives value to the other. The other is, by definition, valued since he or she is defined in terms of those values that also define the knower.

Empathy, on the other hand, is more complex. It consciously combines sympathy with an explicit acknowledgment of the "otherness" of the other. The perception of persons as persons invariably involves just such sympathy/empathy. Persons are not known as persons, as entities with whom we can communicate, in the absence of this kind of sympathy/empathy. To know a person *as a person* requires that the knower be conscious of the one known *via* sympathy/empathy.

Furthermore, I claim that the sympathetic/empathetic perception of persons is sufficient for the recognition of ethical obligations toward those persons. That is, if we see persons in a direct sympathetic/empathetic sense, we know as a direct phenomenal fact that we are under ethical obligation toward them. Accordingly, the fact upon which psychology is based, the phenomenological fact of persons, carries with it direct knowledge of an ethical obligation toward those persons.[25]

It is not that persons, as defined in terms of extensively derived cultural forms, evoke in us a perception of an ethical order. Rather, it is that a *direct* phenomenological perception of a particular person involves a sympathy/empathy with the directly perceived person that is sufficient to ground ethical considerations. The phenomenal realm in which we find persons is also a realm in which we find ourselves ethically related to them. We find that it is a property of our *own* personhood that we have regard for the values and purposes of persons in such a domain.

It is important to see that their status as rational beings determines the most fundamental identity and the difference between ourselves and other persons. As rational beings, persons must be understood as simultaneously identified with one another and autonomous from one another. The intelligibility we find in the experience of sympathy/empathy is grounded in our recognition, however dim, that the object of such intuition is, like us, both free and self-revealing because of its grounding in reason. It is persons' common access to reason that is, in the final analysis, the ground of personal community.

Moreover, since the sympathetic/empathetic recognition of personhood carries with it a self-evident ethical obligation to the persons so recognized, to deny the validity of this perspective (as classical reductionists do) is to deny one's ethical obligation to those persons. In the end, this denial is proscribed by the perspective under consideration. First, the requirement that the psychologist understand his or her own understanding in terms that do not deny the validity of that understanding rests upon the primal recognition by the psychologist of his or her own personhood. It depends on the psychologist's refusal to deny the validity of the perspective in terms of which one is seen by one's self to have value. That perspective finally grounds the value of all action, including the search for truth. As such, rejection of reductionism depends, in large measure, upon the psychologist being willing to maintain a fundamentally ethical attitude toward him- or herself. Second, since the perception of other persons carries with it a self-evident ethical obligation to the perceived persons, and since acknowledgment of such obligation *is* a fundamental ethical obligation, the knower is ethically prohibited from denying the ultimate objectivity and value of the subject's subjectivity while claiming, explicitly or tacitly, something more for him or herself.

The knower-actor who sees and acts in terms of such a primal phenomenal point of view can never compromise with a way of seeing that explicitly denies the objective value of those persons, including the self, whom he or she values. Hence, from this primal and universal point of view, the ad hominem argument reveals a fundamentally ethical constraint that obligates one to subordinate all perspectives to the condition that they not contradict evaluations assigned from the personal or ethical point of view. On the other hand, putative perspectives are to be valued insofar as they are appropriate vehicles for the expression or the achievement of the values that constitute the primal point of view.

The ad hominem argument involves the recognition that we always argue from a personal context within which the reasons and values of ourselves and other persons have significance and meaning. As we noted, this means that we argue in a framework in terms of which we and they are viewed in an ethical way. The ad hominem prohibits us from denying the validity of the personal or ethical point of view while at the same time presupposing it. Thus, the primal phenomenal personal perspective under discussion is self-valuing in that it obligates our ideas about it to affirm its primacy. For this reason, the constraint that the primal perspective imposes on any representation of persons is ethical as well as logical. In this context the ad hominem takes on moral as well as logical force.

We already see, at some level, the value of our own persons and of the others we know as persons. A conception of personhood that correctly elucidates and affirms that primitive but absolute point of view in which we know and value persons will be, from that same point of view, known to be valid—absolutely valid. On the other hand, a conception of the person that denies or ignores the value of persons will, from this primal perspective, be rejected on ethical as well as logical grounds.

Ethics and the Development of Knowledge of Persons

Recall the fundamental epistemological emphases of realism and idealism. Realism insists that the object of knowledge is somehow distinct from the knower. The to-be-known must be confronted as something that is genuinely other in relation to the knower. The presupposition that the to-be-known is fundamentally distinct from the knower entails that knowledge is more than mere projection or self-deception. This is the only adequate ground of the value of knowledge as against error, illusion, or self-deception.

But precisely this sense of the otherness of the to-be-known is, at the same time, the ground of skepticism. The realist thesis, most completely explicated in the second stage of knowing, if taken by itself results in the conclusion that knowing is impossible. Accordingly, although realism is partly true, it is not fully adequate.

Nevertheless, unless the other is first recognized as different and therefore mysterious, it is impossible to see value in knowing the other. Although the second stage tends toward skepticism, it does necessary service by establishing once and for all the problem and value of knowledge, the consequent proscription against self-deception, and the mystery inherent in the to-be-known. Although in its skeptical moment the second stage of consciousness views the object of knowledge as a sort of unknowable "thing in itself," it is only through assenting to the otherness of the to-be-known that consciousness is able to apprehend its object. In the second stage of epistemic development, the knower recognizes a truth that is essential to know if he or she is to approach the problem of knowing properly. The knower must begin by knowing that he or she really does not know. The sense of the otherness and mystery of the other is necessary in the development of understanding.

At the same time, what is achieved parallels the condition for an ethical orientation toward the other. As noted earlier, we ethically approach the object of ethical orientation, a person, by recognizing as a condition for empathy the fundamental otherness of that person. We are required to recognize the essential mystery of the other to know the other as personal. Accordingly, part of the ethical perspective we are attempting to explicate is grounded in achievement of the second stage of knowing.

Although the project of knowing persons requires the recognition of, and respect for, the otherness of the other, its ground and end is in a sense of sympathetic identity between the knower and the known through which the sense of the absolute otherness of the other is transformed into a kind of empathy for the other. As we have seen, recognition of the distinction between the knower and the known is grounded in a tacit axiological identity between the knower and known. Consciousness of this sympathetic identity is attained in the movement into the final epistemic stage. As the sense of identity emerges in the continuing context of a sense of distinction, the knower experiences empathy with the to-be-known. The motive of idealism, to affirm the *possibility* of knowledge, is realized in our claim that the knower achieves a conscious sense of sympathy, or identity, with the other. That is, the knower achieves a conscious sympathetic identification with the to-be-known. At this juncture, it is understood that the autonomous other freely reveals itself to the knower. By granting the otherness of the to-be-known, the knower meets the condition necessary for the self-revelation of the other. Self-revelation of the other is experienced by the knower as an increasingly conscious identity, or axiological sympathy, with the known. Moreover, because it is understood as the other's self-revelation, the otherness of the known is not denied. The movement to self-consciousness by the knower is understood to be complemented by the self-revelation of the other to the knower.

The simultaneous identity and difference between the knower and the known are precisely what are recognized when we engage the personal in a sympathetic/empathetic way. Further, the relation between the self and the other as described here determines a community of persons who are, on one hand, irreducibly distinct from one another (realism) and, on the other, fundamentally identical (idealism).

In summary, if I am correct that the third stage of understanding opens up a personal world, then the culmination of epistemic development reveals a world in which ethical considerations constrain knowing. The knower comes to understand that the perspective in terms of which he or she doubts is, in fact, that of an objective presenting person with whom he or she is identified. At the same time, this perspective, in grounding doubt, is the source of recognition of the distinction between the knower and known. Such understanding is a sufficient condition for a kind of sympathy/empathy with the other and for taking an ethical attitude toward that other.

The experience of human persons results from a three-stage process similar to that previously described. In particular, our knowledge of human persons, to the extent that it ends in a conscious experience of the person or personal presence, is dependent upon the development of consciousness into a third epistemic stage. That is, in the degree to which we become conscious of the perspective in which we find a person's activity to be intelligible, we discover the presupposition of an axiological ground of that activity. We have all along known this axiological ground directly through the tacit sympathy discussed earlier. Insofar as this a priori presupposition has entered consciousness, insofar as we have entered the third epistemic stage with respect to the domain ordered by a given person's activity, we become aware of the self-revealing personhood, or personal presence, of the person in question. We discover a communion with the other that is sufficient to ground recognition in ourselves of ethical obligation toward that other.[26,27]

The point of view from which we recognize the existence of human persons, and from which the psychologist must begin analysis, is to be explained by the psychologist. We have just explained the source of our perception of person-hood, or personal presence, and thus have given the beginnings of an understanding of the realm of persons.

Toward a Unified Psychological Theory

Action in a world of persons will be interpreted in the context of sympathy/empathy with those persons, which is the context in terms of which actions are ethically evaluated. The possibility of right action requires psychological explanation. The explanation of action would be analogous to that involved in the case of judgment. In judgment we have seen that knowing is assumed to be possible because the knower assumes that he or she has access to the principle of the true from the beginning. Likewise, in action, the knower assumes right or ethical action to be possible because he or she assumes access to the principle of the good from the beginning.

Valid action is approached as the actor consciously comes to will the will in terms of which his or her actions have all along been evaluated. The actor comes to see that action is evaluated from the perspective of the other, as well as from his or her own. The actor becomes, through stages that parallel the three epistemic stages, conscious of his or her essential axiological identity with the other. The result is that the actor takes up a consciously held ethical orientation to the other. Thus sympathetic identification, which first tacitly and later explicitly grounds the possibility of true knowing, also grounds the possibility of right action. As self-consciousness develops, both knowing and acting are seen to take place in a community of persons. This context places a priori ethical constraints on both intentionality and judgment.

This chapter does not explore the problem of action in detail. Nevertheless, it is clear that the solution proposed for the epistemic question makes possible a parallel solution for the problem of action. Moreover, intentionality and judgment are brought together and unified since they are grounded in the complementary giving and receiving aspects of an identification that is capable of providing judgment and intentionality with a common ground. In this way, we may expect to approach a unified psychological theory.

PSYCHOLOGY AND THE NATURAL AND HUMAN SCIENCES

We have attempted to discover the place of the personal in the natural order. We have found that instead of viewing the personal as derivative of the natural order, we must see the natural order as somehow depending upon and expressing the personal. This grounding of nature in the protopersonal is introduced as an a priori element in a theoretical account of the whole. It is neither supportable nor refutable by empirical means. Nevertheless, it is required if we are to see the whole as intelligible. The antireductionist position taken here has extensive implications for both the natural sciences and the humanities. My purpose in this section is to point to a few of them.

Two Views of Natural Structure

First, I wish to draw a distinction between two views of structure that correspond to alternative paradigms of science at the most general level of analysis. They are grounded in antagonistic cosmological assumptions. The more or less conscious assumption that value-free structure per se is the sole constraint on the empirical world grounds practically all modern scientific understanding. On the other hand, the assumption that the world structure is the expression of a generative axiological ground would provide the proper framework for science if my unpacking of the knower's presuppositions has been correct.

An important manifestation of the received position is that the personal significance or value associated with an empirical domain is said to be projected onto that domain from without. Value is extrinsic to the structural world. The valuing observer is seen as outside of and separate from the domain of inquiry. Put crudely, values are only subjective. Of course, the corollary is that objectivity is without any value. By way of contrast, from the perspective that takes structure as expressing value, observed events are not fully defined except with respect to their broader personal, axiological context. Thus, the meaning and definition of observable events ultimately depends on the personal and axiological level of analysis. Personal significance and value are understood as being inherent in the structural domain. In opposition to the common view, rather than being merely subjective, values are the ground of the objective world. Objectivity is understood to be *intrinsically* significant and valuable.

If knowledge is possible, what is perceived directly, because of its significance *for* us, is the ground of the whole—the ultimate personal significance or value of the whole in relation to ourselves as knower-actors. That ground is, as we have seen, necessarily protopersonal and self-revealing. Particular structural features of the whole emerge as expressions of its global protopersonal significance. The whole will ultimately be coherent as its assumed ground is explicitly postulated to be its source and to define its goal. What must be finally postulated is not structure per se, but the significance or value for the knower of the whole. *Personal value* will then be explicitly understood to ground and generate the whole.

Note that the foregoing discussion in no way denies the possibility of a mathematical-structural account of the whole from within the perspective of science proposed here. It may yet turn out that the form of the personal significance we wish to consider can be fully characterized in mathematical terms. What *is* being denied is that such an account would represent anything other than persons with all their irreducible valuing.

The Reunion of Value and Objectivity

We find in psychology the key to a unified understanding of the whole. Through psychology, as understood here, we come to see the epistemic project of the natural sciences as revealing an objectivity that is intrinsically valuable. On the other hand, because we are able to avoid the reductionism traditionally associated with natural science, we see the subjective valuing that is the object of humanistic inquiry as having intrinsic objectivity. This chapter has focused on the scientific and epistemic problem. However, it is clear that the results presented here have extensive implications for the humanities. The personal values that have traditionally concerned the humanities can no longer be viewed as arbitrary projections or as wholly subjective and lacking in objective validity because they are finally reducible to biological necessity. This subjectivization of value is, I think, a primary source of the radical relativism and irrationalism that characterizes much humanistic work.

I suggest that the appropriate place to heal the breach between the humanities and the natural sciences is psychology. The separation between value and objectivity, which is the source of the split between the humanities and the natural sciences, is a typical second-stage condition. Its logical consequence is nihilism. In contrast, we require a psychology that insists, against the reductionist-behaviorists in preserving the objectivity of the valuing person and against the radical irrationalists whose views are also entailed by reductionism, on preserving the value of scientific objectivity.

We are faced with a problem that cannot be solved unless we can apprehend some objective value that grounds both the study of value and of objectivity. This objective value is the value of the person. The present perspective, in seeing the final objectivity as personal, solves the characteristically second-stage dilemma by bringing to consciousness the personal ground of both the humanities and the sciences. The sought-for reunion is made possible through establishing a metaphysic that grounds the objectivity of natural science in the objectivity of personal value.

Such an understanding is attained through a transition into a subsequent or third epistemic stage. The theory presented is itself the initial step into that valued end of the process of epistemic development. By explicitly acknowledging the objectivity and value of the protopersonal ground of the world, we place ourselves forever beyond the reach of modern nihilism.

Reflections and Recapitulations

Instead of being unnatural, the development suggested here represents the direction in which we should expect to find a culmination of the scientific motive. Modern scientific inquiry found its first extensive development in the study of the "other"—either physical or biological nature or other human beings. Even in those rare instances in which scientists studied their own minds (as in introspectionism and psychoanalysis), the point of view inspected was not that from which the inspection was being made. Nevertheless, it was inevitable that the motive to understand should turn upon itself. Then the content of scientific theory would include a characterization of the normative epistemic context within which science is carried out. The presuppositions so characterized would then become the a priori basis for the postulates that elucidate the first principles of the intelligible world.

The result of such inquiry shows that personhood is the presupposed ground of scientific analysis. Therefore, self-revealing foci of valuing must be expected to emerge as fundamental objects of a self-reflective scientific inquiry. Personhood can never be reduced to an impersonal level of analysis because, as science becomes self-conscious, persons will emerge as the objective ground of any impersonal domain that science has hitherto investigated.

The order of personhood is not preserved from reductionist distortion by maintaining that the order of persons is not systematically related to other orders of analysis. In the real world, persons do interact with the sorts of structures described by the natural sciences. Rather, the order of personhood is independent of other orders by virtue of being related to them in terms of *priority*. Personhood is independent of other orders of analysis in that those other orders are dependent upon the order of personhood. The order of personhood, on the other hand, is only dependent upon other orders of existence insofar as those orders are themselves expressions of, or dependent upon, personhood.

The conception I am suggesting, instead of reducing personhood to the valueless structures of physics, alters the standard view of the world in another way. It allows us to see even in the structures of physics a dimension of protopersonal significance. There is an inversion of the reductive process: Personhood is conceived as grounding and unifying and as yet remaining distinct from other levels of analysis. Personal significance is not projected onto what is an intrinsically valueless structural world. Instead, what is viewed as intrinsic is personal significance. The structural world finds not only its intelligibility but its being in the fact that it expresses patterns of personal significance or value.

It is important to see that these issues have more than purely detached theoretical interest. Questions about the relations between a person and entities other than him- or herself are no doubt motivated by deeper concerns that center on the significance of particular persons and their relation to the world in what has generally been taken to be a nonscientific, philosophical, or even a theological sense.

By introducing a fundamentally personal cosmology, I am able to ground the validity of what can be called a dramatic understanding of reality. From the point of view of presentationalism, events ultimately possess a meaning that is best understood in terms of categories of dramatic analysis (cf. Proffitt, 1976). Such an analysis would not negate more traditional scientific approaches but would correct and ground traditional analyses by providing a context for them. It makes possible a discussion within scientific psychology of the significance and meaning of persons.

A most important point here is that psychology, properly understood, has *as a science* not only the capacity but the obligation to invade such hitherto forbidden territory. Before psychology, science did not take as its task to explain the scientist. Scientists were, therefore, not explicitly required to be conscious of their own presuppositions and motives. On the other hand, a prime requirement of the completed psychological theory is that it offer a plausible account of its own origins as well as those of science in general. As soon as such a goal is assumed, questions of significance and value—which have traditionally been seen as only implicit in, or extrinsic to, the scientific project—can be seen as a manifestly explicit and intrinsic part of that enterprise. Scientific theories must take on, as explicit content, statements concerning the ultimate meaning and value of human existence and activity.

TOWARD A THEORETICAL PSYCHOLOGY: PSYCHOLOGY AS THEOLOGY

We began with the recognition that the task of theoretical psychology is to state the place of the person in the world. We have seen that this endeavor requires us to consider not only the nature of the person but also the nature of the world and the nature of the relation between the person and the world, a world that contains the persons related to it. This section indicates the outlines of our solution to the psychological problem.

Theism as the A Priori Base for Theoretical Psychology

The solution presented thus far has involved showing how the various intelligible domains that constitute the world are assumed to be subject to self-revealing systematic axiological constraints. It has been argued that the world as a whole, including the knower learning about it, is assumed to be grounded in an absolute systematic axiological constraint that guides the knower's coming to know the whole. But I have defined protopersons as self-revealing foci of valuing, or systematic axiological constraint on structure. Therefore, insofar as theism is the thesis that the whole intelligible world is the expression of a protopersonal world ground, the presuppositional analysis presented here entails that the knower-actor assume a kind of theism as the ground of his or her assumption that the world is intelligible.

But it is one thing to argue that the knower-actor presupposes a theistic ground to the world; it is another to show how that presupposition makes possible the solution of the psychological problem. There are at least three lines of connection between the presuppositions of the psychological subject and the solution to the psychological problem. First, one goal of psychological analysis is to provide a true account of the determinants of judgment. Theistic presuppositions are here argued to be fundamental causes of judgment. Second, we have seen that a theory of the person must, among other things, be a theory of the psychologist proposing it. Insofar as the presuppositions we have adduced are, in fact, universal and necessary, they are made by psychologists as well as everyone else. It is in terms of these assumptions that the psychologist discovers intelligibility in his or her world, including the psychological domain. Therefore, to avoid ad hominem attack and to attain self-conscious understanding, the psychologist must begin by postulating the truth of the universal presuppositions in question. Third, because we want to account for the existence of relatively *competent* or *true* judgment, we must postulate the objectivity of those values that are, by definition, realized in true judgments. The meaning of those values involves the presupposition of a self-revealing ground or presenter of the whole. By tacitly participating in the metaphysical assumptions already explicated, the psychologist has all along been able to conceive the possibility of, and to recognize the development in the psychological subject of, competent judgment, or learning. Theoretical psychology must be grounded in the a priori postulation of the presuppositions without whose validity psychological phenomena, such as learning, would be impossible. If it can be shown, as I believe it has been here, that what is presupposed is an absolute and self-revealing axiological constraint on—or protopersonal ground of—the whole, then theoretical psychology must be based on the a priori postulate of a theistic metaphysic.

It must be emphasized that the postulate in question involves neither the result of a deductive scholastic argument nor a God hypothesis invoked to explain the empirical fact of order or intelligibility in the world. On the contrary, it is postulated as the indubitable first principle of understanding the intelligible world. It can be neither supported nor refuted by either empirical fact or scholastic argument. The self-revealing epistemic ideality of the real is the first axiom of thought, the final and indubitable presupposition whose postulation is necessary for explicit intelligibility. Given the presented definition of protopersons, the fact that the to-be-known is *defined* in terms of self-revealing value entails the postulate of a protopersonal ground of the to-be-known, or theism.

Learning as a Creative Act

It is possible to develop further the account of the growth of consciousness begun earlier. We have seen that attempts to construct an account of epistemic becoming in terms of notions typically utilized by the natural sciences lead to logical and ethical disaster. Any theory that understands personal change by ignoring or "seeing through" the values and motives that constitute that change is doomed from the outset.

Nevertheless, most conceptions of the evolution or development of mind involve attempts to give a reductionist account of the emergence of mind and self-consciousness. At the phylogenetic level of analysis, the prime example is the materialist neo-Darwinian theory of evolution. As it has usually been understood, neo-Darwinian theory shows how life, and ultimately self-conscious mind, could develop out of the matrix of unself-conscious, value-free "natural" causes. That is, the theory sees the relationship of the adaptation that exists between an organism and its environment as resulting from the value-free mechanisms of natural selection. Therefore, the higher mental processes, so essential to the adaptation of humankind, must be seen as depending entirely on the matrix of mechanistic causes assumed by Darwin. Learning itself, necessary for the adaptation of the human organism, is thus said to be finally grounded in the order of natural, mechanistic cause. Consequently, neo-Darwinian theory proposes to explain learning in terms of precisely the framework that has been demonstrated to be inadequate. The traditional version of the theory of materialist evolution *cannot* ground a self-reflective account of mind.

Moreover, not only must we reject the physicalist reductionism of neo-Darwinian biology, we are also forced to discount other attempts to describe the development of mind in terms of value-free laws. Such "laws," whether historical, economic, sociological, biological, or psychological, are seen as imposing a necessity on the knower according to which his or her valuing can be exhaustively explained as resulting from certain value-free causes. Whether phylogenetic or ontogenetic in focus, all such accounts are reductionist. They are incompatible with a self-reflective conception of the persons doing the explaining.

In fact, the learning process is not fully intelligible in terms of the conscious perspective, however teleological in character, of the learning person. This follows directly from considering that an understanding of the learning process requires an account of the values that, *by definition,* remain unclear until the process of learning (or development of full self-consciousness) is completed. Until he or she has attained self-conscious understanding, the pattern of good reasons that direct learning is not fully explicated by the learner. The learning process is only explicitly intelligible from the point of view of *full* explication of the values that guided it. Learning is only intelligible from the perspective the learner seeks to attain. Therefore, to attempt an explanation of learning solely in terms of those reasons of which the learner is discursively aware before he or she has learned would be one kind of reductionism.

Having rejected such "bottom-up" accounts of mind as reductionist and unintelligible, I propose a "top-down" theory that, when fully unpacked, shows the dialectical process that results in learning as a kind of creation—creation of the discursively self-conscious knower by a self-revealing ground of the knower, the known, and the whole. As shown earlier in attaining final self-consciousness, the knower sees the ground of the whole as the self-revealing and self-evident source of his or her consciousness of it.

Further, the self-evident and self-revealing perspective is not only the assumed ground of the intelligible world (which includes the knower–known relationship); it is also the *only* point of view from which that world and its ground are fully intelligible. Through his or her direct access to this self-revealing rational perspective, the knower is able to discover discursive intelligibility in the world. As we have seen, this perspective has all along been the knower's hidden inner guide toward his or her recognition of itself as the objective ground of the intelligible world. The final, self-revealing perspective is both the goal of development and what determines and guides that development.

Thus the final object of knowledge, simultaneously the final ground of the whole, must be viewed by the self-conscious knower as the source or ground of the self-conscious knower as well as the rest of the to-be-known. Therefore, the presenter of that whole (which includes the knower) is, from the perspective of the self-conscious knower, understood to be the self-revealing determiner, or creator, of that whole. The development of self-consciousness is thus intelligible as the self-revealing creative act of that absolute ground.[28]

A Final Comment

In *Beyond Realism and Idealism* (1949), W. M. Urban notes three recurrent presuppositions explicated by perennial philosophy—first, the existence of being, which is independent of its being consciously known by us; second, the capacity of reason to apprehend being; and third, the inseparability of value and being. These presuppositions typify the Western intellectual tradition until approximately the time of Locke. They continued as the driving force in Kant (taking critical philosophy as a whole) and in Objective Idealism. They are, however, antithetical to the modern point of view—a point of view grounded in naturalism and made confident by the success of physical science.

There are indications, however, that the modern point of view is bankrupt. The logic of the very sciences that provided its primary justification has been directed toward the person. What the modern perspective sees when it analyzes the person is a piece of meat—an interesting kind of meat, perhaps, but basically, just meat. The final result of this view must be nihilism—a fundamental loss of intelligibility in epistemology, ethics, and aesthetics, because of a denial of the value of the personal context from which these projects derive significance.

It is not that persons who hold the modern point of view have stopped thinking, behaving ethically, or appreciating beauty. It is that when seen from the modern perspective, these activities have become meaningless. The distinctions between truth and falsehood, kindness and cruelty, and beauty and ugliness—the valuing of truth above error, kindness above cruelty, and beauty above ugliness—cannot be taken to have any objective significance in the world from the modern perspective.

Adherents to the modern perspective engage in epistemic, ethical, or aesthetic activity only by maintaining an artificial compartmentalization. The personal grounds of epistemic, ethical, and aesthetic activities are kept conceptually distinct from a world view within which they cannot be seen as having any objective value. This artificial distinction is the final line of defense against a complete absence of epistemic, ethical, and aesthetic intelligibility—against nihilism.

It is possible to avoid both nihilism and the intellectual self-deception required for this compartmentalization. But there is an associated cost—the modern world view. We must take up again the perennial project of the Western tradition. The members of that tradition have been distinguished by unanimous recognition of their own rational, ethical, and aesthetic natures as integral aspects of the universal mystery. Their response to this mystery has been to attempt to locate and appreciate it, not to deny it.

In this context, the task of psychology is to continue to extend our understanding of human action and thought by seeing how they are grounded in the character of human persons as well as that of the world those persons know, and in which they act. The result of such inquiry will not be a mere technology of learning or behavioral change. It will be an understanding of the development of human consciousness toward an explicit realization of those values that, for example, define truth, goodness, and beauty—toward explicit recognition of the protopersonal source of those values.

It is that source that, as the absolute and final perfection, realizes all our valuing. In the epistemic case, for example, the desire to know is not fully realized in mere knowledge of the world but, rather, in knowing the self-revealing world ground that reveals itself in and through the world—and thus makes the world it presents intelligible. Moreover, that ultimate object of epistemic valuing constitutes, in its own self-revealing nature, the perspective in which our valuing of it is valued and given objective significance. It is, therefore, the hidden inner ground as well as the self-revealing goal of the development of the consciousness of persons.[29]

CHAPTER NOTES

[1]The phenomenological experience of persons no doubt includes a sense of personal *presence*. The sense of personal *presence* is the root of the phenomenological experience of persons.

[2]I am indebted to W. M. Urban's (1977) *The Intelligible World*, C. S. Lewis' (1963) *Miracles: A Preliminary Study*, and B. Blanshard's (1964) *The Nature of Thought* for lucid discussions of the difficulties inherent in naturalism and for demonstrating the use of the ad hominem in refuting it.

[3]It might be claimed that a reductionist learning theory would at least be capable of predicting its own acquisition. Consequently, if prediction of the acquisition of beliefs were a sufficient condition on learning theories, then we might ignore the difficulties introduced by the question of good reasons as essentially irrelevant to scientific analysis.

This move is mistaken because it ignores the meaning of the term *learning*. The difficulty is manifest when the learning theorist is asked to demonstrate that learning has taken place. This is a reasonable request inasmuch as a scientist ought to be able to demonstrate that the event chosen for explanation has actually occurred. For example, the learning theorist must be able to convince us that the psychological subject has actually arrived at a *judgment* and is not arbitrarily guessing. Presumably, such guessing (even when correct) is not judgment.

A belief (or judgment) is, by definition, a proposition that is not merely entertained as a possibility; nor is it simply held provisionally to establish a base for action—as an arbitrary guess might be. A belief is a proposition that is understood to be, to a degree, plausible because it is viewed as warranted in a context of good reasons. Judgments have this characteristic: When they are made, they are viewed as relatively plausible from the viewpoint of the one who makes them. That is, judgment involves hypothesizing the most plausible characterization of some situation, given the limitations and perspective of the judge.

Thus, our learning theorist must convince us that from the viewpoint of his or her subject, the allegedly learned proposition is more valid than other alternatives the subject has tacitly or explicitly considered. But this is just to say that the events the learning theory must predict are defined in relation to a context of good reasons. It is therefore impossible to ignore the phenomena of good reasons in a scientific analysis of learning.

Accordingly, learning involves coming to know (acquire beliefs for which there are good reasons), albeit in a limited and incomplete sense. Learning theories must state those conditions under which the psychological subject can be said to know—that is, to possess *warranted* belief. Further, those conditions must refer to the subject's *own* reasons for belief—that is, to the epistemic context in which they were chosen. To repeat, a *learning* theory must demonstrate that the allegedly learned beliefs are, from the perspective of the learner, warranted. Such warrants are not only defining characteristics of judgments; they are also necessary causes of judgment. Therefore, it is only by showing that learning is grounded in good reasons that we can give an adequate explanation of it.

On the other hand, it is never an argument for the validity of a claim to say that it is the result of nonnormative causes. Indeed, to assert that someone is making a claim solely as a result of such causes is *usually* to deprecate the validity of the claim in question. The good reasons for, and the nonnormative causes of, making a claim are logically distinct matters. Reductivist accounts must therefore remain inherently incomplete in that they can never, by themselves, address the normative issue of the goodness of the reasons that constrain the beliefs of the psychological subject.

If such considerations tempt the reader to yearn for the simpler days of yesteryear, when subjects were not conceived as thinking but as responding according to certain laws of association, remember that one will still have to demonstrate that the laws of association produce valid inference if one wishes to show that those laws result in genuine learning. Only by defining learning to exclude explicitly any question of the appropriateness of what is learned can the issue of the warrant for belief be sidestepped. However, such a definition would eliminate any study of the question of learning as such and is therefore too high a price to pay for resolution of the problem. Such a move would simply deny the significance of what psychologists have studied extensively since the days of Thorndike.

[4]This ad hominem attack is extremely powerful. W. M. Urban (1977) quotes Lowes Dickenson as saying that it is "the only argument possible and, indeed, the only one which anyone much believes [p. 45]."

Urban then makes a series of points so appropriate to our argument that I quote him at length here:

> Rightly used, and with a proper understanding of its nature, this type of argument does, I believe, . . . enable us to establish certain presuppositions of all thinking which are above the differences of the schools. Let us try, therefore, to get to the heart of the argument.
>
> Taken as a characteristic device of formal logic, as a means of establishing abstract logical axioms, the method of self-refutation suffers under a genuine disability which the slightest logical acumen serves to make clear. The skeptic, for instance, is said to refute himself when he asserts with conviction that there is no knowledge. And he certainly does. But this self-refutation is immediately applied by the unwary not to the skeptic, where it rightly belongs, but to the abstract proposition which he enunciates, where it does not belong.
>
> It will be worth our while to examine this a little more closely. Whoever claims that there is no valid knowledge, in this very claim expresses a "case" of knowledge for which he presupposes objective validity. So far he contradicts or refutes himself. X makes the assumption A, that he possesses no valid knowledge. This has as its consequence merely that X himself can have no valid knowledge of this assumption A, for if he had this knowledge, he would possess in it a case of valid knowledge. It is not the assumption A (that X possesses no valid knowledge) that contains a contradiction, but rather a further assumption B (namely, that X possesses a valid knowledge of A). From this contradiction there follows as a consequence, however, not the falsity of A, but merely the falsity of B. To repeat, when one claims to know that he knows nothing, he contradicts himself of course, but one may not, therefore, conclude that he knows anything, but only that this which he claims to know he does not know. And how can it be otherwise, since from the principle of contradiction, viewed as a principle of abstract logic, only "analytical" propositions can be inferred? The proposition that we possess objectively valid knowledge is, however, obviously of a synthetic character.
>
> Now, the importance of this conclusion is immensely more far-reaching than appears at first sight. It by no means follows from this criticism of the principle of self-refutation that it does not do its work, but merely that it does not do a kind of work it was never intended to do. . . . In general, it may be said that it *is one of the determining principles of intelligible philosophical discourse.* It is concerned with those presuppositions which the thinker cannot deny without making himself unintelligible, the values, logical, and alogical, that must be acknowledged if communication from mind to mind is to be possible. The possibility of intelligible communication is the ultimate postulate of all thought, all knowledge. It itself cannot be explained, but is the presupposition of all knowledge and science [pp. 45-46].

The ad hominem can only be used in those cases in which a self-reflectivity of argumentation or understanding is aspired to. The contradiction arises when the conclusion of an argument (e.g., "that a man knows nothing") refers to the epistemic context in terms of which the argument is formed. As Urban shows, the contradiction arises when one claims to know something where that "something" is that one knows nothing. Similarly, reductionist accounts of mind are open to the ad hominem only because they, too—at least tacitly—necessarily aspire to self-reflectivity (cf. Johnstone, 1959).

The condition of self-reflectivity, then, involves the requirement of a kind of *argumentative coherence.* Negatively, *via* the ad hominem, it is required that arguments not contradict the presuppositions of the one making them. Positively, it is required that arguments be grounded in the explicit postulation of the arguer's most fundamental presuppositions. The explicit argumentative coherence attained in the realization of this ideal is what I mean by truth.

[5]The hypothesis of an *emergence* of persons, mind, value, or consciousness from the material realm does not seem to me to be a significant improvement on the traditional

reductionist view. Proponents of the emergence of mind claim that there are properties of systems that cannot be deduced from a knowledge of the parts of those systems (and their interrelationships). This claim is supported by a set of examples drawn from domains as diverse as chemistry and economics. It is then claimed that mind, reason, or consciousness is just such an emergent phenomenon.

It should be clear that this claim is gratuitous. Insofar as a property *is* emergent, knowledge of the system's components and the relations among them can, by hypothesis, in *no* way constrain our expectations concerning the character of that emergent property. Accordingly, by hypothesis, there is no good reason to believe that persons, consciousness, or minds (for example) are emergent properties of brains.

To show that rationality is emergent, one would have to demonstrate that brains should be expected, on the basis of our knowledge of their physical structure, to exhibit rationality as an emergent property. But this is precisely what the thesis of emergence denies the possibility of doing. Therefore, the assertion that rationality is an emergent property of brains must, by its nature, be forever unsupported.

[6]To repeat, if it is not reason per se that finally determines belief, but the nonnormative laws of physics and biology, then we have lost the universally necessary warrant for belief. If we think that our beliefs are determined not by good reasons, but by nonnormative law, we will be inclined to discount their validity, because we understand directly that our beliefs are *only* warranted by good reasons.

Suppose it is suggested that there exists a correlation between reasons and the physical causes of belief such that when a sequence of physical causes results in a particular belief, there usually exist good reasons for that belief. The proponent of this view, while insisting that the causes of a given belief state are entirely (value-free) physical-chemical, would also claim that there would be, because of this correlation, ample good reasons for holding such a belief. The hypothesized correlation between good reasons and the physical cause of belief states would have been established by a process of natural selection. Presumably, only organisms that hold warranted beliefs have any chance for survival.

The difficulty is that this view is, in effect, an empirically based hypothesis intended to support the validity of thought. However, because of this, it is circular. It is an example of those arguments that David Hume has forever discredited. The theory of natural selection presupposes the validity of thought. It is therefore obviously unwarranted to assert that on the basis of natural selection, we may expect thought, even though governed by a nonnormative law, to be valid. Any attempt to ground epistemology in a scientific hypothesis, such as natural selection, begs the question at issue.

The point is that epistemic value has an explanative priority. It cannot be reinterpreted as nonnormative law or viewed as derivative of such nonnormative law. It is value, not nonnormative structure, that has explanative primacy. We may interpret what is usually assumed to be nonnormative structure as being derivative of epistemic value (it is one main purpose of this chapter to do so). We may not, however, do the converse. Epistemic value is itself an undoubted ground of experience. It requires no empirical validation—derivation of it from other levels of analysis is both unnecessary and impossible.

[7]One must be definite from the outset concerning the nature of presuppositions. It is possible to distinguish at least two distinct but related uses of the term *presupposition*.

Consider first the usage of Urban mentioned in Note 4. The skeptic's statement "I know nothing" is associated with an implicit claim—that the individual knows something (that he or she knows nothing). Urban's point is that if we accept the truth of the skeptics' explicit claim, then we must deny their implicit claim. It follows that skeptics do not know that they know nothing. Urban uses the term *presupposition* to designate the implicit claim of the skeptic. Because this type of presupposition deals with implicit claims, I call this category *rhetorical* presuppositions.

We may explicate the relevant rhetorical presupposition as follows: There exists objectively valid reason such that if I claim "*x* is true," then I also claim reason has determined my claim "*x* is true"; moreover, if I claim "*x* is false," then I also claim that reason has determined my claim "*x* is false." That is, the claim "*x* is true" presupposes the existence of objectively valid reason such that if one claims "*x* is true," one claims that reason determines the claim "*x* is true", and if one claims "*x* is false," one claims that reason determines the claim "*x* is false." If I deny the existence of such belief determining reason, then I deny what is implicit in every claim and its denial. Accordingly, I deny what is implicit in my denying the existence of belief determining reason, as well as what is implicit in my affirming the existence of such reason.

In the foregoing, the self-contradiction demonstrates the argumentative incoherence of the denial of the first type of presupposition. As Urban points out, it does not follow directly from this argumentative incoherence that the implicit claims of the skeptic or the reductionist are true. What does follow is that the skeptic, the reductionist, and everyone else are argumentatively responsible for their implicit as well as their explicit claims. When there is inconsistency between them, the one making those claims is being incoherent.

Even though, in a logical sense, the self-refutation of the skeptic and the reductionist does not imply that the skeptic knows something or that the antireductionist thesis is true, it is clear that we can never have argumentative coherence if the implicit claims of the arguer are contradicted by what he or she explicitly claims. Accordingly, if we were able to discover a set of implicit claims (presuppositions) that were necessarily universal (implicit in *all* explicit claims), those implicit claims could be made explicit assertions about reality. Such newly explicit claims could not be denied except on pain of self-refutation. But we would be taking such claims to be true because they explicitly affirm what is implicit in the very act of making them (as well as all other claims). Thus, since the ad hominem argument is used to uncover what is universally implicit in judgment, that argument reveals a set of assumptions that we must take to be true whenever we make judgments concerning a domain whose scope includes ourselves in the act of making those judgments.

In denying that judgments or beliefs (the claims one makes to oneself) are determined by objectively valid reason, reductionists deny their own rhetorical presupposition—a presupposition that must be true if one is either to affirm or deny the truth of reductionism. On the other hand, to assert the existence of belief determining objectively valid reason is to affirm the presupposition of that assertion as well as the presupposition of its denial. It is, moreover, to make a statement about the cause of beliefs—a statement that would be an indubitable ground of a nonreductionist explanation of belief and thus, a basis for psychological theory.

A second kind of presupposition is discussed in more recent literature. It is usually said that a presupposition of a proposition is a proposition that must be true in order for the proposition (of which it is a presupposition) to be either true or false. To use a classical example, the claim "the present King of France is bald" involves the contingent presupposition that there exists presently a King of France. Obviously, in the absence of a present King of France, the claim that ''the present King of France is bald'' is neither true nor false.

Although of the same general type, the presupposition Hume considers is distinct from the King of France variety. The presupposition that the empirical world is a causally integrated system is an example of what I call an *argumentative presupposition* or a *presupposition of judgment*. Such presuppositions are characterized by the fact that within the domains defined by them, they ground the distinctions between valid and invalid arguments.

For example, suppose we discover a watch on a desert island. From this we might conclude that a human being had, at one time, been on the island. We presuppose that the presence of the watch has a cause. The existence of the human being is taken to be that cause. In effect, we argue: ''The presence of the watch was caused, and the probable cause of a watch is a human being, therefore, it is probable that a human being was on the island.'' On the other hand, if we do not conclude that a human being has been on the island, it is not because we doubt that the presence of the watch has a cause. It is because we have not yet been persuaded that it was a human being that caused either the presence of the watch or anything else we have observed. The presence of the watch may have had another cause.

Thus, within the domain assumed to be defined by causality (the empirical world), we discover that arguments possess a particular kind of validity or invalidity. If we deny that the principle of causality is operative in this domain, the arguments we have been considering cease (in this particular sense) to be either valid *or* invalid. The beliefs, or judgments, that those arguments warrant are not merely brought into question; they are rendered neither true nor false, since both truth and falsity have been defined in relation to the presupposition of causality.

[8]The rhetorical presupposition mentioned in Note 7 stems from a proscription against self-deception, the obligation to intellectual honesty. That condition requires that the claims I make to myself (my beliefs, or judgments) be determined by reason. I understand that to claim to myself that a proposition is true while being conscious of the absence of good reasons for it would be to engage in explicit self-deception. The claim implicit in all my judgments is that they have been determined by good reason. This is not to say that those beliefs have, in every case, been reasonable—only that I at one time thought they were and that this fact determined my adopting them.

[9]Denial of an a priori presupposition would subject the denier to ad hominem attack. To deny *any* presupposition on the grounds of having made it would be inadmissible. A priori presuppositions are indubitable from within the domain of discourse that they define. On the other hand, there is no noncircular argument *in favor* of the truth of a priori presuppositions. Such propositions are, therefore not contingent but necessary within the domain of discourse defined by them.

[10]These a priori presuppositions embody sine qua non conditions on the intelligibility of *all* experience. More specialized learning capacities may be developed as a function of experience, or they may be innate. In either case, my claim is that they participate in the fundamental presuppositions discussed here.

An example of the relation of such a priori assumptions to intelligibility is found in the argument David Hume made concerning causality. As Hume argues, within his system causality is a sine qua non of the intelligibility of the empirical world. If he doubts the causal integration of the empirical world, then he must doubt that the empirical world is intelligible. This presupposition has the status of an a priori assumption *about the object of learning*—in this instance, the empirical physical world. This is generally the case in regard to a priori presuppositions: They are presuppositions *about* the systems being experienced—*about* the learning context. The assumed intelligibility of those systems (the assumption that one can learn about them) depends upon the assumed *truth* of a priori assumptions. For this reason, such presuppositions can be made the nonempirical explanative ground of the domains with which they are associated.

[11]The value of learning, or judgment, depends in two ways on the foregoing conditions. First, for judgment to be correct requires the assumption of idealism that the "thing in experience" is developing under the constraint of the same values that are realized by the "thing as it is." If the object of learning were only a "thing in itself" (unconstrained by the a prioris), knowledge would be impossible. Learning in such a context would be viewed as an impossible and valueless enterprise.

Second, to account for the possibility of ignorance and error requires the realistic condition that the "thing in experience" be distinct from the "thing as it is"; that is, we recognize that the "thing in experience" may not fully realize the values in terms of which it is developing. If the object of knowledge were merely the "thing in experience," error would be impossible.

[12]*Person* is used here because I intend to indicate that world structure is assumed to be constrained by rational value. By *persons,* I mean foci of self-revealing, global, axiological constraints on structural domains. The term *person,* however, has an unfortunate ambiguity, elaborated by cultural meaning. For example, in jurisprudence, persons have certain prescribed rights and obligations. The meaning of *person* is extensively developed in every cultural context. What I intend might be more appropriately named *protopersons.* Protopersons do not necessarily possess the elaborations of a particular culture but make such elaboration possible. At the very least, they constrain structure in terms of epistemic values.

[13]This theory of the idea has been proposed in this century by both Josiah Royce (1901) and Brand Blanshard (1964). Although these authors are known to be idealists, I do not think that this theory of the idea here proposed is exclusively idealist. It is, in Urban's sense, beyond realism and idealism.

In presentationalism the object is, *by definition,* for being known. Therefore, the *fully explicit end* of the presentation *is* the presentation as fully and explicitly understood—the presentation as *actually in* the experience of the knower. But getting the object into experience is also the goal of the knowing process. Accordingly, the knower's idea is becoming precisely what the presentation is becoming—an entity that is simultaneously the fully realized idea and the fully realized presentation.

Further, argumentative coherence, already mentioned in connection with the nature of truth, is required for truth because it is only through argumentative coherence that discursive ideas can come to manifest fully the values that have constrained their development and that define the to-be-known. It is through argumentative coherence, therefore, that the idea becomes its object.

[14]The kind of complementary knower-known relationship alluded to here is like what Shaw, Turvey, and Mace (Chap. 10, this volume) call a *specification* relationship. Note, however, that I am claiming that the knower necessarily specifies the epistemic value of the to-be-known *only* at the most global level of analysis. The world is for the knower in order that he or she may know it. It is reason, not a hand, that grasps reality. It is only because I make a distinction between specification in terms of epistemic values and

momentary or transient representation that I am able to characterize the intuition that it is possible to be wrong.

It is not clear how Shaw et al.'s doctrine, "specification but not representation," explicates the intuition that error is possible. Moreover, the meaning of error depends upon a distinction between the object of knowledge (the "thing as it is") and our knowledge of it (the "thing in experience"). I have argued earlier that the knower specifies the epistemic value of the intelligibile world. It is, however, necessary to distinguish between such specifications and representations, since the epistemic values of the world that we know through specification are only imperfectly realized in our present conception of the world. Our present conception of the world is, therefore, not our specification of it. I have chosen the conventional term *representation* to signify our imperfect conceptions of the world. As already noted, however, a conception of the world that fully realizes those values whereby we specify the world would not merely be a representation.

To avoid the obvious problems associated with error, deception, and so on, specificationists assert that specification is carried out over time. That is, it is said that an organism specifies its environment through the process of interacting with it. It might be claimed that objections to the specificational view on the grounds that the organism can be mistaken are spurious, because the organism cannot be mistaken if it has enough time and access to the structures that it specifies. The difficulty with this view is that it entails that specification is impossible in real time. Obviously specification precluding the possibility of error would require more time than any mortal organism possesses. Therefore, specification of the environment, in the sense under consideration, simply never occurs. Clearly, however, something occurs. That something is, I assert, representation.

Note in passing that the Gibson-Shaw account assumes that evolutionary constraints do not permit a permanently deceptive relation between an organism and its environment: Organisms regularly deceived by their environments would not survive. The truth of this assumption is not at all obvious. The assumption is grounded in the view that evolutionary processes favor species in which individual members approach an ideal homeostasis. But this is false: That organisms die, and how they die, is just as important, ecologically, as the fact that they live. Mechanisms for species survival no doubt often include population feedbacks that act to limit the life span of individual members. There is no reason to believe that evolution in every case operates to improve the affordance relations between individual organisms and their ecological contexts. It is not inconceivable that an organism's capacity to be deceived in some contexts could actually *facilitate* the survival of its species. Moreover, it is evident that the survival of certain organisms depends on their capacity to deceive other organisms.

In general, any ecologically valid psychology must take for granted the fact that misperception of the environment does occur and that it may have great biological significance. Homeostasis, as a metaphor for the individual organism's relation to its environment, is not ecologically valid.

Direct realist theories of perception have traditionally had difficulty with the problem of error. The facts of error and deception require us to make a distinction between the "thing as it is" and the "thing in experience." We are thus forced to reject Gibsonian realism if we aspire to a psychology of perception consistent with what we know about the ecological context within which perception normally takes place.

[15]This point receives further qualification in the final section. It appears that there is a sense in which the knower, as one who is becoming, has a derived status in relation to the ultimate object of knowledge. Nevertheless, for the time being, it is important to see that

the intelligibility of the to-be-known rests on the fact that what is to be known is *defined* in relation to the knower's epistemic valuing, and conversely.

[16]I intend that the distinction between the first and second moments of the second stage corresponds to the distinction between the Representative and the Significative epistemic functions described by Ernst Cassirer (1965).

[17]In making the claim that psychology ought to be conceived to be self-reflective, I am giving psychology a unique place among the sciences. Typically, scientific theories are not explicitly required to characterize as a part of their *content* the context of presuppositions in terms of which they are chosen. Psychological theory, on the other hand, is unique, since the act of constructing and accepting the psychological theory is one fact that such a theory must explicate.

[18]The ideal of intelligibility that I assume the knower to seek is self-consciousness. The mind seeks a vision of the whole that is consistent with the tacit ground in terms of which mind seeks that vision. That is, mind seeks a conception of the whole that is grounded in a priori postulation of what it assumed all along in seeking a conception of that whole. This motive for a self-reflective view of the whole determined our use of the *argumentum ad hominem* in the first section.

Further, such an account, which grounds the to-be-known in the a priori, sees the world as necessarily the way it is. Such necessity can only derive from the explicit postulation of a priori assumptions. As we move toward full self-consciousness, as the presuppositions that inform our inquiry become explicit postulates, we achieve a vision that is not only self-reflective but also one in which the whole is subject to a systematic necessity. This is why the final stage of thought, the stage at which truth is acquired, requires a self-reflective coherence.

[19]The dialectical process is beautifully illustrated in the Platonic dialogues, especially in the *Meno*. Recall that as the dialogue begins, Meno uncritically assumes that he knows the character of virtue. Therefore, Socrates' first task is to show Meno that he, Meno, does not know the nature of virtue. Socrates is so successful that Meno concludes not only that he does not know what virtue is but, further, that he could *never* know. His reason is simply that since he does not know what virtue is, he would not be able to recognize the correct answer to the question even if it were given to him. In response to Meno's confession of absolute ignorance, Socrates does a remarkable thing. He tells Meno a story—a myth. The point of the story is, of course, that Meno *already knows* the nature of virtue. He has only forgotten it. He may become conscious of it through a process of recollection.

Plato does not tell us how one may distinguish between correct and incorrect recollection. Apparently he assumes that the truth, when fully or directly seen, possesses a kind of self-evidence. In this, he is doubtless correct.

[20]It is important to see the structure of the argument clearly. First, it is evident that to learn is to develop toward a *true* understanding about some domain. Even the development of superstitious behavior is to be explained by showing how, in a limited context, the learner has good reason for believing what, in a larger context, is certainly false. Second, an explanation of learning will therefore involve showing how it is possible for the learner to come to the truth about the to-be-known domain. Third, to show how the learner could regularly come to truth about his or her world, it is necessary to demonstrate that the learner's thought is competent to know that world. Fourth, if we are concerned to give an account of our own learning as psychologists, as well as the learning of other intelligent persons, it will be apparent that we cannot *demonstrate* the validity, or competence, of

thought to know the world. Such a demonstration, which would be governed by thought, would presuppose the competence of thought. Accordingly, the competence of thought is an ultimate presupposition of thought. The values that guide thought are assumed to be fully realized in the world thought aims at knowing. The immanent and transcendent ends of thought are assumed to be one.

As will be seen, this presupposition is self-evident. Although we cannot go beyond this ultimate presupposition in attempting to explain learning, we must nevertheless construct our understanding of the knower–known relationship around it. Thus, we explain the possibility of learning by grounding that explanation in the explicit postulate of the competence of thought.

[21]Note that the presentationalist metaphysic is no more than an exact reflection of the methodology of the experimental psychology of learning. In a psychological experiment, the to-be-known domain is, quite literally, a presentation, defined for the knower in order that he or she may come to know it. The psychologist *defines* the to-be-known as being intelligible in terms of a set of good reasons. The to-be-known is explicitly constructed to conform to the epistemic values of the learner. Psychologists recognize and explain learning in terms of what they know to be true about the domains they have defined and presented.

We can extrapolate the results of experimental studies of learning to settings in which there is no obvious experimenter-instructor only because we conceive the environment to which the subject responds *as if* it had been presented by us. We assume that we know the epistemic values in terms of which that domain is defined in order to recognize and explain learning about it.

A psychological experiment is, in the final analysis, defined in a communicative context. The interaction between subject and experimenter is certainly a form of communication. Thus, the experimental, or empirically oriented, psychologist is forever denied the possibility of seeing the subject as responding to a nonpersonal context.

[22]Because we recognize the fundamental status of value in psychological phenomena, we are committed to a somewhat unorthodox approach to data. The classical psychological method has been to inspect elementary examples of the phenomenon of interest. It has been thought that what is essential to a class of psychological events will be most readily apparent in its rudimentary examples. More elaborate examples would be expected to confuse and obscure what may be clearly observed in elementary cases. Thus, a psychologist studying musical behavior would typically investigate folk songs and the songs of children, assuming that more sophisticated musical expressions would contain nothing that is not already more evident in very simple examples.

Classical methodology is in error: Since we are dealing with the realization of value, it is precisely in the fullest expressions of a given motive that we see clearly what is only dimly expressed in rudimentary examples. It will be impossible to understand the expressions of a value until that value is sufficiently realized to be explicitly recognized as constraining the expressions in question. Accordingly, we should expect to decipher more about the psychology of music from an examination of the productions of J. S. Bach than from the spontaneous songs of children. Having attained, in this way, some conception of the ideals music is an attempt to realize, we would expect to find children's songs intelligible as less perfect realizations of those ideals.

Examples of learning typically studied by psychologists must be classified as rudimentary in the extreme. Accordingly, we should not expect to discover in them any clear expression of the real nature of learning. On the other hand, if we examine the achievement of Galileo in his discovery, or learning, of the law of inertia for example, we will be amply rewarded.

Similarly, the question of how the learner decides that he or she has learned something is one central issue learning theory must address. Unfortunately, so far as I know, this has never been the explicit subject of experimental inquiry. One reason is that the examples of learning studied by psychologists have not resulted in sufficient self-consciousness for this issue to become significant for either psychologists or their subjects.

Until psychologists understand the methodological principle stated here, we cannot expect that psychology, as an empirical science of cognitive functioning, will develop far. Neither should we expect to see the relevance of the present theory to the empirical literature on learning.

[23]Note that although the demand for coherence is grounded in reason, reason as here understood is not purely formal or abstract. That is, in that the presupposed context is argumentative and rhetorical, it is necessarily concretely personal and communal. The use of the *argumentum ad hominem* necessarily presupposes a community of persons who are responsible to themselves and to one another for the coherence of their arguments. Such a community of reasoning persons (or rational beings) is, in the final analysis, what I take to be the concrete locus of reason. A conception of reason that abstracts from such a community of intelligences may be useful for some purposes, but it is necessarily incomplete. Reason, as a concrete reality, inheres in a community of persons (a community of beings who are, by definition, related to themselves and to one another in terms of reason itself).

In the last analysis we are concerned to define the presuppositions, logical and alogical, that are necessary to actual reasoning. In this way, we return to the concrete and present context of *reasoning together* about the psychological problems at hand. This concrete and present context has been taken for granted in the present study. It is this same context of our reasoning together to which we have made reference when invoking the *argumentum ad hominem*. Therefore, as our analyses become increasingly explicit, the self-consciousness we may expect to achieve will not involve mere metaphysical abstractions but, instead, a progressive transformation of the tacit, yet concrete, life-world within which we think and act into an intelligible and consciously present reality. The absolute ground of knowing is not to be found in abstraction but in the discovery of what has been immediately present all along. We have not engaged in this critical enterprise in order to avoid the concrete. On the contrary, the *goal* of this work is to replace the empty abstractions of modern empirical psychology with an explicit vision of the concretely real.

[24]Understanding the idea to be becoming its object enables us to draw the distinction between the idea and its object necessary to establish the possibility of error. On the other hand, by understanding the idea to be becoming its object, we make truth, or degrees of truth, possible because we see the idea and its object as realizing the same value. Accordingly, by understanding the idea as becoming its object, we explicate the presupposition that grounds all criticism and, in doing so, make for a meaningful distinction among varying degrees of truth and error. This presupposition is, in effect, the context within which we meaningfully say that it is possible that a given judgment may be either true or false. It is, therefore, a presupposition that cannot be denied without making it.

Every project (e.g., epistemic, aesthetic, etc.) begins with an axiologically defined distinction. The values that create this distinction are the source of the project. In the case of the epistemic project, for example, the distinction distinguishes between truth and falsehood (the object and its representation).

We have seen that a set of arguments have been developed (naturalism) that entail epistemic nihilism because, in the final analysis, naturalism denies the values that ground the distinction between truth and falsehood. We have also seen that those who hold the reductionist–naturalist perspective presuppose precisely what they deny.

In this context, I have distinguished between my antinaturalist position and that of the self-refuting naturalists. I have argued that my position is true and that theirs is false. That is, their theory is not merely meaningless; it is false, since it denies the existence of the ground of the true/false distinction, the existence of which is the presupposition of all judgment.

But I have made a distinction between my position and the naturalists' in terms of a point of view. This point of view is defined by the presupposition that a true account of the whole must be grounded in explicit postulation of the presuppositions that have grounded the epistemic project. It is apparent that this presupposition refers to itself as well as other presuppositions and, therefore, requires its own postulation.

[25]The recognition of personhood is the ground of ethical obligations because it is itself the primal ethical response. That psychologists have yet to discover the centrality of ethics to their enterprise is symptomatic of the fact they they have failed to see persons as the subject of their inquiries.

[26]When speaking of the third epistemic stage with respect to knowledge of other human persons, I do not mean the third stage involved in knowing the absolute. First of all, human persons are not fully self-conscious. Second, although they define, to various degrees, intelligible wholes, they do not define *the* whole.

Rather, I mean that the self-revealing personal presences of human persons are discovered through our becoming conscious of the tacit, sympathetic identification that has all along grounded our understanding of such persons' activities. Insofar as we achieve a self-conscious communion with them, persons and their activities become intelligible to us. In this way the movement toward full recognition of persons can be seen as progressing through three stages directly parallel to the stages described earlier.

In fact, it is characteristic of the development of *any* project to move through three stages. In the final stage, the object of value begins to take on autonomy—the kind of autonomy we associate with persons. The sense of separation from the realization of value that is the product of the second stage is replaced by a concrete experience of the self-revelation of the valued end. This is a self-revelation that does not deny the distinction established in the second stage; it presupposes that distinction. To achieve the third stage of consciousness with respect to any project is to become conscious of an objective, self-revealing, reality.

[27]Through insisting that the only real unity is a self-conscious personal community, presentationalism sees the world as a real unity and diversity. We discover, in self-conscious community, a personal diversity that is more than mere appearance because it is, *at the same time*, the personal unity we have been seeking. In emphasizing the truth in both realist and idealist epistemologies, we have conceived knowing to involve a kind of *coincidentia oppositorum*. The radical opposition between the knower and known is explicit in the second stage of the development of consciousness. In the third stage, that radical opposition is in no way denied but is understood to ground and be grounded in a communion of the knower and known.

[28]As already shown, we reject any notion of the determinants of consciousness that asserts that the ultimate reasons for our beliefs about the world are grounded in a set of irrational (e.g., Freudian) instincts. It is impossible to claim consistently to know the truth of such a

view. On the contrary, we must adduce ultimate reasons for belief that, if we postulate them, do not make postulation of them absurd. Such principles must be self-grounding in the sense that they are the grounds for their own discovery and postulation. The good reasons that remain obscure to us until the end of our investigation of a domain, and that guide our inquiry into that domain, must also guide our discovery of themselves.

Thus, we must see the final point of view as contriving to reveal itself to the everyday perspective we erroneously call self-conscious. The final perspective reveals itself from within, as well as from without. The result is both the self-consciousness of the knower and the apprehension of a self-revealing presenter. Again, the best metaphor for this self-revelation involves seeing the developing consciousness as a kind of creation of a self-revealing presenter who is simultaneously the ground of the presented world and the only perspective from which that world is fully intelligible.

[29]The present account corresponds with perhaps the most ancient mode of apprehending reality. What I have presented is reminiscent of the structure of a number of religions and myths. In these we enter a realm in which the problem of identity is understood as more fundamental than the problems of knowledge and action. Moreover, identity is explicitly understood to be the ground of knowing and acting.

In the context of these ancient traditions, the development of such identity through identification parallels (in a remarkable way) the stages of development already described. Thus, in descriptions of the creation of the world, humanity is often characterized as beginning in a stage of innocence. Subsequently, persons are described as entering a second stage in which they are conscious of *not being* the full realization of the values which constitute their natures. Value has created a problem. Persons are aware of a distinction between their valuing and the realization of those values. In terms of the Biblical story, for example, they have eaten of the tree of the knowledge of good and evil. Finally, the account describes a third stage in which there is an identification between persons and an object of ultimate value. Persons consciously participate in the axiological nature of the valued other. Again, in terms of the Biblical example, they are described as eating of the tree of life.

Religions and myths of the foregoing dramatic pattern characterize a *history;* they refer to a moment of consciousness in which unity between humanity and the absolutely valuable other is unrealized, as well as to a moment in which that unity is realized. The religion or myth is understood as presenting a solution to the (second-stage) dilemma faced by persons who understand themselves to be not-absolute, and, therefore, not-wise and not-good. The problem of identity is solved by understanding that separation and disunity to be transcended in a moment in which value is achieved, *not through wisdom or right action, but through explicit identification* (e.g., in terms of the Biblical tradition again, through consciousness of one's self as partaking of the divine nature).

Further, the consciousness of personal value thus provided does not eliminate traditional epistemic, aesthetic, or ethical projects. On the contrary, it grounds them by making them possible. Thus, for example, from the beginning of this chapter, the argument has depended upon the fundamental presupposition of the *value* of the persons who engage in epistemic, aesthetic, or ethical activity. It is, I take it, the goal of religious or mythic consciousness to attain explicit recognition and affirmation (or postulation) of that value at the most fundamental level of analysis.

The terms *religion* and *myth* are not here understood (as they usually are from the modern perspective) to mean what is necessarily falsehood or fable. On the contrary, I view the present theory as providing a context within which religious-mythic consciousness may be seen to be the ultimate means of knowing. The present theory is not, however, either a religion or a myth. It is an initial exploration of the presuppositions of thought that take us back *to* religion and/or myth. It reveals a context within which we might take a particular religion or myth to be *objectively* (if, in some respects, allegorically) *true*—within which we might, at last, discover and articulate the objective value of both ourselves as persons and the Reality that constitutes the perspective in terms of which we are valued and, thus, given objective value. Precisely that final and objective perspective has all along been the hidden inner ground of our recognition of the value of ourselves as persons.

REFERENCES

Blanshard, B. *The nature of thought*. New York: Humanities Press, 1964.

Cassirer, E. *The phenomenology of knowledge*. New Haven, Conn.: Yale University Press, 1965.

Hegel, G. W. F. *The phenomenology of mind*. New York: Harper & Row, 1967.

Hume, D. *Inquiry concerning human understanding*. Indianapolis: Bobbs-Merrill, 1955.

Johnstone, H. W. *Philosophy and argument*. University Park: The Pennsylvania State University Press, 1959.

Kant, I. *Critique of pure reason*. New York: St. Martin's, 1970.

Lewis, C. S. *Miracles: A preliminary study*. New York: Macmillan, 1963.

Proffitt, D. R. *Demonstrations to investigate the meaning of everyday experience*. Ph.D. dissertation, The Pennsylvania State University, 1976.

Royce, J. *The world and the individual*. London: Macmillan, 1901.

Urban, W. M. *Beyond realism and idealism*. London: Allen & Unwin, 1949.

Urban, W. M. *The intelligible world: Metaphysics and value*. Westport: Greenwood, 1977.

7 On Listening: What Does Rhetoric Have to Say to Cognitive Psychology?

Carroll C. Arnold
The Pennsylvania State University

My presence on the program of this conference surprised me. I'm a professional rhetorician, a student and teacher of oral communication. I took up this profession almost 40 years ago, partly by a quirk of personal interest and partly in defiance. As a fledgling student of English literature and history, I discovered that questions about how communicative *choices* correlated with what people came to believe went unanswered and, at worst, were deplored by my mentors. Historic documents were just there, like shards and other artifacts; and Wordsworth's poems, written to express views about the worth of the French Revolution, were aberrations—not really "literature." Only a small, rather esoteric group of academicians who called themselves "teachers of speech" welcomed my questions about how pragmatic communication works on audiences and tried, in then limited ways, to help me answer such questions. So, in defiance of more "traditional studies," I cast my lot with the professionals whose declared concern was with the nature, methods, and possible effects of oral communication. Imagine a South Dakota farm boy's surprise at finding that his pragmatic questions had been asked and, in some instances, given pretty sensible answers by the pre-Socratic Sophists, Aristotle, St. Augustine, Cicero, Francis Bacon, George Campbell—motivated by Humean psychology and philosophy—and other figures of lesser note!

You are not interested in my autobiography. I say as much as I have only to point out that 40 years ago, about the only place where practical influence through practical language—which is my definition of rhetoric—was seriously regarded was among a coterie of teachers and students of public speaking. Lasswell didn't get down to basics in studying content analysis until the Second World War, and George Gallup confined himself largely to market research until

131

that time. Examples could be multiplied, but the heart of the matter is that scientific study of the workings of practical communication in social settings got its real beginning during and immediately after World War II.

Not being a scientist, I make no pretense of evaluating the attainments of studies of practical communication that social psychologists have laid before us in 30 years. Because of my own peculiar background, the thing that intrigues me is that the sometime harlot of academe, Dame Rhetoric, has now risen to the standing of at least an influential courtesan in the academic world. One may now introduce her at conferences on cognition and symbolic processes, among teachers of English, among classicists (who have always sheltered her on some nights, because she could converse in their languages), among at least some philosophers, and even some sociologists and semiologists now admit to acquaintance with her. Yet who is she that she should speak to cognitive psychologists?

To define rhetoric is almost as hard as to define cognitive psychology! In both cases, Humpty Dumpty understood the situation: "Words mean what I say they mean. It's a question of who shall be master, that's all!" The term *rhetoric,* as I use it, refers to the regulative principles and the strategies by which we render communication influential in predetermined ways. That covers an enormous territory, and I don't pretend to command it all. The part about which I can talk with some information is that part of the territory where we find regulative principles and alternative strategies by which to render *oral* communication influential in predetermined ways. Accordingly, I want to diminish the question assigned to me, making it read: "On listening: What does thought about *oral* rhetoric have to say to cognitive psychology?" Indeed, realism and proper modesty require reducing the question still further to: "What do *some* thoughts about oral rhetoric have to say to cognitive psychology?"

Let us begin by dwelling briefly on speaking and listening as a human experience. I propose that speaking–listening experiences have important dimensions frequently overlooked in our still print-oriented age. (I have more fully developed some of the following ideas in Arnold, 1968.) Part of the complexity of the act of speaking seriously was seen in the 1st century A.D. by Quintilian (1958).

> The mind [must] . . . grapple simultaneously with such manifold duties and be equal at one and the same time to the tasks of invention, arrangement, and style, together with what we are uttering at the moment, what we have got to say next and what we have to look to still farther on, not to mention the fact that it is necessary all the time to give close attention to voice, delivery, and gesture. For our mental activities must range far ahead and pursue the ideas which are still in front, and in proportion as the speaker pays out what he has in hand, he must make advances to himself from his reserve funds [p. 10].

For most rhetoricians of the classical era, it seemed sufficient thus to conceptualize rhetors as *makers.* Converted to Christianity and committed to teaching the new faith, St. Augustine made a foray of considerable depth into the psychology of communicative *inter*action; but the spirit of investigation crumbled with the Roman Empire, and we cannot really say that speaking-listening as collaborative experience became again the object of philosophical or scientific thought until the second third of this century. True, British empiricism arising from the thought of Bacon, Locke, and Hume yielded valuable insights into the nature of communication in general, but visual perception and the experience of reading writing held most attention. Since World War II, speech as action and listening as perception and information processing have received considerable, new investigation; however, attempts to conceptualize speaking-listening as holistic, *inter*active experience have been few. It is because some elements of such a conceptualization can be drawn from the lore called "the art of rhetoric" and from work in what may justly be called "philosophy of rhetoric" that a chapter such as this one can claim a place in your deliberations.

The framework within which I want to think in the remainder of this chapter was very well expressed in an essay by Maurice Natanson (1965):

> The philosophy of rhetoric . . . has as its subject matter . . . the critique of . . . presuppositions which characterize the fundamental scope of rhetoric: presuppositions in the relationship of speaker and listener, the persuader and the one persuaded, judger and thing judged. The specific object of inquiry . . . is not the technique of speaking or persuading or judging but the very meaning of these activities [p. 100].

You will agree, I think, that these particular aspects of rhetorical experience are aspects minimally addressed in psychological investigations, and I must confess that it is only in the past 20 years or so that they have had serious attention from students of rhetorical theory. Let us come, then, to some speculations about presuppositions that inhere in the relationships of apparently persuading speakers and listeners—people who perceive that what they hear is probably intended to persuade them.

We do not need laboratory experiments to demonstrate that where there is speaking *and* listening, a certain division of responsibilities is presupposed and tacitly understood. As I read this chapter aloud, we are demonstrating that in such an arrangement as we have here, a talker allowed to talk is assigned a special burden. You, my listeners, may not have articulated it, but in every moment of our speaker-listener relationship, you are allying with me or withdrawing from me, according to whether you perceive me as *earning* the right to occupy your time, your space, your aural-visual sensory experience. Having allowed me to invade your space and time, you demand that I bring to life on *your terms* whatever black marks I have on these pages. You know and I know that I bear special responsibilities because I have come with, because I am standing with and for, my ideas in *your* space and time. I must even counteract your after-lunch lethargy. Or what? Or you will mark me down as a faulty *person* who has violated a never-spoken contractual term of ordinary speaking-listening: He or she who holds forth shall submit both thought and person to the unchallenge-able judgment of the listeners, whose price for attention is that *their* interests shall at all times be served.

How different our relationship is from the relationship of author–reader! Sup-pose that after lunch you had adjourned to this room, received a Xeroxed copy of these pages, and quietly *read* what is here while I remained in my office across the campus. Would you then judge *me* as you do now? As author, I would risk, too, of course; but the risk of ideas would surely be more serious and the risk of my personhood as an object of judgment far less. Your criteria for judging my message would be only partly those you are using at this moment.

My message would stand alone before you. In a sense, *its* integrity would be peculiarly at risk, as Plato (1956) wryly said toward the end of the "oral culture" of Greece. Said Socrates to Phaedrus:

> Once a thing is put in writing, it rolls about all over the place, falling into hands of those who have no concern with it just as easily as under the notice of those who comprehend; it has no notion of whom to address or whom to avoid. And when it is ill-treated or abused as illegitimate, it always needs its father to help it, being quite unable to protect itself [pp. 69–70].

Socrates goes on to extol the greater usefulness and nobility of dialectical ex-change, where people and their ideas can be tested in face-to-face relationships. I am trying to press that point still further, asserting that it is a unique feature of all speaking–listening relationships that the personhoods of speakers are always placed at risk before the untrammeled judgments of the listeners.

If you accept such a notion, it becomes necessary to inject into studies of the psychology of human communication some precautions not usually exercised. (1) It becomes necessary to specify and control for the characteristics of the *responsibilities* and *privileges* implicit in the human relationship called forth by the mode of communication; and (2) it becomes necessary to recognize that the criteria against which a communicator *earns* credibility may differ from one mode of communication to another—as well as from setting to setting and from subject matter to subject matter. On the other hand, what is typical in research in psychology and general study of communication is that generalizations are drawn about "appeals," credibility, attitude change, and the like from studies in which the modes of communication were unlike. I am not suggesting that all such generalizations are unsound. I am suggesting that kinds of responsibilities and privileges and criteria of credibility are *variables* in communicative relation-ships, and they deserve study as variables. From the vantage point of rhetorical theory, the presuppositions of communicative relationships differ inevitably from mode to mode of communication, with the presuppositions of face-to-face speak-ing and listening invoking the highest possible risk of personhood for the speaker.

The phenomenologists' notion of *presence*, in the French sense of *being present to*, also draws attention to uniqueness in speaking–listening relationships. The Belgian writers, Chaim Perelman and L. Olbrechts-Tyteca, make the point happily in their *The New Rhetoric* (1969)

> What we have in mind [as *presence*] is illustrated by this lively Chinese story: A king sees an ox on the way to sacrifice. He is moved to pity for it and orders that a sheep be used in its place. He confesses he did so because he could see the ox, but not the sheep [p. 1116].

A more thoroughgoing phenomenological philosopher (Ihde, 1976) expresses the special *presence* of speech with both more detail and more poetry

> The other speaks to me in the "singing" of the human voice with its consonantal clicklike sounds and its vowel tonalities. It is a singing which is both directional and encompassing, such that I may be (auditorily and attentionally) *immersed* in the other's presence. Yet the other stands *before* me. Speech in the human voice is between the dramatic surroundability of music and the precise directionality of the sounds of things in the environment [p. 77].

The powers of words and their arrangement to give special presence to ideas and nuances of meaning have been a focal point for rhetorical theory for centuries. But borrowing from phenomenologically oriented theorists, I am suggesting that person-originating sound generates a very special kind of stimulative presence to listeners—an affective presence very little attended to in psychological or other communicative research.

Consider a simple fact we all know. Most of the presumably scientific information we have about listening is based upon experimentation with more or less disembodied voices. For obvious, practical reasons, most experiments concerning aural perception and oral persuasion have used audio recordings of tones and voices—occasionally video recordings, which are iconic at best. But have we good grounds for assuming that the *presence* generated by a recorded voice or a recorded voice together with an iconic image of the speaker gives prominence, presence, to ideas and feelings in substantially the same ways and in the same degrees as live speakers sharing space and time with live listeners and combinatively confronting and surrounding those listeners with the presence of personhood? The phenomenologists' contributions to rhetorical studies make me think not.

My argument is, then, that to experience orality in any form is to experience relatedness and presence uniquely, and that within that uniqueness—or beyond it—additional distinctivenesses are generated by the different ways we can experience the source of human speech. A striking thing is that so conceiving the natures of human speech and the alternative experiences we may have in listening to it clears away a major impediment to scientific exploration of listening.

A decade ago Charles M. Kelly (1967) advanced trenchant criticisms of 20 years of research in listening. He charged that it is probably an error to presuppose that to listen is to engage in *a* distinctive, unitary process unless one means that to listen is to engage in complex, variable activities while attending to something heard. Other investigators have responded—begging the question, I think—"that listening capacity is a unitary process of handling data" (Weaver, 1972, esp. pp. 9-12). But this doesn't seem to me to address Kelly's most salient point—that there exists an array of studies showing dramatically that the mental sets with which listeners listen yield different reports about what the listeners listened for and about what they heard. There are plenty of data arguing that we listen selectively and some data arguing that we listen purposively though our purposes may vary.[1] This implies that the process of listening to speech need not always be precisely the same. And even though we may have some basic, unitary "capacity" that, say, enables us to transpose sequential stimuli into meaningful patterns (whatever that may mean), it still will not do to say that such a capacity alone accounts for the differences in the ways sequences of aural data *mean* to us.

One thing seems agreed to: Something *more* than just processing temporally sequential sounds is involved in listening to speech. Firm behaviorists are apt to say, with Furth and Youniss (1967), that: "Mastery of the temporal and combinative aspect in sequences is thus implicit in the perception of language apart from hearing sensitivity or symbolic significance [p. 345]." Phenomenologically oriented psychologists go further. Erwin Straus (1969) asserts:

> Time is not experienced as a sequence of now-points. The actual moment is a phase in my state of becoming. In a sentence, words follow one another. The phonemes recorded on a tape follow one after the other; each one strictly separated from the other, but in listening to a speech we understand the words as parts of a whole deployed in time. The first word opens the sentence pointing forward to those still to come. The grammatical subject will be defined by the predicate that follows, the end referring back to the beginning. Yet, this temporal sequence of words is apprehended as a whole presenting one definite meaning [p. 311].

The sequential stimuli of speech do not come to mean, just additively; somehow they mean contextually and predictively, as they die to sensory reception. That much seems agreed on all sides, but at that point the empirical evidence begins to give out, and incompatible hypotheses about how we find meaning in or make meaning of spoken words occupy the field. In those circumstances why should a rhetorician who is no scientist fear to enter the fray? I can scarcely do harm!

Let us take as given the three strongly confirmed propositions about listening to speech: (1) Mind set will influence the ways I process what I hear or hear-see in listening; (2) I can perceive patterns or something like them in temporally sequential speech sounds; (3) what I will derive from those sequential stimuli as meaning depends on more than ability to accumulate the sequenced sounds. Now let's bring a little rhetorical theory and some bits of philosophical psychology to bear on these presumed facts.

Since the time of Aristotle, at least, rhetorical theory has posited that communicative experience is *inter*active. Listeners to discourse are alleged to perceive the talkers as *acting toward* them. This is the basis of Aristotle's (1954) conclusion that the *ethos* (the character, intelligence, and apparent goodwill) of a persuasive speaker "may almost be called the most effective means of persuasion." It is also the ground for Perelman and Olbrechts-Tyteca's (1969) saying that "the speech, considered as an act of the speaker, deserves special attention [p. 316]." The theory goes that if I perceive a talker, I shall perceive him or her as doing actions toward me; and if I think the talker is making rhetoric, I shall perceive that individual as acting for the purpose of changing me in a predetermined manner.

This seems to me a very easy notion to defend. Surely we have all had the experience of listening to an auto salesperson, a preacher, a political candidate, or some other speaker while being consciously satisfied that the talker was talking because he or she wanted us to *be* different—to become a car buyer, to live differently, to vote in a certain way. That we at least sometimes are aware of speakers and listen to them with this kind of conscious awareness seems to me undeniable. That we may so perceive mistakenly or that we can have other kinds of perceptions of speakers' intentions and actions makes no difference for my present argument. I wish to concentrate here on the first kind of perception of speech as action. Let us look to its nature.

If I assert that a speaker is speaking in hopes of changing my outlook, and if I continue to listen, I do so granting that he or she *could* cause me to change in consequence of my listening. And if I am consciously or subconsciously aware of this possibility of change, I shall sense that my present way of being is being risked as I listen. And there is more.

If I perceive a speaker as acting toward me with both hope and possibility of changing me, I shall be forced to see this action—the speaking—as *instrumental* to his or her hope of altering me. Now a paradox arises. I can no longer treat the talk as a "fair" reflection of how the speaker perceives "reality" in moments when he or she is not trying to change me for personal purposes. I may even, as all of us have in some moments, perceive *all* that is said as strategic. At this extreme, no aspect of the speaker's actions toward me will seem likely to be true to his or her perceptions of the way things "really" are—except as the individual perceives the necessities of purposiveness. To get at the clearest case, let us focus on this extreme, though not inevitable, kind of circumstance.

When I define a speaker as a thoroughly rhetorical speaker—one whose purpose is dominantly one of changing me in some preconceived manner—I shall have to treat what I hear as strategy, but at the same time I shall have to treat what I hear as truly a presentation of what I *could* become *in fact*. Put more crudely, I shall at one and the same time treat my rhetorical speaker's speech as a "selling job" and as a true imaging of my actual possibilities. I shall on one hand deny full seriousness to what I hear and on the other hand grant full seriousness to it. There is a paradox here, and I think it is one we have all experienced. We've all believed we were being "sold" while being fully conscious that we could "buy."

One thing this paradoxical condition of listening to acknowledged rhetoric shows us is that at least this kind of listening cannot be passive. The best rhetoricians since Aristotle have argued that listening can never be passive, but for my present purpose, it is enough if we grant that there can be *some* listening that involves inner activity in pursuit of resolving a problem concerning one's way of being. If we admit just this much, we must doubt that the strands of literature in psychology and philosophy that depict listening as passive experience can explain *all* listening. And we shall have to posit that in some circumstances, at least, listeners become explorers of ways out of a paradox, rather than defensive strugglers against versions of reality that run counter to their own. We shall have to admit that active listening is possible and that problem solving is a possible goal of that activity. Let me put this image of listening to rhetorical speech in the form of a simple example.

Let us suppose I enter a store and ask a salesperson to show me some sports shirts. The clerk replies by pointing to a display section and uttering the words, "This is our most popular line." Recognizing the clerk as a salesperson, I interpret the move and the remark as actions made toward me for the purpose of encouraging me to buy this kind of shirt instead of some other. Let us further suppose that I entered the store with inclinations toward choosing a shirt made of a certain kind of fabric and in a certain color. But now I have heard the clerk's rhetorical remark. It asserts to me that I *could* buy a shirt for its general popularity. I confront this paradox. No matter how strongly I feel that the clerk's actions toward me were self-serving, selling actions, I cannot expunge popularity-of-line as a possible value in shirt buying. No matter how much I devalue popularity-of-line, it must now have *some* place in my scheme of values. There is no way I can buy any shirt at all until I have disposed of the notion of popularity-of-line by placing it somewhere in my hierarchy of values—in the *real* scheme of valuings on the basis of which I next shall act and be. In a very real sense I must *re*define myself as a shirt buyer. The reason is that the clerk's rhetorical actions, though instrumental for the clerk's purposes, have inescapably pointed to a reality I can only cope with by giving it a value in relation to other realities I formerly recognized as possibilities.

This seems to me a fair paradigm of coping with what is acknowledged to be rhetorical as it is heard. If we accept it as being fair in at least some cases, we shall need to abandon as universal explanations of rhetorical relationships those many widely accepted, polar conceptions of how people respond to persuasion. Assent–dissent, acceptance–rejection, consonance–dissonance explanations of speaking-listening relationships will not, alone, explain the kind of listening to rhetoric that I have described. If my paradigm can ever be true, we shall need to admit the possibility that exploration of potentialities, reassessment of prior judgments, and realignments of value structures *can* be among the activities of listening.

In at least some circumstances, we may want to borrow Sartre's (1956) metaphor for listening:

> The world (is) mine because it is haunted by possibles, and the consciousness of each of these is a possible self-consciousness which *I am;* it is these possibles as such which give the world its unity and its meaning as the world [p. 104].

I am not enthusiastic about following Sartre's counsels very far, but his notion that I can in a given moment be conscious of alternative ways of being next helps me to grapple with my condition in the presence of the clothing-store clerk's actions toward me. The clerk's rhetorical actions placed before me a new "haunting possible." I could no longer *be* a shirt buyer until I chose anew from within my now expanded world of possibilities.

But that very choosing process remains perplexing because to accomplish it, I took very seriously actions I had already defined as actions done instrumentally and, in that sense, not done as really serious representations of realities. I assert both reality and unreality of the clerk's actions. But I must respond *in* reality. How can I get that done? It seems to me it is necessary to admit here the existence of some reflexive processes similar to those that George Herbert Mead (1967, esp. Part III, pp. 135-152) denominated "the self" that can be "an object of itself." But Mead envisioned the self primarily as the mechanism by which an individual resolves the paradox of being at once an individual and a social being. Henry W. Johnstone, Jr., among others interested in theory of argument, has helpfully extended that concept of self to incorporate the processes by which problems of ideational or logical conflicts are resolved. I think his kind of extension can help us conceptualize how listeners to acknowledged rhetoric resolve their paradox.

Johnstone envisages a philosopher who has a view about some philosophical problem but comes upon a counterview and some argument for it. The philosopher decides to refute the counterview. But as soon as he does this, he finds he has to take the counterview seriously—treat it as potentially true—in order to deny it. Johnstone (1970) claims:

> The philosopher who sees an opposing view as both logically impossible and logically possible stands both inside his view and outside it. The assessment of the opposing view as logically impossible is one that the philosopher must take from *within* his own view. The assessment of the opposing view as logically possible on the other hand presupposes that the philosopher stands *outside* his own view [pp. 143-144].

Johnstone is not sure he wants to extend this analysis of dealing with reality-unreality paradoxes as far as I do, but I propose that a listener's situation on hearing acknowledged rhetoric is analogous to Johnstone's philosopher's situation. Listeners aren't always coping with *logical* possibilities and impossibilities, of course. It seems nearer the truth to say they are coping with alternatives that are not necessarily dichotomous. If they reflexively inspect their prospects, they may see that they can separate the rhetor's *intentions* from their own, now revised array of possibilities. *Their valuation* of the option or options the rhetor proposed is their *own*. The possibilities for response become products of *their* valuing. Accordingly, they can, without a sense of paradox, choose between *re*affirming what they were before taking in the rhetoric or *realigning* their valuative structures and acting in new ways. In short, if listeners can be present to themselves, they can dissociate a rhetor's actions and intentions toward them from realities implicit in their *own* valuings. Though they cannot escape their rhetors' identifications of "haunting possibles," they can maintain their own consistency as evaluators and choosers.

Speculative as it certainly is, this conceptualization of what it is to listen to speech we perceive as intended to change us allows us to evade some theoretical difficulties concerning the nature of listening in general. It also renders certain equivocal and contradictory findings about persuasion less embarrassing. It accomplishes the first because it invites us to suppose that listening activities may be different in different situations. It accomplishes the second because it asserts that listening can be exploratory and evaluative rather than either passive or defensive.

As I have already hinted, four decades of sporadic, empirical study of listening have ended in an impasse over whether listening is a unitary process or an execution of special activities called into play by special demands of special situations. It should be added that virtually all research on listening in these decades has focused on which phenomena of communication correlate with the *amount* of information listeners *retain* from what they hear.

If one may say that patterns of listening can be variable and that reflexive exploratory and evaluative activities are or can be part of listening activities, there need be no conflict between "unitary-ists" and advocates of the "variable activities" conceptualization of listening. Surely we read cues to mean that speakers are trying to influence us, and doubtless we invoke certain "rules" for evaluating and otherwise processing those kinds of stimuli.[2] Could we not, then, invoke other sets of listening "rules" upon perceiving different cues? The evidence regarding the influences of mental sets upon listening would then be explainable. On this view invocation of varying complexes of activities could be expected. We have only to hypothesize that human beings are capable of categorizing actions-through-speech according to learned classes. Listening could, indeed, appear "unitary" or systematically patterned with respect to a given class of actions-through-speech, but seem a complex of varying activities when looked at across situations.

The root question is whether or not actions of sources toward receivers are in fact "classed" by receivers. Do we "hear rhetoric," "overhear," "hear poetry read," "hear lyrics sung," and so on? I can push the issue no further, but if we can demonstrate that listening is a systematic but differential response to *classes* of aural stimuli, we would really be demonstrating simply that listeners are as adaptive as we know experienced speakers are. Whether listeners *do* categorize in order to determine how to listen is a question quite open to empirical investigation, but we have had almost none of it. That it would make sense to try to pursue this issue is one thing rhetorical theory suggests to cognitive psychology and to all investigators of human communication.

We also have a large body of evidence on persuasion derived from experiments, but this evidence is so confusing that we are given new theories of persuasion every three to five years.[3] Many of the experiments we depend on were conceived under the influence of dissonance theory, approach–avoidance theory, congruency theory, and other conceptualizations presupposing that we respond to persuasion by planting ourselves somewhere along a straight line of thought whose poles are "yes" and "no" in answer to a *proposition*. A further presupposition of a good deal of this experimentation is that listeners or other perceivers of persuasion are decidedly defensive and protective of whatever their initial states of belief are. The trouble with the data derived from experiments of these two types is that the data account for only *some* of the behaviors of the people exposed experimentally to rhetoric.

A good many findings concerning oral persuasion appear coherent rather than contradictory if we suppose that listening is an exploratory, classificatory, reflexive activity. For example, Arthur R. Cohen (1959), discussing data from about a half dozen studies, found that persons of low self-esteem responded to apparent failures to influence other people by becoming unusually responsive to the group's expectations. Convinced that protection of one's own self-structures is a basic inclination of being, Cohen could only conclude from his and other similar studies that different levels of self-esteem appear to induce different patterns of protective reaction to experiences of failure. But his principle of self-protectiveness could not at all explain the fact that subjects with low self-esteem, after failing to influence others, were exceedingly *accepting* of others' attempts to influence them. Cohen could only say: "People of high self-esteem may be less willing or able to permit their self-picture and views of the social world to be vulnerable to influence from others [p. 115]."

But are notions of protection and vulnerability even necessary to explain the behaviors Cohen and others identified? If we suppose that listening to attempts to influence involves reflexive exploration of alternative ways to be, the findings Cohen was discussing are not perplexing. Persons chosen for their measurable levels of high self-esteem would be searchers after ways of becoming to a much smaller degree than persons chosen for their measurably low self-esteem. In the presence of oral rhetoric, we ought to expect that those of high self-esteem would: (1) be especially sensitive to the instrumentalism of would-be influencers, and (2) be likely to devalue alternatives rhetorically offered. Conversely, persons with low self-esteem would be, by definition, searchers for "ways to be," and they would probably be even more so after having failed to exert influence on their peers. For them, it would not be remarkable if the instrumentalism of other people's rhetoric were minimally observed and if the "haunting possibles" of rhetoric heard were perceived as inviting ways to become. Positing differences in sensitiveness to instrumentalism and differences in readiness to incorporate new valuations of proffered and formerly known alternatives makes the behaviors of *both* sets of subjects understandable—even predictable.

Some recent studies support this notion that listening to rhetoric can be reflexively exploratory and evaluative. Buchli and Pearce (1974) reported that they found listeners altering the character of their listening according to whether they found their predictions of arguers' positions confirmed or mistaken. Listeners were placed in situations where some found predictions of disagreement with the arguers confirmed and others found their predictions of agreement confirmed; some found their predictions of disagreement with the arguers disconfirmed, and others found predictions of agreement disconfirmed. The results of the experiment dramatically argued that "poorest listening [measured by ability to identify factual statements heard] is done when predicted agreement with the other is confirmed. As these authors point out, their findings cannot be explained within the framework of dissonance theory or any approach–avoidance formulation. Referring to their own and to other, similar experimental inquiries, Buchli and Pearce (1974) observed:

> The suggestion here is that a little "imbalance" is a good thing. Specifically, either expected disagreement or a surprising discrimination seems to have had an "alerting" function for the subjects . . ., signaling them to attend to the judge's rationale rather than assuming that they already knew what he was going to say. [Of course], where a little imbalance may facilitate good listening, too much imbalance may hinder it [p. 69].

Details of the Buchli and Pearce study, and others, argue that we ought, indeed, to conceive of listening to rhetoric as an active, probing process that is "cued" by some as yet unclear perceptions of the qualities of speakers' action-through-speech.

Another series of studies (Stamm & Pearce, 1971) involving conversing speaker–listeners showed that college students conversing in pairs listened and spoke to *explore* one another's positions when they found their partners espousing ideas different from their own. It was as though the listeners were unwilling to accept difference until they had an opportunity to probe and weigh the others' positions. Whether this was the overt aspect of a more complicated inner process of reflexively reevaluating options for belief and being, one cannot discover from the evidence. But certainly the overt behaviors hint at that kind of inner experience.

What is striking to me in the evidence I have just reviewed is that none of it requires us to suppose that the relationships between even rhetors and listeners are necessarily those of antagonists, of communicators in the presence of passive listeners, of aggressors and self-protectors, or of tempters and tempted. The evidence and arguments drawn from a variety of sources argue that, at least sometimes, the relationships of even rhetors and listeners can be of the sort Merleau-Ponty (1973) described:

> Between myself as speech and the other as speech, or more generally myself as expression and the other as expression, there is no longer the alternation which makes a rivalry of the relation between minds. . . . I am not passive while I am listening; rather, I speak according to . . . what the other is saying [p. 143].

For myself, I would want to alter Merleau-Ponty's last sentence to read: "I am not passive while I am listening; rather I speak according to what the other is saying and also according to the reasons I think he or she is saying it."

There is a notion so fundamental to traditional rhetorical theory that it is seldom expressed in words. It is that practical communication is at one and the same time a process and the development of human relationships. I have tried in this chapter to offer some variously founded arguments on behalf of that notion. I have stressed alternatives to visions of this relationship as adversarial. In doing so, I have tried to inspect the "hard" case—the case of listening to what one believes is deliberate, rhetorical communication. If there is ever a circumstance in which uncoerced listeners might conceptualize speakers as aggressors or—as one of my friends used to express it—as having "alien properties," it is surely when listeners sense that their speaker is a rhetor deliberately trying to change them. I hope I have shown here, in several ways, that even in this circumstance, it is neither theoretically inevitable nor empirically true that the relation of rhetor and listener is always adversarial.

As alternatives to the adversarial conception of rhetorical relationships, I propose that the following postulates are at least worthy of systematic investigation.

1. The normative way we listen to what we think is intended to change us involves designating at least some of the communicator's behaviors as *strategic*—as not representative of the communicator's permanent conceptions of "reality." By so designating, we are, perhaps, forearmed against too ready accession to what we hear.

2. This distinction between strategic and presumably "real" elements in communication injects paradox into the experience of listening. What is designated "instrumental" may contain hints of real possibilities, and vice versa.

3. To resolve the paradoxical in listening to acknowledged rhetoric, we reflexively revalue the "haunting possibles" of our existence now, and either reaf-

firm our former belief-value structures or realign them to create altered ways of being in future moments.

4. We arrive at ways of being by discriminating our perceptions of instrumentalism from our perceptions of values—the actor from our valuations of the implications of his or her actions. As selves, we judge and act upon the "real" merits of expanded possibilities we have made our own by dissociating them from the instrumental intentions that may have brought them into our view.

This is a conceptualization of listening that stems from rhetorical rather than logical tradition. It recognizes that *both* human relationships and substantive notions are embodied in human communication and the experiencing of it. It is a conception that does not deny that automatism, self-protectivism, acceptance-rejection, or even antagonism *can* characterize the experiencing of rhetorical communication. It only asserts that even in the "hard case" of listening to acknowledged rhetoric, collaborative relationships can be experienced. Because it presupposes that discrimination, reflexivity, and evaluation can occur in responding to what is heard, this conception of listening renders some otherwise contradictory behavioral findings compatible. Because it supposes that listeners are no less adaptive than communicators, it allows for the possibility that however unified the *capacity* to listen, the presence of situational and personal cues may evoke alternative patterns of listening activities.

But none of this establishes the validity of the conceptualization I have been proposing. The legitimacy of that view rests ultimately, I think, on the answers to two questions about cognition: (1) Do we or do we not classify speech-generated, interpersonal relations in ways that "cue in" alternative patterns of perception and interpretation? (2) Does communication evoke "haunting possibles" for being, of which perceivers become conscious? If answers to these questions are affirmative, explanations of relations between the qualities of communicative stimuli and the characteristics of situational responses to those stimuli can, I think, be readily refined. If the answers are negative, it appears to me that virtually all Western thought about psychology of communication and theory of communicative influence falls to the ground.

From the days of the pre-Socratics to the present, rhetorical theory has generally presupposed that listening is a *social* experience, that what is taken in *means* relative to the relations of communicator and respondent. One of the advantages of thinking about oral, rhetorical communication and about the activities of listening is that the Other and the perceived meanings of the Other's actions-through-communicating come into sharp focus. The question of how we cognize a communicating or otherwise acting Other is thus given prominence. Since what rhetoricians most want to say to cognitive psychologists is that this aspect of cognition must not be overlooked in the study of human perception, I have focused on it specially in this chapter. Those of us who profess the study of practical communication are dependent upon your willingness to explore social and socializing perceptions as well as perception in the abstract. And may I be so bold as to suggest that giving attention to perception through listening as well as to perception through seeing and touching might not just complicate—it might enrich—the study of cognition?

CHAPTER NOTES

[1]See, for example, Brown, 1959; Kelly, 1962.

[2]After reviewing a considerable body of research on relations between preparation and response, Steven W. Keele (1973) concludes that "alerting signals" decrease reaction time and increase errors in routine tasks; but he adds:

> In everyday situations less controlled than the laboratory setting, warning signals may actually improve information processing. When a signal is likely to occur in a particular place, the warning may cause a person to fixate on that area. Finally, warning signals may encourage a person to interrupt temporarily another task that might interfere with the processing of a more critical signal [pp. 152–153].

For present purposes, what is at issue is whether it is conceivable that listeners find cues to *how* to listen *within* actions-through-speech. This seems possible, since it has been demonstrated that they pick out and respond specially to more obvious cues such as warnings.

[3]My statement is hyperbolic, of course, but Cronkhite (1969, Chap. 3) points out that since 1946, psychological explanations of persuasion have been attempted on the basis of balance theory; Osgood and Tannenbaum's congruity hypothesis; Festinger's theory of cognitive dissonance; Roger Brown's concept of differentiation; cognitive consistency as variously conceptualized by McGuire, Milton Rosenberg, and Fishbein; an assortment of theories about traits and personality patterns; judgmental theory as developed by Sherif and Sherif; and Kelman's "processes of social influence."

REFERENCES

Aristotle. Rhetoric. In [*Rhetoric and poetics*] (W. Rhys Roberts, trans.). New York: Modern Library, 1954.

Arnold, C. C. Oral rhetoric, rhetoric, and literature. *Philosophy and Rhetoric*, 1968, *1*, 191–210.

Brown, C. Studies in listening comprehension. *Speech Monographs*, 1959, *26*, 288–294.

Buchli, V., & Pearce, W. B. Listening behavior and coorientation states. *Journal of Communication*, 1974, *24*, 62–70.

Cohen, A. R. Some implications of self-esteem for social influence. In I. L. Janis (Ed.), *Personality and persuasibility*. New Haven: Yale University Press, 1959.

Cronkhite, G. *Persuasion*. Indianapolis: Bobbs-Merrill, 1969.

Furth, H. G., & Youniss, J. Sequence learning: Perceptual implications for the acquisition of language. In W. Walthen-Dunn (Ed.), *Models for the perception of speech and visual form*. Cambridge: M.I.T. Press, 1967.

Ihde, D. *Listening and voice: A phenomenology of sound*. Athens, Ohio: Ohio University Press, 1976.

Johnstone, H. W., Jr. *The problem of the self*. University Park: Pennyslvania State University Press, 1970.

Keele, S. W. *Attention and human performance*. Pacific Palisades, Calif.: Goodyear, 1973.

Kelly, C. M. *Actual listening behavior of industrial supervisors as related to "listening ability," general mental ability, selected personality factors, and supervising effectiveness*. Unpublished Ph.D. dissertation, Purdue University, 1962.

Kelly, C. M. Listening: Complex of activities—and a unitary skill? *Speech Monographs*, 1967, *34*, 455–466.

Mead, G. H. *Mind, self, and society*. Chicago: University of Chicago Press, 1967.

Merleau-Ponty, M. [*The prose of the world*] (John O'Neill, trans.). Evanston, Ill.: Northwestern University Press, 1973.

Natanson, M.   The limits of rhetoric. In M. Natanson & H. W. Johnstone, Jr. (Eds.), *Philosophy, rhetoric, and argumentation*. University Park: Pennsylvania State University Press, 1965.

Perelman, C. & Olbrechts-Tyteca, L. [*The new rhetoric*] (John Wilkinson & Purcell Weaver, trans.). Notre Dame, Indiana: University of Notre Dame Press, 1969.

Plato, [*Phaedrus*] (W. C. Helmbold & W. G. Rabinowitz, trans.). New York: Liberal Arts Press, 1956.

Quintilian. [*The institutio oratoria of Quintilian*] (H. E. Butler, trans.). Cambridge, Mass.: Harvard University Press, 1958.

Sartre, J. -P. [*Being and nothingness*] (Hazel E. Barnes, trans.). New York: Philosophical Library, 1956.

Stamm, K. E., & Pearce, W. B. Communication behavior and coorientational relations. *Journal of Communication*, 1971, *21*, 208–220.

Straus, E. W. Norm and pathology of I–world relations. *Diseases of the Nervous System*, Monograph Supplement, 1961, *22* (No. 4), 57–68. Also in P. W. Tibbetts (Ed.), *Perception: Selected readings in science and phenomenology*. Chicago: Quadrangle Books, 1969.

Weaver, C. H. *Human listening: Processes and behavior*. Indianapolis: Bobbs-Merrill, 1972.

8 Argument and Intellectual Change: Comments in the Context of Arnold's Chapter

Charles N. Cofer
University of Houston

When I was asked to comment on a paper concerning rhetoric and cognitive psychology, my first reaction was one of puzzlement: What *does* rhetoric have to do with cognitive psychology or, for that matter, with anything except ornamental language, figures of speech, and types of arguments? And are not these topics those on which Samuel Butler commented: "That all a rhetorician's rules /but teach him how to name his tools''?

Consultation of a paper by Weimer (1977), however, soon put another perspective on the assignment. Weimer, concerned (as he often is) with how theories in science are chosen or with the preference for one over another theory, has seemed to conclude that argument and persuasion are central factors in such choices and preferences (see also Shaw & McIntyre, 1974, p. 338). Indeed, he refers to science as a rhetorical transaction and cites a number of writers in the tradition of the "new rhetoric" (cf. Perelman & Olbrechts-Tyteca, 1969) who, in a geneal way, appear to subscribe to something like this thesis. I return to this point later.

As I read his chapter Arnold does not deal with this issue; rather, he is concerned with the auditor in a rhetorical interaction and with whether the reaction of the auditor to the rhetor's argument is a passive one, an antagonistic one, or whether the reaction is self-protective or defensive. Arnold clearly holds that there are many ways of listening, including those just mentioned. He suggests that we may *discriminate* between the rhetor's strategies or instrumental means of persuasion and the presumably real or valid elements in the message; these elements may constitute for us " 'haunting possibles' of existence'' that we may reject or accept. Acceptance of these possibilities alters us because they modify our belief-value structures. We judge "the 'real' merits of expanded possibilities

147

that we have made our own by dissociating them from instrumentalism.'' In stressing listening by an audience, Arnold sides with the new rhetoric in contrast to classical rhetoric, which was designed to train the orator.

In taking this view of the audience—that it can differentiate between what is real and what is instrumental—Arnold differs from the view of many earlier social psychologists, who saw the auditor as the victim of persuasive endeavors, because the auditor seemed to be easily manipulable. This view appears early. For example, in one experiment, a text was attributed in different groups of subjects to Thomas Jefferson or to Nikolai Lenin. Judgments of this text were much influenced by the author to whom it was attributed (Asch, 1952, p. 419). Results such as these were taken as showing that people have no opinions of their own concerning something they have read but are gullible and easily persuasible (but see Asch, 1948, 1952). Later work on persuasion apparently suggested that persuasive techniques are so effective as to lead to the development of a subfield in this domain—immunization against persuasion (McGuire, 1969, p. 258 ff).

This view of the auditor as passive is not shared by Arnold and cannot in principle be accorded validity in cognitive psychology. To cognitive psychologists, as to Arnold, the auditor is active, and any apparently passive compliance to persuasive communications must receive a cognitive interpretation, such as was afforded by Aşch (1952, pp. 419–425) for the results arising from attribution of authorship to Jefferson or Lenin in the example just cited. If we have no knowledge of the text involved and, further, no reason to doubt the attribution of authorship, then that knowledge of authorship provides a context in terms of which to evaluate the passage. We can hardly fault anything attributed to Jefferson, a founding father, author of the Declaration of Independence, and important to the political philosophy of our country. On the other hand, at the time the study was done, Lenin's views—for many of the experimental subjects—were inimical to their own. The differential evaluations of the text, then, are perfectly rational. In the case of conformity to expert or majority opinions, a similar case can be made for the reasonableness of conforming.

A major thrust of Arnold's chapter is concerned with the evaluation of the intentions and motivations of the rhetor by the listener (or reader). The speaker, of course, must ''know the audience''; that is, there must be a conception on the part of the speaker of the ''psychology'' of the audience—perhaps a common-sense or naive psychology. The listener probably reacts to the speaker in terms also of a common psychology people have for explaining the actions of speakers. All this sounds very much like Heider's (1958) naive psychology and attribution theory. Naive psychology can be summarized as having the following features: (1) The ordinary person assumes that there is a real world that that person perceives and with which she or he interacts; (2) the person perceives that events in the world are caused; (3) in order to deal with the world in an orderly manner, the person wishes to know what the causes in the world are; (4) since causation is not directly perceptible, the person *attributes* causes for the events that are experienced; further, (5) the attributed causes probably confer some predictability on what will happen so far as the individual is concerned.

Attribution of causation is not limited, of course, to the nonpersonal world. It applies also to the explanation of why people do what they do, especially in their interactions with us. It should be remembered that the causes attributed for personal or nonpersonal events may be invalid. One could believe that the sun rotates around the earth, producing day and night; or that Chinese communists in Mexico are responsible for the occurrence of crimes in Texas. Neither of these attributed causes is true, but if they are one's attributions, they constitute the environmental field in which one's behavior, to some extent at least, occurs.

The study of naive psychology is, I think, a form of cognitive psychology, because the person in this view functions within an environment to which causation is attributed by the person. Harold Kelley (1973) has suggested that attribution theory is related to a broader field that he calls "psychological epistemology [p. 107]." Unfortunately, to my knowledge, this phrase has not received further explication at Kelley's hands.

Another aspect of attribution theory, developed by Kelley (1971, 1972, 1973), is the way in which a person evaluates information and reaches attributions of causality. Kelley conceives the individual as operating as an intuitive statistician who uses, informally, an analysis of variance paradigm when there are sufficient data to permit it. When the data are not sufficient for this course of action, the person uses causal schemata that are in an incomplete ANOVA form. Kelley's assumption here is not unlike the view that the individual manages to interact with the world by acting more or less as a hypothetical scientist would—developing constructs and testing them, as George Kelly (1955) said, or, to paraphrase Craik's assertion (1943, p. 53), using the brain to model external processes in the world.

The auditor, I wish to suggest, attributes causality to the speaker; that is, the auditor will try to discern the motives or intentions that guide the speaker to say what is said and to wish to influence the auditor in a certain way. Heider has distinguished between attributions that relate to external and to internal causes. Internal causes correspond to intentions. When we listen to a speaker, I think we usually attribute the speaker's actions to internal factors; that is, they are under her or his control. Hence we perceive these actions as intentional. We may also wish to go further to find specific causes or motives that underlie the intentions. On the other hand, if we can infer that the speaker has been *forced* to follow the line of persuasion taken, we are not so likely to make attributions involving intentionality.

As I said earlier, Kelley has suggested that we follow an analysis of variance model in making attributions. What he means is that we construct, implicitly, a table of data (or even a cube if there are more than two variables), with the effects as the dependent variables and the presumed causes of the effects as the independent variables.

Kelley goes on to say that in cases in which the data are inadequate or cannot easily be obtained, we make attributions in terms of causal schemata. Kelley's notion of the schema is not unlike those of Piaget and Bartlett, although he specifies his usage to say that "a causal schema is an assumed pattern of data in a complete analysis of variance framework" (1972, p. 2). That is, the person has learned "how certain types of effects tend to be distributed in a matrix of relevant causes." Further:

> Causal schemata reflect the individual's basic notions of reality and his assumptions about the existence of a stable external world. . . . Derived from the individual's sensory and manipulative experience with the external world, the causal schemata enable him to integrate and make use of information gained from temporally and spatially distinct occasions. Once it is learned, a schema may be activated by any of a number of appropriate sets of data or cues, and it thereby has "mobility" in that it is applicable to a broad range of objects and situations [p. 3].

Kelley gives examples of kinds of causal schemata, and he suggests that it may be possible to construct a taxonomy of causal schemata (p. 18). I do not follow this line of discussion any further here, but I feel some confidence that such a taxonomy and an attributional analysis might have value in ordering our knowledge concerning the evaluations we make of rhetors. These evaluations, I should make clear, seem to me to fall in the category of attributing intentions to the rhetor—intentions that, we think, lead the rhetor to use strategies and instrumentalities in order to persuade us of something. These evaluations do not really pertain to the rhetor's arguments. However, the evaluations may have a significant effect on our willingness to hear the argument or to entertain the haunting possibilities of which Arnold wrote. Attribution theory, as it has developed, does not seem to me to be concerned with cognition in the sense of knowledge, aside from the interpersonal domain.

These comments about naive psychology and attribution theory were intended mainly as a kind of response to Arnold's chapter. He has said some things that psychology must deal with if it is to contribute to understanding of rhetorical transactions. I have suggested that this understanding may come from attribution theory as a kind of cognitive psychology.

I should like to return now to the matter of argument in science—specifically the idea that in science, the fate of a theory or even a paradigm may not be so much a matter of evidence or logic as it is of argument. Of course, the argument can be logical and can be evidentially supported. But logic depends on premises, and evidence can be given numerous interpretations. Hence, Weimer (1977) can assert: "Science instructs us in how to conceive the universe in which we find ourselves, and it does so rhetorically since the adjunctive claims of scientific theory can only be given support by argument [p. 13]."

Since 1957, I would say that there have been two paradigm shifts in psychology and one in linguistics. The phrases "cognitive psychology" and "information processing'' mark the shifts in psychology as ''transformational grammar'' marks the one in linguistics. In psychology the paradigm that was rejected is the S–R paradigm or the empiricist–associationist–reductionist view that held sway for several centuries. It is interesting to speculate about the role of argument in these paradigm shifts. I confine myself, however, to one shift in psychology after first distinguishing between the shifts that have occurred there.

Many writers would not distinguish between cognitive psychology and information processing, and it is true that Neisser's (1967) book laid out the information-processing approach as cognitive psychology. However, the sources of such concepts as capacity limitation, the sensory register, short-term store, long-term store, and control processes (Atkinson & Shiffrin, 1968)—all central to the information-processing approach—do not lie in linguistics. Rather, they lie in laboratory and practical situations—as presented, for example, by Broadbent (1958). Neisser's more recent book (1976) disassociates his own cognitive psychology from information processing, as I understand him.

A cognitive psychology that derives from Chomsky (1957) is concerned with the contrast between underlying and surface structure, as seen in the ability to detect ambiguity, and with the abstractive and generative powers of the mind (see Weimer, 1973). These ideas are reflected in the first Penn State Conference (Weimer & Palermo, 1974), where there was little or no reference to information processing.

Intimations of trouble for some of the presuppositions of the S–R paradigm in the realm of verbal behavior and verbal learning appeared in 1959 (Cofer, 1961). In a conference held that year, Jenkins provided a list of references to linguistic units for the edification of the investigators there. But it was in the next conference (Cofer & Musgrave, 1963) that the S–R approach came under attack. In summarizing that conference, Wickens (1963, pp. 374–380) found that the participants could be classed into two camps: the S–R group and what he called the non-S–R or the anti-S–R group. The latter group, he said, does not get its intellectual stimulation from S–R theory. Rather, its members find their inspiration more broadly, even from other disciplines, such as linguistics and engineering. They also ''are quite receptive to using theoretical formulations which are new to psychology and drawn from other disciplines [p. 375].'' Their concepts are not rooted in physiology and can come from any discipline; Wickens noted the important differences between this group and the S–R group in attitudes toward the computer: ''The S–R group sees in it a way of processing data. . . . In contrast, the Antis view the computer as the father of a new language, a language which may be used to express behavioral terms, and whose grammatical laws may thereby lead to new insights into behavioral relations [p. 376].''

The non-S–R viewpoint presented arguments; these arguments consisted primarily of identification of important problem areas to which the methods and theoretical ideas of S–R psychology seemed irrelevant. Some of the issues involved language. Others concerned problems within verbal learning itself. Among these were the problems of one-trial learning, stimulus selection, mediated associations, purpose, and associative selectivity. The S–R theorists rejected the evidence in favor of one-trial learning on methodological grounds and essentially modified the classical theory in relation to the other problems.

It was actually the Kentucky conference in 1966 (Dixon & Horton, 1968) at which the problems with S–R theory became very obvious, both from within the area of its own interests and from the area of language. In the former case, as Horton and Dixon (1968, p. 673) have observed, Robert Young could point out that no explanation of serial learning developed from S–R theory is adequate. Further, William Battig found current theory inadequate for paired-associate learning (p. 574). These two tasks, of course, were the methodological mainstays of the verbal learning tradition and have turned out to be much more complex than the prevailing theory considered them to be. Young's and Battig's points have the force of arguments, of course, because no one can say with certainty that the conventional theory could not be modified in ways that would make it applicable to these tasks. Maltzman (1968), too, held that S–R theory greatly oversimplified the complexities of classical conditioning.

These criticisms and objections were addressed to tasks whose ecological validity could also be questioned. What, one could ask, can be learned about important problems such as language acquisition and constructive processes in memory from list-learning experiments? Implicit here is the rejection of the idea that complex processes can be understood by looking at simpler processes first, given that list learning is in fact a relatively simple process.

More telling arguments against the paradigm were those provided at Kentucky by the linguists and psycholinguists. Perhaps the most important one was made by Bever, Fodor, and Garrett (1968; see also Chomsky, 1957; Fodor, 1965). This argument is that, in principle, S–R associative theory—even one that includes mediational processes—is inadequate to deal with language. This argument did not convince everyone, but it was decisive for many. Other ways of making this point, perhaps, were more convincing for others, such as the distinctions between surface and deep structure and between competence and performance. It was also argued persuasively that no available theory could account for language acquisition.

I am sure that the various arguments I have just listed were central to the rejection of the old paradigm (and it was not rejected by all), in part because they made the point that important problems were being neglected and that their study would simply not arise under the old paradigm. For those interested in these problems (mainly related to language), these considerations mandated a paradigm shift.

Perhaps the nature of the argumentation was important. The linguists pulled no punches. Some of the flavor of the way in which they advanced their views can be seen in the following account by Jenkins (1968):

> The psychologist's position became more and more painful. Having worked hard to
> build his bridge to linguistics, it was difficult (to say the least) to hear that the

discipline was no longer there and that no one had really ever said that it was there anyway. Accompanying this was the consequent charge that the psychologist had been wasting his time by trying to do what he felt he had just done. The words "trivial" and "uninteresting" (even though used in their logical sense) are scarcely palatable. As one tries to understand what has happened, it is not helpful to be beaten about the ears or to be told that the thing one does not understand is "obvious" [p. 540].

Of course, this tone was present in Chomsky's (1959) review of Skinner's book, but for many students of verbal behavior, the approach of that book had not been convincing anyway.

The kinds of arguments to which I have alluded have appeared in the last 20 years and have effectively forced a paradigm shift. It would seem that the time is ripe to mount a study of the effects of these various kinds of arguments on those to whom they were directed. Which ones were effective and which not? Why were certain people affected by arguments and others not? Was it argument, or was it the neglect of certain problems that led to a change in view? These and a host of other similar questions can still be answered by study of the personae involved during the last 20 years, most of whom are still alive.

REFERENCES

Asch, S. E. The doctrine of suggestion, prestige and imitation in social psychology. *Psychological Review,* 1948, *55,* 250–276.

Asch, S. E. *Social Psychology.* New York: Prentice-Hall, 1952.

Atkinson, R. C., & Shiffrin, R. M. Human memory: A proposed system and its control processes. In K. W. Spence & J. T. Spence (Eds.), *The psychology of learning and motivation* (Vol. 2). New York: Academic Press, 1968.

Bever, T. G., Fodor, J. A., & Garrett, M. A formal limit of associationism. In T. R. Dixon & D. L. Horton (Eds.), *Verbal behavior and general behavior theory.* Englewood Cliffs, N.J.: Prentice-Hall, 1968.

Broadbent, D. E. *Perception and communication.* London: Pergamon, 1958.

Chomsky, N. *Syntactic structures.* The Hague: Mouton, 1957.

Chomsky, N. Review of B. F. Skinner, *Verbal Behavior. Language,* 1959, *35,* 26–58.

Cofer, C. N. (Ed.). *Verbal learning and verbal behavior.* New York: McGraw-Hill, 1961.

Cofer, C. N., & Musgrave, B. S. (Eds.). *Verbal behavior and learning: Problems and processes.* New York: McGraw-Hill, 1963.

Craik, K. J. W. *The nature of explanation.* Cambridge: Cambridge University Press, 1943.

Dixon, T. R., & Horton, D. L. (Eds.). *Verbal behavior and general behavior theory.* Englewood Cliffs, N.J.: Prentice-Hall, 1968.

Fodor, J. A. Could meaning be an r_m? *Journal of Verbal Learning and Verbal Behavior,* 1965, *4,* 73–81.

Heider, F. *The psychology of interpersonal relations.* New York: Wiley, 1958.

Horton, D. L., & Dixon, T. R. Traditions, trends, and innovations. In T. R. Dixon & D. L. Horton (Eds.), *Verbal behavior and general behavior theory.* Englewood Cliffs, N.J.: Prentice-Hall, 1968.

Jenkins, J. J. The challenge to psychological theorists. In T. R. Dixon & D. L. Horton (Eds.), *Verbal behavior and general behavior theory.* Englewood Cliffs, N.J.: Prentice-Hall, 1968.

Kelley, H. H. *Attribution in social interaction.* New York: General Learning Press, 1971.

Kelley, H. H. *Causal schemata and the attribution process.* New York: General Learning Press, 1972.

Kelley, H. H. The processes of causal attribution. *American Psychologist,* 1973, *28,* 107–128.

Kelly, G. *The psychology of personal constructs* (2 vols.). New York: Norton, 1955.

Maltzman, I. Theoretical conceptions of semantic conditioning and generalization. In T. R. Dixon & D. L. Horton (Eds.), *Verbal behavior and general behavior theory.* Englewood Cliffs, N.J.: Prentice-Hall, 1968.

McGuire, W. J. The nature of attitudes and attitude change. In G. Lindzey & E. Aronson (Eds.), *Handbook of social psychology* (2nd ed., Vol. III). Reading, Mass.: Addison-Wesley, 1969.

Neisser, U. *Cognitive psychology.* New York: Appleton-Century-Crofts, 1967.

Neisser, U. *Cognition and reality: Principles and implications of cognitive psychology.* San Francisco: Freeman, 1976.

Perelman, C., & Olbrechts-Tyteca, L. [*The new rhetoric: A treatise on argumentation*] (J. Wilkinson & P. Weaver, trans.). Notre Dame, Indiana: University of Notre Dame Press, 1969.

Shaw, R., & McIntyre, M. Algoristic foundations to cognitive psychology. In W. B. Weimer & D. S. Palermo (Eds.), *Cognition and the symbolic processes.* Hillsdale, N.J.: Lawrence Erlbaum Associates, 1974.

Weimer, W. B. Psycholinguistics and Plato's paradoxes of the *Meno. American Psychologist,* 1973, *28,* 15–33.

Weimer, W. B. Science as a rhetorical transaction: Toward a nonjustificational conception of rhetoric. *Philosophy and Rhetoric,* 1977, *10,* 1–29.

Wickens, D. D. Summary and evaluation. In C. N. Cofer & B. S. Musgrave (Eds.), *Verbal behavior and learning: Problems and processes.* New York: McGraw-Hill, 1963.

9

Arnold–Cofer Discussion

Member of Audience: Dr. Arnold, I'd like you to clarify what you mean by change. Why is it that poetry and music don't change you when you listen to it, or am I not understanding what you have said?

Arnold: I'm afraid you're understanding all too well. Obviously, I've got to have some kind of definition of human change in order to talk about what I'm defining as rhetoric, and I haven't done that well. I simply plead for the proposition that there are dimensions of difference between the change a preacher wants in me or a change that you may want when you argue with me, and the kind of change that a concert violinist seeks to create in me. Consider pragmatics versus aesthetics—it's something like that distinction that is the problem with the way I put the matter. I'm asserting that there are some kinds of changes that are sought, changes in my understanding of reality that will affect me.

Member of Audience: It seems to me that when you talked about the listener (or ways of listening, types of listening), another way of putting that would be to characterize the roles or subpersonalities in the listener and similarly in the speaker.

Arnold: You may be quite right. However, role always makes me uneasy in the sense that by calling it a role, you predefine the very construction that you'd like to come to know. It's as if I have little packages of personality. It scares me when one wants to go at this question either via the route of role adoption or personality types, because that presupposes such packaging.

Member of Audience: When you deal with the listener probing as opposed to having a negative or positive reaction, does this fit in with the rhetoric of the speaker; is this a goal of that speaker; or is this an outcome of what he's doing?

Arnold: The problem with the tradition of rhetoric is that it has focused almost entirely on the speaker's side and tried to describe him or her. So one must now plunge beyond what is traditional in rhetorical theory. Surely when I am talking to you—hoping to make a significant change in your perceptions of reality—if I plan at all, I plan to get you to respond according to patterns that I have preconceptualized. But obviously I may be totally mistaken. You retain your own autonomy. Only in my dreams do you play my game. And so we have to conceptualize the listener as running his or her own show. Another image of listening was proposed by Merleau-Ponty—that there is really a kind of identity of interest between communicator and respondent. He says listening is not passive: I speak as the other speaks. If that occurs, you have achieved the identification, the communion, that Jim Martin was talking about this morning, that Sartre said you could never achieve; and I wonder if you can. I wonder if you can keep your independence and I, mine, and yet achieve quite that "loveliness." And yet surely identification is not a silly notion.

Member of Audience: I feel that you're talking primarily from the point of view of an orator or politician rather than, say, a teacher or actor. I have an uneasiness when a politician is speaking. I actually feel somewhat defensive, because I know he's going to change my view because of his identity. As teacher or actor, I don't feel that way.

Arnold: First of all, we've got a much more complex problem when we're thinking about listening to an actor, because now there are wheels turning within the wheels in our heads. The actor is acting the role of somebody else, and my colleagues in drama always make that quite clear to me. Whoever delivers Mark Antonio's speech over Julius Caesar's body is neither Shakespeare nor Mark Antonio. For the present, I want to put that aside as too complex to treat adequately. Now, as to the orator or politician, I think my own view is (and my belief is so empirically evident that we don't need to experiment about it) that one often seeks out the political persuader by whom one would like to be persuaded. It's the ones you don't like that you're defensive about. You didn't like them when you started, and therefore you're defensive. I'm not arguing that that doesn't happen. I'm just saying that surely we are mistaken to suppose that the whole personal relationship of listening and speaking, even when it's rhetorical, must necessarily be the defensive versus the committed. Much literature in psychology and rhetorical theory (and general folklore) is based on that, so I'm not denying that we are defensive in many circumstances. I'm just saying that if that's all we tell ourselves about when listening to the rhetoric that we are conscious of, we have not told ourselves about our whole experience. Take a very simple case, when I bought a car about a year and a half ago. I wanted those guys to make really good pitches to me. I knew they were salesmen, but the ones that didn't make me any sales talk likewise didn't give me any information. I wasn't totally fighting them as I went from dealer to dealer. But our image is that this is a dissonance situation requiring a balance theory, and that suggests to us that it's an either-or proposition. Now the third kind of rhetor was the teacher. I think every pedagogical activity, if properly carried out, is a rhetorical activity.

That kind of situation, when it's well done, is a good example of the exploratory probing, redefining experience that goes on in the listener.

Member of Audience: I have a related question. What means of causality are you talking about? The general question is, what does the listener have to have contact with when he or she is being persuaded?

Arnold: I'm no scientist (and no psychologist), and I couldn't with any authority answer that. It may be subconscious much of the time, and what I was emphasizing was that even when the recognition is conscious, there can be—in Merleau-Ponty's phrase—a speaking to one's self as the other speaks. That's as far as I want to go. I'm sure much of it is unconscious. One thing I'm driving against is the notion we see that rhetoric is perceived as deceit. I don't think that's so. We couldn't buy any clothes if that were really so. Sometimes, undoubtedly it is deceitful; but many times the rhetoric is there and I don't know it, and I'm influenced no less.

Member of Audience: It seems there is room for a category of what one could call friendliness in your theory.

Arnold: I think it's highly interesting that when Aristotle wrote his *Art of Rhetoric,* he said there are three things that are observed relative to the ethos (that is, the credibility) of the speaker: trustworthiness, intelligence, and goodwill. Hundreds of years later, at Yale in the 1950s, when studies on credibility were done, what did they come out with? Trustworthiness. Then they incorporated some intelligence and what they called dynamism. Intelligence, trustworthiness, and now dynamism. This presence I was talking about has to have some of those qualities if there is going to be a kind of collaborative listening in the presence of rhetoric. I suspect we could turn that around and say that when it's there, the collaborative kind of listening is probably present; and when one comes up against one's own favorite politician, it isn't there and only defensive reactions are.

Member of Audience: Would you say that psychotherapy is a form of rhetoric, and how would you characterize that situation?

Arnold: That's a can of worms I'll only open a little way. I think we've proved to Mike Mahoney that some of his psychotherapy is some of the best debating that ever was carried out. If one were really a true Rogerian and didn't read Carl Rogers' latest works, and really affirmed all the time and did nothing else, I don't think one would find much rhetoric. I don't think that unconditional affirmation would be subject to analysis from the point of view of examining a rhetorical act. Now in other schools, I have no idea. My answer is simply that certainly some schools of psychotherapy are rhetorical.

10 Ecological Psychology: The Consequence of a Commitment to Realism

Robert Shaw
University of Connecticut

M. T. Turvey
University of Connecticut
&
Haskins Laboratories

William Mace
Trinity College

INTRODUCTION: BARRIERS TO REALISM

Science assumes a real world whose existence is not a matter of mental fabrication. Animals, by further assumption, are said to know this reality, at least in part. They know those aspects of the world that bear on their individual existences; and what one (kind of) animal needs to know, another (kind of) animal need not. Though the claim is easy to make—that an animal is perceptually in contact with reality—it is not a claim that can easily be defended. Realism as a philosophical point of view has required constant and sophisticated defense.

Yet it would seem that some form of realism must be captured in any theory that claims to be a theory of perception. To do otherwise would render impossible an explanation of the practical success of perceptually guided activity; and it is this aspect of perception, its role in successful activity, that we take to be the focal problem. For psychologists, a realist stance should seem to be a truism. There should be fairly general endorsement of the view that the causal relations that hold between the physical world and the physiological mechanisms of an organism guarantee that the animal is, indeed, sensitive to its environment. However, belief in a form of perceptual realism and the construction of a theory that actualizes such a belief are two very different things. Historically, it has proven very difficult to design a theory of perception that is intrinsically realist; that is, a theory that identifies the objects of perception with objects that can be said to be present when no perceiving is going on.

Elsewhere (e.g., Mace, 1977; Shaw & Bransford, 1977; Turvey, 1977) we have discussed the issue of direct realism versus indirect realism as a major issue dividing perceptual theorists on the assumption that most are realists and that virtually all perceptual theories are realist theories. We are no longer so certain of this assumption, particularly with respect to the theories. The issue of whether a perceptual realism is direct or indirect may well be a subordinate issue—one that may eventually take care of itself. The overarching problem, as we see it, is whether or not one can devise a perceptual realism at all. The reason we think a realism in perceptual theory is so hard to come by lies not so much in the complexity of the problem as in the assumptions that we bring to it. These assumptions have created formidable barriers.

What are the major conceptual barriers to a successful realism? They appear to be several, all firmly grounded in traditional thinking that treats the animal and its environment as logically distinct (Turvey & Shaw, 1979). There is, to begin with, the assumption that the distal object and the proximal stimulus—say, the environment and the light reflected from it to the eyes—relate equivocally. Stated more strongly, the assumption is that the mapping of distal object properties onto proximal stimulus properties is destructive; the structuring of the light by the laws of reflection does not preserve the structure of the environment. On this assumed failure of the proximal stimulus to specify the distal object, it is a simple matter to generate skepticism about an animal's knowledge of what is real. Given the nonspecificity assumption, perception must be a matter of making propositions (about what the proximal stimulus stands for) with neither a guarantee of their truth nor any apparent way to determine their truth.

A second related barrier to realism is raised by the mind–body subtheme of animal–environment dualism. It is the promotion of two kinds of objects—that which perception is with reference to, the physical distal object; and that which perception is an experience of, a mental object representing the distal object. They are two kinds of objects because, it is argued, to talk about them, one must use two different and irreducible languages. Given the assumption of these two object kinds, skepticism arises about the animal's ability to perceive what is real, because the perception of reality depends on two object kinds—the physical and the mental—being coordinated. It has seemed in the past a relatively trivial matter to show slippage between the object of reference and the object of experience.

Animal–environment dualism thwarts realism in another, though more subtle, way: It invites a science of psychology largely separate from a science of physics and vice versa, a science of the animal as a perceiving/acting agent indifferent to a science of environments and indifferent to a science of the energy patterns created by environments. Realism is hamstrung to the extent that the sciences hold distinct the knower and that which is known.

Consider, however, a program of theory and research committed to realism. It would have to advocate a physics in which the descriptors of the environment and the energy as patterned by the environment would be animal-referential; and a biology in which the descriptors of the animal would be environment-referential. It would have to seek a single language in which the object of reference and the object of experience receive the same description, thereby dissolving the distinction between them. With respect to the first barrier, a program committed to realism would have to promote a contrary assumption—namely, that the proximal stimulus necessarily specifies the distal object. On the assumption of a necessary specificity holding between, say, the light as structured and the properties of the environment inducing that structure, a realist program would pursue alternative descriptions of the structured light in search of such specificity. The search would be unfettered by a priori claims as to *the* proper spatiotemporal grain of analysis.

But closely related to the conceptual barriers already noted are others, made conspicuous by the preceding responses of a program committed to realism. There is, quite noticeably, the issue of describing what is real. If we choose to hypostatize the conventional variables of physics, then it is a simple step to argue that how things appear to an animal and what those things really are, are sometimes—perhaps often—largely distinct. Either the animal's experience is not of reality, or reality for the animal has been incorrectly defined. A program committed to realism would claim the latter. Paraphrasing a point of the preceding paragraph, the program would have to seek a definition of reality that would be animal-relative, but no less real for being so.

There is also, and again quite noticeably, a realization that if the proximal stimulus specifies the distal object, then perception need not be a proposition-making activity. That perception might be nonpropositional would also follow from a conflating of the objects of reference and of experience. But the notion of perception as nonpropositional is more than simply a suggestion on which other parts of a realist program converge. It is, we believe, a necessary response to a major barrier to realism—precisely, the assumption (belief?) that perception can err. Perception as a proposition-making activity can be either true or false and is therefore suspect as a source of knowledge about what is real. But if perception is nonpropositional, then it can be neither true nor false, neither right nor wrong. When conceived as nonpropositional, perception is a state of affairs, a fact of existence—and, therefore, incorrigible.

By and large, these introductory remarks summarize the thrust of the present chapter. The chapter is a *first* pass at dismantling two conceptual barriers to realism already identified—namely, the assumed distinction between the object of reference and the object of experience, and the assumption of perception as propositional and error-prone. In the sections that follow, the conceptual barriers are fleshed out, and in measured steps we try to delineate the conceptual tools needed for dismantling them. Simultaneously we attempt to develop a case for the realist alternatives.

An overriding theme of the chapter is that a commitment to realism and an ecological approach to psychology go hand in hand, and it is to the character of this ecological point of view that our attention is first directed.

ECOLOGICAL PSYCHOLOGY

The ecological approach to psychology is a functional approach. It construes psychological problems as instances of biological adaptation. The ecological treatment of perception defines perception as awareness of the environment and thereby focuses attention on an animal's veridical experience. (Where veridical means that an animal's experience of the environment is sufficient to allow the animal to live and reproduce, one might say that the experience is ecologically correct. It is not "correct" in any absolute, philosophical sense.) Because the animal's environment constitutes part of this definition of perception, it is not possible to study varieties of meaningful experience as instances of perception unless the environmental component is included as an intrinsic part of the object of study. Awareness of the environment is not composed of two things that can be isolated and separately scrutinized—first, awareness and, second, the environment. For the ecological psychologist, to study perception without the environmental component would be like studying one hand clapping. A full account of clapping must necessarily include a sufficient study of that one hand, but increasingly detailed analysis of the hand does not continually increase knowledge of clapping. Nor will it help to divide the labor among those who study right hands and those who study left hands. Under this scheme of things, the phenomenon of clapping will be conspicuously absent.

Treating perception functionally makes it what philosophers have called an achievement word, not a process word or a word referring to the qualities of experience *qua* experience. Visual experience as a result of a blow on the head is not visual perception. Dreams and hallucinations are not perception. Awareness (including tacit awareness) of a real environment—the one in terms of which effective action must take place—is perception. The functional definition of perception reflects the opinion that experiences such as those found in dreams, hallucinations, and imagination are derivative and not likely to be fully explained until perception of the environment is understood.

Contrasting views of perception in psychology treat it in terms of characteristics that do not necessarily involve achievements. Observe that the common references to *perceived* size, *perceived* distance, *perceived* duration, and so forth not only fail to denote a sense of veridical experience but actually connote a lack of correspondence with reality. Instead of treating perception as something like hand clapping, the traditional approach treats it like hand anatomy—at least in the sense that the problem allows a division of labor among those who study characteristics of hands and those who study the uses to which hands may be put. Thus they may agree that the study of environments is an important topic for perceptual psychologists to acknowledge but also believe that the labor can be divided between those who study the experience or process of perception and those who study topics about the objects of perception. As we said earlier, the ecological approach does not define its problem in a way that would allow such a division of labor to preserve the essential object of study.

In short, the ecological focus is different from the conventional, and in consequence the ecologically oriented scientist soon discovers that there are many conceptual issues to work out that are not usually discussed in modern psychology. It is not that the issues do not inhere in all psychology but that there has been tacit agreement to keep the issues out of harm's way. Preeminent among these is the issue on which we focused our introductory comments—that of realism. What does it mean to say that an animal perceives its environment? The answer must be that it perceives some of what is actually there in the world. But *what?* Atoms, molecules, quarks? Tables, chairs, oranges, waterfalls? Time, space, motion? Cubes, lines, pyramids? Each of these answers leads to conceptual difficulties that make it impossible to reconcile a theory of the causal processes (physical, physiological) involved in perceiving with the behavioral level of adaptive activity.

For most psychologists the problems that assume preeminence in the ecological perspective belong to philosophy and should not properly cut into the psychologist's work schedule. But it is a simple enough matter to show that the problems *are* inherent in the phenomena psychologists seek to understand. The fact that they have been addressed most often in philosophy rather than psychology, and the fact that they are often problems of clarifying concepts rather than making empirical discoveries, should not mislead one into thinking that as problems, they do not belong to the science of psychology.

BACKGROUND

The framework for our discussion of realism and ecological psychology builds on traditional approaches to the question: "How is knowledge possible?" We sharpen the question by giving it the form: "How is knowledge of the world (environment) possible?" Traditional answers, with successors in modern psychology, have been selected from a general set of characteristics of animals or humans that can be called mental processes. Thus the available pool of candidates includes sensation, perception, memory, reason, association, and various subdivisions of these processes. Theorists who stress the primacy of sensation or perception in knowledge gathering can be crudely lumped together as empiricists. Theorists who stress reasoning processes such as inference or prior knowledge contained in a type of memory can be collectively designated as rationalists. In pursuing realism, we argue for the primacy of perception, thus casting our lot with empiricism. It becomes apparent, however, that an empiricism committed to realism will differ radically from familiar varieties of empiricism, sufficiently so to consider the ecological approach its own new category. Indeed, it is argued that the familiar forms of both rationalism and empiricism share a commitment to two features of dualism that a committed realist must oppose. These features are simple to describe and familiar to all psychologists despite the less familiar descriptive labels we have selected. We touched upon them in the introduction, and in the following discussion we refer to them as the doctrine of intractable nonspecificity and the incommensurability of natural kinds. These are two different ways to designate gaps between the knower and that which is known that must be bridged (or barriers that must be overcome) to have a complete scientific theory of knowing. In this background section, these gaps are discussed together with the recalcitrant problems facing not only the rationalist and conventional empiricist approaches to bridging the gaps but also the representational approach, which shares characteristics with both rationalism and empiricism and is currently a dominant feature of theories in cognitive science.

Intractable Nonspecificity

There is a belief of some antiquity that holds that the inputs to an animal's nervous system are an inadequate basis for knowing the world. This inveterate belief is fundamentally an assertion that energy media cannot convey meaningful information for animals about the world in the sense that the media, as patterned, are not specific to properties of the world taken with reference to animals. We have referred to this belief as the doctrine of intractable nonspecificity (Turvey & Shaw, 1979).

Traditionally, the doctrine is complemented by the claim that an animal has at its disposal the means for processing energy media to make them meaningful. What an animal is said to have, in short, is knowledge about the world; and debate has focused on whether the knowledge comes from stored memories, innate schemata, or reason. The debate has been intensive and oftentimes eloquent, but it has always begged the question that characterizes the traditional explanations of an animal's knowledge: All traditional accounts of how an animal knows what it knows presuppose the very knowledge of the world they seek to explain. What remains fiercely at issue for empiricism and rationalism as alternative perspectives is precisely the origin of the knowledge that the animal is said to have.

We may, if somewhat crudely, compare empiricism and rationalism with respect to three questions: (1) What is the proper vocabulary in which to describe the structured energy in which the animal is immersed? (2) What is the proper vocabulary in which to describe the mental entities corresponding to the structured energy descriptors? (3) What is the relation between these mental entities and knowledge?

With respect to the first question, empiricism has tended to adopt the stance of nominalism and has assumed that the vocabulary cannot be of abstract relations and the like, but only of simple, concrete particulars. Thus the structured energy might be described—say, in the case of light—as rays of given intensity and wavelength. The answer to the second question follows: The corresponding mental entities are at the same elemental grain-size as the energy descriptors and, similarly, must be simple, concrete particulars. In earlier forms of empiricism, these latter, simple particulars were sensations; in more contemporary perspective, they can be fine-grained features without violating the explicit mental nominalism of classical empiricism. The gist of empiricism's answer to the third question is that the complex, abstract particulars that comprise the animal's knowledge of the world must be induced from the simple, concrete particulars provided by sensory experience. Association has been the commonly promoted mechanism of induction.

Our portrayal of rationalism's response to the three preceding questions can be brief. With respect to Question 1, rationalists would probably be unanimous in their agreement with the answer from empiricism; and with respect to Question 2, empiricism's answer might not be palatable to all rationalists, but it would be tolerable for most. It is with reference to Question 3 that the two points of view diverge. In contrast to empiricism's claim that abstracta are induced from concreta, rationalism argues that concreta are interpreted—given meaning—by abstracta; for rationalism, knowledge of the abstract must be anterior to experience with the concrete.

There are two points to be emphasized. One is that with respect to nominalism, empiricism and rationalism part company only on the last of the three questions raised. The other point is that empiricism promoted "sensing" as the source of knowledge and thereby sought to ground the origin of knowledge in experience, whereas rationalism traditionally denied the primacy of sensory contact in favor of reason. The sensory mechanisms, rationalists often argue, are just sources of phenomena; it is by the instrument of reason, working on the phenomena of the senses, that reality is made known.

But it would seem that to impugn the primacy of sensory contact with the environment is self-defeating, for it leaves no means by which knowledge could originate. If an animal's awareness of what is real (real, that is, for its purposes) is wrought through a process of reasoning from the inadequate data made available by the senses, then we should suppose that the constraints on this reasoning are neither indifferent to the features of the environment, as they relate to the animal's behavior, nor to the laws that relate these features to the patternings of energy that they create.

Now by evolutionary theory, at any point in the evolution of a given animal's species, there must have been an ancestor that knew reality in order that an adaptive relation between this animal and its environment held (to support the successful production of offspring). That is to say, for any point in evolution that we choose, there must have been an ancestor whose reasoning abilities were tightly constrained by the significant features of its environment and the manner in which those features modulated energy media. What will always remain unexplained is how the constraints arise. Indeed, if the argument sketched here is run to conclusion, we would have to suppose that the requisite environment-specific tailoring of reasoning is extraevolutionary in origin. And that ought to be an unsatisfactory conclusion.

It is of some importance to the point being made that the distinction between nativism and evolutionism be made clear. Nativism has been a classical response to the doctrine of intractable nonspecificity: Concepts available at birth and matured in development define the medium in which inadequate sensory data become meaningful percepts. But nativism did *not* identify, either by design *or by intent,* the mechanism for the origin of said concepts. Whereas nativism regards knowledge as a priori, evolutionism views knowledge as a product of the history of the species, a response to the pressures of natural selection. We see, in short, that nativism and evolutionism distinguish on just this point: Evolutionism is a programmatic orientation to the question of *how knowledge originates,* a question left unasked by nativism. But the point of the immediately preceding paragraphs is that an argument from evolutionism with respect to the origin of knowledge converges on a priorism (and thus nativism) when one of the premises of the argument takes the form of a denial of the primacy of perception—that is, a denial of perceiving as *the* source of knowing.

We should ask, therefore, where empiricism failed in its attempt to found knowledge in experience. The reasons seem to be primarily two, and they are closely related. The first is the doctrine of intractable nonspecificity; given this as the received doctrine, it was necessarily the case that some process other than sensory contact with the environment was needed. Sensory contact per se could realize only equivocal and inadequate dividends. The second is the distinction between sensation and perception, with sensation relating to simple dimensions of physical energy, and perception relating to environmental and animal events; and with perception said to be predicated on sensation. Empiricism in its classical form failed because in order for perceiving to be *the* means by which an animal comes to know what it knows and justifies what it knows, it cannot be the case that perceiving is mediated *by knowledge,* however defined. Classical empiricism was forced by the doctrine of intractable nonspecificity and an entrenched nominalism to appeal to memories and sense data as mediators of perception. Paradoxically, empiricism's platform was undermined by its very assumptions.

But it is clear—at least to us—that *an* empiricism is needed, that the central problem is to unpack successfully the idea of perceiving as *the* means of knowing, whether the focus be the perceptual experience of a present animal or the perceptual experience of its ancestors.

This sought-after empiricism, though consonant with classical empiricism in spirit, would differ substantially from the classical view in detail. A sharp contrast on the basic assumptions is to be expected. Thus, for example, a successful empiricism could not be built on the assumption of intractable nonspecificity, but it might be built on the assumption of necessary specificity (Turvey & Shaw, 1979)—that for any given (species of) animal, energy media must necessarily be structured by the world in ways that are specific to properties of surfaces and substances taken with reference to the (species of) animal (Gibson, 1966, 1977; Mace, 1977). The concepts of affordance and effectivity that are discussed in the next main section are expressions of this unconventional doctrine.

Incommensurability of Natural Kinds

We see, in short, that one method of overcoming the nonspecificity dealt with earlier is to change part of the theory to build in more specificity. This is what James Gibson proposed to do in 1950 with his program of perceptual psychophysics. With respect to vision, Gibson (1950) showed examples of structured optical descriptions of an animal's surroundings that were more appropriate than traditional descriptions to the categories of what is perceived. Gibson's suggestion, then and now, is that a concerted effort to discover more such environment-specific structures in the light might reveal enough to support a theory of visual perception based on specificity among; (1) the structure of the animal's surroundings, (2) the light as structured by those surroundings, and (3) the animal's perception of those surroundings. Thus, in the program advocated by Gibson (1950, 1966), both specificity and tractability are assumed. Because we do not know the true structure of the "givens" of perception that support specification, it is taken to be a major task of empirical science to discover this structure. There would be no such scientific task for students of perception committed to nonspecificity as a matter of doctrine (cf. Turvey & Shaw, 1979).

There is a second problem, however—one that tradition might have us believe is a problem that would remain untouched by the demonstration of specification. No matter how much the description of structured energy media is enriched, it might be argued that this enrichment cannot alter the *kinds* of entities involved. Is it not the case that the problem of knowing the environment contains an essential gap between physical and mental entities? This is a *qualitative* gap, one that separates incommensurable entities. It is known more commonly as the mind–body problem.

The metaphysical dualism of traditional psychology and, indeed, of most 20th-century science divides the natural world into two kinds of objects: physical phenomena and psychological phenomena. This division, as noted in the introduction, poses a barrier to realism. A committed realist is justifiably uncomfortable with a kind of realism that is true to dualism, a realism that proposes epistemic entities as mediator between a world that is claimed to be real and experience—a realism that might be dubbed "indirect." Many scholars would argue that the kind of realism that would make a committed realist comfortable, a realism in which there are no epistemic mediators—that is, direct realism—is nothing more than a form of naive realism, the belief that the perceived world is all that is real. If so, then it must be admitted that a commitment to realism that rejects the dualism-tainted, indirect realism leads nowhere useful. However, it is argued here, as it has been elsewhere (Shaw & Bransford, 1977), that this pessimistic evaluation is by no means warranted: Direct realism and naive realism are not equated; there are a variety of direct realisms, *one* of which is naive realism. What must be demonstrated is that a form of direct realism exists that can satisfy the committed realist who desires a footing for knowledge firmer than mere belief, by allowing perceptual experience to be a direct "contact" with *some portion of what is real in nature*—namely, that which has relevance to the life-style of the percipient.

Scientists have been justifiably reluctant to take seriously philosophical answers to scientific puzzles. Bertrand Russell most eloquently voiced these shared misgivings among scientists when he observed that metaphysics is to scientific investigation what thievery is to honest toil. Consequently, before launching full throttle into the brambles of the problem of incommensurability of natural kinds (i.e., of physical and psychological phenomena), a few words may be in order to soften the ordeal for the scientist and to allay any fears that the search for an acceptable form of direct realism is in any way an attempt to void Russell's remarks.

The fundamental problem of perceptual epistemology, and hence of psychological approaches to the problem of knowledge, would be solved if it could be shown that the entailed dualism was not necessary. Admitted and unavoidable, however, is the realization that if this dualism is to be dissolved, then the dissolution must take place at a level somewhat deeper than epistemology. It must take place at a level where decisions are made regarding the objects to which perception is with reference and the objects of which perception is an experience—respectively, the so-called physical and mental objects of mind-body dualism.

However, no absolute answers need be sought. All that is needed is a realization that our task is to explain experience both in terms of the reference it makes to the world and the intentional means of doing so. There are apparently two kinds of objects whose ontological status must be elaborated—reference objects and intentional objects. The descriptions of these objects that we seek must satisfy the requirements of scientific explanation, but they need not be philosophically "rock-bottom." That is to say, the deeper problems of constructing an absolute metaphysics can be left to the professional philosopher. As scientists—more precisely, as scientists taking an ecological stance—we need only seek a compromise position that lies somewhere between the absolute concerns of metaphysics, regarding what must exist if anything exists at all, and the relative concerns of epistemology, regarding what must exist if (perceptual) knowledge is to be possible.

Thus, we would argue, the goal of the ecological psychologist is more modest than the goal of the philosopher who pursues ontological analyses: Whereas the philosopher seeks grounds for inferential knowledge that must be necessarily true in spite of the contingent properties of the world and the experiences of humans, the ecological psychologist seeks only those grounds for experience that make possible a perceiver's evolutionary specialized knowledge of a rather restricted world. Thus grounds for knowledge are sought that possess relative or ecological validity rather than grounds for knowledge that possess absolute metaphysical validity.

This is not to say that the task is any less difficult than that of the philosopher. On the contrary, the logical tools that have been developed over the past 2000 years to aid philosophical inquiries are valuable armaments for the ecological psychologist as well, because the tasks are so methodologically similar. Whatever aids straight thinking in one domain most likely will do so in the other.

Representation as Presupposing a User and as Presupposing Specification

A compelling strategy that has been adopted to sidestep partially, if not to solve, the problems raised by the doctrine of intractable nonspecificity and the incommensurability of natural kinds is to posit representations that contain the essence of knowing. If an animal can be said to know or perceive or remember by virtue of its own representations of its surroundings, the theorist might ease the transition between the physical and mental world. It has become increasingly popular, with the growth of the information-processing perspective, to explain perceiving, remembering, and behavior by *internal* representations. Consequently the call is out for a completely general theory of representation (e.g., Bobrow & Collins, 1975; Dennett, 1977; Fodor, 1975) in order to understand better how one thing can represent another. A representation may be defined, tentatively, as a structure—either abstract or concrete—the features of which purportedly symbolize the features of some other structure (MacKay, 1969). And *to represent* entails the thing represented, the representation, and *the device for which the representation is intended*. The latter aspect of representing has been the cause of much concern.

Long before the information-processing perspective took hold, philosophy and psychology (with a few exceptions, such as behaviorism) claimed that the only kind of psychology with a chance of success was one that posited internal representations. But since a representation entails a user, an interpreter or agent with psychological traits such as comprehension and goals, the claim that a psychology without internal representation cannot succeed is equivalent to the claim that a psychology without internal animal-analogues cannot succeed. In short, to advocate the necessity of internal representations is to advocate the necessity of homunculi; but to advocate homunculi is to doom psychology to an infinite regress. And a psychology with unexplained or uninterpreted, internal animal-anologues is no psychology at all.

Let us distinguish between "representation *for*," which necessarily implies a user, and a "representation *by*," which does not (cf. Cummins, 1977 [appendix]). Suppose that we are talking about a skill of some kind (such as striking a baseball). This relatively complicated activity can, in principle, be decomposed into a number of relatively less complicated activities that, when suitably organized, produce the skilled striking of the ball. Taken collectively, the component activities and the order and manner of their interlacing may be said to identify a "program," and learning to hit a baseball can be described, in part, as memorizing that program. We can speak, therefore, of the program as a kind of knowledge that can be examined and followed by some separate mechanism to execute baseball batting much as a cook might examine and follow a recipe to execute the preparation of a gourmet meal. Herein lies the sense of representation *for:* The internally represented program must relate to the mechanism that executes it in much the same way that a recipe, as a part of a cook's environment, relates to the cook. The analogy underscores the properties that the user of the internal representation must have, and they are the very properties that a science of psychology would seek to explain.

Is there a way in which these properties can be discharged that preserves the notion of internal representation as a source of knowledge? The problem is an old one, and it was tackled unsuccessfully by Hume (Dennett, 1977). Hume, however, did point in the direction of what, to some, appears to be the solution—precisely, the idea of self-understanding representations. It has been suggested (e.g., Dennett, 1977; Fodor, 1975) that the "data structures" fashionable in artificial intelligence research are just such creatures or, at least, that they come very close to being just such creatures: Data structures are said to be (kinds of) representations that understand themselves. The trick to discharging an intelligent device—an animal-analogue that manipulates internal representation—is to devolve that intelligence on *many* fine-grained devices that are marked by their ignorance and myopic outlook. This is not the whole trick, however, For paralleling the devolution of intelligence, there must be a differentiation of any given representation into representations of considerably lesser sophistication, each tailored to the stupidity of its respective user(s). And paralleling this paring down of sophistication in representation and user-ability, there must be an increasing sophistication in organization. Hence it is by such means that, in theory, markedly intelligent activity can be achieved by a collection of markedly unintelligent subsystems.

The thrust of self-understanding representation is to slur intentionally the distinction between representation and user. Additionally, it would seem to slur the distinction between representation *for* and representation *by*. Referring back to the baseball-hitting program, saying that the program is represented *by* a device is to intend something quite different from saying that the program is represented *for* a device, as the following example (after Cummins, 1977) illustrates.

Given a complicated electronic circuit, one could draw a schematic diagram of the circuit as a way of expressing the circuit's style of functioning. And it would be legitimate to say that the circuit is represented by the schematic diagram, and vice versa. Similarly, one could write a computer program to express analytically the circuit's behavior, and in like fashion it would be legitimate to say that the circuit is represented by the program, and vice versa. In both these cases exemplifying representation *by*, representation is used descriptively rather than imperatively. That is to say, in both cases, representation is used as a theoretical tool for analyzing behavior rather than as a cause of behavior (Cummins, 1977). In neither case could we internalize the representation, for although we can say that the schematic diagram or program is represented *by* the circuit, it would be nonsense to say that the program or schematic diagram is a representation *for* the circuit that can be used to direct the circuit's performance.

Clearly, representation in the sense of representation *by* is a userless concept: A representation, in this sense, is not information, not a source of knowledge, to be used by some agentlike device. When representation is interpreted in the sense of representation *by*, we cannot ascribe to the representation of X the status of a thing perceived when one is said to perceive an object or event X; nor can we ascribe to the representation of Y the status of a thing controlling and coordinating behavior when one is said to perform the activity Y. A representation of X by the nervous system of an animal might be discerned by the neuroscientist or by the information-processing scientist when the animal is perceiving X (as might a representation of Y when the animal is doing Y), but it is not discerned *by the animal or any of its parts*. To be purposely redundant, when we speak of representation in the sense of representation *by*, there may be a representation of an environmental situation X by an animal's nervous system when the animal sees X, but it is not a representation *for* the animal (or any part of the animal) as perceiver; and there may be a representation of an activity Y by an animal's nervous system when the animal does Y, but it is not a representation *for* the animal (or any part of the animal) as actor.

Ideally, the concept of self-understanding representation, as intimated already, eliminates the representation/user dichotomy. A question arises, however: On eliminating this dichotomy, do we relinquish the rights to the notion of representation as a source of knowledge (a source for whom?) and to the use of the prefix *internal*? And does it not invite a consideration of the possibility that self-understanding representation is logically equivalent to representation in the sense of representation *by*? In this case, there would be no imperative sense in which representation can be used, only a descriptive sense. That is to say, in short, that representation would refer (simply) to the way in which an animal is structured when, say, the animal is perceiving, acting, or remembering and not to a causal determinant of the animal's perceiving, acting, or remembering.

The conundrum on which the preceding remarks have focused is the time-honored one of representation presupposing a user, and the remarks are intended to convey the flavor of the debate to which the user presupposition has given rise. There is another conundrum to be considered—one that is far less heralded but no less important—that representation presupposes specification. Following Mac-Kay (1969), we tentatively defined a representation as a structure, the features of which symbolize the features of some other structure. Of any posited internal representation, we could ask: how did it arise? More to the point, however, we could ask: Why did that *particular* representation arise, symbolizing *those* particular features and not some other? Presumably, it must be argued, by those who would posit internal representations as determinants of perceiving (or acting, or remembering), that the internal representations are "made" during the course of phylogeny and/or ontogeny. The underlying puzzle is how the to-be-made internal representations are selected—that is, how they are specified.

We may highlight the specification presupposition through a brief consideration of the mechanics of using representations. A conventional argument, motivated by the doctrine of intractable nonspecificity, is that proximal stimulation is interpreted in terms of the distal object that would most normally give rise to it. The idea is that the perceiver has at his or her disposal internal representations of "normal" situations and brings these representations to bear on the proximal stimulation. Helmholtz (1925) and William James (1907) were early proponents of this idea, which currently receives expression through a number of scholars (e.g., Gregory, 1966; Minsky, 1975). Suppose that normal situations are represented in the form of structural descriptions exemplified by frames or schemata (cf. Bobrow & Collins, 1975). The assimilation by a frame of a preliminary description of the proximal stimulus yields the perception of the distal object. There are, of course, many frames, and how the proper frame for assimilating the proximal data is arrived at presents a problem. We may suppose that several frames are tried before the correct one is hit upon. But how is the first frame chosen? It would be undesirable if the first frame did not approximate the correct frame, for we may suppose that a blind choice of frames would then ensue. Theory at this point seeks succor in "context," assigning to context a significant role in narrowing the initial choice of frame. Roughly and intuitively, the way in which context may be presumed to work is like *pointing:* Context *points to* (or specifies) the ball park of relevant representations. Hence selection of a frame presupposes specification by a context. Whether an epistemic entity that is framelike is necessary or not, we take it that in representational theories, *there will always be* some relation of specification between the structure of stimulation and the putative epistemic entity.

At all events, a little thought suggests that a case can be made for a completely general theory of specification, so that we might better understand how one thing can be said to specify another. Such a theory might be thought of as a natural accompaniment of a completely general theory of representation, but it need not be—at least not with respect to such matters as perceiving, acting, and remembering. We have touched upon the deep-seated difficulties of positing epistemic mediators for perception, and we have identified problems for a concept of representation interpreted in the sense of representation *for*. It may well be that an adequate theory of specification would obviate the need to postulate internal representations; in short, perhaps it is a theory of specification rather than a theory of representation that is of primary concern.

The Problems of Representational Realism (as the Principal Form of Indirect Realism)

Conventional psychology (largely under the influence of positivism) expresses limited interest in metaphysical issues; this attitude has been generalized to epistemological issues as well—a case of throwing the baby out with the bath water. This attitude is exemplified by the lack of concern for the questions of whether memories are true representations of past experiences and whether perceptions are truly distinguished from appearances (e.g., sense data). In keeping with this studied disinterest in epistemological issues is the contemporary eminence of a theory of representation on which we have just remarked: The central concern of cognitive psychology appears to be how knowledge is represented and organized (e.g., Anderson & Bower, 1973; Bobrow & Collins, 1975).

Not surprising, either, is the fact that little concern is shown for determining how such representation may express valid knowledge about objective occurrences. That is, they do not inquire into the problem of how representations "interface" with the world; and, *a fortiori,* they do not inquire how representations can yield knowledge of the world with which they are interfaced. To a great extent, cognitive representations are left dangling, semantically hinged to nothing more solid than other cognitive representations.

To be fair, contemporary cognitive theory tacitly assumes some form of the correspondence theory of meaning and imputes a degree of resemblance, or isomorphism, between the cognitive structure and the thing it represents. If pressed to explain whether such a resemblance is necessary or only contingent, the most apt response is that since perception can sometimes be in error, as when viewing illusions or mirages, then the correspondence at best is only contingent.

But how valid is the knowledge possible under such a view? The only answer that can be given is to invoke a version of the causal-chain theory of perception, which, in the case of vision, asserts that *somehow* (a somehow that is never quite explained), the image experienced is of a real fact if the causal chain from object–to light wave–to retinal image–to brain–to homunculus remains unbroken and undisturbed—say, by intrusions in the media (e.g., light, eye, nerve tract, or brain) supporting the perceptual process. However, the percipient can never know whether such intrusions are present and to what extent perceptual experiences may be of something other than the reference object for which the representation was intended.

Involved in the de facto structure of the foregoing argument are de jure questions of considerable epistemological importance arising from the assumed incommensurability of natural kinds: To what does a perception refer? To the cognitive representation? Or to the reference object in the world? If the answer is that it refers to the object in the world, then why the need for a representation at all—why not just let the object of experience be the object of reference? Although such a solution avoids the need for representational stages in perception, a ploy that a committed realist should endorse, it seems to fall down on the issue of error in perception, an issue that the traditional theorist is not likely to ignore given the large body of research devoted to the study of illusions.

On the other hand, if it is argued that the perceptual experience refers to the "object in the head," it is still unclear whether this means the cognitive representation *qua* psychological entity or a function of the neural substrate *qua* physical entity. Furthermore, whichever is meant still requires a referential theory to explain how the correspondence with the world referent is achieved so that perceptual knowledge is possible. Such a referential theory must be causal if the representation is deemed to be a physical entity (e.g., a brain state), leaving theoretically vague how the homunculus, as a psychological entity, is to be related to a physical entity. On the other hand, if the representation is deemed to be a cognitive structure, the same problem remains; namely, although a representation might be a content of the homunculus's "perceptual" experience, how is it to be related to the chain of causal support that guarantees the possibility of perceptual knowledge of the world?

As tiresome as this old philosophical chestnut may be to those who have muddled through the mind–body problem in Philosophy 101, it serves to point out exactly why the traditional approach to the problem of perceptual knowledge is fruitless. It is fruitless not simply because it chooses to be vague on the issue of how physical entities may be related to psychological entities but rather because it cannot avoid being vague; it is vague by necessity, not by want of cleverness on the part of its proponents.

The difficulty for representational realism appears to reside chiefly in two assumptions—first, that the object of perception (a representation) corresponds to its reference object by a causal process. This assumption requires that physical entities in the world must somehow be coordinated with psychological entities. (At a more subtle level of analysis, it confuses causal support for an epistemic act with the epistemic act.) For future discussion, we call this the *problem of referentiality*. A second major assumption is that an internal representation, as the object of perceptual experience, is an *intentional object* in the quasi-technical sense originally proposed by Brentano (1874/1925). This term, *intentional object,* figures prominently in the ensuing discussion, and we would do well to preface its usage here. It is of no little significance that the idea of intentional object promotes the incommensurability of natural kinds independent of any arguments about the ontological status of mental entities (cf. Dennett, 1969).

By way of a quick (and dirty) explanation of intentional objects, note the argument that statements about intentional objects cannot have the same truth conditions as statements about nonintentional objects. Here are some statements about intentional objects: I want X; I hope for X; I imagine X. And here are some statements about nonintentional objects: I throw X; I walk through X; I eat X. The point about an intentional object, therefore, is this: It does not or need not exist in the fashion of nonintentional objects such as those thrown, walked through, and eaten; after all, it does not follow from imagining a pint of Guinness stout that there is a pint of Guinness stout that I imagine. In short, intentional objects do not have ordinary existence; rather they have—as Brentano expressed it—"inexistence." On the representational (indirect) realist's view of perception, it is evident from this intuitive explanation that the representation intermediary between the reference object and experience is an intentional object, and the possibility arises that perception does not imply some ordinary (that is, real) thing perceived. We refer to the problem of elaborating on what is meant by an intentional object as the Problem of Intentionality.

Distinguishing Between Direct Realism and Indirect Realism (a Phenomenalism)

It is fair to ask if the direct realism favored by a committed realist fares any better with respect to the epistemological puzzles that infirm indirect realism, which we now appreciate is more aptly termed a phenomenalism. Clearly, the problems the two kinds of realism face cannot be identical since their goals and fundamental epistemological assumptions differ radically. In fact, the main problem of direct realism is complementary to that of a realism mediated by phenomena or representations in the following way: If knowledge of what is real is to be possible, then the content of the perceptual experience of some object x must refer to object x. For representationalism, a representation stands intermediary between the experience and the reference object x. Hence under the representational view, the referential relationship is indirect in that the intentional object of the experience, the representation, is not the same as the referential object x. However, under a theory that perception is direct, the intentional object cannot be something other than the referential object, and perception, therefore, is of an object in the world and not of some extraordinary object "in the head." If no representation exists and perception is direct, then there can be no slippage between the experience and that to which the experience refers. Thus, the possibility of knowledge of the world being obtained through perceptual means is logically assured. If this argument is valid, then direct realism is the only reasonable epistemological position—the only reasonable position that a committed realist could endorse.

But notice that *if* error can be introduced into perception by some means, then no logical assurances can be given to guarantee the possibility of knowledge. *If* perceptual experience may contain erroneous information about the world, uncertain knowledge is all that is possible. Uncertain, or contingent, knowledge is of course nothing more than beliefs that may be either true or false.

Surely there is undeniable evidence proving that perceptual experiences are sometimes the breeding place of error. Consider the case of so-called misperceptions, as in magic shows where one fails to perceive what really takes place, or in masking experiments where seeing one of two closely presented displays precludes seeing the other. Also, what of illusions where one sees something that, from the standpoint of physics, is not really there? We can see straight lines as spuriously bent (the Hering and Wundt illusions or the stick-in-water illusion), size discrepancies between objects that are truly of equal size (the Ponzo, Müller-Lyer, and Jastrow illusions), or a lack of alignment where alignment is really perfect (the Poggendorf illusion).

Thus the concerned realist who desires a firm perceptual foundation for knowledge seems trapped between the compellingness of erroneous experience, on one hand, and the necessity of valid experience, on the other hand.

It is now possible, in the wake of the preceding discussion, to move to a deeper level of appreciation of the dilemma facing a viable realism, regardless of which of the two views is advocated: Direct realism and indirect realism (phenomenalism) are horns of the same dilemma; to deny one is to affirm the other and, unfortunately, at the same time to inherit all of its attendant epistemological puzzles. A popular tactic for avoiding dilemmas is to deny that they represent the only alternatives—which means, so to speak, to pass safely between the horns without being ensnared by either self-contradictory position. As appealing as this solution might be, it does not seem viable since no third alternative form of realism is possible. Between the two horns of direct and indirect realism, there does not seem to be sufficient room to pass.

If we are essentially correct in our appraisal, then the only strategem left open to the psychologist *qua* committed realist who stubbornly refuses to be cynical about the possibility of knowledge is to demonstrate that a change in the relative acceptability of one of the two positions is possible. Such a change must be wrought at a level of argument deeper than epistemology—namely, at the level of ontology that furnishes common ground for both views. Direct and indirect realism can only be placed at loggerheads at the level of epistemology (i.e., regarding perception-as-knowledge versus perception-as-belief) if they are commensurable at the level of ontological commitment. For instance, both views (as already portrayed) share a common belief with respect to which aspects of perception are physical entities—namely, the reference object in the world—and which aspects are psychological entities—namely, the contents of experience. Since they are essentially in agreement on these ontological matters, we must look elsewhere for an issue that can be used to pry them apart. Metaphorically speaking, this cement of shared ontological framework allows the objectively stronger of the two positions unwittingly to provide support for the other. By logically separating the two positions at their ground of support, it is our belief that the weaker position will topple under its own weight, leaving the logically sounder position upright.

It remains only to ascertain the divisive issue: Recall from the earlier discussion, in addition to the contents of experience and the referential object from which such contents draw their meaning, that there is the intentional object—a cognitive representation for indirect realism—and the object of reference—as captured in a conventional physical description—for the naive form of direct realism. It is here that the required ontological wedge is to be found.

THE REALIST INTERPRETATION OF PSYCHOLOGY AND ITS PROBLEMS

Perceiving as Knowing Rather than Believing

An almost universal opinion about the epistemological status of the information about the world that perception provides asserts: "Seeing is believing." We hold this view to be seriously misleading because it imposes on perceiving the logic of believing rather than the logic of knowing. Only the latter logical analysis is acceptable, since the former makes it impossible to distinguish knowledge of reality from knowledge of appearance. To avoid this epistemological conclusion, the adage should read: "Seeing is knowing." The argument to be made can be schematized as a formal analogy: *Perceiving* is to *appearing* as *knowing* is to *believing*. The most fundamental distinction between direct and indirect (representational) realism inheres in the strong epistemology of direct realism, which endorses perceiving-as-knowing, and the weaker epistemology of indirect realism, which accepts perceiving-as-mere-believing.

The crucial distinction between the two forms of realism is not so much that one believes knowledge of the world through perceptual means is possible whereas the other does not, but that they disagree as to what the constituents of knowledge are—facts or beliefs. Their differing characterizations of knowledge retroact on their respective views of perception, forcing each faction to adopt a theory consistent with its peculiar form of realism and at odds with the other. Furthermore, even theories at this level have inevitable implications for the design and interpretation of experiments. For instance, one does not attempt to measure quarks unless one believes that they exist in a state sufficiently real to be measured. Neither does one attempt to investigate the organization of the imputed cognitive structures presumed to represent knowledge or perceptual experiences unless these, too, are believed to be in a state sufficiently real to be investigated.

The question of the ontological status of the intentional and referential objects of perceptual experience and of the nature of their epistemic accessibility has serious consequences for one's *scientific* realism and entails constraints that are passed down to the selection of methodology and experimental goals. Therefore, it would be a serious mistake to dismiss the issue of what form of realism is most plausible, since regardless of what ultimately proves right or wrong, the position chosen has significant practical ramifications.

If one defines knowledge as *true* belief, then the possibility of *false* belief is also implied. Following the foregoing analogy, perception would be defined as true appearance and misperception as false appearance. Something that happens to be true but could just as well have been false is contingent. Thus perception as defined by the analogy would be considered a source of contingent knowledge about the world. In this case, perception would assume the same logical status as occupied by judgment or inference: To perceive that "some *x* is *y*" would be tantamount to inferring that some *x is y* is a fact about the world that may or may not be true; at least, if true, it might have been otherwise. Such a view, as Helmholtz realized, makes perceiving a species of judgment (an unconscious inference, perhaps) as fallible as any other source of belief. It is extremely important to notice that this assumption—that perceiving and believing can be treated as logically equivalent—allows error to creep into perception just as readily as it might creep into judgment. In more technical terms, this traditional characterization proclaims perception to be the assertion of contingent, a posteriori facts about the world.

As we shall see, this traditional characterization of perception is not acceptable, since it permits certain philosophically queer conclusions to be drawn—such conclusions as importing existence to mere fictions—and it gives other vagaries of imagination the same ontological status as real objects: Unicorns and sphinxes become ontologically indistinguishable from horses and lions and hallucinations indistinguishable from perceptual experiences. A stronger commitment to realism than the anemic form endorsed by representational realism is needed in order to avoid such confusions. What is knowable must be more tightly bound to what is real than is admitted by the claim that perceiving is believing. To see what this means, let us consider, in some detail, various issues separating the perception-as-believing and perception-as-knowing positions as held by indirect and direct realism, respectively.

Avoiding Inexistent Objects

The accusative form of sentences involving verbs specifying psychological attitudes has led many philosophers and psychologists to postulate a shadowy realm of entities to be taken as direct objects of these verbs. Such ghostly entities are to be distinguished from those objects needed to define relationships among physical objects. "John *believes* Mary lied"; "Bill *saw* the snake"; "The detective *knew* who the murderer was"; and "The wife *desired* a change" are all sentences that employ verbs referring to psychological attitudes regarding the objects involved. Such objects, however, may or may not exist in the sense intended by the sentence: Mary may not have lied to John, so there is no lying Mary who exists to be the intentional object of John's believing. Yet the accusative form of the statement clearly requires that the verb take an object. Similarly, the objects intended by each of the other psychological attitudes may not really exist: Bill's snake may have been a stick; the detective's victim may have been a suicide; the wife's desire for a change may forever go unfulfilled. But if the objects of the main verbs may not refer to things in the ordinary world, where are the objects intentionally specified by the corresponding psychological attitudes?

Brentano (1874/1925) suggested (but later recanted) that such objects, because they may not exist as physical objects do, must exist in some other way; they have, he argued (and as we noticed earlier), *intentional inexistence*. Intentionally inexistent objects, required to satisfy the accusative form of statements about psychological attitudes, have an immanent—or mental—origin and, therefore, should be distinguished from physical objects, which exist independently of any psychological attitude.

Of course, physical objects also enter into statements having an accusative form, such as ''The boy hit the ball'' or ''The dog bit the mailman''; here the interpretation of the direct object of the verb is quite different: In order for the boy to hit the ball, there must be a ball to hit; and for the dog to bite, there must be something that can be bitten. Hence, physical phenomena, as opposed to psychological phenomena—according to Brentano's thesis—cannot ''intentionally contain objects in themselves.'' Rather, the statements using physical verbs seem to have the form of relational statements. ''Diogenes sits in his tub'' specifies a relationship between a man and his tub. Such propositions are said to be *extensionally* existent rather than intentionally inexistent.

Many philosophers and psychologists have attempted to treat propositions involving intentional objects like those involving extensional objects, assuming that they, too, specify a relationship between two kinds of real objects—objects of a physical kind and objects of a psychological kind. This leads to difficulties to which phenomenalism or representational realism is particularly susceptible because of the assumption that *knowing* and *perceiving* are psychological attitudes like *believing* and, therefore, must intentionally implicate some kind of immanent (mental) object—a representative cognitive structure.

But this view, to a wary and committed realist, seems too literal a confusion between the accusative grammar of certain statements involving psychological predicates and the intentional logic required to analyze psychological attitudes. Where the verb grammatically requires direct objects, psychological attitudes logically may require no objects at all. Although respect for grammar has run deep in philosophical analysis, it should not be allowed to lead to false conclusions regarding metaphysics.

The nonmediated or direct realism favored by the committed realist avoids this danger by arguing that, to the contrary, perceiving is more like *knowing* than *believing;* whereas *believing* may invite the assumption of intentional objects with immanent existence, or inexistence, *knowing* does not.

To anticipate the committed realist's argument: Our goal is to show that although *knowing* and *perceiving* are indeed intentional, the objects they specify are quite real in an ordinary sense and, therefore, commensurate with the physical objects required to define extensionally an animal's, or human's, environment. We call this the *ecological* thesis—a thesis that, so far as we know, was first raised for psychologists in a different form by James J. Gibson (1966). As the logician Hintikka (1975) observes:

> The conceptual moral [i.e., of Gibson's thesis] is that the perceptions that can surface in our consciousness *must be dealt with in terms of the same concepts as* what we perceive. The appropriate way of speaking of our spontaneous perceptions is to use the same vocabulary and the same syntax as we apply to objects of perception. If there is a general conceptual or philosophical point to Gibson's book, it is surely this [p. 60; italics added].

Fundamental to the ecological thesis put forward by Gibson (and under elaboration here) is the precept that *perceiving* is a form of *knowing* rather than a form of *believing*. Whereas beliefs must be translated from the mind to the world of reason to register a fit, perceptual knowledge does not. It derives its "fit" from the directness of the act of experiencing in part what truly exists. Thus, it is the lack of translation of perceptual experiences by cognitive mediators that allows a description of perceptual experiences and the reference objects perceived to share a common basis in both meaning and syntax, as Hintikka (1975) remarked and as we have made explicit elsewhere (Turvey & Shaw, 1979).

In this way, the significance of the direct realism position for theoretical psychology is that it provides a framework in which the problem of the incommensurability of natural kinds might be resolved. In very large part, the subsections that follow identify necessary steps to that desired conclusion.

Laying the Ground Rules of Argument

Assume that two convicts, Mr. X and Mr. Y, handcuffed together, are lost in the desert and are on the verge of dying from thirst. After peering expectantly in various directions over the hot desert sands, Mr. X gleefully cries that he has spotted a lake off in the distance. Mr. Y, a thirsty but avowed philosophical skeptic, disagrees that what his friend sees is water at all; rather, he insists it is only a mirage—a shimmering optical display caused by waves of hot air rapidly rising off the furnace floor of the desert. But Mr. X, an eternal optimist who trusts his senses, doggedly persists, and the two thirsty felons at last start out in the direction of the watery appearance. To take their minds off their ordeal, we can imagine that a classical argument fills the interim.

They agree that they both detect an optical display of the sort described, but they disagree as to its nature. Is it water or a mirage? Is one perceiving correctly and the other perceiving incorrectly? Or are they each perceiving correctly what is there, say, an optical display at a distance that resembles water—with error arising not from perception but from a willingness—say, on the optimist's part—to jump to conclusions unwarranted by the evidence at hand? In the former case, error would originate in perception; in the latter case, error would not be intrinsic to perception but would originate from inference, with further perception as the basis for verifying or falsifying the inference made. (We should note that on the view of perception as an inferential process or, similarly, an act of asserting propositions to be tested, the distinction just cited is nonexistent; on this Helmholtzean view, error must be intrinsic to perception.)

At this point, we offer a simple logical hypothesis: Whichever realism, direct or representational, can meet the challenge of the foregoing puzzle will be logically the sounder realism. In order to decide a winner, however, criteria for recognizing a solution must be agreed upon: We declare the winning position to be the one that provides the firmest foundation to the knowledge a perceiver can have. This means that the winning position will have to overcome the problem of how to build a sturdy semantic bridge to span the ontological gap that separates the intentional objects of psychological experiences from the referential objects of the world from whose existence perceptual meanings are drawn. However, such a semantic bridge can be neither "fish nor fowl"—neither wholly intentional nor wholly referential. Neither can it be merely a third kind of object, in violation of Occam's razor, because this would compound the ontological problem by proliferating potentially incommensurate kinds.

Before attacking this serious problem, it will be useful to consider carefully the major arguments for why the realism favored by a committed realist and representational realism (a phenomenalism) differ with respect to whether perception is a source of knowledge or only a source of beliefs about the world.

Being True by Force of Existence Rather than by Force of Argument

Although we may ask of a knowledge claim put forward: "How do you know?" or "Why do you believe?" we cannot ask "Why do you know?" or "How do you believe?" (Austin, 1946). The difference in what questions are appropriate suggests that the logic of propositions entailed by *knowing* that something is true is quite different from that entailed by *believing* that something is true. A similar distinction must be made between propositions entailed by perceiving that *x is y* and those entailed by the claim that *x appears* to be *y*.

We attempt to show that where the proposition purporting to describe a perceptual experience is known to be true by virtue of the existence of the state of affairs in which the percipient perceives, by contrast the proposition purporting to describe the appearance of something can only be known true by virtue of argument. Thus, by this claim, perceptions draw whatever validity they have as knowledge *from the force of existence,* whereas appearances draw whatever validity they have as true beliefs *from the force of argument.* This distinction is of sufficient importance to be considered more carefully.

A noticed resemblance is a prime example of something that draws its validity from the force of existence. If you identify one object with another because they share a resemblance, this fact of resemblance can be usefully cited as evidence for the validity of the belief in the identity only if it is obvious to all parties concerned. For instance, eyewitness testimony in a court of law has no legal merits if it can be contradicted by other eyewitness testimony. Similarly, the claim that one thing is to be identified with another because they share a certain resemblance is impeached if the facts of resemblance are disputed.

The ultimate evidence for the belief that one thing resembles another is the perceptual evidence that the resemblance exists. Such perceptual experiences in which resemblances are noticed are by that fact alone sufficient to guarantee their weight as evidence for beliefs. Although a belief can be impeached by other evidence, the fact that a resemblance is noticed cannot, because it is by the perceptual experience alone that a resemblance can be recognized to exist.

The noticing of resemblances shares with beliefs held, pains felt, and other "noticings," a privileged epistemic position in that unlike the propositions asserted about other things, they cannot be impeached by argument or by any other source of evidence; for to notice them at all is to notice that they exist.

Following Brentano, most theorists have assumed that all such "noticings," since they are intentional, necessarily refer to some immanent object, such as an image, sense datum, or other mental representation. We eventually dispute this claim after considering further why the logical analyses of *perceiving* and *believing* differ in just the same way as do those of *knowing* and *believing*.

Let (1) "*x* is *y*" stand for the proposition that is true if and only if *x is y* is indeed a fact about the world. Now let *p* be a proposition whose truth value requires that the proposition "*x* is *y*" be true; hence *p* can be true only if (1) is true, and (1) is true only if a certain fact about the world holds—namely, that *x is y* is the case. In this way, proposition *p* draws its truth from existence vis-à-vis proposition (1). Proposition (1) can be modified by introducing an intentional qualifier, or modal prefix, as follows: (2) APPEARS (*x* is *y*) is a schema representing the claim that "*x* appears to be *y* to someone." Similarly, we can modify (1) with another intentional qualifier: (3) PERCEIVES (*x* is *y*) is the schema representing the claim that "someone perceives that *x* is *y*." The question we wish to explore is which of the two modal propositions, (2) or (3), may be logically identified with the nonmodal proposition *p*, the proposition that is true *by force of existence* (i.e., from the fact that *x is y* is a fact).

In addition to modal propositions (2) and (3), we introduce two more modal propositions also constructed by prefixing intentional qualifiers to the original proposition (1): (4) BELIEVES (*x* is *y*) and (5) KNOWS (*x* is *y*). Again we ask if either proposition (4) or (5) may be logically identified with the nonmodal proposition *p* so that either is true if *p* is true.

The logical distinction between the species of realism favored by a committed realist and representational realism can be sharpened by using the foregoing analysis: Representational realism as a form of phenomenalism claims that the logic of (2) APPEARS (x is y), (3) PERCEIVES (x is y), (4) BELIEVES (x is y), and (5) KNOWS (x is y) must be the same. Moreover, realists of any persuasion must agree that the reference object of any of the preceding intentional kinds of modal propositions must be some fact that is true of the world as specified by proposition (1). Consequently, because of their approach to the problem of reference (or meaning, in the extensional sense), indirect realists must argue that all the modal propositions—(2), (3), (4), and (5)—should have exactly the same truth conditions as (1): that is, they must be logically identified with proposition p. This follows, of course, from the twin assumptions of phenomenalism that knowing and perceiving are both species of believing (i.e., *true* beliefs and *contingent* beliefs, respectively).

If the identity of these propositions (truth-functionally) with p should, however, turn out not to hold, the program for indirect realism is severely jeopardized, for then there would exist no basis for explaining or adjudicating knowledge claims (i.e., the claim that "x is y" would refer equivocally to both factual contingencies x *is* y and x is *not* y.)

Furthermore, if a specific subset of the modal propositions can be shown to be truth-functionally equivalent to p whereas another subset cannot—say, (3) and (5) can, but (2) and (4) cannot—then a case can be made for the viability of the direct realist's program. In order for the direct realist's program to be supported, it must be the case that (3) PERCEIVES (x is y) and (5) KNOWS (x is y) are logically equivalent to p and thereby draw their meaning (truth) from the existence of a fact about the world.

Let us return to the example of the two thirsty convicts marooned on the hot desert: Merely for the optimistic convict to believe that a shimmering optical display seen in the distance is water in no way entails that it *is* water, since it may be—as his pessimistic friend declares—a mirage. Thus beliefs no more entail facts than wishes entail their fulfillment. Clearly, to believe that x (a shimmering optical display) is y (water) in no way entails that "x is y" is necessarily true. This means, of course, that the representational realist's claim that proposition (4) can be identified with proposition p must be false, since (4) BELIEVES (x is y), unlike p, entails the disjunct that proposition (1) asserting "x is y" is either true or false.

A similar analysis holds for proposition (2) APPEARS (x is y): Just because the optical display appears to be water in no way entails that it *is* water; it might, as already argued, be a mirage. The similarity of these conclusions should in no way be surprising given that beliefs are naturally founded on appearances; if they were founded upon reality, then they should never lead us astray as they sometimes do.

As a consequence of the preceding analysis, it is clear that neither proposition (2) APPEARS (x is y) nor (4) BELIEVES (x is y) can be identified with proposition p. Therefore such propositions cannot be said to refer directly to what exists but at best can refer only indirectly, by argument, to what may or may not exist. Thus, the epistemic thrust of *appearing* and *believing* is propositionally that of contingent, a posteriori facts.

The viability of the realism sought by the committed realist, here termed *direct*, rests upon showing that modal propositions involving *perceiving*, like those involving *knowing*, are necessarily true "by force of existence" because they intentionally specify nonmodal (extensional) propositions like *p*, whose truth value (and meaning) necessarily entails existence (i.e., facts about the world). To see that this is so, we need only observe under what conditions we should be willing to admit that something is known rather than merely believed. The argument is not difficult, but it is subtle and deserving of careful consideration.

We are willing to say that one *knows* some proposition is true—say, that *x* (the optical display) is *y* (water)—if and only if certain conditions are satisfied: (a) One must understand what the proposition means; (b) one must affirm (accept) the proposition; (c) one can offer adequate evidence for it; and finally (d) the proposition is indeed factually true.

This definition contrasts with what must be satisfied simply to say that someone believes in the truth of a proposition. To believe *p* requires only that conditions (a) and (b) be satisfied and that (c) be modified. As already shown, (d) need not be satisfied, since the proposition does not have to be true to be believed. Condition (c) has to be modified, since what is important to believing a proposition is not whether one can adequately defend it, but that one accepts some form of evidence (cogent or otherwise) in its favor.

The optimistic convict presumably demonstrated his belief that the shimmering optical display specified water by satisfying these three conditions in just the way prescribed: He tacitly demonstrated all three conditions by recognizing that water is a significant substance with which to quench one's thirst (condition a); by setting out in dogged pursuit of it (condition b); and by arguing against and opposing the belief of his pessimistic friend (condition c).

But what would have been required of him to illustrate that he had knowledge rather than mere belief that what he and his friend saw was water rather than a mirage? Let us assume that conditions (a) and (b) could tacitly be satisfied in exactly the same way as before. We must now consider what would constitute adequate evidence that he *knows* that there *is* water. The committed realist has no option but to recognize the following as the key to the argument: Whatever evidence is sufficient to satisfy the strong version of condition (c), it must derive its cogency from "the force of existence"—condition (d)—rather than from argument.

This means that the fact that water exists must be recognized by all parties concerned, just as a resemblance purported to exist between two objects must be so recognized if the fact is to have any weight as evidence. As argued earlier, such weight that resemblances have must arise *directly* from the noticing by all concerned rather than *indirectly* by arguments. This follows because arguments may have contingent outcomes whereas "noticings" carry a necessary force because of the existence of the property to which they intentionally refer (i.e., the resemblance). In other words, to know a proposition *p* is simply to notice that the conditions that make *p* true necessarily obtain. For the form of realism favored by a committed realist, perceiving is a kind of noticing; it is, as we describe later, a primary fact of experience.

Thus, it follows from this discussion of the logical difference separating *believing* from *knowing* that *perceiving* is a necessary condition for *knowing*, although it is not necessary for *true* believing. It is the failure to recognize that *knowing* may entail *true believing* without being in any sense a species of *believing* that has led so many theorists with presumably realist sympathies to endorse a phenomenalism—precisely, representational realism.

If valid, then the preceding analysis demonstrates that modal propositions (3) KNOWS (x is y) and (5) PERCEIVES (x is y) are logically equivalent to propositions like p, whose truth depends upon existence, whereas propositions (2) BELIEVES (x is y) and (4) APPEARS (x is y) are not. Herein lie the ontological roots of the logical separation from which the schism between the warring forms of realism grows. It is sufficiently deep and pervasive that no verbal sleight of hand can conjure it away.

In arriving at this conclusion, we have exploited several ideas and notions of some considerable significance with little discussion of them individually. It is the task of the remaining parts of this main section to provide that discussion and, ideally, clarification. In addition, the remaining parts underscore the evolving claim for the incorrigibility of perception: Perception is a fact of existence; it is necessarily what it is and not something that can be either right or wrong.

In preview, the remaining parts contrast the following: true by force of existence with true by force of argument; necessary a posteriori facts with contingent a priori facts; and the nonpropositional and propositional uses of the term *perception*.

The Futility of Skepticism Regarding Realism (or Perception as the Court of Last Appeal)

Recall the story of the two thirsty convicts: They were left, engaged in philosophical debate, walking toward what may or may not be an oasis. For the sake of argument, let us assume that they are indeed approaching water, which becomes increasingly more apparent to them with every step. The rather nondescript, shimmering optical display takes on the wavy texture of a semitransparent, liquid blue surface. The optimistic convict proclaims that he was correct all along; it is water.

However, let us assume that his skeptical friend refuses to yield this point and stubbornly denies that he is yet convinced. Soon they are at the water's edge and can hear its rippling sound and feel the coolness of the desert breeze as it wafts across the pond's surface. Still the skeptic stands his ground. Finally, the two find themselves standing knee-deep in water, splashing and drinking; but still the skeptic refuses to recant. Besieged by ill humor and a singular lack of objectivity, the optimist thrusts the skeptic's head under the watery surface, intent upon drowning him unless he gives some tacit sign of agreement. The skeptic, unresisting to the last and refusing to acknowledge the water by word or deed, alas, drowns.

The moral of this vignette is that often what cannot be settled by force of argument is settled by force of existence—in this case, by the existence of the water. We would scarcely endorse the optimist's method for curtailing the skeptic's regressive argument—namely, the argument that no number of empirical tests are ever logically sufficient to prove the certainty of perceptual knowledge—although we must admit that the optimist has cogently demonstrated a point: The only possible stopping-rule for the skeptic's regress issues, not from reason, *but from the existential power of well-chosen acts to impress the relevant primary facts of experience on all concerned.* This is the last court of appeal in arguments where no rational criteria for settling the debate can be agreed upon.

Similarly, given the problematic nature of using deductive or inductive criteria to verify or falsify evidential claims, scientists invariably fall back on observational experience as the final arbiter of theoretic disagreement. Corroborated (i.e., replicable) eyewitness testimony of experimental outcomes carries immense weight scientifically, just as it does legally. (This is by no means to imply that noncompeting theories are necessarily accepted on the weight of empirical evidence alone, nor that these are the only grounds for their acceptance, but to emphasize that in most cases of competing theories, such observational evidence plays a primary, even necessary, role in their scientific adjudication. Nor is it meant to suggest that theoretical attitudes may not color data interpretation; on the contrary, they most assuredly do.)

The perception-as-direct theorist and the perception-as-indirect theorist are equally susceptible to the Socratic skeptic because they share a commitment to perceptual realism; the skeptic's attack cannot be tolerated by either position, for to question the veridicality of perceptual experience is to cast doubt on the last stronghold of realism. Any attempt to appeal to extraperceptual evidence is to worsen one's case, since it is a move from things that are known by acquaintance and are, therefore, true by force of existence to things that are known by description and are, therefore, believable only by force of argument. It is instructive to see how poorly each type of realist fares against a truly unrelenting skeptic.

Assume the debate is over whether in principle one can have sufficient grounds to say with certitude that one perceives a particular object—say, a kitchen table. The perception-as-indirect theorist is forced to agree with the skeptic that if the table is experienced at all, then it must be accomplished by virtue of some intervening process—an epistemic mediator, some image, or other representational surrogate of the table. This assumption allows the skeptic to ask: "But by what evidence can you be certain that the experience of the epistemic mediator reveals the true properties of the table [say, its solidity and hardness]; moreover, if it does not, then perhaps what you are really experiencing is something else—say, a soft cushion."

The theorist most likely will reply by taking the skeptic very carefully through some form of the causal-chain argument, dramatically gesturing in a knowing manner at the final step where the brain state somehow gives rise to the perceptual experience. However, to this explanation, the skeptic merely repeats the thrust of the original question: "But by what evidence can you be certain that the causal chain projects into awareness the true properties of the table? For even if we accept the assumption, although you have not truly justified it, that the causal process is isomorphic with the table at every stage from the eye to the brain, it does not follow that the representation created spontaneously in awareness necessarily has the properties of the table such as its size, shape, solidity, texture, color, and so forth. To argue that it must is to commit an egregious error of semantics—namely, confusing the properties of a symbol with that which is symbolized." In this way, the skeptic legitimately dismisses the *raison d'être* of the causal-chain argument.

Furthermore, with the causal-chain argument removed from contention on grounds of not being materially relevant, the theorist arguing with the skeptic might just as well be a direct realist rather than an indirect realist. It matters not at all whether the weak link in the realist's argument is the last link in a lengthy mediational chain or the first and only link binding the object perceived to the state of awareness; the skeptic's criticism is equally devastating.

Neither does it help for theorists to appeal to extraperceptual evidence—say, by arguing that they know that the representation, or contents of experience, capture the significant properties of the table because they can match the current experience against remembered experiences of tables and thus verify it. Clearly, this is also a mistake, for it permits the skeptic, in gadfly fashion, to enter a regressive line of Socratic interrogation: "But by what evidence can you justify the claim that your memory is correct? Does not memory knowledge originate in perceptual experience? If so, then it must be heir to two possible sources of error: the potential lack of fit of the original perceptual experience with the object upon which it is based, as well as the potential lack of fit of the memory to the original perceptual experience. Thus it seems your appeal to memory (or to inference, for that matter) worsens your position, for surely memory (or inference) can be just as faulty as perception.

Must the debate end here, with the skeptic smug and triumphant? Not necessarily, because the perceptual realist (of either persuasion) has one last reply that, if used at the opening of the debate, could have stymied and frustrated the skeptic. Where it is futile to argue for the veridicality of perceptual experience from *in*direct evidence, it is not futile to argue from *direct* evidence. Indeed, the only stopping-rule for this kind of debate is the following reply: "What justifies me in believing that I experience a table when I perceive a table is simply the fact that the meaning of such experiences is self-evident and neither requires nor allows appeal to any higher authority. Such experiences are no more capable of being falsified than they are capable of being verified." As surprising as it may seem, perceptual experiences, like the awareness of one's pains and beliefs, are self-presenting facts—that is, facts that neither require nor allow any justification by argument since they draw their validity from the force of existence itself. I know I perceive a table whenever I *notice the existence* of the object in front of me, while at the same time *noticing that it possesses properties of a certain sort* that by convention we call a "table." For someone not to grasp this argument is not to understand the difference between appearance and reality. Not to understand this difference is to be thoroughly ignorant of the topic of the debate.

On the other hand, if the skeptic is not ignorant and truly understands the distinction between appearance (as knowledge by description) and reality (as knowledge by acquaintance)—as must all who live with some degree of sanity and success—then he or she is either unreasonably obstinate (as was the skeptic who drowned in the oasis) or a liar. This being the case, further argument would be pointless.

However, if the foregoing ploy should fail to silence the skeptic, then you may resort to striking the individual sharply about the head and shoulders with the table, denying all the while that you are doing so. If the skeptic should protest, you may then turn the tables, so to speak, and ask in the name of heavens what evidence led him or her to conclude such a thing. The individual cannot, of course, take exception to your argument except on pain of tacitly renouncing the original skeptical position.

Such pragmatic solutions to epistemological puzzles have never been popular with professional philosophers, not because they lack the stomach for *argumentum ad mayhem,* but because such arguments lack logical cogency. Nevertheless, we may observe that for all living creatures, neither evolution, learning, nor other forms of adaptive change progress by the rules of philosophical debate; rather, they progress by more pragmatic means. Whatever success such epistemic functions of ecosystems achieve, they must do so in an eminently practical way. The decision rule for adaptive choices made must satisfy existential rather than logical criteria.

The Primary Facts of Experience

If it can be shown that perception provides self-presenting (directly evident) truths—that what is perceived *is* necessarily what *is*—then the stopping-rule invoked to curtail the skeptic's attack discussed earlier would be justified and a legitimate basis for knowledge found. But what is the nature of such self-presenting truths about the world upon which no skeptical doubt can legitimately be cast? Leibniz (1949) characterized the directly evident as follows:

> Our direct awareness of our own existence and of our own thoughts provides us with the primary truths *a posteriori,* the primary truths of fact, or in other words, our primary experiences; just as identical propositions constitute the primary truths *a priori,* the primary truths of reason, in other words, our primary insights. Neither the one nor the other is capable of being demonstrated and both can be called immediate [direct]—the former, because there is no mediation between the understanding and its objects, and the latter because there is no mediation between the subject and predicate [Vol. 4, Section 9, p. 2].

Although a committed realist might wish to claim that perception in general satisfies Leibniz's notion of direct awareness, it is not at all obvious that it does. Nevertheless, we argue that perception provides us not only with primary truths a posteriori, or "primary facts," about ourselves but also about the environment with which we have evolved strong mutual compatibilities (Shaw & McIntyre, 1974; Turvey & Shaw, 1979). Moreover, such primary facts, although not propositions in themselves, provide the stuff about which propositions might be asserted and on the basis of which propositions might be evaluated. Neither empiricists nor rationalists truly avoid the assumption of direct evidence in their respective versions of phenomenalism. The empiricist appeals to a direct awareness of sense data, retinal images, or brain states, whereas the rationalist similarly appeals to a direct awareness of self-evident truths about logical inference. Thus, the major difference in this regard between the realism favored by a committed realist and the realism that is a variant of phenomenalism does not depend on the assumption that direct evidence for the truths of experience is available, but on the evaluation of the import such directly evident truths may have for our knowledge of the world. An evaluation of the degree of objectivity such direct evidence may or may not have takes us into a very subtle but terribly important argument regarding the relationship of necessary and contingent truths to a priori and a posteriori facts. We follow Kripke (1972) in distinguishing these concepts. Our drawing of the distinction is less than complete, but ideally, it is sufficient to clarify the nature of direct perceptual evidence. Tentatively, we accept the idea that perceptual facts are both necessary and a posteriori.

Truths about which there might be knowledge—direct or otherwise—traditionally include such categories as "analytic," "necessary," "contingent," "a priori," and "a posteriori"—categories that have been referred to frequently in this chapter without explicit interpretation. The distinctions among these categories are often very difficult to define; consequently, some philosophers defend the distinctions vociferously, whereas others work just as hard to dissolve them. For present purposes, however, we need only consider the notions of necessary truths or facts and a priori truths or facts. Quite often these are said to be synonymous, or at least they are used interchangeably.

By calling a truth *necessary,* we simply mean that there is a state of affairs that is described truly and could not have been otherwise. Conversely, a *contingent* truth refers to a description of some state of affairs that is true but could nevertheless have been otherwise. This category distinction belongs to metaphysics, the branch of philosophy that attempts to assay what must be necessarily the case.

By contrast, the notion of an a priori fact refers to something that can be known to be true independent of experience. Or, conversely, the notion of an a posteriori fact refers to something that can only be known to be true through experience. This category distinction—if we care to assign it—belongs, not to metaphysics, but to epistemology—that branch of philosophy that studies how we can know certain things to be, in fact, true.

As Kripke (1972) points out with respect to the category distinction between the a priori and the necessary: It may, by some philosophical argument, follow from our knowing, independently of experience, that something is true of the actual world, that it has to be known to be true also of all possible worlds. But if this is to be established, it requires some philosophical argument to establish it. Similarly, one might argue the converse: That anything that is necessary is something that can be known a priori. Since the identification of these two concepts would obviously require considerable philosophical argument, on prima facie grounds we are justified to assume, at least until proven otherwise, that a priori facts and necessary truths are not the same.

To avoid belaboring the distinction, we give but one example to show why the two concepts are not logically coextensive. Goldbach's conjecture asserts that every even number is the sum of two primes. This is clearly a mathematical statement that, if true, must be necessarily true. However, since the conjecture has not been proven, no one at this time knows a priori or a posteriori whether it describes a fact about mathematics or not. On the other hand, no one doubts that if it is true, it must be a necessary truth of mathematics.

Now someone might quibble over the fact that the definition of an a priori fact says that if such a fact is true, we *could* know it independent of experience although we need not. But it is difficult, as Kripke (1972) points out, to know exactly what this reservation means. Does it mean that all a priori facts must be provable? If so, then we know from Gödel's famous theorem that not all necessary truths of mathematics are provable theorems. Hence by the provability criterion, not all necessary truths can be known a priori. On the other hand, the claim that a priori truths may be known by intuition rather than proof is essentially a nonargument until some cogent theory of intuition is given.

Thus there is good reason for believing that the conceptual categories of necessary truths and a priori facts are based on logically distinct notions. At least it is not at all clear that the difference is just a trivial matter of definition; their apparent distinction seems sufficiently real to require that anyone be taken to task who callously ignores it.

The importance of the foregoing discussion for present purposes is to provide just cause for tentatively accepting the claim that some a posteriori facts may indeed be necessary truths. At least this possibility cannot be rejected out of hand for the following reason: Presumably we have shown that it may be a mistake to identify a priori facts with necessary truths; therefore, this suggests that it may be equally mistaken to identify a posteriori facts with contingent truths. Furthermore, although perceptions reveal by definition a posteriori facts, there is no reason to assume that what they reveal must be contingent truths rather than necessary truths.

To return to our main topic: On purely logical or philosophical grounds, there is no reason to accept the skeptic's primary premise that what is known through perceiving must be considered, at best, contingent knowledge about the world. If not contingent, then no evidence is required to establish the "truths" of an animal's environment as revealed by perception; they could be true, as argued earlier, by force of existence (i.e., self-evident truths) rather than by force of argument. In other words, perceiving may be considered to reveal, in Leibniz's words: "the primary truths a posteriori, the primary truths of fact"—requiring—"no mediation between the understanding and its objects."

The Propositional and Nonpropositional Uses of the Term *Perception*

We have been pursuing a realism that would be agreeable to a committed realist. This section collects the arguments developed thus far and contrasts the propositional and nonpropositional uses of the term *perception*.

A careful distinction must be drawn between "seeing *that* a shimmering optical display over the hot desert sands *is* water" and "*seeing* water in the desert"; the former is the so-called propositional use of the term "seeing" and connotes the weighing of evidence, the drawing through inference of a conclusion, and the insight that the evidence is probable or conclusive support for the inferential claim. Thus this usage of the term "seeing *that*" (or, more generally, "perceiving *that*") is the *propositional* use of the term—a usage that connotes judgment and logically permits error to arise. The second sense of "seeing" involves no propositionizing at all; that is, it is in no sense judgmental or inferential and neither requires nor allows for probabilistic surmise from evidential support. Rather, "seeing water" (or, more generally, "perceiving *x*"), like water itself (or *x*), *is* a state of affairs or an existential fact about the world (including the "percipient" as part of that world).

Notice carefully, however, that the claim is that "seeing *x*" *is* a state of affairs that either *is* or *is not*, rather than a proposition that *may* or *may not* be affirmed by evidence. Let us call this latter locution, "seeing water" (or "perceiving *x*"), the nonpropositional use of the term. We can now formulate the contrast, separating the positions of indirect and direct realism with respect to the nature of perception in terms of the foregoing distinction: The indirect view assumes that perception necessarily takes the locutory form "sees that x is y" (e.g., sees that the shimmering display is water), which entails the identification of the act of perceiving with that of inferring, the propositional use of the term.

In sharp contrast to this indirect or phenomenalist view is the direct view, which assumes that perception necessarily takes the locutory from "sees x" *as it is* (e.g., sees water rather than seeing that x is water is a possibility, a resemblance). Thus the direct view, unlike the indirect view, identifies perceiving with an existential fact about the world (i.e., the percipient and its environment) rather than with an inferential conclusion. Under the direct view, the object perceived cannot be other than what it is, since to perceive it is to relate existentially to it; whereas under the indirect view, the object judged could conceivably be other than what it is taken to be. The former is an *experience* of what is, whereas the latter is a *surmise* of what is *from* an experience of what is.

Thus we must conclude that the indirect view of perceiving draws whatever truth and meaning it might have ultimately from the experience of what *is* and deviates into error, illusion, falsehood, or maladaptiveness whenever the judgmental act of surmise deviates in an unwarranted, invalid way from the experience of what is. In short, "perceiving that x resembles y" is true and meaningful whenever it correctly draws on "perceiving x" and is false whenever it abridges that direct experience by unwarranted inference. That is, the propositional use of the term *perception* is dependent upon the nonpropositional use of the term for its semantics. The problem that must now be resolved is twofold: First, can we be certain that the nonpropositional sense of perceiving ever occurs; and second, if it does occur, can we be assured that it must be a direct experience of what exists rather than an indirect experience of what is surmised from evidence about whatever exists? Let us consider the last question first.

If our judgments are to be based on what exists, then there must exist an experience of what does in fact exist; otherwise there would be no way even in principle to gather evidence in support of the judgment. We submit that judgments about which no evidence even in principle can be forthcoming are both meaningless and irrelevant to the percipient's ongoing relationship to its world (e.g., its actions). Such a view trivializes the role of reason. If one's judgment that x is water does not necessarily entail circumstances under which x as water constrains one's ongoing experiences in a way specific to x being distinctively water (e.g., I can quench my thirst or drown in it), then x might just as well be said to be a powder puff, a scorpion, or nothing at all. Hence, if there is to be the possibility of knowledge (propositional or otherwise), there must exist experiences that provide evidential bridges between *knowing* and *doing* or between knowing and *being done to*. Knowing or believing must be efficacious; it cannot be vacuous. By definition, assertions that pertain to null experiences are not more than empty wishes or imaginings. A theory of knowledge based entirely on such effete concepts or judgments would be a denial of realism and a degenerate solipsism.

Given that experiences of what is the case must to *some extent* be possible if knowledge is to be possible, it only remains to show that these must be perceptions rather than judgments; that is, they must be perception in the nonpropositional sense rather than perception in the propositional sense. But this conclusion is necessarily entailed by the assumption of realism required to preserve the efficacy of judging as already argued. If *judgment* is to be possible (as opposed to merely wishing or imagining), then experience of the states of affairs of the world must necessarily exist. Anything that necessarily exists *is* a state of affairs of the world rather than merely a judgment *about* those states of affairs. Hence perception, unlike judgment, by being a direct experience of some state of affairs, is itself a state of affairs and must be counted among the existential facts that necessarily constitute the world. On the other hand, a judgment is merely an experience *about* but not *of* the world. In other words, judgments may be true or false and, therefore, refer to contingent facts of the world rather than necessary facts.

A different but related point: We may assume that knowledge of the world (i.e., realism) is possible without entailing that judgments exist, but we may not do so without assuming that (direct) perceptions exist. For instance, we can imagine situations in which we experience what *is* but do so without (consciously or unconsciously) judging it to be true—that is, without inferring that our experience *corresponds* somehow to what exists. Moreover, we can also assume that lower species of life are sensitive to or irritated by aspects of the world without being able to venture judgments or draw inferences at all. Therefore we must conclude that direct experiences may exist even though judgments or *indirect* experiences do not.

But now we come to the main point of the argument: Judgments do *in fact* exist, for we know of cases where we judge or believe it proper to say others judge. But if judgments contingently exist, then perceptions must necessarily exist. This follows from two things: first, the assumption that realism is possible; and second, from the argument given earlier showing that for realism to be meaningful and judgments nonvacuous, non-(epistemically) mediated perception of the world must exist. To deny the directness of experiences of the world, what we called the ''nonpropositional'' use of the term *perception,* leads to a hopeless regress where judgments feed parasitically off other judgments, which ultimately feed off nothing. For knowledge to be ''living,'' judgments must ultimately draw sustenance directly from the world. That is, whether judgments are true or false, meaningful or meaningless, depends upon the existence of perceptual experiences that directly draw upon the ''facts'' of the world.

Thus, since direct perceptual evidence is required to adjudicate judgments, perception cannot be in any sense judgment (propositional). That which is nonpropositional is not *about* anything, but *of* something. Perception, then, is *of* the world—an existential fact of it; but although judgments are *about* the world, they either do or do not correspond to such facts. This means that perception is of *necessary a posteriori* facts whereas judgments, insofar as they relate to the world at all, are about *contingent a posteriori* facts.

In summary, we see from the foregoing argument that nonpropositional perception, as a direct experience of existential facts, is a necessary consequence of the possibility of realism. The argument has brought together three distinct lines of thought in the present chapter:

1. The claim that the truth or meaning of perception necessarily derives from the force of existence rather than the force of argument.
2. The claim that perception is a source of necessary a posteriori knowledge about the world.
3. The claim that perception, unlike judgment, is *of* the actual (necessarily true) world rather than *about* possible (only contingently true) worlds.

To deny any of these claims is, we believe, tantamount to undercutting the foundations to a realistic theory of knowledge and thereby flies in the face of the claim that animals live adaptively because they experience their worlds truly.

ECOLOGICAL PSYCHOLOGY AS A POSSIBLE-WORLDS SEMANTIC

This final section considers the logical and semantic grounds for the ecological thesis already identified—a thesis that asserts that the objects of reference and of experience may be described in the same theoretical vocabulary, thereby making commensurate two concepts traditionally treated as dualistic. However, no attempt is made to resolve the issue of metaphysical dualism by proposing either a reduction of one category to the other, as in the case of physical reductionism, or by proposing that the two dichotomous categories be subsumed under a third neutral category, as in the case of neutral monism. Instead, our tactic is to show that rather than psychology and physics being incommensurate parts of a dualism, they are distinct but complementary, and hence quite commensurate, poles of a *duality* (Shaw & Turvey, 1981; Turvey & Shaw, 1979).

The crucial distinction to be emphasized is that the parts in a dualism are not only distinct but logically independent; although the poles of a duality may be distinct, they are reciprocally dependent—with one pole drawing on the other for its meaning and identity. Thus, the view that psychology and physics are logically independent is consistent with the notion of an animal–environment dualism; as contrasted with the ecological approach, which—in the attempt to treat psychology and physics as two different but mutually dependent perspectives of the same object, the ecosystem—is consistent with the notion of an animal–environment synergy (Turvey & Shaw, 1979).

A chief difficulty that the ecological approach must overcome is the semantic prejudice that there is only one possible grain of analysis to be applied to physical reality and that such analysis is necessarily provided by physics. There is a strong propensity to believe that the description of things at the atomic and molecular scale is metaphysically more real and scientifically more natural than their description at a level of ordinary perceptual experience. This bias holds sway in spite of the obvious fact that the furniture we sit upon, the ground we walk upon, the food we eat, the people we embrace, and the tools we handle provide a greater feeling of substance, solidity, and support than can be adequately reflected in the popularized physicist's image of them as probabilistic clouds of swirling particles.

Clearly, here, the grain of theory is at odds with the grain of experience; yet there exists a strong and pervasive prejudice in favor of the theoretical physicist's picture of reality, which emerges whenever most people are forced to choose the scientifically most accurate description of an animal's environment. Theoretical biology was once solely concerned with macrophenomena (e.g., flora and fauna). But with the advent of electron microscopy, it has rapidly descended to microlevels of analysis, leaving the coarser-grained phenomena by default to ethologists, agriculturalists, and animal psychologists.

Furthermore, coarser-grained analyses are typically considered superficial, inaccurate, and, perhaps, at best practical or heuristic; whereas finer-grained analyses, by contrast, are considered deeper, more accurate, and, hence, more scientific. The ecological orientation disagrees with this assessment and proposes instead that "most scientific" should be considered synonymous with "most appropriate" rather than with "most fine grained." Indeed, detail and degree of precision are relative terms, being attributes of analysis whose grain is most revealing. A coarser-grained analysis that captures the coherence of a phenomenon (e.g., as in the parable of clapping hands in the introduction) is to be scientifically preferred over a finer-grained analysis that dips so far beneath the surface as to destroy the integrity of the phenomenon studied (see Fowler & Turvey, Chap. 1, this volume).

Thus a basic tenet of ecological psychology is the suggestion that we trade in the microstructuralism of these sciences (recognizing while doing so, however, that they may provide quite valid analyses of the causal support of psychological processes) in favor of a more pragmatic, macrofunctionalism that preserves the integrity of the animal–environment synergy (see Fitch & Turvey, 1978; Fowler & Turvey, 1978; Turvey & Shaw, 1979).

Affordances and Effectivities

In order to avoid the dualism reflected in the assumptions of intractable nonspecificity and the incommensurability of natural kinds, appropriate new categories must be fashioned. A first step is to describe the "physical" dimensions of the world within which the animal has evolved relative to the animal's capacity for activity. These dimensions are what Gibson (1977) calls *affordances*. Thus, places that *afford* locomotion or objects that *afford* grasping are regarded as being values on perceptually relevant dimensions, in contrast to the more usual use of color and bidimensional form as basic dimensions underlying perception. The concept of an affordance relation is a treatment of meaning; it is intended as a way of describing the surrounding surfaces and substances in animal-*relevant* dimensions, so that an individual animal does not subjectively have to *add* meaning or value to that which is "merely" physical.

Gibson's notion of an affordance may be schematized as follows (see Turvey & Shaw, 1979): *A situation or event X affords action Y for animal Z on occasion O if certain relevant mutual compatibility relations between X and Z obtain.* With Gibson we would like to maintain that animals perceive affordances rather than animal-neutral dimensions. What we hope to emphasize in this schematic sharpening of Gibson's idea is that an affordance is not merely a mapping of surface and substance states onto animal states—that is, a two-term or binary relation. Rather, an irreducible minimum of three logical terms is required to define an *affordance*—a term that references surfaces and substances, an animal activity term, and a term indicating relevant dimensions of compatibility. A major task is to understand how the set of affordances—the affordance structure—of an ecosystem might be specified; the spirit of such an inquiry is essentially geometric and would result in a theory of *what* there is to be perceived by a particular animal.

An ecological definition of an environment as a set of affordances is very similar to a functional definition; namely, it makes no attempt to answer the ontological question of what the environment *is* in any absolute sense (i.e., metaphysics), but rather attempts to answer the pragmatic question of what an environment means to an animal. The answer given is that it means what an animal can in principle do or is in practice constrained from doing in that environmental context. It is insufficient, however, to focus on the question of what the environment is as construed with reference to the animal (i.e., affordances); there remains the question of what an animal might be when construed with reference to an environment. Both these questions must be considered, because the bidirectionality of the mutual (reciprocal) compatibility relation imputed to hold between animals and their environments demands it (Turvey & Shaw, 1979).

Gibson (1977) asserts: "Subject to revision, I suggest that *the affordance of anything is a specific combination of the properties of its substance and its surfaces taken with reference to an animal* [p. 67]." When generalized, this is to say that the environment from an ecological viewpoint (but not from a physical, biological, psychological, or metaphysical one) is a complex set of relationships among various affordances—what was called an *affordance structure* earlier.

Correspondingly, a similar ecological definition is required of an animal as the complementary component to an environment in the ecosystem. Therefore, it is suggested that an animal consists of a complex set of relationships among effectivities, or what might be called an *effectivity structure*. What is meant by the concept of an effectivity? The following definition is proposed; it complements the definition of affordance that Gibson provides. We suggest that subject to revision, an effectivity of an animal (or human) *is a specific combination of the functions of its tissues and organs taken with reference to an environment.* The notion of effectivity may be schematized as follows: An *animal* Z *can effect action* Y *on an environmental situation or event* X *on occasion* O *if certain relevant mutual compatibility relations between* X *and* Z *obtain* (See Turvey & Shaw, 1979).

It seems to us that the laws of learning and memory, as they emerge, will have to be written in complementary terms not unlike affordance and effectivity. Consider the contemporary scene in animal learning theory. The belief that guided the earlier and well-known attempts to establish a theory of learning was that there were certain to-be-discovered principles of learning that could be applied uniformly and universally across all kinds of learning and all kinds of species. We might say that these principles were thought of as context-indifferent, activity-indifferent, and species-indifferent. Thus learning might be due to contiguity or to reinforcement.

It was this article of faith that justified attempts to build a general theory of learning by studying only one response system in one animal. That article of faith has been rudely shaken. The current impression (Bolles, 1975; Hinde & Stevenson-Hinde, 1973; Seligman & Hager, 1972) is that learning depends in very important ways upon the kind of animal that is being considered, the kind of behavior that is required of it, and the kind of situation in which the behavior occurs. On the current view, it is an empty claim that learning is a function of contiguity or reinforcement contingencies.

A brief overview must suffice to make the point. The celebrated Garcia effect (Garcia & Koelling, 1966) is that an animal can rapidly learn to avoid a situation that made it ill even where the situation and the onset of illness are not temporally proximate. Importantly, the situation the animal learns to avoid under these conditions is not species-neutral: For the rat, the situation must be chemically distinct; for the quail, it appears that the situation must be distinguished by a dimension that is detected by sight rather than by taste (Wilcoxon, Dragoin, & Kral, 1971).

Avoidance behavior, of course, has always been a thorny issue for learning theory, especially where the theory emphasized reinforcement; there is no reinforcement that can be explicitly defined, and an appeal to the nonoccurrence of, say, shock is logically embarrassing since a good many other things besides shock do not occur. What makes learning to avoid an especially recalcitrant puzzle is that there appears to be no consistency in the patterning of the experimental contingencies relating to the learning (Bolles, 1970, 1975). Bolles (1970, 1975) pinpoints the required avoidance behavior as the all-important factor. But to require of an animal in a given experimental setting an avoidance behavior with a high operant rate or one that is successful in some other setting is not to guarantee that the avoidance behavior will be learned without difficulty, if at all. More precisely, what is important is the relation between the given situation and the given avoidance behavior. A behavior easily learned by a given animal in one situation may be unlearnable, or at least very difficult to learn, by that animal in another situation. Situation and avoidance behavior are coimplicative, and the ease with which an experimenter-chosen behavior is learned depends—or so runs the argument of Bolles (1970, 1975)—on whether the animal perceives the situation as implicating the chosen behavior.

To return to the Garcia effect: It is a phenomenon that contravenes the premise of equivalence of associability—that any conditioned stimulus can be connected with any unconditional stimulus and that any response can be connected with (modified by) any reinforcement (Seligman, 1970). For the rat, illness contingent on bright and noisy water does not result in avoidance of the water. Learning, it would seem, is not a general-purpose plasticity. On the contrary, learning is a special-purpose plasticity that operates within the constraints defined by the relation between a species and its environment. Echoing this theme, the coimplication noted earlier—of situation and avoidance behavior—cannot be species-indifferent; the behavior implicated by a given situation for a given species of animal will not necessarily be the behavior implicated by that situation for another, different species of animal.

Consider the following curious observation. Where either food or the song of conspecifics is contingent on the behavior of pecking a key, a chaffinch will learn the behavior with respect to the food contingency but not with respect to the song contingency. In contrast, the chaffinch will learn to perch at a particular location with conspecific singing as the reinforcement but not with food as the reinforcement (Stevenson-Hinde, 1973). In the light of this observation and others, it is easy to venture the claim (Bolles, 1975) that "the proper understanding of learning requires us to know something about an animal's ecological niche; we must know how it solves its problems [p. 176]."

In part, this brief aside into contemporary puzzles in animal learning theory is intended to shore up, with distinctively different conceptual materials, the claim that psychology must be ecological. What is meant by this claim can now be summarized.

The theoretic language required for launching the enterprise of ecological psychology should be one in which the terms used to describe the animal's environment as perceived and acted upon (i.e., its econiche) constitute an "ecologized" physics whereas those terms used to describe the animal as a perceiver and actor constitute an "ecologized" biology. Ecological psychology will be the common language where the terms of an ecological physics and an ecological biology are symmetrical and reflexive—that is, where descriptions of the animal are always given in reference to the environment and those of the environment, in reference to the animal.

"Possible-Worlds" Semantics

The "possible-worlds" approach to perception and action constitutes a radical departure from traditional conceptions, which are implicitly based upon correspondence theories of semantics and truth. In classical logic, a statement is evaluated as meaningful or anomalous, or as true or false, based on how well that statement corresponds to some specified state of affairs that obtains. The statement "Snow is white" is meaningful if and only if there is an object, snow, that has properties such that the designated property, whiteness, might conceivably be found among its property set; similarly, the statement is true if such a corresponding property *is* indeed found among its property set.

By contrast, the "possible-worlds" approach evaluates the meaning and truth of statements about the world in terms of their coherence when elaborated, rather than their correspondence to isolatable simple facts about the world somehow objectively ascertained. This approach has the virtue of avoiding the need to evaluate prematurely the meaning or truth of statements, before an internally consistent scheme of description is attained. Admittedly, the "possible-worlds" approach, unlike the correspondence approach, does not promise to deliver immediate assessments of the truth or falsity of statements considered in isolation by somehow comparing them against observed facts of existence. Rather, it offers only a conception of meaning or truth based upon a very carefully constructed model that exhibits coherence in the account given of reality, much the same as a cogent legal case can be built upon circumstantial evidence. In other words, it produces no absolute, objective account of what is true or meaningful but produces an account to be evaluated against other accounts to see which is most "fit" to survive at advanced stages of elaboration. The view that can incorporate the most consistently meaningful statements wins the crown of reality.

Thus the difference between the two approaches that is important for our purposes is the implicit dependence of the correspondence approach, as opposed to the coherence approach, on some means of objectively determining what states of affairs may obtain in the world to which the correspondence of the statements holds. The only method that ultimately holds is ostensive specification, which depends by definition upon the establishment of perceptual rapport between the content of the statement in question and the relevant state of affairs. But clearly, the existence of semantic correspondence relationships between statements and states of affairs necessarily depends upon an epistemic act that establishes perceptual rapport with existing states of affairs, a process typically termed *ostensive specification*. Thus the correspondence approach to semantics is ultimately circular: It assumes ostensive specification to get correspondence going and then attempts to explain it by correspondence. Thus, it follows that the correspondence that depends upon perception *qua* ostensive specification cannot itself provide an explanation of perception as a fundamental epistemic act.

Consequently, some other logical approach to modeling reality is needed that does not depend on perception as an ad hoc or a priori means of assessing reality. The technique required must be a posteriori like perception but must be existentially more primitive than perception. In other words, it must be the means of rooting perceptual experiences in existing states of affairs without prejudging the nature of those states of affairs prior to experience. As argued earlier, the required approach should rest on the force of existence to shape experiences (knowledge from acquaintance) rather than on the force of argument (knowledge from description). This means in the final analysis that the coherence of consistent statements that may be offered as surrogates of experience by the "possible-worlds" approach must ultimately *be* the experience of the content; where meaning and truth by correspondence can only be argued for indirectly and after the fact of experience, coherence of experience is direct and sui generis of meaning and truth. We experience the meaning of perceptions and the felicity of actions as we experience the cogency of a mathematical proof—by its coherence, not by how it corresponds to something outside itself.

This direct apprehension of the experience of reality as coherence is much like our ability as native speakers of a language to recognize what utterances are grammatical and therefore capable of meaning and what utterances are ungrammatical and meaningless. In this sense, taking a leaf from Chomsky's book of syntax, we can view the "possible-worlds" semantics as an attempt to provide a theory of one's intuitions—as a native of the real world—of what is real, just as a formal grammar is meant to provide a theory of one's intuitions—as a native speaker—of what is grammatical in English. It is the native's intuition of its species' reality, like a speaker's intuition of his or her language, that is to be explained by the "possible-worlds" approach. This is the primary datum for what is real and cannot be abrogated by perception, since perception is founded upon the act of apprehending and comprehending this datum.

The remainder of this part presents a more detailed discussion of the "possible-worlds" approach to semantics.

The idea of a "possible-world" can be grasped intuitively through an analogy. We might call a "complete novel" a set of sentences in some given language that is consistent but that cannot be enlarged without making it inconsistent. A "possible-world" would be described by such a complete novel. Usually, however, "possible-worlds" are less than completely specified; such partial specification, nevertheless, can be very useful so long as what they purport to describe is really *possible*. Hintikka (1969) has called such partial descriptions of "possible-worlds" "model sets"; in this chapter they are referred to, more simply, as "semantic contexts."

In the case of virtual objects—that is, energy displays that produce spontaneous effects in experience that resemble those effects typically produced by other displays—we might speak of "possible-worlds" as the different semantic contexts or world situations that must be assumed to make each appearance of the virtual object consistent with the appearances of other virtual objects. Thus in all cases where an energy display resembles other energy displays, the resemblance relation specifies—as a self-presenting fact of experience—"possible-worlds" in which the percipient may be living. Such "possible-worlds" have no necessary existential import but are mere *virtual* worlds that resemble the world to the extent that they remain internally consistent when elaborated. The elaboration takes place through actions or inferences—but with the former having power to compel through the force of existence whereas the latter receives its power from force of argument.

The *real* world, as opposed to a virtual or merely possible world, is defined as whatever remains consistent *across* all "possible worlds" after they have been elaborated by action (or reason). By definition, we speak of *right* action (like right reason) as the activity the percipient-as-actor engages in whenever the elaboration increases the consistency of a selected "possible-world" over the others—that is, when the agent's actions are consistent with the interpretation of the world that his or her primary perceptual experiences entail. Thus, the *real* world, properly speaking, is not a possible-world per se but a set of resemblances that is invariant over all possible-worlds. The real world garners existential import from the consistent or mutually compatible properties that hold across all "possible-worlds." In this sense, ecologically valid knowledge an animal has of its world is knowledge of these "transworld" consistencies discovered through perceptions and elaborated through actions. For instance, an open-minded traveler on the desert who experiences a virtual object, or objects, disambiguates the situation by following appropriate patterns of action; namely, the individual elaborates the possible-world specified by what may be the case, if the virtual object should prove real, by walking toward the shimmering optical display and investigating it.

The shimmering optical display is an existential fact, a primary fact of experience, or necessary a posteriori truth and, therefore, must be a property of all possible-worlds—that is, all the consistent semantic contexts specified by taking the virtual object to be a real object and acting toward it accordingly (e.g., walking toward the water). The resemblance of the shimmering optical display to water is also a datum of primary experience and cannot be impeached. What can be impeached by further experiences is the premature judgment that the display *is* indeed water. To be real water, all primary experiences of the virtual object, arising through elaboration by appropriate actions (e.g., the primary experiences of splashing in the water or drinking it), must be consistent with the affordance structure of water. That is, the actions specified in reference to the virtual object of experience must be felicitously realized. The effectivities that *are* the percipient-as-actor must be logically consistent with the affordances of the object specified to the actor-as-percipient. The *real* world of the animal-as-actor/

percipient is designated by the mutual compatibility, or reciprocal consistency (or *duality*, in the technical sense), between the affordance structure of the possible (or virtual) world (that only partially specified semantic context) and the effectivity structure of the animal by whom the affordances are noticed and acted upon.

Of course not all objects of experience at every moment get disambiguated by right action; sometimes the actions are wrong or irrelevant. Thus we must recognize the fact that since experience is broader than perception, the world we truly experience—and to some extent know—is never fully specified nor completely disambiguated from other "possible-worlds." The validity of knowledge an animal possesses of its world that determines the quality of life rests upon the possibility of identifying true (logically consistent) knowledge with useful knowledge (i.e., knowledge that prompts right action). Consequently, humans—like other animals—live in the seams between all "possible-worlds," a realm from which actions unfold previous unseen paths into new semantic contexts. Hence, under this view, truth is dynamic rather than static, for facts struggle for existence in the same competitive way that species do.

"Possible-worlds" that reveal inconsistencies when elaborated through appropriate actions receive no ontological status. But this does not prevent them from being the intentionally specified object (semantic contexts) of false belief. This must be allowed because false propositions may still entail meaningful propositions and, therefore, require some kind of context of interpretation and evaluation. However, by definition, false belief cannot arise from perception or memory, since it gives rise to inappropriate action whereas they do not. For instance, a delusional system constructed as a "possible-world" in the imagination of a paranoid schizophrenic reflects true fears and has real connections with the patient's prime facts of experience. But such delusions do not constitute knowledge, since they lead inevitably to inconsistencies when elaborated more fully. Thus possibility of inconsistency is predicated on the ability of the real world to intrude existentially into the possible-world of the schizophrenic and make its presence known in such a way as not to be ignored or doubted. That the reality of such intrusions is so recognized by the patient as both salient and indisputable is evidenced in the fact that he or she tends to treat it as a real threat to be acted against. In other words, the patient seeks right action, usually in the form of aggressive acts, by which to ward off the intrusion or, failing this, to redesign the delusional system to accommodate it.

So are we all, animals and humans, like the paranoid in this one regard: We feel the intrusive force of the real world as primary facts of experience, which can neither be ignored nor doubted. Doubting, contrary to some opinion, is not at all a psychological attitude as easily assumed as others—say, as lying. It is an immense burden to be lifted, not a cloak to be put on and off lightly. Doubt, too, must be earned; it is never a gift. Doubt arises because the experienced inconsistencies of actions intrude upon us with the force of existence, not merely the force of argument. We cannot doubt the import of our perceptual experiences because we cannot ultimately fail to acknowledge them in our deeds.

Token-Reflexive Expressions: A Modal Operation for the Semantic Schema of Perception and Action

To approach an understanding of the relation between affordances and effectivities, we pursue the preceding assumption—that perceiving is a modal operator that qualifies propositions asserting facts about the world—and the assumption, which we now add, that action is a modal operator of like kind. Following Hintikka's (1969, 1975) suggestion and consonant with the theme of the immediately preceding part, these modal operators will be viewed as involving a reference, albeit tacit, to more than one "possible-world." Our hypothesis is that perceiving and acting, as modal operators, qualify the same schemata of variables. They do so in reciprocal, or complementary, ways; moreover, they are only intentional in a very special non-Brentano sense. Where intentionality in Brentano's sense referred to some kind of inexistent, immanent object, perception and action operators refer to the same object over all "possible-worlds." That is, the object they refer to is a *necessary truth*. (A contingent truth is one that is *not* true in all "possible-worlds" but is true in at least one.)

Our primary task, then, in this part and the next is to introduce a way of talking about perception and action that befits the hypothesis just forwarded and that, on elaboration, promises to dispel the problem of incommensurability of natural kinds. Let us consider again the notion of affordance and, at the risk of being repetitive, why a notion of this kind is necessary and unavoidable from the perspective of a commitment to realism.

The assumed dualism of animal and environment seduces the perceptual theorist to distinguish between what a thing *is* and what a thing *means*; a thing that simply *is* inhabits the physical domain, whereas a thing that *means* inhabits the mental domain. In this vein, Koffka (1935) distinguished between the geographical world (noumena) and the behavioral world (phenomena) and proposed the latter as the framework for behavior. Thus, Koffka (1935) would say that a handle "invites" or "demands" grasping. But a physical description of the surface and substance properties that constitute the material nature of a handle contains no animal-referential or activity-relevant terms; the physical dimensions used to describe the handle are animal-indifferent. So what is the status of the characteristics of surfaces and substances to which behavior is in reference? Since they are not characteristics or dimensions of the geographical or physical environment, they must be dimensions of the behavioral or phenomenal environment. The claim is that the dimensions of surfaces and substances that behavior is in reference to *are not ordinary physical dimensions* and therefore *are not real dimensions*. These dimensions that invite behavior owe their very existence, on Koffka's (1935) reasoning, to an animal's needs. Thus a configuration of surface and substance properties (that make up a handle) has the character of being grasp-able only when an animal needs to grasp it; a mailbox, Koffka would say, invites letter mailing only when there is someone in its vicinity who needs to mail a letter; and so on. Here we have, in plain language, the incommensurability of natural kinds: The reference object, the mailbox as an object described in physi-cal terms, is logically distinct from the intentional object, the mailbox as an object that invites a particular behavior. And though the reference object may have (for a phenomenalism of Koffka's kind) an existence independent of percep-tion, the intentional object cannot.

From the perspective of a commitment to realism, the foregoing conclusions are anathema. They can be avoided, however, by taking the following as a fundamental precept for realism: The dimensions of configurations of surfaces and substances that behavior is with respect to may not be ordinary physical dimensions, in that conventional physical language fails to describe them; but they are, none the less, real dimensions. It would seem that conclusions opposed to realism arise from describing the reference object in a physical language that is committed to a reality but is noncommital or neutral with regard to animals as epistemic agents, and from describing the intentional object in a phenomenal language that is noncommittal on reality but *is* agent oriented. Another way of putting this distinction is that the physical language is in the impersonal third person (*it* causes *it* to happen; *these* things caused *these* things to occur), whereas the phenomenal language is in the personal, first-person singular (*I* had such and such an experience when *I* was in such and such a situation)(Shaw & Pittenger, 1977). This distinction, we can appreciate, is in the spirit of animal-environment dualism. What is needed is a *single* theoretical language—in the spirit of animal-environment synergy (Fitch & Turvey, 1978; Turvey & Shaw, 1979)—that manages to incorporate both the objectivity of the physical language and the agent orientation of the phenomenal language.

We see, in short, that a concept such as affordance is not optional; rather, it is mandated by a commitment to realism. That commitment also mandates that the affordance of a given thing is always there to be perceived. An affordance exists as a real property of the ecosystem and not by virtue of its being perceived; nor does the affordance of something change with a change in the animal's needs (see Gibson, 1977). What does change with an animal's needs is the *attensity* or perceptual salience (Shaw & McIntyre, 1974) of an affordance, its likelihood of being attended to. In sum, at any given time, a configuration of surface and substance properties may afford several behaviors for a given animal; which behavior occurs (which affordance is individuated) depends on the occasion in which the animal finds itself—that is, whether it is hungry, afraid, involved in nest building, etc.

We can now partially anticipate the task that the present part and the next must address if the hypothesis advanced at the outset of this part is to be supported and a commitment to realism preserved. In the schematic sharpening of the affordance notion already given, four terms were identified: a term referring to an aspect of the surroundings, a term referring to the animal, a term referring to the mutual compatibility between the preceding two terms, and a term referring to the occasion. (We take these first three terms to be irreducible and the fourth term as a partitioning on the set of mutual compatibility relations.) In perceiving an affordance, an animal perceives a relationship—a symmetry—between its action capabilities and the properties of the surfaces and substance(s) of an aspect of its surroundings. More formally, in perceiving an affordance, an animal perceives, as a single particular, the complex coordination of the four terms identified in the foregoing. By the realist program, this perceiving is unmediated. What is needed, therefore, is a way to model perception as an act that directly apprehends the affordance schema.

Let us proceed with an attempt to provide a modal operation for *noticing* as a self-referenced or *self-directed* act of *ostensive specification* after due consideration of the italicized terms. From a realist point of view, to perceive something is to notice that it exists; to notice something, however, is not logically equivalent to *perceiving* that it exists—although it is necessarily the case that whatever the object, it must exist before it can be noticed. All this is to say that perceiving x entails that x exists; similarly, noticing x entails that x exists; but *noticing* does not necessarily entail *perceiving,* although *perceiving* necessarily entails *noticing.* Thus *perceiving* is *noticing* of some special kind, not to be confused with *noticing* of other kinds (e.g., feeling one's pain, examining one's belief).

Ostensive specification is a technique for making another person, or animal, notice what you notice. A technique that fails to achieve this outcome, no matter how arduously applied, is not ostensive specification. If, as Wittgenstein suggests, you point to an object you wish your dog to retrieve and your dog—rather than retrieving the object—bites your finger, we say that pointing is not a technique that achieves ostensive specification for your pet. On the other hand, if your Irish setter points its nose toward the fallen duck and you notice where it is, then the dog's technique qualifies as ostensive specification. Noticing is ostensive specification sui generis; and as far as epistemic acts are concerned, there can be none that are logically more primitive.

However, noticing is neutral with respect to whether the source of control over the "pointer"—the vehicle for the ostensive specification—is based in the self (that is, is self-directed) or in the world. A loud noise or garish color points to itself by capturing one's attention, whereas a lost thimble in a haystack may require hours of arduous sifting to be noticed. Thus whatever means successfully objectify or segregate one thing from a background of other things is ostensive specification—whether self-initiated or other-initiated. Self-initiated means of ostensive specification are desires, wants, intents, interests, fears, and, perhaps, attitudes in general.

Let us consider how the evaluation of a special type of linguistic act, token-reflexive expressions, can be used to characterize a very special case of noticing—namely, the noticing of speech acts. This concept of token-reflexive speech acts is generalized in the following part to define the concept of *event-reflexive operations*—a set of operations that apply to acts of any sort and that, by doing so, provide exactly the kind of intentional schemes needed to characterize perceptual acts in general. Such intentional schemes are later shown to specify necessary a posteriori truths.

Semantically distinct individuals (particulars) are such things that none can be substituted in the place of another without altering the meaning of a token-reflexive expression. *Token-reflexive expressions* contain indefinite terms whose semantic evaluation requires the ostensive specification of a coordinated reference complex. This complex consists of the designation of the person using the expression and the designation of the circumstances (where, when, how, and why) under which the expression was used. For example, "I shall become President of the United States next election" is a token-reflexive expression requiring knowledge of who the speaker is (or was) and the circumstances under which it was uttered. If the "I" designates Abraham Lincoln and the assertion was made just prior to his successful presidential campaign, then the expression is both meaningful and true. On the other hand, if it was uttered by Thomas Dewey prior to his unexpected defeat by Harry Truman, then the expression is meaningful but *not* true. But if this token-reflexive expression was uttered by a cocky young politician whose boast to be his party's next candidate is unfounded, then it is both meaningless and false (in the sense that it has no reference to satisfy the intention). (It would be as if Polly Parrot or the speech synthesizer at Haskins Laboratories had said it with the qualification that the parrot and synthesizer are not capable of true speech acts.)

In general, token-reflexive expressions need not be self-reflexive in the preceding first-person sense; nor do they always refer to people; they may also be second-person assertions about other people, animals, inanimate objects, situations, or places. For instance, *this* book, *that* camel, *her* home, *its* number, etc., are all token-reflexive expressions whose meaning and truth value can only be evaluated when an operation is given (e.g., pointing, describing) that ostensively specifies *when, where* and *by whom* the expression is used.

In the earlier example, regarding the pledge to be president, the ostensive specification of who authored the statement (e.g., Lincoln, Dewey) was indirectly given by linguistic description. However, the ultimate validity of the stipulated evaluation must come from direct acquaintance with the occasion on which the expression was used. In a sense, token-reflexive expressions are like confessions; they must be witnessed to count as valid testimony. For this reason, such expressions are self-presenting in that the evidence for their proper evaluation *is* evident in their presentation. For instance, the reference for the ambiguous assertion "Pass me that!" is semantically *opaque* if you do not understand the circumstances under which and by whom the request is made. On the other hand, being a witness to the assertion, in the sense of understanding who is speaking and what is being pointed to, is to be privy to the information needed to evaluate the speech act. In this case we would say the reference of the token-reflexive expression is semantically *transparent* rather than opaque.

The meaning of the token-reflexive expression is ostensively specified in the very act by which it comes into being. And for this reason, to perceive this particular kind of speech act is to know what it means by the very force of its existence. A word of caution: The semantic content of such an expression, as a token-reflexive expression, does not refer to the proposition or propositions to which the expression may be affixed. For example, in the statement, "He confessed to the killing of his wife," we must distinguish the token-reflexive, "He confessed to it," which—whether true or not—cannot be evaluated simply by witnessing the confession since the truth or falsity of the confession rests on other grounds, such as: Was his wife actually killed? Or did he only imagine he killed her? Moreover, the portion of the statement containing the token-reflexive expression always entails an explicitly or implicitly defined modal prefix expressing a psychological attitude of the person uttering the proposition.

Notice that the ostensive specification, required to make transparent the otherwise opaque reference of token-reflexive expressions, directly entails the existence of both an agent (the person who utters the expression) and the semantic context in which the agent is inserted. This semantic context includes a designation of the *situation* (time and place) within which, and the *occasion* (psychological attitude) upon which, the expression was uttered or written. Thus, three variables must be stipulated in the evaluation of a token-reflexive expression: an *agent* variable, a *situation* variable, and an *occasion* variable. We refer to the complex coordination of these three variables as a *complex particular*.

The main point of the preceding discussion to be generalized, to account for the perception of a wide variety of events, can now be anticipated: The reference of a token-reflexive expression is to be evaluated in terms of a scheme of three semantic variables that, taken collectively, intentionally specify an object, a complex particular. This complex particular is therefore both the intentional object of the schema as well as its reference object; it is both that which is evaluated and that by which evaluation is given. In other words, the complex particular specified by a token-reflexive expression is *self-presenting* (it represents itself) rather than being representational (representing something outside itself).

Because of this property required for a person to evaluate a token-reflexive expression, it suffices that that person *notices* precisely who says what, about what, where, and when. No representational knowledge—say, as derived from memory or inference—is necessarily required for this task; perception alone suffices. But because perception can achieve, in a direct fashion, the evaluation of this special form of speech act, something important is revealed about its nature: Perception in the case of speech events is revealed to be *an act that directly apprehends a speech event as a complex particular*. Even more precisely, we can define *perception as an indexical act that ostensively specifies a self-presenting object* (the complex particular), *an object that is both its own intention and reference*. In this way perception can indeed be a source of necessary a posteriori truths about the world.

But are these primary facts of experience to be restricted to this admittedly peculiar type of speech act, or may they not extend over a wide range of ecologically significant events? In the next part, it is shown that indeed they can.

Event-Reflexive Operations: A Way of Satisfying the Ecological Thesis

Linguistic acts are but a particular kind of event. Hence token-reflexive expressions can be considered a special case of a more general class of event-reflexive operation, whose evaluation involves noticing self-presenting, complex particulars, which may or may not be speech acts. In this way, it may be argued *mutatis mutandis* that if perceiving provides necessary a posteriori truths about semantic evaluation of token-reflexive speech acts, then it may also provide such truths about other events—whenever circumstances make available perceptual information for ostensively specifying, to a properly attuned agent, the state of affairs in which and the occasion upon which the agent is presented with such information. For instance, the occasion upon which someone is hungry—that is, in a psychological attitude of DESIRING (x) where x is food—happens to be the situation in which the person also notices (i.e., indexes) that on the kitchen table there is both a piece of apple pie and a newspaper.

Under such circumstances, ceteris paribus, it is reasonable to argue that the intentional object, ostensively specified by the event-reflexive schema for the agent on the occasion in question (being a hungry person) and in the situation depicted (being in the kitchen, noticing the table and its contents), is that object whose reference (affordance structure) receives the highest attensity (i.e., when the *edibility* of the pie receives greater attensity than the *readability* of the newspaper). On the other hand, if the person's psychological attitude (occasion) had been different—say, one of boredom rather than hunger—then this attitude would selectively specify a different reference object to interpret the intention—namely, the newspaper, whose affordance structure (readibility) was more relevant (attensive) to the appropriate effectivity structure of the agent (i.e., piqued interest in acts that dispel boredom, such as reading).

Hence, in general, the intentional object of the schema—namely, a desire for something that dispels boredom or something that dispels hunger—is also the reference object, something that affords reading or something that affords eating. Notice, however, that although the intentional object specified by the schema takes an opaque reference (i.e., *something* that), the proper evaluation of the schema, through some form of ostensive specification (e.g., noticing the relevant properties of the situation), makes transparent the reference object with the affordance property (e.g., the *edible* object, the *readable* object) that satisfies the effectivity intended (e.g., the eating of something or the reading of something). Consequently, this allows for a very brief rendition of the pragmatic rule required to satisfy the ecological thesis: Ecologically valid knowledge of its environment arises for an animal whenever the animal acts in such a way (and circumstances permit) that a mutual compatibility is created between its effectivities and the affordances of the environment. These conditions will be found to prevail whenever the semantic schemata for perception and action, whereby the reference object (affordance structure) and intentional object (effectivity structure) are defined, *dually* specify one another.

The semantic scheme needed to specify ecologically valid knowledge of events in general is what may be called an affordance/effectivity schema and consists of a compounding of the *dual* schemata for perception and action as discussed earlier: X affords Y for Z, *and* Z effects Y on X, if and only if X and Z are mutually compatible in certain ways to be specified (i.e., specified as the values required of the agent, occasion, and situation variables for the appropriate compatibility relation to hold). Furthermore, since the variables implicated in the perception schema by which the reference object (affordance structure) is specified are the same as those implicated in the action schema by which the intentional object (effectivity structure) is specified, then the two semantic schemata and thereby the objects they specify, must be commensurate. We take this to mean that theoretical psychology, by being rendered an ecological science, has at its disposal a single language in which to describe perceptual experiences and the objects perceived. Ideally, this dissolves the traditional dualism in psychology and, consonant with the ecological thesis, lays to rest the perennial problem of the incommensurability of natural kinds.

Ecological Knowledge

Ecological knowledge is a qualified form of knowledge; it is neither metaphysical nor logically perfect. Because it is not logically perfect, a significant issue in the study of the specification of an environment for an organism is: "How much is enough?" The answer to this question should be sought within a theory of affordances and effectivities.

Consider the locution "Z perceives x" to be true, it is not incumbent upon Z to notice *every* characteristic of x. Indeed, perceiving an object cannot realistically require noticing every property of that object—an impossible task given that the property set for any real object is probably infinitely dense. Rather, what is called for is simply that Z notice certain *significant* properties of x. The troublesome term, of course, is *significant;* consequently, a theory of significant properties seems called for.

Essentialism is the metaphysical doctrine that purports that every object has essential, as opposed to accidental, properties that are both necessary and sufficient to its definition as a kind. A most popular theory of significance has been simply to endorse essentialism. Under this view, the perception of any object merely entails noticing that every property on the essential list is ostensively specified sui generis. This is tantamount to claiming that perception must provide knowledge of the objective properties of objects independent of any psychological attitude on the part of the percipient. Under such a view, it would not matter if the percipient Z were a human, a horse, or a hermit crab; if Z perceives x, then whoever or whatever Z may be does so by noticing the very same property list.

There is considerable evidence showing that various species of percipients do not perceive the same objects in the same way, and that even the same percipient does not perceive the same object in the same way on different occasions. Perception does not seem to be so cut and dried an activity but one that is modulated by evolution and by experience (what Gibson [1966] has called genetic preattunement and the "education of attention," respectively). Indeed such Platonism is anathema to the ecological thesis, since the latter proposes that psychological attitudes (such as fear, thirst, love, or anger) act as modal operators on the potentially infinitely dense property set of objects to ferret out the appropriate properties to be noticed on a given occasion.

Support for this ecological concern—namely, to keep the animal and its world bound together in a harmonious synergy—can be provided simply by considering the way the verb to perceive can be used (Chisholm, 1957). This verb is not at all like the verbs to carry, to own, or to contain. A truck cannot carry a box without carrying every part of the box; a baron cannot own a country estate without owning all of it; and a plot of land cannot contain a garden unless it contains every square inch of it.

The grammar of perceiving is rather like that of biting or inhabiting: A dog can surely bite a postman without biting every part of him, and a tribe of Indians can inhabit the state of Utah without inhabiting every nook and cranny of it. Similarly, if Z sees x, this does not require that Z see all of x or that Z perceive every characteristic of x. We say that the mother saw her child hiding behind the sofa when nothing more than the child's hand or foot was noticed. Clearly, a friend can truly be said to have seen his smiling, nattily dressed neighbor without having noticed whether his teeth were newly capped or what he wore.

To quibble that this is merely an imprecise manner of speaking suggests that the mother really noticed only a disjointed hand or foot without an owner, and that our friend saw his neighbor toothless and naked. Is it not more appropriate to say the mother saw the occlusion of her child by the sofa, and that our friend saw his neighbor with unspecified teeth and clothing? Amputated limbs and edentate mouths are totally distinct perceptions with property sets that include information for discontinuities and abrupt changes in texture gradients. Like public nakedness, the attensity of these properties of objects is so high that it is unlikely they would go unnoticed.

Thus significant properties of objects, as opposed to trivial ones, are those specifying the true nature of the objects to which they belong and that possess great attensity for the circumstances under which they are perceived. However, since these circumstances may vary, the property set of the object may be partitioned differentially by the psychologized attitude of the percipient. For example, a less concerned mother may not have noticed the childlike appendages behind the sofa; and a different friend, who is a fashion buff or a dentist, may have been quick to notice the wardrobe and cosmetic changes of his neighbor.

The ultimate criterion for whether Z perceives x is not how many properties of x that objectively define its essential nature are noticed, but what properties Z can notice that are appropriate to the nature of Z and the attitude Z assumes on a particular occasion with respect to x—say, on the occasion of being hungry, thirsty, cold, angry, lonely, bored, curious, and so forth. Again we see, as in the preceding parts, that for the ecological approach, the perceived object is functionally defined in reference to both the animal's nature and the particular psychological attitudes held, rather than being structurally defined in terms of so-called objective essences. What a collection of surface and substance properties means for a given animal is specific, in part, to the nature of the animal and what it intends and, in part, to the properties that can be noticed by the given animal. To reiterate, what is knowable ecologically is neither metaphysically nor logically perfect. To grasp the form of what is ecologically knowable, we consider doxastic logic an important branch of intensional logic, which studies the logic of belief acts, belief attitudes, and belief propositions.

Doxastic logic can be traced in its origins to Plato's dialogues, especially the *Meno* and *Theaetetus*, where the distinction between knowledge and belief are debated. Here we find some of the earliest discussions of the pragmatic doctrine that truth is what is *useful*. Earlier we argued that successful evolution, adaptation, and coping may not require that an animal or species have perfect perceptual knowledge of its surroundings but only that such knowledge be ecologically valid in the sense that it "works" to protect the animal from harm and to enrich its life appropriately. The criterion for determining what counts as ecologically valid knowledge therefore requires a pragmatic rule to specify the notion of "working." A prototype of such a rule was suggested by Plato in his original study of *doxa,* or opinion, in the later parts of the *Meno* dialogue (Ryle, 1967).

Socrates is portrayed as despairing of trying to prove that virtue is teachable and, consequently, is a kind of knowledge. He reminds Meno that in the course of daily affairs, correct opinion, or *doxa,* serves just as well as knowledge. For instance, the guide who only *thinks* that this is the road to Larissa but who is quite right gets us to Larissa as surely as one who actually knows it. Thus *doxa,* as correct opinion or true belief, is a form of pragmatic "knowledge" differing from true knowledge in that it can be shaken by criticism, conflicting evidence, authority, etc. Plato makes a great deal of this contrast, devoting much of the *Theaetetus* to its discussion.

It should be noted, however, that *doxa* is more general than our "opinion" of things; it also includes the case of seeming or appearing (e.g., APPEARS [x is y]). Moreover, the experience of a virtual object is a case of *doxa,* such as the appearance that the earth is flat, that the sun moves across the sky, that Necker cubes reverse, and so forth. Similarly, the convict who took the optical display to specify water, since he had no knowledge from that distance, was providing *doxa*. The fact that his opinion, unlike that of his unfortunate skeptical friend, was indeed proven true does not make it any less a case of *doxa*. Therefore, we consider *doxa* to be any case where evidence is insufficient to specify with logical certainty the nature of that referred to by the *doxa*.

The question that must be addressed with respect to ecological psychology is this: Is perception a case of correct *doxa*, or pragmatic ''knowledge,'' in the sense of the guide's true and useful opinion that *this* is the road to Larissa, or in the sense of the convict's true and useful opinion that the shimmering optical display *is* water? Or is it a case of philosophically certain knowledge, in the sense that the available information is logically sufficient (perfect) for making all ontological distinctions that can be made? Both questions are of course offered rhetorically since arguments have been given throughout the paper against both extreme views.

On the other hand, there is a nuance to Plato's concept of correct *doxa* that is not perfectly reflected in the translation of it as mere opinion. Correct *doxa* is not idle opinion that is fortuitously true, but connotes efficacious opinion that not only is true but is true for the right reasons—namely, that it conforms to reality at least to the extent that it motivates useful actions. The guide's correct *doxa* gets us to Larissa, or the thirsty optimist to an oasis, not merely by chance decision but by constrained and motivated choice. The guide does not randomly elect to set out for Larissa down the chosen road by mere happenstance, but chose this road because going down roads in this general region, rather than roads in another region, is more likely to lead to success than just sitting around idle or wandering aimlessly. Similarly, the thirsty convict pursues a course through the desert that is motivated by the existence of what might be water. He does not set out in random directions, nor does he randomly select between not seeking and seeking water. Not *to choose* to choose is a forced option, the alternative choice being death by thirst.

In all cases of correct *doxa*, choice is constrained rather than random; a choice is made under mitigating circumstances that direct opinion down paths of decision that are relevant to given goals. A ball park for constraining the formation of opinion is given, no matter how marginal the constraint might be. This ball park of constraint provides the semantic context, a ''possible-world,'' in which *doxa* may be logically interpreted with respect to relative standards of truth and meaning.

Doxa may or may not achieve pragmatically desirable outcomes, but unlike mere opinion, they are never totally irrelevant either. Thus *doxa* may not qualify as unmitigated knowledge; indeed it would be unwise even to call it *probable* knowledge (as some perceptual theorists might); but *doxa*, unlike fortuitously correct opinion, *may lead to* knowledge. The guide who thinks *this* is the road to

Larissa and acts upon that belief, like the thirsty man in the desert who seeks water in the direction of the shimmering optical display, is engaged in appropriate action that may result in knowledge; thus *doxa*, at least as opinion taken sufficiently seriously to be acted upon, is more likely to be validated or invalidated than the mere holding of idle opinion. More importantly, unlike idle opinion, correct or otherwise, where no actions necessarily follow, no "ball parks" of constraint obtain, and no "possible-worlds" are entered; the holding of *doxa* is relevant to the possible attainment of knowledge since if the entailed actions are appropriate, then knowledge is forthcoming.

Indeed, in the *Meno,* Plato has Socrates recognize the fact that correct *doxa* may, under appropriate circumstances, be transformed into knowledge:

> True opinions are a fine thing and do all sorts of good so long as they stay in their place, but they will not stay long. They run away from a man's mind, so they are not worth much until you tether them by working out the reason . . . Once they are tied down, they become knowledge, and are stable. That is why knowledge is something more valuable than right opinion. What distinguishes one from the other is the tether . . . so that for practical purposes right opinion [doxa] is no less useful than knowledge, and the man who has it is no less useful than the one who knows. (p. 571–82).

We have labored over these distinctions among correct *doxa*, merely true opinion and perfect knowledge, because the distinctions are crucial to an understanding of the special nature of ecologically valid knowledge, a form of knowledge that differs from mere correct opinion in the fact that like correct *doxa*, it can be "tied down" to a relevant semantic context—a "possible-world"—by means of a pragmatic principle of right action. Right action has the felicitous effect on correct *doxa* of bringing about a change in the existential circumstances of the agent (e.g., by reaching the desired goal), so that belief is transformed into knowledge—opaque references of beliefs are rendered transparent—whenever the effectivities of the person-as-actor are mutually compatible with the affordances of the situation experienced by person-as-percipient.

Thus ecological knowledge, like all forms of knowledge permitted under critical realisms, is trapped somewhere between totally perfect knowledge of noumena and mere opinion of phenomena. Ecological knowledge is no more than correct *doxa* in the sense of motivating pragmatically true (useful) action that leads to success as relatively defined in a given semantic context. But this is enough.

This ecological account of knowledge as correct *doxa*, defined relative to a given semantic context, is close, but not identical, to the pragmatist's doctrine that an idea or proposition is true if it "works" to achieve some warranted end. John Dewey (1916) illustrated it this way: A man lost in the woods uses his idea as a working hypothesis to guide his action. Not until he succeeds or fails to find his way home can he ascertain whether or not his idea is true. Thus by the pragmatist's account, *doxa* (e.g., a thought, perception, plan, belief, and so forth) is true in an instrumental sense only; it is true *if* it motivates actions that are felicitous to some desired or required end. This instrumental criterion for valid knowledge is close to the tenor we want for ecologically valid knowledge in one sense—namely, that right action is necessarily entailed by knowledge; but it is seriously inadequate in another sense—that having to do with how successful or right action should be defined.

Arthur O. Lovejoy (1908) criticized William James' (1907) pragmatic theory that truth is what works because the concept of "working" and being true do not seem logically synonymous. The Jews' belief in the coming of the Messiah *worked* in the sense that it sustained them and gave them hope as a people during hard times. But the belief did not work in a second sense because the Messiah failed to appear to save them. Thus the belief was useful but untrue.

Bertrand Russell (1910) raised the same criticism in a different way: That other people exist is a true proposition. However, this proposition is in no way entailed by the proposition that it is useful to believe that other people exist. As argued earlier, BELIEVE (*x is y*) is a contingent proposition that does not necessarily entail that *x is y*. Consequently, if the notion of ecologically valid knowledge is *true doxa*—and "true" here means *pragmatically* true (i.e., useful)—then the ecological program is in serious difficulty unless it can answer these criticisms of the pragmatic doctrine.

Again we try to show how the "possible-worlds" semantic of modal logic comes to our rescue. But let us recognize that Russell's and Lovejoy's criticisms are incisive and not to be extenuated; a serious rebuttal to their points is sorely needed if the ecological program is not to be stillborn. Such a rebuttal must demonstrate the tenability of ecologically qualified knowledge—namely, useful knowledge that, like Plato's correct *doxa,* is less than perfect but more than idle opinion and that springs from veridical perceptions and leads to felicitous actions.

But Plato's concept of *doxa* is peculiarly human. Thus we must depart from his treatment and show *doxa* to be appropriate propositional attitudes of animals as well as humans. Socrates' provocative claim that correct *doxa* "tied down by reason" becomes knowledge implies too narrow an anthropomorphic bias. If ecologically valid knowledge is to be possible for all species—the lowest to the highest in intelligence—then reason, at least of the human variety, can play no necessary role. Rather, we argue that since all that is needed to "tie *doxa* down"—and thus transform it into valid (ecological) knowledge—is appropriate action, an animal's perspective is just as valid for its circumstances as the human perspective is for his or her circumstances. All forms of ecological knowledge draw whatever validity they have from the force of existence rather than the force of argument (reason) and, in this sense, qualify as primary facts of experience, or necessary a posteriori truths.

Ecological Knowledge at Different Grains of "Possible-Worlds" Analysis

Ecological knowledge must be a nested affair since animals function adaptively at various levels of competence to survive and maintain health: Species evolve because they persist over generations; generations of animals survive because offspring adapt sufficiently well over lifetimes to become parents; lifetimes are traversed because they consist of shorter episodes in which individuals successfully cope with the demands of existence. Consequently, no single grain of analysis of an ecosystem has a monopoly on ecological knowledge; its validity must range over nested "possible-worlds," a Chinese-boxes arrangement of semantic contexts where the *truth* of one level may not be the *truth* of another level.

Thus let us consider the issue of how "possible-worlds" semantics may provide contexts of interpretation at more than a single grain of analysis. By our previous arguments, it should be clear that for ecological knowledge to be possible, the affordances of X must be commensurate with the effectivities of Z at *all* grains—that is, where X ranges from econiches to objects and Z from species to individuals on particular occasions, respectively. To illustrate this fact, consider three grains of analysis that are significant for ecological psychology: those of species, individuals, and distinct episodes of experiences.

The "possible-worlds" context for species refers to the distinct econiches they live in because of differences in genetic preattunement (i.e., evolution). An econiche is a partitioning of the world into affordances or "possible-worlds" of action and determines perceptual experiences that are invariant (or pragmatically true in the sense already described) over all members of a single species. The "possible-worlds" context of individual members of a species refers to how distinctive attensity values highlight particular configurations of affordances specific to subsets of individuals who possess the same skills, such as those who belong to the same language culture or profession, possess the same artistic talents or athletic abilities, and so forth. As already noted, Gibson (1966) has called such differential attunement to affordances by experience the "education of attention." And finally, there are the "possible-worlds" of episodes of experiences specified by the various psychological attitudes that arise on different occasions for the same individual, such as going from anger to hunger or from desiring to knowing.

In a purely abstract vein, we can consider all the foregoing cases as propositions that have been qualified by a modal operator, a propositional attitude, just as in our previous discussion of psychological attitudes; namely, for S OPERATOR (x), where S can be species, individual, or psychological state, OPERATOR is the appropriate intentional qualifier for the S involved (e.g., EVOLVES when S is a species, ADAPTS OR LEARNS when S is an individual, and KNOWS, BELIEVES, etc., when S is an individual involved in a particular situation on a given occasion). Here, of course, x refers to the intentionally specified propositional object—such as the action consequent required to specify the correctness or incorrectness of the *doxa* in question.

Whether a convenient formal notation can be worked out to capture these different grains of analysis for the "possible-worlds" (semantic contexts) in which animals live and learn remains to be seen; the differences, however, are no less real. The different grains of "possible-worlds" analysis specify some of the different types of knowledge attunement an animal may have with respect to its environment of nested perceptual information and action opportunity. Furthermore, it seems clear that a different modal operator must apply to the propositional descriptions of the animals' ecosystems considered at different grains of analysis. The emphasis here is on *ecosystem* rather than *environment* because: (1) each propositional description must be qualified by a pair of *dual* operators—one specifying the intentional object of perception (a "possible-worlds" of affordances) while the other specifies the intentional object of action (a "possible-worlds" of effectivities); and (2) the fact that the dual modal operators apply to the same propositional description of the environment to represent a single propositional attitude held by a single agent on a particular occasion guarantees that the perception and the action specified will be commensurate (mutually compatible) and that ecological knowledge is possible. It is in this sense that all the propositions in the domain of this ecological approach to psychology take the abstract form of an event-reflexive operator prefixed to a scheme of the three variables discussed earlier—namely, the situation, agent, and occasion variables.

We appreciate that without extensive elaboration, the foregoing discussion may itself be logically opaque; consequently, some degree of intuitive transparency may be gained by considering examples of "possible-worlds" semantic contexts defined at three different grains of analysis. Such illustrations should provide a glimpse of the formal relationships between these dual modal operators that any more extensive treatments must honor.

Illustrations

In addition to the points just mentioned, the cases discussed also serve to illustrate the relativity of ecological knowledge over species and to clarify the concept of error. It should be clear by now, however, that the ecological thesis does not preclude animals and humans from being mistaken about what their experiences truly mean where the available evidence is insufficient. On the other hand, the ecological thesis also admonishes us that all such experiences that entail incorrect *doxa* are a fortiori not perceptions, since perceptions necessarily entail correct *doxa*.

The first case illustrates why *doxa* that is correct for one species may not necessarily be correct for another; and, similarly, why *doxa* that is "globally" correct for a species, in the sense that it entails a pragmatic principle that has long-range validity for every member of the species, may not always entail correct decisions at a more local level where the individual members must deal with short-range, variable environmental contingencies.

Case 1: The Frog and the Fly.   A frog that preys on flying insects, say houseflies, is genetically preattuned to strike at any small, dark object that darts within range of its sticky tongue. However, when the object attacked is not a housefly but an experimenter's decoy, then it is tempting to say that the frog misperceives or has made a perceptual error. The ecological thesis would disagree with this assessment, for the frog does not misperceive in this situation nor engage in judgmental error of any kind. Indeed, it is not even proper to say that the frog experiences the experimenter's decoy as a *virtual* object because of its noticed resemblance to actual houseflies.

The experience of a virtual housefly entails that the frog notice a resemblance between two real things—the small, dark, darting object and a particular type of flying insect. Whereas the former has been shown to be a perceptual object within the possible-world of experience for frogs (Lettvin, Maturana, McCulloch, & Pitts, 1959), the latter most likely is not. The articulate level of detail that humans use to differentiate houseflies from small, darting, dark objects may not be a possible level of perceptual detail for frogs. Frogs are known to strike readily at moving insects but to ignore static (dead) ones; whether they see them at all has been questioned. Thus, there is no paradox in claiming that the frog "sees" the darting object but does not perceive it to be a virtual housefly.

By contrast, at a coarser grain of perceptual analysis, the decoy target is a *virtual* object for the frog. For the frog, small, dark, darting objects typically afford eating; the decoy is a small, dark, darting object and, therefore, specifies this same affordance property. Moreover, if the frog is to be consistent with its knowledge of edible targets, it *must* strike at the decoy, for that is the right action that its *doxa* calls for. In fact, it would be an error at the species level of possible-worlds analysis for it not to do so. Yet this raises an apparent paradox since for the frog to strike does not result in a successful action. The apparent paradox is easily resolved, however, if we distinguish species *doxa* from the *doxa* held by a given individual on a particular occasion, in keeping with the claim that what is valid knowledge at one grain of possible-worlds analysis may not be so at another.

Presumably, frogs and other species thrive because the pragmatic principles they live by as a species are correct *doxa,* entailing actions that are more likely to be successful than unsuccessful. The attensity value of certain properties—such as being small, dark, and darting—is higher than that of others because the perception of them entails correct *doxa* for the animal. The fact that the same properties, when displayed artificaly under contrived experimental context, do not result in correct *doxa* on such exceptional occasions in no way detracts from the pragmatic truth of those same perceptions or actions on other, more natural occasions.

Thus, the unsatisfactory performance is explained as a valid instance of satisfactory functioning in the animal's normal environment. An animal is constrained and motivated to right action in its own econiche by the same perceptual information that may be essentially undefined in someone else's econiche—say, that of a human experimenter. When the semantic context of its experiences is altered, then their meaning varies accordingly. The possible-worlds of experience of one species or one individual may not be those of another. No puzzles for epistemology or psychology, however, are entailed by this fact unless one holds to a rigid, universal theory of truth rather than a more flexible, relativistic one.

Given sufficient time, however, a species or individual may learn to accommodate to such changes in context, to transform incorrect *doxa* into valid ecological knowledge; but the process is never instantaneous. Hence, attempts at instant science—as represented in the arbitrarily contrived "possible-worlds" of experimentation, where the problems of ecological validity of stimuli and responses are often ignored—may prove more misleading than revealing, especially if the data gathered receive only a narrow anthropomorphic interpretation—namely, where the criterion for error is based on human *doxa*.

Case 2: Environments for Cartwheeling.   A second case considers how experience may attune given members of a species to experience the same configuration of surfaces and substances in different ways. Since different experiences support different *doxa,* such experiential differences specify distinct varieties of "possible-worlds" in which the animal's behavior must be interpreted. Just as we must avoid the *species-specific fallacy* of treating animals anthropomorphically (as living in the same semantic contexts as humans), indicative of human perceptions, we also must avoid treating members of the same species as sharing exactly the same set of "possible-world" contexts. They surely share the semantics of their econiche, as one among many "possible-worlds" at the species level; but different experiences may educate members in ways that are only suitable to interpretation in distinct "possible-worlds."

For instance, a person who learns to cartwheel may seek out places where this playful activity is possible. The "possible-worlds" context for a cartwheeling human is therefore distinct *in part* from that of a noncartwheeling human. The cartwheeling aficionado will perceive affordances of terrain that escape the eye of the more sedentary person. The correct *doxa* for cartwheeling hence partitions the properties of the environment into affordances specific to this view of right action (e.g., having a nonrocky, fairly smooth surface without too many trees or shrubs and, perhaps, possessing a very slight declination in one direction). Moreover, the *doxa* for cartwheeling also raises the attensity level of the relevant properties of the terrain as a direct function of the psychological attitude assumed by the person (e.g., "I'm bored. I think I'll cartwheel for a while").

The principles for determining correct *doxa* for cartwheelers can of course be generalized to other activities that may be more subtle and complex. For instance, the task of determining the sex of chickens at a young age is very difficult. Even those who are successful "chicken-sexers" cannot articulate clearly and sufficiently the tacit knowledge that allows them correct *doxa* in their choices. This perceptual skill is not so different from that of the expert microscopist who recognizes cancerous from noncancerous tissue samples; the expert air-traffic controller who accurately anticipates dangerous problems in crowded air corridors on the radar screen; the art connoisseur who detects forgeries of Rembrandt's style; or the radiologist who correctly diagnoses broken or displaced bones when no obvious anomaly is visible to his or her colleagues. None of the perceptual skills of experts can be easily explained to a novice. A novice only becomes an expert through the "education of attention" that permits correct *doxa*.

The ability to decide wisely in such situations is not to be explained by reason, but by a requisite change in the attensity of certain properties that specify to the percipient the relevant affordances of the situation. In this way, judgment is a form of right action, not of inferential reasoning. The perceptual knowledge of animals achieves correct *doxa* in the same way. Wolves who track the caribou by their scent, like birds who seek shelter because they anticipate an oncoming storm by detecting changes in air pressure, and the giant green sea turtles who follow meandering courses to avoid choppy water at sea in their homing voyage to lay eggs on the Galápagos beaches are all demonstrating correct *doxa* spawned by attunement.

The final example shows how a change in the psychological attitude individuates the affordances of the affordance structure that is a given animal's environment. Such changes require a host of distinct "possible-worlds" in which the success or failure of actions may be semantically interpreted. Moreover, the next illustration also specifies in more detail exactly what is meant by the duality of action and perception and shows how the event-reflexive operator applies to the dual action and perception schema to define the relevant "possible-worlds" contexts.

Case 3: The "Possible-Worlds" of Hermit Crab Perceptions. As argued earlier, the notion of perception as an event-reflexive function is quite general, applying to lower animals just as well as to humans. This can be seen in the case of hermit crabs, who seem to perceive sea anemones as affordance objects rather than merely as crass physical objects (von Uexküll, 1957). On one occasion, a hermit crab that has been robbed of the actinians that it normally carries on its shell for protection against its enemy, the cuttlefish, perceives the sea anemone as a replacement for the lost actinians in the sense that it perceives the anemone as something to be planted on its shell. By contrast, on another occasion, if the hermit crab has lost its shell, it often attempts unsuccessfully to crawl into the sea anemone. Finally, on the occasion that the crab has been left to starve for some time, it will proceed hungrily to devour the sea anemone. Thus, we see that on at least three separate occasions, different propositional attitudes toward the same (physical) state of affairs (the sea anemone) can intentionally specify three distinct affordance objects for the same agent (the hermit crab)—a protective shield, a portable enclosure, or a tasty repast. Let us now illustrate more precisely our definition of perception as an indexical, or event-reflexive, operation. We begin with the affordance description of the circumstances that must prevail if the hermit crab is to perceive the sea anemone in either of three "possible-worlds"—the worlds in which it is a protective shield to be worn on its shell, a tasty repast to still the crab's hunger, or a portable enclosure to be worn in place of a shell. The first two cases qualify as perceptions that entail ecologically valid knowledge or correct *doxa* for the crab since they allow it to carry out a line of action that is pragmatically true. However, in the third case, the sea anemone resembles something it is not—namely, a potential portable enclosure to replace a lost shell. Since this *doxa* leads to an unsuccessful attempt by the naked crab to enter the apparently hollow body of the sea anemone, the sea anemone display functions as a virtual object (a virtual shell). Unlike the first two situations, this situation intentionally specifies a "possible-world" without existential import; hence, the psychological attitude qualifying the propositional schema cannot be Z PERCEIVES (x *is* y) but must be Z EXPERIENCES (x *as* y). As pointed out in the case of the frog, this situation would traditionally be treated by the representational realist as a case of perceptual error.

By contrast, a committed realist who is averse to phenomenalist forms of realism would argue that it is a case of the theorist mistaking the intention of the crab's action because of an anthropomorphic bias rather than a case of the crab misperceiving. Since trying to enter things that afford any degree of access (which the sea anemone does) will eventually lead the naked hermit crab to don a protective covering, it would be inappropriate to call this case of appropriate species *doxa* a misperception. The maxim of the act, regardless of its success or failure, is both right and relevant and, therefore, is motivated by ecologically valid knowledge, correct *doxa,* that the crab has of its environment.

Recall from our earlier discussion of "possible-worlds" semantics that although "possible-worlds" are intentionally specified by propositional (e.g., psychological) attitudes, such specification does not automatically bestow existential import on them. The "possible-world," which receives existential import, does so because the agent's primary experiences of it are sufficiently veridical as to lead to right action. If the "possible-world" situation experienced by the agent on a given occasion receives existential import, the experience is said to be a perception and thereby to provide necessary a posteriori truths about the agent's environment; such truths are of course synonymous with correct *doxa,* or ecologically valid knowledge.

Let us now attempt to characterize formally the event-reflexive operation that specifies "possible-worlds" and delivers existence to them whenever certain mutual compatibility relations hold between an agent and its environment.

If we consider the two felicitous occasions abstractly, then it is possible to identify the variables, relations, and operations required to give a precise definition of perception, action, and ecologically valid knowledge in terms of event-reflexive operations on schemata containing exactly the same variables. Put differently, correct *doxa* will be shown to be specified by those "possible-worlds" situations in which perception and action function as *dual complements* because certain symmetries hold between effectivities and affordances.

1. "Possible-World" Where the Anemone Affords Eating. The sea anemone, X, *affords* eating, Y, *by* the crab, Z, on the occasion of its being hungry, O, if and only if the ingestive/digestive system of the crab, *fZ*, is mutually compatible with nutritional properties of the sea anemone, *gX*.

The preceding schema fits the general form: X *affords* Y *for* Z *on* O *if and only if certain symmetries hold between the properties of* X *and those of* Z. This reduced form can be translated into an event-reflexive formula as follows:

$$P\ (X_i, Z_j, O_k | \ gX \ \Diamond \ fZ) = Y_1$$

where X_i = a particular situation—i.e., a state of affairs in the animal's surroundings.

Z_j = the agent as perceiver.

O_k = the occasion upon which a particular propositional (psychological) attitude holds.

gX = a particular set of properties belonging to the situation that is relevant to the occasion in question.

fZ = a particular set of properties of the agent that is also relevant to the occasion in question.

$|$ = a symbol designating that the expression on its right is the semantic context of the expression on its left.

$\Diamond$ = a symbol designating that a mutual compatibility relation or symmetry holds between the terms on its left and right.

$| \ gX \ \Diamond \ fz$ = the mutual compatibility condition that must be satisfied if the event-reflexive function $P(\quad)$ is to be defined.

Y_1 = the affordance–property or affordance structure, as the case may be, that is intentionally specified by the P-function when all the variables are properly evaluated.

The preceding intentional schema for perception as an event-reflexive function of three variables can be transformed into an intentional schema for defining action in an analogous manner. The only changes required are that the agent variable Z is now interpreted as actor rather than perceiver; the variable Y_1 as an intentionally specified effectivity or effectivity structure of the agent Z rather than an affordance or affordance structure of the situation X; and finally, we change the ordering of the variables in the argument of the function and its designation from P (for perception) to A (for action). Thus we obtain the new event-reflexive schema:

$$A(Z_j, X_i, O_k| \; g \; X \; \Diamond f \; Z) = Y_1$$

Read: *The agent Z effects Y on X on the occasion O if and only if certain symmetries hold between the properties of X and Z.*

The two formulae for defining perception and action, logically speaking, are *duals* of one another. A *duality* is a transformation T such that when applied to some object x, it transforms it into some new object y and when applied to the new object y, will transform it back into the object x. Hence $T(x) \rightarrow y$ and $T(y) \rightarrow x$. It is clear that such a duality exists for transforming the action schema into the perception schema, and vice versa. Indeed, the simple syntactic transformation mentioned earlier by which we derived the action formulation from the perception formulation is precisely of this nature: $T(P) \rightarrow A$ and $T(A) \rightarrow P$ represents $T: P(X, Z, O|X \Diamond Z) \Rightarrow A(Z, X, O|X \Diamond Z)$ and $T: A(Z, X, O|X \Diamond Z) \Rightarrow P(X, Z, O|X \Diamond Z)$, respectively.

Moreover, since the intentional schemata for action and perception are duals, so are the intentional objects they specify—namely, effectivities and affordances, respectively. This simply means that in our preceding example, the affordance property of the sea anemone, its *edibility* for the crab, is a dual expression of the effectivity of the crab, *its ability to eat* the sea anemone. As trivial as this may sound, it has profound implications for promoting the ecological thesis, for it provides the basis for proving that there can indeed be a common theoretical language in which perception and the objects perceived may be precisely described: The objects perceived are not crass physical objects but intentionally specified objects in a "possible-worlds" semantic context.

2. A "Possible-World" Where the Anemone Affords Shielding. The sea anemone, X, affords use as protective shielding, Y, for the crab, Z, on the occasion of its loss of actinians, O, if and only if structural properties of the crab's shell, gZ, are mutually compatible with the attachment and support properties of the sea anemone, fZ.

Again the abstract formulations for action and perception in this perception in this "possible-world" of experience for the hermit crab are duals of each other. The possibility of such a duality holding guarantees that the semantic context ("possible-world") so stipulated is ecologically real for the animal and, therefore, that it potentially entails correct *doxa*. The action formulation would be as follows: The hermit crab, Z, can effect the planting, Y, of the sea anemone, X, on its shell to serve as protective shielding if and only if . . . etc. This intentional schema specifies a realizable felicitous action because of the same mutual compatibilities holding between the crab and the anemone that make the crab's perceptions of the anemone, as a potential shield, veridical. Thus, the event-reflexive operators $P(\ )$ and $A(\ )$, for perception and action, respectively, are propositional attitudes having to do with an agent *noticing* that certain properties (resemblances or symmetries) hold between itself and its world and *intending* to act upon them accordingly. These propositional attitudes are *duals* of one another because the affordance properties of the world are written in a perceptual language that can be read by the agent as an action language, and vice versa. And as argued earlier, *the noticing of resemblances and the intending to act upon them,* like knowing one's beliefs or pains, are primary facts of experience and thus provide the necessary a posteriori truths upon which to build an ecological psychology.

At the risk of belaboring the obvious at this point, let us round out our discussion by considering the case where the hermit crab appears, at least to a human observer with human *doxa* rather than crab *doxa,* to be thwarted in its attempt to enter the sea anemone and wear it as a "shell." We give two "possible-world" versions of this same case—one where an asymmetry, or incompatibility, is defined to hold between the perception and action of the crab with respect to the sea anemone; and the other where a symmetry holds.

We call the first version the *spurious* version because it ignores species *doxa* in explaining the actions of the hermit crab: It assumes, first, that the crab "sees" the anemone as affording a shell function when, in fact, it does not lead to felicitious action, since the crab's body cannot fit into the sea anemone; secondly, it also assumes that the action of the crab is an attempt to don the sea anemone like a shell.

3. The Spurious "Possible-World" Interpretation. The sea anemone, X, affords use as a portable enclosure, Y, for the hermit crab, Z, if and only if the structural properties of the sea anemone (e.g., size and shape), gX, are mutually compatible with those of the hermit crab, fZ.

What makes this version the specification of a spurious "possible-world" is that no matter how hard the hermit crab attempts to enter the body of the sea anemone, it will fail because, presumably, *in principle* no member of the hermit crab species can enter the body of any member of the sea anemone species. Therefore, if the affordance defined is a true affordance Y for Z with respect to X, then the possibility of right action must exist, for it is only in this duality that the "possible-world" can become actualized. Hence it is improper to say of the crab that it *sees* the sea anemone as affording something that it in principle does not. This is a misuse of the term *affordance.* To clarify this term, consider a different case.

Let us now try to formulate the felicitous interpretation of what the naked hermit crab must be intending when it notices the sea anemone and approaches it from the standpoint of crab *doxa* rather than human *doxa.*

4. The "Possible-World" in Which Hermit Crabs Are Investigators. The object, X, affords being investigated in a particular manner, Y, by the hermit crab, Z, on the occasion of its being naked if and only if the object has certain properties, gX, that are mutually compatible with certain properties of the crab, fZ.

Notice that in this formulation, the object could be anything that has a certain size, shape, texture, rigidity, etc; it need not be a sea anemone per se. Species *doxa* for the crab, like species *doxa* for the frog, has it act toward objects as a member of a rather grossly defined equivalence class. The object only has to invite investigation by the crab, or being struck at by the frog, in order to satisfy the criterion for right action. It is as if you were in a dark hallway, fumbling for your door key, which is one of a large collection of similar-shaped keys on your key chain. You cannot know which key is which merely by feeling the grooves; you must try to see which fits. Your fumbling attempts nonetheless constitute right action under the circumstances, since to do nothing leaves you stranded in the hallway. It matters not whether, unknown to you, the key has been surreptitiously removed from the key chain, since this is execution of an act that is entailed by ecologically valid knowledge of door opening in architectural environments.

Similarly, the naked hermit crab also exhibits a grasp of what is appropriate when it investigates in its fumbling manner various objects whose details are presumably not perfectly differentiated. This is correct action as entailed by its species *doxa*. No perceptual error is involved because the crab cannot take the sea anemone to be more than an object to be investigated, just as you might take a randomly selected key as one to be tried. The action is as felicitous as the perception is veridical: Since they are duals, it could scarcely be otherwise. How else can a "possible-world" among many become existentially actualized?

Reality of this ecological sort draws its force of existence from correct *doxa*, which as a form of knowledge has the same ability to compel appropriate action as Socrates claimed of virtuous knowledge: *One cannot know the good (veridical) and do the evil (nonfelicitous).* Only ignorance of what is afforded can lead to inappropriate action, and this is certainly not to be confused with knowledge—perceptual or otherwise.

On this point we conclude our arguments. We have attempted to flesh out what a commitment to realism entails for a theory of perception. In so doing, a number of serious problems have been addressed, and ideally, the directions in which their solutions might be sought have been identified. For the student of cognition whose interest is memory, the arguments we have made should not be construed as simply germane to perception. Remembering is a kind of knowing that relates animal and environment, and the issues we have raised for perceiving as knowing must be raised *pari passu* for remembering as knowing. Put bluntly, we believe it a mistake to treat the objects of remembering as numerically distinct from the objects of the original experience. From the perspective of a commitment to realism, talk about remembering cannot be talk about a present representation of a past event; rather, it must be talk about (a possibly special sort of) knowing of past events themselves (Locke, 1971). What the precise nature of this direct knowing may be remains a problem; but at least it is just one problem in comparison to the several mysteries (such as how to resolve the problems of referentiality and intentionality) that inhere in the characterization of memory from the stance of that form of phenomenalism that assumes a reality—namely, representational (indirect) realism.

REFERENCES

Anderson, J. R., & Bower, G. H. *Human associative memory*. Washington, D.C.: Winston, 1973.

Austin, J. L. Other minds. *Proceedings of the Aristotelian Society,* 1946, Vol. XX (Supplement).

Bobrow, D. G., & Collins, A. (Eds.). *Representation and understanding*. New York: Academic Press, 1975.

Bolles, R. C. Species-specific defense reactions and avoidance learning. *Psychological Review,* 1970, *71,* 32-48.

Bolles, R. C. *Learning theory*. New York: Holt, Rinehart & Winston, 1975.

Brentano, F. *Psychologie vom empirischen Standpunkt* (3rd ed.). Vienna: 1874; Leipzig: F. Meiner, 1925.

Chisholm, R. M. *Perceiving: A philosophical study*. Ithaca, N.Y.: Cornell University Press, 1957.

Cummins, R. Programs in the explanation of behavior. *Philosophy of Science,* 1977, *44,* 269-287.

Dennett, D. C. *Content and consciousness*. London: Routledge & Kegan Paul, 1969.

Dennett, D. C. Critical notice. *Mind,* 1977, *86,* 265-280.

Dewey, J. *Essays in experimental logic*. Chicago: University of Chicago Press, 1916.

Fitch, H., & Turvey, M. T. On the control of activity: Some remarks from an ecological point of view. In B. Landers & R. Christina (Eds.), *Psychology of motor behavior and sport*. Urbana, Ill.: Human Kinetics, 1978.

Fodor, J. A. *The language of thought*. New York: Crowell, 1975.

Fowler, C. A., & Turvey, M. T. Skill acquisition: An event approach with special reference to searching for the optimum of a function of several variables. In G. Stelmach (Ed.), *Information processing in motor control and learning*. New York: Academic Press, 1978.

Garcia, J., & Koelling, R. A. Relation of cue to consequence in avoidance learning. *Psychonomic Science,* 1966, *4,* 123-124.

Gibson, J. J. *The perception of the visual world*. Boston: Houghton Mifflin, 1950.

Gibson, J. J. *The senses considered as perceptual systems*. Boston: Houghton Mifflin, 1966.

Gibson, J. J. The theory of affordances. In R. Shaw & J. Bransford (eds.), *Perceiving, acting, and knowing*. Hillsdale, N.J.: Lawrence Erlbaum Associates, 1977.

Helmholtz, H. von [*Treatise on physiological optics*] (J. C. P. Southall, trans.). Rochester, N.Y.: Optical Society of America, 1925.

Hinde, R. A., & Stevenson-Hinde, J. (Eds.). *Constraints on learning*. New York: Academic Press, 1973.

Hintikka, J. Information, causality and the logic of perception. In J. Hintikka (Ed.), *The intentions of intentionality and other new models for modalities*. Dordrecht, Holland/Boston: D. Reidel, 1975.

James, W. *Pragmatism: A new name for some old ways of thinking*. New York: Longmans, Green, 1907.

Koffka, K. *Principles of Gestalt psychology*. New York: Harcourt Brace, 1935.

Kripke, S. Naming and necessity. In D. Davidson & G. Harman (Eds.), *Semantics and natural language*. Dordrecht, Holland: D. Reidel, 1972.

Leibniz, G. W. *Nouveaux essais sur l'entendement humain* [*New essays concerning human under-standing*] (A. G. Langley, Ed. and trans.; 3rd ed.). Lasalle, 1949.

Lettvin, J. Y., Maturana, H. R., McCulloch, W. H., & Pitts, W. H. What the frog's eye tells the frog's brain. *Proceedings of the Institute of Radio Engineering*, 1959, *47*, 1940–1959.

Locke, D. *Memory*. Garden City, N.Y.: Doubleday, 1971.

Lovejoy, A. O. The thirteen pragmatisms II. *Journal of Philosophy*, 1908, *5*, 29–39.

Mace, W. M. James J. Gibson's strategy for perceiving: Ask not what's inside your head, but what your head's inside of. In R. Shaw & J. Bransford (Eds.), *Perceiving, acting and knowing*. Hillsdale, N.J.: Lawrence Erlbaum Associates, 1977.

MacKay, D. M. *Information, mechanism and meaning*. Cambridge: MIT Press, 1969.

Minsky, M. A framework for representing knowledge. In P. Winston (Ed.), *The psychology of computer vision*. New York: McGraw-Hill, 1975.

Plato. The Meno. In E. Hamilton & H. Cairns (Eds.), *The collected works of Plato*. Bollingen Series LXXI, Princeton, N.J.: Princeton University Press, 1961.

Quine, W. V. Quantifiers and propositional attitudes. *Journal of Philosophy*, 1956, *53*, 177–187.

Russell, B. Pragmatism; also, William James' conception of truth. In *Philosophical Essays*. London: Longmans, Green, 1910.

Ryle, G. Plato. In P. Edwards (Ed.), *The encyclopedia of philosophy* (Vol. 5). New York: Macmillan, 1967.

Seligman, M. E. P. On the generality of the laws of learning. *Psychological Review*, 1970, *77*, 406–418.

Seligman, M. E. P., & Hager, J. L. (Eds.). *The biological boundaries of learning*. New York: Appleton, 1972.

Shaw, R., & Bransford, J. Introduction: Psychological approaches to the problem of knowledge. In R. Shaw & J. Bransford (Eds.), *Perceiving, acting and knowing: Toward an ecological psychology*. Hillsdale, N.J.: Lawrence Erlbaum Associates, 1977.

Shaw, R., & Turvey, M. T. Coalitions as models for ecosystems: A realist perspective on perceptual organization. In M. Kubovy & J. Pomerantz (Eds.), *Organization of perception*. Hillsdale, N.J.: Lawrence Erlbaum Associates, 1981.

Shaw, R. & McIntyre, M. Algoristic foundations to cognitive psychology. In W. B. Weimer & D. S. Palermo (Eds.). *Cognition and the symbolic processes*. Hillsdale, N.J.: Erlbaum, 1974.

Shaw, R. & Pittenger, J. Perceiving the face of change in changing faces: Implications for a theory of object perception. In R. Shaw & J. Bransford (Eds.) *Perceiving, acting, and knowing: Toward an ecological psychology*. Hillsdale, N.J.: Erlbaum, 1977.

Stevenson-Hinde, J. Constraints on reinforcement. In R. A. Hinde & J. Stevenson-Hinde (Eds.), *Constraints on learning*. New York: Academic Press, 1973.

Turvey, M. T., & Shaw, R. The primacy of perceiving: An ecological reformulation of perception as a point of departure for understanding memory. In L. -G. Nilsson (Ed.), *Perspectives on memory research: Essays in honor of Uppsala University's 500th Anniversary*. Hillsdale, N.J.: Lawrence Erlbaum Associates, 1979.

Turvey, M. T. Preliminaries to a theory of action with reference to vision. In R. Shaw & J. Bransford (Eds.), *Perceiving, acting, and knowing: Toward an ecological psychology*. Hillsdale, N.J.: Erlbaum, 1977.

Uexküll, J. von A stroll through the worlds of animals and men. In C. H. Schiller (Ed.), *Instinctive behavior*. New York: International Universities Press, 1957.

Wilcoxon, H. C., Dragoin, W. B., & Kral, P. A. Illness-induced aversions in rat and quail: Relative salience of visual and gustatory cues. *Science*, 1971, *171*, 826–828.

11 Gibson–Shaw Discussion

Martin: Shaw's notion of neutrality is absolutely right. That is precisely the notion that I had in mind when I said that, in fact, one could not give independent definitions of specifications of the known. They are distinct, but they are not defined independently—which in effect is a relationship as complementary as Shaw has in mind. The metaphor I used in the figure–ground relationship is an example of a complementary relationship. Concerning *representation* as a definite ambiguous term, I reject a certain version of representation that goes like this: If I knew, say, chalk as being strictly representational, I think I would have to have a representation of something in order to see it. The question, then, is how will I see my representation? I will need another representation for that, and how would I see that representation, etc., etc? But that's not the representation that I had in mind or I think that any intelligent scientist has. It seems to me that if one uses the metaphor of grasping for the way we know, it is quite clear that in a grasping of something, there is a hierarchy. In effect, I am a hierarchy of graspings and in so being, for example, moving my body, etc., so that I can, in fact, finally grasp particular objects, I have become, in fact, what we mean by representation. What is important to see is that lower-level "grasps" presuppose the possibility of higher-level "grasps," but they also presuppose that the world forms the higher-level grasping.

One point about the mobility of a whole that came up. The claim that I made was that we assume that the world is defined in some sense in order that we may know it. That is to say, the world forms the possibility of a cosmology. In effect, facts—whatever they are—are defined in a conceptual context. We all know about the conceptual relativity of facts. There must be assumed an apprehension of the whole context. Since I am a part of a whole, this requires finally a level of self-grasping, and that's the level at which the whole is grasped. It's grasped with a self-grasping that is, in fact, a third term of the system that we are proposing. It can't be derived from any other level of analysis, and yet without it, knowledge of any particular part is impossible. So we're talking about a priori analysis, not about particular empirical facts. This level of analysis brings us to the personal, the empathetic, to the ethical. One final point about Gibson: If you take him seriously, he says that you begin with some direct knowledge relation in which you recognize states, etc. That is a reductionist view of the higher-level processes. The meaning that takes place indirectly is somehow transferred down for its validity to a lower level of knowing, and of course, that is a version of the empiricist and reductionist conception of knowing. It doesn't really account for a person's total activity, such as what is involved in creating the theory itself.

Shaw: When you were speaking of the self-grasping, I was reminded strongly of the dog chasing its tail. I don't think that the self-grasping of the something or other is an essential aspect of what I mean.

Martin: You don't think you're a part of intelligence?

Shaw: I'd like to focus on self-grasping as a fundamental category of existence.

Martin: That's exactly the problem. In one way or another, it sets the grounds for it. Within any attempt to give an account of a basic logic, a basic framework in terms of which we should account for the world, we invariably encounter problems unless we begin with the conceptual structure of self-grasping.

Pribram: It seems impossible that anything could grasp itself.

Martin: That's precisely Spencer-Brown's point. His claim, finally, is that we need just that kind of understanding. My point is that in order to get that kind of understanding, one has to begin with it. The problem that Spencer-Brown raises with respect to the imaginary in mathematics—which, in effect, is self-grasping—comes back to Pribram's question: "How can the context apprehend itself?" This can only be solved by beginning with self-grasping with the double cross—not the cross but the double cross. If one doesn't, it's possible to show that Spencer-Brown's system doesn't work.

Turvey: I think you have to assume it from the start in order to get it into your system at all, which means that it's an absolute fabrication, and I don't see any point in that.

Martin: The only point is that we will understand the psychology that will explain ourselves in the act of doing psychology.

Turvey: It seems there are essentially two ways in which we have conceived representation—one of which I like and the other I am opposed to. Traditionally, I think, representation is running opposite something like a schema or a frame. Essentially, I already have a description of the frame that I am going to conceive in presenting terms. What I seek to do is collect some data through my visual system, bits and pieces, and take those data and assimilate them. That is, I match them to the scheme that I have when those pieces are assimilated, and then I try to recognize the object. That use of representation I find very difficult because it always leads to the curious puzzles of how do I know which schema I need to use for a given circumstance, and it also presupposes that for anything I see, I have a schema for that very thing. That use of representation is very widespread today. But for the second conception, suppose that what I seek is to understand how I discover some property of an object—to discover, for example, that this platform is smoother than the surface of Lila's arm. In order to do that, I would rub my hand over this surface like so. This particular activity—it's a particular transformation over the skin's surface and over the pieces of my arm—reveals to me the property in question and reveals to me the information I need to distinguish whether this surface is smoother than that surface. Or suppose I want to find whether or not the shape of one surface is different from another. Now I transform differently: I do some different operation on the object in question. What I do is again enclosed in a different transformation. If we view perception in general as the detection of the variance revealed under relevant transformation, then in part, what we might mean by schema is not an entity into which things are assimilated but rather a way of approaching the world that reveals the properties in question. I don't approach the world knowing or ready when those properties arise, but I have ways of revealing those properties to myself.

Pribram: It doesn't seem that the problem of knowing which schema to use is any different from the problem of knowing which action to use to gather that information. What you haven't said is how is a *revelation,* which is the new term, different from a representation? You have revelations, we have representations. I guess in the information being revealed, we're talking about the information being detected. This is not to say that the information is being represented in another form.

Martin: Michael, you have got the wrong idea about representation.

MacNamara: That's what I'm trying to tell him. A representation is a construct of a scientist that lets us know the world. Now what one knows is the world; one doesn't know the schema nor the representation. I gave a simple example of that before, about looking in the mirror to see if my hair was tossed. In that particular case, I am normally attending to my hair and seeing it tossed. Thus what I can't possibly become aware of is the representation of me. When I'm looking out at you, I can't become aware of the representation of you; I am only aware of you. But I have a construct to explain how I come to know you from that input. I mean how else can I know you? Something like representation must form something in my head. I don't know it directly, but I know *of* it. Consider meaning: I talk about the world, and there must be some way in which the world out there gets tied up in my world. It's in our minds.

Member of Audience: What's the relationship between a presentation and a representation?

Mace: The way that Martin talked about affordance, he was using good English, but he was not using affordance the way Gibson would. For Gibson, there are very severe restrictions on the notion of affordance, even though it's certainly not a very precise term as yet. We say X affords Y for Z where Y is the grasping or the affordance. But the thing that is important is that it has to be a real embodied act on the part of the organism: moving around in the world, doing something like grasping or walking. It cannot be a mental act. It cannot be perceiving, knowing, recognizing. Mental acts are metaphors adopted from familiar overt acts. If you allow yourself to say that something like recognizing, perceiving, or knowing really exists then you go back to the schema—saying things like, "This chair affords perceiving or knowing by me." But then one wants to say that affordances are the things that are perceived, and one winds up with statements like the claim: "I perceive the perceivability or the recognizability." It is perfectly good English to say that something affords recognizing or knowing, but it is not appropriate in Gibson's framework to say that the universe affords knowing.

I want to amplify the point Michael was making. The question, to rebuff Turvey's point, is on the mark: There has to be some way of choosing the kind of transformation one will discover in certain dimensions of properties. This does lead us into the same kind of problem that the schema people face, in terms of the selectivity of the schema and selectivity of the transformation. That's not to say that the two approaches come down to the same thing. It's to say that they share a recalcitrant problem that doesn't go away when one shifts from one framework to the other. I would still want to press the notion of schema just exactly the way Michael did. Is the schema "in the head"? One needs a schema that is an abstract formula, but it is in the head. I take that as counting one term. The second term will be that which gets schematized. I don't care whether it's the event in the world, or whether it's the object in the world, or whether it's an elementary property in the world: The issue isn't one of elementarism versus holism. The issue is whether we have counted a second thing that is not the first thing. What is the relationship of the thing in the head—the first thing—to that second thing in the world? Either one believes that those are two separate things and that some explanatory operation somehow allows them to come together for recognition, or one doesn't believe that. Now I maintain that Turvey's example about running your hand over the floor, over the arm, or any other part of the body really sets us up in a kind of paradigm if we go into it a bit deeper. I'm perfectly willing to accept the word *schema,* but is the schema in the head? I would rather say the schema is defined on the ecosystem. The schema's defined on the environment and what we call the person. To just reaffirm: Yes, there is a problem of what transformation I will select in order to test the object. You want to see which falls faster, and I don't want to say that's not a problem; but I want to say that that problem exists in this framework just as surely as it exists in the other framework.

Weimer: I have a historical question. Characteristic of the Gibsonian position is a slogan: Surfaces are where it's at. This was one approach that Mace used at the last conference to try and make this point. Now my question to Mace and

Shaw is: In a Gibsonian framework, are you attempting to differentiate or to enrich "surfaces as where it's at" in saying what you just said?

Shaw: I did say surfaces are where it's at, because that's where the contact is. If we make the concept of surface alone more abstract, then we can even get to communication and other things. But the transformation to fill out the "schema" is not being applied; one transformation of one surface, another transformation of the other, and then one puts those two kinds together. So I'm just emphasizing what comes under Gibson's view of perception as an exploratory, investigatory activity, and I am calling that the transformation.

Weimer: Would you say that we don't know anything that we're not in physical contact with?

Shaw: We're not talking about physical contact now.

Weimer: Would you say we don't relate to anything we're not in direct contact with?

Shaw: I guess I would have to say, no, we don't know it. I have to explain why I say that, because that's a very hard question. The question is, *can* I know anything or *do* I know anything? I'm trying to speak to the question of what are the conditions of knowing. You're asking me about a particular case of knowing. I'm not sure how I would answer any particular example, but I know how we go about sketching an answer to any particular example. There must be dimensions of affordance that will allow for the compatibility to be specified. If those dimensions don't exist, it's like not knowing how to get the thermal dimension together with the radiant light dimension, which I would call contacts; because there is no place where there's a gap between the thermal and the light. When I come into physical contact with an object, what we mean by contact is that I have immediately adjacent values on some kind of dimension. So I don't see how I could know anything without that contact.

MacNamara: I'll give you an example of knowing without contact—triangularity.

Shaw: Gibson has often cautioned us about taking geometric models as our model for structures. I'd say the same thing about triangles. You can't untie a triangle.

MacNamara: Oh yes one can. I'm saying that I'm contacting something very abstract right now called surface. It's not this floor that I'm contacting at every grain of analysis. I'm contacting a plane or surface, which means that there are several kinds of transformations that can be defined on it. Do you understand what I'm saying? There are two kinds of displacements.

Shaw: You must end up saying that that stage is an abstract as a triangle. But I mean one can bump into that stage, and one can't bump into a triangle.

MacNamara: But I can bump into the triangle. However, I can't bump into the concept; I don't bump into schemata.

Weimer: I'm going to rephrase the issue in quasi-historical context. One thing that got us all to being other than stimulus–response psychologists was that we came to realize that triangles both are and are not, in a very important sense, perceptual entities. They are also conceptual. A triangle, within the confines of Euclidean plane geometry, is a three-sided figure, the sum of whose interior angles is 180°. Now in that sense, triangles are neither perceptible nor bump-into-able or anything else that surfaces are. But I can touch a particular—say, plastic—triangle, and it turns out, from the Gibsonian perspective, to be a surface that affords certain things. Now when I encounter triangles, I can perceive, in traditional terminology, that they are triangular. This discussion is crossing these two modes of description and asking, "How abstract is abstract?" We have reached a point at which the sort of knowledge that the Gibsonian framework requires is unbelievably abstract. That's the improvement Gibson has made over any other approach to the "stimulus." By definition, the stimulus is particular, and that's why it isn't going to work. Now the question we all face is this: Since an adequate account requires this degree of abstraction, how does the CNS or the cognitive apparatus "represent" (pardon that term) such abstract information? How is it that our heads work such that they work with that degree of abstraction? And this problem faces the Gibsonians just as much as the schema theorists as soon as one admits that perception is meaningful. The concept of affordance appears to beg all the questions of meaning. One cannot explain understanding by saying that perceiving is an organism-environment interaction that picks up affordances. That is, at best, a paraphrase of the real problem.

Shaw: My point must have gone unheard. Let me just say it again. My point is that there's a schema in the head and on the world that allows us to know triangles, and that's the boundary condition I still believe to be the unanswered question. The question that the gentleman asked earlier is, how do we have selective knowledge? Now I thought this is what MacNamara was getting at. How is it that I am somehow in contact with the triangle when I'm not paying attention to triangles? My answer to that is that we're speaking of a potential transformability of the world. This would be the ecological schema, and when the triangle does appear at the physical intersection—and indeed I am there in this relationship to it—I could perceive it. That means that we can coparticipate in the event schema. And that event schema is what I'm looking for, as a Gibsonian—the specification of (or the revelation of) it and not the representation of it in the sense of being in the head. My theory allows representation but not in my head.

Pribram: When the Gibsonians say something positive, it's great. But when they say something negative, like there is nothing in the head, it isn't. Try to cut out the schema, if you will. A classical case is the motor cortex and the control of action. Cortical ablation debilitates skilled action and comprehension. Now you say okay, but if you take off a hand, then one can't do it anymore either. You have contact at the hand. However, if I stimulate the motor cortex, you can still feel as if you were doing it with the hand that isn't there. And so we have two kinds of evidence. One is removal of whatever you want to call "it"—and I prefer the word *complement* to the word *represent*.

Shaw: When you say it that way, I have no trouble with it. The complement is a line that's not drawn between the animal and the environment. It's not the line drawn there that gives you this unholy dualism. What we're talking about is something that has to do with the mirroring, if you will, of the transformation that can be performed on the schema in which we participate by the environment that you may correspond with. Your transformations and their body development complement one another.

Pribram: Yes, all that is true, but there is a special place that the brain has in all of us.

Shaw: The point is that the phenomenon we seek to understand can be defined on an ecosystem. To say: "Isn't it amazing—when I do something to the brain, something breaks down in this relationship," is not surprising. Of course it does—the brain is one of the pieces.

Pribram: But it's a very special piece.

Turvey: What do you mean when you say the brain is really special?

Pribram: It's really special in this sense—it determines what we can know of the world. I pushed Gibson when he said, "How much information is in the world?" He replied, "an infinite amount of information." Now Lashley would say that if there's an infinite amount of information out there, that means there's an utter chaos. So how will we discover the affordance structure if what's in the world must be determined by the head? If there's an infinite amount out there, there must be certain constraints determining what an organism can pick up. But many theorists take the exact opposite view from Gibson and say that all the constraints are inside the organism. Unlike Gibson and those extreme constructionists, I think there are constraints both in the environment and the organism, and the brain is special because it constrains what we can know.

Shaw: One can't specify an environment except in reference to an animal; species implies an environment and an animal. Now what you're saying is that there's a way of describing the world in terms of environment where an environment is to be regarded as a center for an animal. The animal is in the process of evolution. We can think of this animal becoming that kind of biological substrate that is attuned to that particular description of the environment. Again, these are two terms—the species and the environment—and they are reciprocally related and cannot be separated. The organism and the environment are both mutually constrained or not constrained at all.

Pribram: The question really is which had precedence: Does the animal fit the environment, or does the environment fit the animal?

Shaw: Two pieces of the same jigsaw puzzle.

Pribram: Right. But who does the fitting? Would you say that this one fits this piece, or what?

Shaw: Both pieces?

Pribram: I don't know. But mankind creates the environment. We create the environment to fit ourselves.

Shaw: Your point, I surely agree with. One problem of the change of evolution, the reorganization of knowledge, is how we keep the abstract ideal condition of the mutual compatibility that I talk about as, if you will, the goals for the ecosystem. Evolution happens in a dynamic mode over time, and organisms and environments do get out of synchrony, which can cause an ecological upset. You're right when you say that when we apply it to the real situation, sometimes the fit is not perfect.

Pribram: You've got the problem that chimpanzees don't have meetings like this. Chimpanzees have marketplaces. There's something different about chimpanzees and human beings. Whatever it is—that precedes the fitting into the environment.

Shaw: We say that the chimpanzee can anticipate in a different class of event schemata than humans can. And the action is defined as the event schema into which the animal fits.

Pribram: As long as we are talking about this, you keep jumping into the environment, acting human. There's something in the organism that constructs the environment, if you will, and the importance of the environment such as a marketplace. I think a real difference between the Gibsonians and myself is that the Gibsonians are basically passive on this point.

Shaw: But perception is active investigation or exploration over time.

Weimer: Perhaps Professor Gibson would address what is involved in the organism–environment relation.

Gibson: The relation between the animal and its environment is not one of *interaction* in any sense of that word that I understand. Forgive me, but a few moments ago, Pribram said "interaction." Now what was my position about the interaction between the animal and its environment? It is not one of interaction; it's one of, well, reciprocity's not too bad. A mutual application and a focus point. There are several terms in the ecological approach to psychology that bridge the gap between animal and environment. But such a term that bridges the gap points both ways, like the concept of affordance. Another one is the ambient optic array. It's specified at a point where an observer might stand, a station point, where you have reflected light impinging upon an observer. So with such concepts, I don't have to ask a question about the relation between the animal and its environment. I've defined it out of existence in your own way.

The very notion of a representation in your head of an outside environment assumes automatically a form of dualism—an old-fashioned form of dualism.

MacNamara: I think one trouble with Gibson's system is that he does not like to make a distinction between knowing and perceiving. There is a problem here that one must face. I know the concept of number. I know the number system. But there are no numbers in the world. Numbers are abstracted from the world. There are no numbers in the environment: They aren't there to be found. There is no triangularity there for me to find, and yet I know Euclid. Here's another problem for you: I can say either that I know there is a dog here or that I know there is an animal. Those two things are descriptions of the same events in the environment. One can't stand there, taking in some of the information or the affordances—the entire thing is described. There is nothing at a station point that differentiates dog from animal.

Shaw: We don't want to continue the contrasts between knowing and perceiving, and we do want to separate perception from explicit knowing in words. My belief that the cat is on the mat and the perception of the cat on the mat are professionally different. That's our substitute for knowing versus perceiving. I want to say that animals perceive as we do, but they know differently because we have language. What happened to our species when language developed is a problem for psycholinguists; but before we can get to that problem, you've got to have an account of perception.

MacNamara: Does the word *meaning* mean anything to you?

Shaw: There are two radically different kinds of meaning—semantic meaning, which is what most people mean by *meaning;* and perceptual meaning, for which we substitute the term *affordance.*

Pattee: I have heard a lot of arguing, and it has to do with the notational problem—with the cosmological paradox—concerning complementarity of descriptions. In physics there are two sides to the question. First, there are those who want to separate the observer and the world. But there are also those who see the problem as one of surfaces. The surface always distinguishes two things and is also the union of two things. That is, a surface does not *separate* two things, if you want to look at it that way. All physics involves two psychological processes—cognition and volition. Volition occurs when one decides that the surface is going to "separate" or "join," as in the difference between animal and dog. That's a volitional decision because there is nothing in the outside world telling us that's either an animal or a dog; it's our choice. The same is true in physics. If you want to look at the measurement problem and understand it, then you look at the intersection as a union. You decide what is going on between the measuring device and the thing you measure. The description that you end up with, if you take the view of separation, and the view you end up with if you conceive it as a union—these two descriptions are logically complementary because they don't fit together. I don't think that the positions taken here by the Gibsonians and the constructivists will fit together, for the same reason. They are volitional positions rather than factual issues. The question is, what do I want to explain? If I want to explain certain types of psychological phenomena, one theory is better, and if I want to explain another type of phenomena, the other theory works. The point is that this is constantly going on, and as in physics, this argument has never been resolved. In physics, they say you people, psychologists, had better answer it. So it's kind of "back to you."

Member of Audience: I greatly appreciate the Gibsonian starting point of trying to understand how organisms stay in contact with their environment. However, note that Gibson, Mace, and Shaw all use the rhetorical strategy of indirectly telling us about direct perception. Why didn't they simply take us on a stroll through the campus or the woods? I'd like to know how they use the role of conception in knowledge, for nothing has become more attuned to the environment than our conceptual thought. After saying my theories, for example, help me clarify my experiences in the environment and clarify my groundwork, what role does theory have in the system?

Shaw: In order to answer your question, I want to stay within my rhetorical mode to direct it at what may be only the end. If we were approaching it at one grain of analysis, we would expect to get one type of answer; but if we were approaching it at another, we would expect to get still another. We must be careful not to circumscribe our levels of analysis. I think what Pattee was saying is that there is something like this volitional problem that is one of my three terms. We're arguing about the interpretations imposed on the equation in physics, so that it doesn't seem to me to get us out of the framework at all. When we argue about interpretations of quasi-mathematical equations, that's no different from arguing about the interpretations of the cat on the mat. So when you ask how—that's an interpretation—those are two interpretations, you have the same situation.

Member of Audience: Is a conceptual statement a representation?

Shaw: It's an interpretation. We can use the word *representation* to mean the same as *interpretation;* but again there's Representation 1, Representation 2, etc.

Member of Audience: What would be Representation 2? We say there is a state of affairs out there, and there are some interpretations that are true. That's a volitional question. Volition is an interpretation of what is true. But there must be a correspondence of some sort. One leg of that correspondence is the real world. What's the other leg?

Shaw: The other leg corresponds, in this case, to the role of that surface in this other system.

Pribram: The meaning of the surface is not in that other system. The meaning of the system is in the complementation of its role in this other system and the role of the situation that is the case.

Shaw: That's the problem of truth. The truth is the correspondence.

Member of Audience: But the meaning is another relationship.

Martin: You leave out persons if you leave out meaning.

Shaw: You leave a placeholder for mind.

MacNamara: Suppose I say this is true. I make a judgment that this is the truth. In order for it to be true, there has got to be a state of affairs corresponding to my meaning.

Shaw: You don't make the judgment that that is true until you know the meaning, and the meaning is in the complementation of that situation to the other situation.

MacNamara: How could one "afford" knowledge of the world?

Mace: Let me try and make it simpler. It seems to me that the correspondence theory of perception has nothing to do with true or false judgment. What it "corresponds" to is reality. What we substitute is an adequacy theory of perception of the world that is more or less faithful to the needs of the individual, relative to the potentialities of the affordances of the world. But the criteria of truth or error are not themselves in error.

Member of Audience: I want to know what would happen if I can come to understand Gibson's system. My assumption is it would change the way I perceive the world and the way I act on the world. What's the nature of remodeling? How does your system allow one to change the way one perceives?

Shaw: That requires some kind of theory of the evolution of speciation. How do we get different species? We get different species because they are weighted in a different way. You're asking me for a theory of evolution of the achievement.

Turvey: I think he's also raising the relationship between accurate, explicit knowing and tacit knowledge: How do we so organize our explicit action to bring about a reorganization of our tacit knowledge? Polanyi's account of tacit skill acquisition is perfectly Gibsonian.

Member of Audience: Hayek once wrote that man pursues knowledge or science for reasons of wonder. Can you state how wonder gets into your system?

Shaw: I don't have a good answer to that, but I truly agree that I think for most people, the exploratory is equally important with the performatory. Some theorists argue it is because we are open systems.

Member of Audience: What happens to affordances over time? Can you say something about that in relation to what we call memory?

Gibson: I can answer part of it. The affordances of the terrestrial world are permanent relative to the species of individual to which they relate. Affordances are both objective and persisting and, at the same time, subjective, because they relate to the species or individual for whom something is afforded. We perceive affordances over time.

Member of Audience: Next year someone will be able to say that they remembered your being here. Tell me, if you can, what the affordance structure has to do with that memory.

Shaw: Nothing.

Gibson: The whole idea of affordances is to get rid of the ancient assumption that meanings are attached to sensations by association. We've got to get rid of that ancient model that values and meanings are subjective in the sense of being learned by association or reinforcement as attachments to inputs.

Turvey: I say that I can see that this layout supports the act of locomoting. I can say that I can see that this pen is something I can grasp and use in a certain way. For example, suppose we were standing in a bar and started to argue and I got annoyed, and so I pick something up and I throw it at you. Then I notice that which can be thrown. I think in traditional language, one would say that's conceptual knowledge; however, we would say no, that's the detection of the affordance. When we use the affordance conception, the traditional distinction between sensual knowing (or whatever) and conceptual knowing begins to fade.

Member of Audience: Would it be an oversimplification to suggest that conceptual knowing deals with language systems?

Weimer: That's what Turvey said at the last conference.

Turvey: I did get away with that.

Weimer: You got away with saying it.

Turvey: Right.

Weimer: One thing Turvey could throw at you at the bar is an obscenity, which may have more effect than throwing a glass at you. How does the Gibsonian deal with that?

Turvey: I would say that that's a fundamental problem that ought to have a solution, even when it comes down to that framework. A very good question.

Mace: Shaw has worked on the problem of what we agreed to call—maybe not the happiest choice of words—figural analyses, or figural methods versus symbolic methods. Now he's doing a book on what the relationship is between, if you will, the ground of the figural analogy (which we would argue is affordance) and the ground of symbolic analogy. I think we would want to argue, there again, that there is a ground in that case that will go back to the source of the knowledge that allows us to understand the symbolic form. We don't want to say language is a source of knowledge. We want to say the source of knowledge is in the ground that allows the linguistic instruments to be used. So the issue that we are addressing is, how do we come directly in contact with the source of all knowledge? We think the Gibsonian approach provides a theory of figural analogies and a theory of symbolic analogies to do that.

Shaw: It might be wise to confine the meaning of the term *concept* to vocalized concepts, to eliminate animals.

Pribram: I think the claim you want to make is that what you have to learn from history is how not to repeat its mistakes. I wish you would tell me how to do that.

Mishkin: How can you do that without language or, for lack of a better term, symbolic prophecies?

MacNamara: Up-to-date definitions of human intelligence deal with the symbolic system. How would it fit into Shaw's framework?

Shaw: Let's throw out the word *intelligence.*

MacNamara: I would like to say *intelligence* is the effectiveness with which an animal deals with its environment. But *interaction* is not correct, because as I understand you, the two are interdependent.

Shaw: The word *interaction* is misleading. *Complimentary* or *dependency* is better.

Member of Audience: I see two counterclaims in advance of all discussion. One is the Gibsonian thesis that says I have a framework and it applies to everything. It is a way of looking, a way of perceiving. In that sense, a framework is like a pair of conceptual spectacles that you see through, and if you see through them at all, you see everything. Then the next thing is that somebody comes along and says, "How do we handle phenomena *X, Y,* and *Z*?" The response is, "Well, we can't handle that." My question is, does that mean you can't see it at all, or does that mean that it requires a theory the Gibsonians don't yet have within their framework? The claim is that there are phenomena that cannot be handled by the framework, and that therefore such phenomena impose a limitation on the framework. That is the opposition to the Gibsonian approach and what Gibsonians reply is that when those situations arise, we have got to develop a theory within the Gibsonian framework.

12

Hayek's Approach to the Problems of Complex Phenomena: An Introduction to the Theoretical Psychology of *The Sensory Order*

Walter B. Weimer
The Pennsylvania State University

Friedrich August von Hayek is well known as a Nobel laureate in economics and as an outstanding social and political philosopher. He is also the author of a theoretical psychology, first systematically elaborated in *The Sensory Order* (1952b). Hayek's psychological work, however, is virtually unknown except to certain cognitive psychologists. Furthermore, few economists have attempted to understand Hayek's psychological writings, and hardly any psychologists have read the work for which he is famous. What specialists in one or the other domain appear not to notice is the essential continuity in Hayek's thought: Hayek's approach to the explanation and comprehension of complex phenomena provides a conceptual focus that underlies virtually everything he has written. This chapter attempts to overview several recurrent themes that provide continuity between Hayek's social, political, and economic thought, on one hand, and his psychology, on the other.

The major theme in Hayek's work is that there are constraints upon the nature of our knowledge (and hence upon our explanatory capabilities), and ultimately upon rationality itself, that apply to complex organized systems. These constraints entail that the understanding that science can provide for complex systems—such as the nervous system of the psychological individual, or the interactions of individuals that comprise the social system(s), or the marketplace in the economic system—is considerably different from what has been and is still being provided for reasonably simple phenomena such as those studied by the physical sciences. Hayek has systematically explored the context of constraint that determines what the possibilities are for theoretical understanding and practical control of complex phenomena, and what actions are rational given that our behaviors are both constituents of complex systems (social, economic) and the

241

result of the organization of a complex system (the nervous system). We may begin to understand that context of constraint by looking at the nature of explanation.

DEGREES OF EXPLANATION: EXPLANATION OF THE PARTICULAR AND OF THE PRINCIPLE

The rise of modern science has been due to our ability to understand physical phenomena (phenomena of low complexity). Physics is the paradigm of science, and the majority of analyses of the nature of science attempt to force the model of science instantiated by physics upon all domains that would be "scientific." The recent excesses of Vienna Circle Positivism in this regard truly rival Procrustes' use of his famous bed, but virtually all philosophical analyses assume that the physical sciences, when properly understood, will be representative of all science. Thus far, physics has been remarkably successful in the explanation (and often in the prediction and control) of particulars by theoretical laws. Physicists have been model builders: They use models (either formal or material) to derive quantitatively precise values of the events to be explained or predicted. Explanation, in the physical sciences that deal with simple phenomena, is the (deductive) subsumption of particulars to general or covering laws: It is explanation of the particular.

There is another kind of explanation—explanation of the principle—that occurs in complex systems in which explanatory value is claimed for theoretical models even though they do not enable us to ascertain precise values of the variables involved. For theorists enamored of explanations of the sort for which physics is most famous, these "mere" explanations of the principle are a source of embarrassment—at best, preliminary efforts to be replaced by better accounts when science matures. But what sorts of understanding does explanation of the principle provide? Hayek (1967) answered this way in the essay "Degrees of Explanation":

> We may not be able directly to confirm that the causal mechanism determining the phenomenon in question is the same as that of the model. But we know that, *if* the mechanism is the same, the observed structures must be capable of showing some kinds of action and unable to show others; and if, and so long as, the observed phenomena keep within the range of possibilities indicated as possible, that is so long as our expectations derived from the model are not contradicted, there is good reason to regard the model as exhibiting the principle at work in the more complex phenomenon.... Our conclusions and predictions will also refer only to some properties of the resulting phenomenon, in other words, to a *kind* of phenomenon rather than to a particular event [p. 15].

In contrast to most theorists, Hayek has consistently maintained that explanation of the principle is the rule rather than the exception in complex phenomena such as biological evolution, human culture, and economics and psychology. As "The Theory of Complex Phenomena" argues (1967):

> In general the physical sciences tend to assume that it will in principle always be possible to specify their predictions to any degree desired. . . .
>
> There is, however, no justification for the belief that it must always be possible to discover such simple regularities and that physics is more advanced because it has succeeded in doing this while other sciences have not yet done so. It is rather the other way round: physics has succeeded because it deals with phenomena which, in our sense, are simple. But a simple theory of phenomena which are in their nature complex (or which, if that expression be preferred, has to deal with more highly organized phenomena) is probably merely of necessity false—at least without a specified *ceteris paribus* assumption, after the full statement of which the theory would no longer be simple [pp. 24–25, 28].

Hayek's contention received independent corroboration from the pioneering work in automata theory of John Von Neumann (Burks, 1966). Von Neumann was able to prove, in mathematically rigorous fashion, that for phenomena of high complexity (the precise specification of which need not detain us here; see Burks, 1966), the least complex model of a complex phenomenon would possess a degree of complexity equal to the thing itself. Thus, a model capable of behaving exactly like a complex phenomenon would, for all practical (and indeed theoretical) purposes, be another instance of that phenomenon. When we reach such complexity (such as evolutionary phenomena, the nervous system, social and cultural phenomena, economic systems, and so forth), explanation of the principle is all that we can hope to achieve, granted the finitude of the human condition.

Thus it is no accident that, say, evolutionary theory and biology have not surpassed "mere" explanation of the principle, as Hayek (1967) was one of the first to see, they never can!

> The theoretical understanding of the growth and functioning of organisms can only in the rarest of instances be turned into specific predictions of what will happen in a particular case, because we can hardly ever ascertain all the facts which will contribute to determine the outcome. Hence, "prediction and control, usually regarded as essential criteria of science, are less reliable in biology. It deals with pattern-building forces, the knowledge of which is useful for creating conditions favorable to the production of certain kinds of results, while it will only in comparatively few cases be possible to control all the relevant circumstances" [pp. 33–34].

Precisely the same holds for economics:

> Economic theory is confined to describing kinds of patterns which will appear if certain general conditions are satisfied, but can rarely if ever derive from this knowledge any predictions of specific phenomena. This is seen most clearly if we

consider those systems of simultaneous equations which since Leon Walras have been widely used to represent the general relations between the prices and the quantities of all commodities bought and sold. They are so framed that *if* we knew all the parameters of these equations, we could calculate the prices and quantities of all the commodities. But, as at least the founders of this theory clearly understood, its purpose is not "to arrive at a numerical calculation of prices," because it would be "absurd" to assume that we can ascertain all the data [p. 35].

From these individual disciplines, we may easily move to general consequences for the philosophy of science and methodology of research. The notion of a law of nature as a relationship obtaining between a few phenomena, linked together by a simple relation such as cause and effect, simply will not apply to complex phenomena. Hayek (1967) wrote:

We may well have achieved a very elaborate and quite useful theory about some kind of complex phenomenon and yet have to admit that we do not know a single law, in the ordinary sense of the word, which this kind of phenomenon obeys. . . . It would then appear that the search for the discovery of laws is not an appropriate hall-mark of scientific procedure but merely a characteristic of the theories of simple phenomena as we have defined these earlier; and that in the field of complex phenomena the term 'law' as well as the concepts of cause and effect are not applicable without such modification as to deprive them of their ordinary meaning. . . It would probably have saved much confusion if theoretical science had not in this manner come to be identified with the search for laws in the sense of a simple dependence of one magnitude upon another. . . And the prejudice that in order to be scientific one must produce laws may yet prove to be one of the most harmful of methodological conceptions [p. 42].

Thus it seems that a key to Hayek's views is to be found in his analysis of complexity. The nature and limitations of our understanding of complex systems ramify throughout the topics that Hayek has addressed during his career. Many of his essays and books are attempts to unpack the manner in which the problems of complexity provide a context of constraint that delimits the understanding that we may reasonably expect to achieve in a given domain. It is simply not rational to expect complex phenomena to be causally (or lawfully, or deterministically) related or controlled in the manner in which simple physical phenomena have been explained to be. But what is rationality, and what is a reasonable expectations for the understanding, modification, and control of complex systems?

RATIONALISM, SCIENTISM, AND THE PRETENSE OF KNOWLEDGE

From the foregoing analysis of complex phenomena, one can see that Hayek has little sympathy for traditional or, as I would call them, knee-jerk, progressive attitudes in the social sciences and economics. Transition to this topic is straightforward: Consider the rationality of planning and centralization of "control" for complex systems. Specifically, consider whether or not it is possible for a single, centralized planning board (or committee, or group of determiners of some sort) to accumulate and to utilize all the relevant information available in a complex system. The answer is that it is not possible—and this is Hayek's argument against planned economics, "collectivism", socialism, "fine tuning" of economic systems, etc. The complex phenomenon that is the economic system (essentially, the marketplace) cannot be made rational or subject to rational "control," in that sense. The rationality of complex systems is not localizable in a single locus of control, and it is therefore never "conscious."

Tacit Knowledge and the Nature of Rationality

We may develop Hayek's point by noting similarities to Michael Polanyi's distinction between tacit and explicit knowledge. Polanyi pointed out (in numerous publications—most importantly, *Personal Knowledge* [1958] and *The Tacit Dimension* [1966]) that most knowledge is tacit rather than explicit. Polanyi's (1958) point is that "tacit knowing is more fundamental than explicit knowing: *we can know more than we can tell and we can tell nothing without relying on our awareness of things we may not be able to tell* [p. x]." Our consciousness and explicit awareness, and the rationality that depends upon them, are a thin veneer upon the tacit dimension that, although it operates according to complex rules of determination, *is not consciously rational*. The most mundane psychological examples show the pervasive primacy of tacit knowing: All concept formation, perceptual thing-kind identification, as well as all skilled performances, are tacit. We have no explicit or formal account of how even the simplest instances are accomplished. We can do these things (and with considerable skill), but exactly what we are doing or how we are doing them, we cannot say; our heads are smarter than we are. The executive function of a conscious ego is simply not capable of accounting for (let alone understanding) our most mundane, everyday activity; in this sense our behavior is not rationally planned.

Hayek applies reasoning analogous to Polanyi's account of the psychological individual to the social phenomenon of the marketplace. After citing A. N. Whitehead to the effect that civilization advances when it can relegate more operations to tacit control, he argues 1952(a) in *The Counter-revolution of Science:* that

> Indeed, any social processes which deserve to be called 'social' in distinction to the action of individuals are almost *ex definitone* not conscious. In so far as such processes are capable of producing a useful order which could not have been produced by conscious direction, any attempt to make them subject to such direction would necessarily mean that we restrict what social activity can achieve to the inferior capacity of the individual mind [pp. 87–88].

Does this mean that our behavior (both individual and social-economic) is not rational? To the socialist collectivist, or economic engineer, it often does. And if not irrational, our behavior would seem to them unscientific: "No society can be regarded as fully scientific unless it has been created deliberately with a certain structure to fulfill certain purposes" (Russell, 1931, p. 203). Such theorists would embrace socialism and collectivist planning as the obvious application of "scientific method" to society and would assume that conscious, rational planning is always superior to seemingly unconscious and irrational traditions. This line of reasoning began with the writings of Comte and Saint Simon, and that earlier brand of positivism is part and parcel of the historicism of Marx and the communist planners, as well as the later "logical positivism" of theorists such as Otto Neurath, Joseph Schumpeter, and, to a considerable extent, the interventionist economics of J. M. Keynes.

Hayek argues in *The Counter-Revolution of Science* (1952a) that such reasoning exemplifies *scientism* rather than science and that it is based upon an untenable assumption: that complete specification of all relevant knowledge is not only possible but achievable by a central planning board. "The fact that no single mind can know more than a fraction of what is known to all individual minds sets limits to the extent to which conscious direction can improve upon the results of unconscious social processes. Man has not deliberately designed this process and has begun to understand it only long after it had grown up [p. 100]." Once more we are concerned with the limits of understanding, and a context of constraint that dictates the flow of events in complex phenomena.

But what is the problem that rational planning has presumed to address, and what alternative mechanisms are available? The problem appears to be that of the most efficient utilization of our resources. Hayek (1952a) turns this problem into one of "how that knowledge of the particular circumstances of the moment can be most effectively utilized [p. 98]." No single authority can possess enough knowledge of the particular at any time to succeed. Thus, Hayek (1952a) argues for individualism over collectivism:

> A successful solution can therefore not be based on the authority dealing directly with the objective facts, but must be based on a method of utilizing the knowledge dispersed among all members of society, knowledge of which in any particular instance the central authority will usually know neither who possesses it nor whether it exists at all. It can therefore not be utilized by consciously integrating it into a coherent whole, but only through some mechanism which will delegate the particular decisions to those who possess it, and for that purpose supply them with such information about the general situation as will enable them to make the best use of the particular circumstances of which only they know.
>
> This is precisely the function which the various "markets" perform [p. 99].

The problem of the maximal utilization of information can be handled by the market because it is a distributed knowledge transmitting system—"an instrument for communicating to all those interested in a particular commodity the relevant information in an abridged and condensed form. . . . [Markets] help to utilize the knowledge of many people without the need of first collecting it in a single body (Hayek, 1952a, p. 99). The market, in other words, functions because it decentralizes decisions and therefore militates against any single locus of control. The peculiar problem of a rational economic order, as *Individualism and Economic Order* (Hayek, 1948) argues, is that it is a problem "of the utilization of knowledge not given to anyone in its totality [p. 78]." That is, the problem concerns how we may make maximum use of our tacit knowledge and skill, rather than how to make the tacit component explicit (Hayek, 1948): "The problem is precisely how to extend the span of our utilization of resources beyond the span of the control of any one mind; and, therefore, how to dispense with the need of conscious control and how to provide inducements which will make the individuals do the desirable things without anyone having to tell them what to do [p. 88]."

Let us take stock for a moment. Hayek is concerned with complex phenomena and how they are organized as distributed knowledge and information-gathering and -transmitting systems. A further concern relates to the rationality of such systems: Hayek argues that they are not centralized or collectivized and not consciously rational. This runs directly counter to the constructivist rationalist world view that surrounds and undergirds "knee-jerk" progressivism—and so Hayek denies its naive rationality, its scientistic claim to a guaranteed method, and its pretense to knowledge. But the issue is not one of being pro or con rationalism and rational "control"; the issue is instead what rationality and control actually are, and Hayek is concerned to show the untenability of the dominant viewpoint, not to glorify irrationality. Hayek argues *for reason and against the abuse of reason.*

Two Kinds of Rationalism

To do this, he distinguishes between two kinds of rationalism—the "knee-jerk" variety that is committed to conscious planning and "objective scientific method," which he calls *rationalist constructivism;* and, borrowing the term from Karl Popper (1962), the *critical rationalism* that Hayek (1967) prefers.

Once again, this is constructivist rationalism:

Rationalism in this sense is the doctrine which assumes that all institutions which benefit humanity have in the past and ought in the future to be invented in clear awareness of the desirable effects that they produce; that they are to be approved and respected only to the extent that we can show that the particular effects they will produce in any given situations are preferable to the effects another arrangement will produce; and we have it in our power so to shape our institutions that of all possible sets of results that which we prefer to all others will be realized; and that our reason should never resort to automatic or mechanical devices when conscious

consideration of all factors would make preferable an outcome different from that
of the spontaneous process [p. 85].

The critical rationalism that Hayek (1967) champions acknowledges and even
stems from the context of constraint that limits human reasons:

> That we should not be able fully to shape human affairs according to our wishes
> went much against the grain of generations which believed that by the full use of his
> reason man could make himself fully master of his fate. It seems, however, that this
> desire to make everything subject to rational control, far from achieving the maxi-
> mal use of reason, is rather an abuse of reason based on a misconception of its
> powers, and in the end leads to a destruction of that free interplay of many minds on
> which the growth of reason nourishes itself. True rational insight seems indeed to
> indicate that one of the most important uses is the recognition of the proper limits of
> rational control [p. 93].

Hayek's rationalism is *abstract;* like the abstractness of explanations of the
principle, it is concerned to allow us to "make infinite use of finite means," to
be creative or productive in facing the indefinite range of possibilities that may
confront us. His argument for the rationality of following abstract, and often
unconscious, *rules of determination* (rather than making conscious choices at
each moment) is exactly parallel to Chomsky's arguments against finite state
grammars and associationistic psychologies; we would be incapable of addressing an infinite amount of complexity in perception and behavior unless we rely
on abstract, generative rules that are productive. He explains (1967):

> Since our whole life consists in facing ever new and unforeseeable circumstances,
> we cannot make it orderly by deciding in advance all the particular actions we shall
> take. The only manner in which we can in fact give our lives some order is to adopt
> certain abstract rules or principles for guidance, and then strictly adhere to the rules
> we have adopted in our dealing with the new situations as they arise. Our actions
> form a coherent and rational pattern, not because they have been decided upon as
> part of a single plan thought out beforehand, but because in each successive deci-
> sion we limit our range of choice by the same abstract rules [p. 90].

Hayek (1948) stresses the fundamental importance of abstract rules in the
governance of human affairs in relation to freedom; we can be free only insofar
as we are all bound to follow rules.

> Our submission to general principles is necessary because we cannot be guided in
> our practical action by full knowledge and evaluation of all the consequences. So
> long as men are not omniscient, the only way in which freedom can be given to the
> individual is by such general rules to delimit the sphere in which the decision is his.
> There can be no freedom if the government is not limited to particular kinds of
> action but can use its powers in any ways which serve particular ends. . . . Our main

conclusion is that an individualist order must rest on the enforcement of abstract principles rather than on the enforcement of specific orders [p. 19].

Scientism in the Study of Society

Hayek's reformulation of the rationality of social phenomena, which effectively removes conscious control from its definition, relates to and correlates with his distinction between explanations of the principle and the particular. Explanation of the principle, of the abstract rules of determination underlying the myriad particulars of complex phenomena, is all that we can hope to achieve and all that is involved in the rationality of such systems. Explanation of the principle, rules and abstractness, and rationality are thus interrelated in the complex phenomena with which the social and psychological sciences deal. Together they add up to a profound methodological difference separating the study of complex phenomena from the objectivistic and positivistic methodology that Vienna Circle Positivism assumed constituted "the scientific method" for any discipline worthy of the title "science." Hayek's philosophy of science is remarkably similar to that of Karl Popper, and both are the sharpest of possible breaks from the pseudo-objectivism of logical positivism and empiricism. We discuss some of that later, in historical relation to Hayek's understanding of David Hume, but now let us mention the methodological mistake Hayek sees in the positivistic approach to complex phenomena: *scientism*.

For Hayek (1952a) scientism is

> an attitude which is decidedly unscientific in the true sense of the word, since it involves a mechanical and uncritical application of habits of thought to fields different from those in which they have been formed. The scientistic as opposed to the scientific view is not an unprejudiced but a very prejudiced approach which, before it has considered its subject, claims to know what is the most appropriate way of investigating it [pp. 15-16].

It is the trespass of scientism into the study of society that Hayek regards as *The Counter-Revolution of Science*, the subtitle of which is *Studies on the Abuse of Reason*. Scientism is the Procrustean attempt to make the complex phenomena of humanity and society fit the model of science that positivists have assumed was represented by physics.

The ideal of a positivistic science is based upon "objectively specifiable data" that, when painstakingly gathered by induction into a single body (a central planning board), will eventuate into explanations of the particular. How does one collate all that information?—By utilizing the mathematics underlying "inductive logic,"—that is, statistical inference procedures—is the standard answer. Thus, it should not be surprising that economists who espouse the positivistic conception of science have been among the most ardent admirers and utilizers of statistics, and that they have used statistical models in economic theory and statistical results (especially "indexes" and "indicators") in forcasting and economic policy decision. The complexity and length of calculation in such work rivals that in physics and chemistry, and not surprisingly, economists treat it as being of the same significance as calculation in the physical sciences.

By now it should be obvious that Hayek regards this as scientism, as an instance in which methodology has become methodolatry through the uncritical acceptance of the idea that economics is a science exactly analogous to physics. Hayek (1948) spoke to this in "The Use of Knowledge in Society":

> The sort of knowledge with which I have been concerned [local knowledge of the particular in time and circumstance] is knowledge of the kind which by its nature cannot enter into statistics and therefore cannot be conveyed to any central authority in statistical form. The statistics which such a central authority would have to use would have to be arrived at precisely by abstracting from minor differences between the things, by lumping together, as resources of one kind, items which differ as regards location, quality, and other particulars, in a way which may be very significant for the specific decision [p. 83].

Inquiry into Complex Phenomena

If the phenomena of organized complexity are not susceptible to analysis in the same fashion as the less complex physical phenomena, then we must attempt to specify how and why such domains require a different methodology. To do so, we must become clear on the nature of the "facts" of the social sciences and their relation to theoretical construction and also of, to use Popper's (1957) turn of phrase, the poverty of historicism.

Consider first the problem of our knowledge of the intentions, beliefs, and actions of other individuals. How do we comprehend the behavior of other members of society? The answer is simple: "We invariably interpret their action on the analogy of our own mind: that is, that we group their actions, and the objects of their actions, into classes or categories which we know solely from the knowledge of our own mind" (Hayek, 1948, p. 63). Having achieved such analogical knowledge of other individuals, we can then become social scientists by using these behaviors as elements from which we "construct hypothetical models in an attempt to reproduce the patterns of social relationships which we know in the world around us [p. 68]."

This means that the task of theory in the social sciences is different from that in the physical sciences. Social theories do not discover by observation (or induction) any laws about social aggregates or "wholes" from the action of individuals. Instead they construct such wholes (Hayek, 1948): "Their task is rather, if I may so call it, to *constitute* these wholes, to provide schemes of structural relationships [p. 72]" that the theorists use to interpret the individual action they observe. Thus, theories in complex social domains do not consist of laws (empirical generalizations) about physically specifiable objects. A consequence of their non law gathering character is that no social theory is ever "empirical" enough to be either verified or falsified by reference to "facts."

> The theory itself, the mental scheme for the interpretation, can never be "verified" but only tested for its consistency. It may be irrelevant because the conditions to which it refers never occur; or it may prove inadequate because it does not take account of a sufficient number of conditions. But it can no more be disproved by facts than can logic or mathematics [Hayek, 1948, p. 73].

Our position is quite different when we conduct social science inquiry from when we look at the natural science world. We look at the physical world as "external" objects in relation to which we are on the outside. Physical science concepts are theoretical inferences about the facts of this realm and must be adapted to and corrected by such external facts. When we look at society, it is from the inside, and some of our most familiar concepts are the constituents of which the social realm is made. All that we can understand of this realm is thus already in our own minds, and our theories are in that sense rationalizations of what we are acquainted with. As Hayek (1948) wrote:

> In the social sciences it is the elements of the complex phenomena which are known beyond the possibility of dispute. In the natural sciences they can be at best only surmised. The existence of these elements is so much more certain than any regularities in the complex phenomena to which they give rise that it is they which constitute the truly empirical factor in the social sciences [p. 126].

Any attempt to apply the physical science generalization-from-particulars-to-laws approach to social phenomena will thus be stultifying, since it will find no "laws" that can be "induced" from the chaotic welter of particulars, almost all of which are novel. Historicism, arguing that there are no laws of social phenomena and thus no recurrently identifiable "causes" of social events, will be the result. A thinker such as Marx will then argue that economics, say, is only particular historical development, and that economic "science" is only a description of historical change. Such scientism can lead only to disaster, as "Socialist Calculation" (Hayek, 1948) notes:

> To start here at the wrong end, to seek for regularities of complex phenomena which could never be observed twice under identical conditions, could not but lead to the conclusion that there were no general laws, no inherent necessities determined by the permanent nature of the constituting elements, and that the only task of economic science in particular was a description of historical change [p. 127].

The "poverty" of historicism, then, is self-induced, resulting from the misapplication of hard science procedure to the social realm.

Experimentation or Demonstration?

The natural sciences have been enormously successful in employing the experimental method. Empirical laws are the result of our ability to experiment, which is essentially the ability to simplify and control a situation to the extent that it can be repeated, either under identical conditions or those that we choose to vary systematically. The experimental techniques at the command of the natural scientist are thus designed to isolate and identify the definite regularities in observed phenomena. The elaborate statistical apparatus that has grown under the guise of "inferential statistics" is based upon the possibility of repetition (at least partial) under controlled conditions, and the concept of statistical "significance," so beloved of editors and referees in the social sciences, presupposes that we can control a situation sufficiently to detect deviations from expected distributional outcomes.

In the domains of complex phenomena, however, this conception of experimentation is as impossible to achieve as is the induction of laws from facts. As Hayek (1948) noted, "Experiment is impossible, and we have therefore no knowledge of definite regularities in the complex phenomena in the same sense as we have in the natural sciences [p. 126]." Instead of the experimental isolation of relevant variables, the empirical research in complex social phenomena consists in the construction of situations in which we demonstrate to ourselves that we can produce "facts" of which we are already well aware. Our demonstrations "test" our theoretical models only in the sense already noted; they compare the consistency of our theoretical model with an analogical knowledge of social phenomena, but they neither confirm nor refute them in any logical sense.

Hayek's reasoning on this point is in agreement with both of the classic "fathers" of psychology, Wundt and Brentano. Wundt's original program—as sketched in his *Physiological Psychology* (see, e.g., Boring, 1950, for references) in 1873-1874—defined "psychology" as the experimental study of the "lower" mental processes; the "higher" mental processes were left to the *Volkerpsychologie,* to be studied by historical and cultural anthropological techniques. Brentano, in his *Psychology from an Empirical Standpoint* in 1873, defined "psychology" as the study of the higher mental processes and argued that although it was an empirical discipline, it could not be experimental. Both theorists used arguments similar to those employed by Hayek to make their point. This point of agreement in the otherwise opposed viewpoints, to say nothing of its implication for the conduct of research, was lost with the rise of scientistic positions such as behaviorism, which owed their success in the main to either ignoring the higher cognitive phenomena or reductively defining them in "lower" mental process terms. Since behaviorism as a substantive psychological theory has been increasingly acknowledged to be inadequate in the last decades, it is now time to consider repudiating the behavioristic version of method as well.

But to do so, we will have to realize that it does not represent, as its proponents loudly proclaim, "the only way" to be scientific.

Excursus: The Future of Economics

J. M. Keynes is without doubt the most significant theorist in the recent past of economics. The current scene is all but unintelligible except in terms of reactions, either for or against, Keynes' positions. This chapter need not discuss the substance of those views, but in this context it is appropriate to note that Keynes epitomized the rationalist constructivist approach to economics, both in his doctrines and in his views of his own importance and role within the intellectual community. Methodologically, he was a devotee of the easily measurable as definitive of the economic whole and is in large part responsible for the ascendancy of macro-analysis over micro-analysis as the backbone of technical economics. By now it should not be surprising that Hayek (1978) should say this about the future of Keynes' views:

> Keynes' theories will appear merely as the most prominent and influential instance of a general approach to philosophical justification of which seems to be highly questionable. Though with its reliance on apparently measurable magnitude it *appears* at first more scientific than the older micro-theory, it seems to me that it has achieved this pseudo-exactness at the price of disregarding the relationships which really govern the economic system. Even though the schemata of micro-economics do not claim to achieve those quantitative predictions at which the ambitions of macro-economics aim, I believe by learning to content ourselves with the more modest aims of the former, we shall gain more insight into at least the principle on which the complex order of economic life operates, than by the artificial simplification necessary for macrotheory which tends to conceal nearly all that really matters [p. 289].

THE FUNDAMENTAL PROBLEM OF THE SOCIAL SCIENCES: THE ECONOMY OF KNOWLEDGE

We have been concerned to specify a context of constraint that unifies Hayek's thought on a wide range of topics. Thus far we have concentrated upon methodological points, such as the nature of our understanding of complex systems, scientism and the pretense of knowledge, the tacit dimension, etc.; and also the broader context of the nature of rationality, such as the inadequacies of rationalist constructivism. Now we must mention the problem of knowledge that underlies all economic and social scientific inquiry.

The marketplace acts by decentralizing control: It divides the knowledge necessary for its functioning among its participants. This *division of knowledge,* which is characteristic of complex systems, is the central problem of economic analysis: "The problem which we pretend to solve is how the spontaneous interaction of a number of people, each possessing only bits of knowledge, brings about a state of affairs in which prices correspond to costs, etc., and which could be brought about by deliberate direction only by somebody who possessed the combined knowledge of all those individuals" (Hayek, 1948, pp. 50–51). The central problem of economics is thus one of knowledge—in a wide sense of "knowledge" that includes not only current prices but also broader information such as how different commodities may be obtained and then used, and various other possibilities for future action. From this we can generalize to all the "social" sciences. The problem is (Hayek, 1948): "How can the combination of fragments of knowledge existing in different minds bring about results which, if they were to be brought about deliberately, would require a knowledge on the part of the directing mind which no single person can possess [p. 54]?"

To return to a familiar theme, this central problem must be faced quite differently, from the standpoint of scientific analysis, in the social realm than in the natural sciences. In the natural sciences, the basic phenomena with which we deal are always inferential—that is, theoretical constructions in what Russell (1948) called knowledge by description. When we do "natural" science, it is of necessity "from the outside"; and we gain knowledge by experimentation, which is essentially the repetition of conditions to detect regularities in phenomena of interest. In short, in the natural sciences (Hayek, 1948):

> All that experience shows us is the result of processes which we cannot directly observe and which it is our task to reconstruct. All our conclusions concerning the nature of these processes are of necessity hypothetical, and the only test of the validity of these hypotheses is that they prove equally applicable to the explanation of other phenomena [p. 125–126].

In the social sciences, on the other hand, it is the "facts" that constitute our (Russellian) acquaintance, and if we know anything directly, it is these social "facts." The empirical element in the social sciences is thus *nonphysical,* comprising the functionally (rather than physically) specified ingredients of our acquaintance as social beings. The sort of understanding that science can achieve here is quite different. In the social sciences (Hayek, 1948):

> Experiment is impossible, and we have therefore no knowledge of definite regularities in the complex phenomena in the same sense as we have in the natural sciences. But, on the other hand, the position of man, midway between the natural and social phenomena—of the one of which he is an effect and of the other a cause—brings it about that the essential basic facts which we need for the explanation of social phenomena are part of common experience, part of the stuff of our thinking [p. 126].

The "stuff of our thinking"—that is, knowledge—is thus a key to Hayek's work; the remarkable *economy* of knowledge that results from the division of knowledge in complex phenomena is central to both his economic analysis and his psychology. Indeed one way to understand *The Sensory Order* is that it is an exploration of how a central nervous system, as a complex phenomenon, could effect such an economy of knowledge.

HISTORICAL BACKGROUND: DAVID HUME AND THE BANKRUPTCY OF 18TH-CENTURY RATIONALITY

Hayek's writings have an intrinsic historical quality; every topic he addresses is discussed in sufficient depth of historical development that it often appears as tbough his major points are only restatements and elaborations of positions that his intellectual ancestors have originated and defended. It is not just modesty that masks Hayek's originality; his historical and interdisciplinary scholarship continues the tradition in which great figures in the development of economics were also great figures in philosophy, social theory, and even psychology. Today that fact is often lost upon specialists in each domain. But as he noted (1967):

> It is certainly no accident that, so far as economics is concerned, in England, the country which has so long been leading in the subject, a list of her great economists, if we leave out only two major figures, might readily be taken for a list of her great philosophers: Locke, Hume, Adam Smith, Bentham, James and John Stuart Mill, Samuel Bailey, W. S. Jevons, Henry Sidgwick, to John Neville, and John Maynard Keynes—all occupy equally honoured places in the history of economics as in that of philosophy or of scientific method [p. 131].

Hayek has assimilated a far more comprehensive view of these thinkers than is taught in any of the disciplines alone, and some major themes in his work can be brought into sharp focus by studying the thought of David Hume, whom Hayek greatly admires, as an indicator of the bankruptcy of 18th-century enlightenment.

Rationalist Constructivism and 18th-Century Enlightenment

Hume is of focal importance in philosophy, psychology, and economics, but the pictures one receives of the man's thought in typical history courses of those disciplines are so disparate and disjointed that he appears to be a different man in each. The philosopher learns of Hume, the skeptical empiricist, whose persistent probings into rationalist (in the traditional philosophical sense) method disclosed the problem of the justification of induction, which has devastated justificationist epistemology ever since. It was Hume who relegated "scientific method" and all other inductive inference procedures to the realm of "mere animal belief." The next topic that the philosopher studies is Hume's reduction of causality to "nothing but" the constant conjunction of ingredients in our experience, and then perhaps Hume's contention that the ''self'' is not a substance but rather a bundle of sensations. Such skeptical views led Bertrand Russell (1945), in many ways the epitome of 20th-century constructivist rationalism, to conclude:

> Hume's philosophy, whether true or false, represents the bankruptcy of eighteenth century reasonableness. He starts out, like Locke, with the intention of being sensible and empirical, taking nothing on trust, but seeking whatever instruction is to be obtained from experience and observation. But having a better intellect than Locke's, a great acuteness in analysis, and a smaller capacity for accepting comfortable inconsistencies, he arrives at the disastrous conclusion that from experience and observation nothing is to be larnt. There is no such thing as a rational belief [p. 672].

Thus, rather than rational, human behavior becomes a matter of ''mere animal belief.''

At this point, the psychologist steps in and learns that Hume is the thinker who completed the transformation of British empiricism into British associationism. Hume's psychology—which is a naive associationism not unlike that of his predecessors such as Hartley, Berkeley, and even Hobbes—provides an account of how the *appearance* of rational and well-ordered ideas (such as the doctrine of empiricism) can arise from ''nothing but'' the principles of association. Thus, Hume accounts for mere animal belief in terms of the ''laws'' of associationism (resemblance, contingity, and cause and effect). (Note that this makes causality and induction psychological, not logical, notions.)

It is interesting to note that philosophical and psychological primers dismiss Hume's social and political philosophy, and his economic views, as unoriginal (if they are mentioned at all). Russell (1945) mentioned his ''other'' views as suffering from carelessness and inattention (p. 672) and regarded his history of England as biased: ''He did not consider history worthy of philosophic detachment [p. 660].'' Few other histories of philosophy emphasize Hume's social and economic views (Fuller & McMurrin, 1955, give it two pages); Boring's (1950) famous psychology text fails to mention it at all.

So what could Hayek, trained in the Austrian tradition, find of interest in the thoroughly Scottish thought of Hume? Certainly neither his empiricism nor associationism. Hayek's psychological training (as Chapter 13 in this volume indicates) was sufficient to lead him away from a superficial doctrine like associationism and eventually led him to publish an alternative view in *The Sensory Order* (1952b). Hayek's fellow Viennese, Karl Popper, took Hume seriously about the impossibility of justifying induction, and argued for testability and falsifiability in scientific methodology instead of inductivism (which is, after all, a variant of associationism) in his famous *Logik der Forschung* in 1934 (Popper, 1959). Hayek's own methodology either adopts or anticipates most of Popper's thought, so it is worth discussing the relationship between empiricism, associationism, and inductivism.

Empiricism (in global terms) is the doctrine that "knowledge is a deliverance of sense," that the origin and foundation of all knowledge is the sensory experience of the observer. The empiricist is the one who will *look to see* how many teeth a horse has (in the case of the classical Greek query) rather than intuit or deduce from first principles what the answer should be (as did the Greek rationalist). Empiricism as a metaphysical doctrine thus leads directly to a methodology for the acquisition of knowledge—inductivism. Inductivism claims that knowledge is built up (induced) by the accumulation of sensory experiences, that our theoretical systems are founded upon and result from the accumulation of observational "facts." Inductive "method" is the philosopher's term for how this is supposed to happen. Associationism is the doctrine that the mind "works" by knitting together (associating) basic mental elements (historically, "ideas"; recently, "habits") according to specified conditions (contiguity in place and time, etc.). Hume's critique of inductivism forced empiricism to abandon its pretense of grand philosophical method for cruder psychological support; that is the import of the thesis that knowledge is "mere" animal belief (psychological association) rather than proven truth (via inductive "logic").

Popper's (1959) Humean attack on empiricism is twofold. First, he agrees with and reinforces the arguments against a "logic" that induces theoretical knowledge from facts by showing that "observation" and sensory "experience" are theoretically determined. The conceptual nature of facts, removing its objectivity and foundational features, turns empiricism upside down, forcing one to a theory of the organism to account for how we construct facts. Without developing a psychology in detail, Popper's second attack on empiricism denies its account of the nature of knowledge as proven assertion. For Popper (especially 1963), knowledge is a matter of conjectures—literally, guesses—that are never justifiable (or verifiable, proven true, etc.). Our "empirical" knowledge is thus tentative, subject to revision, forever. We can never prove "for certain" except in logic and mathematics. Instead, science advances by "refuting" theories that do not accord with the evidence when we construct a situation to test them. Testability and falsifiability allow science and knowledge to grow in the total absence of any inductive logic.

Being familiar with Popper's arguments, Hayek has applied the notion of potential falsifiability to the assessment of theories of complex phenomena. In domains that are sufficiently complex to require explanations of the principle, one could never "inductively" establish a theory because one could never get from the welter of particulars to the principles. Falsifiability, even if it can only be conventionally specified, is the only "empirical" assessment available. But unlike Popper, Hayek went on to develop a theoretical psychology to explain how the organism constructs not only its theories but its sensory experience in a nonjustificational, noninductivist fashion. In so doing, *The Sensory Order* adopts much of Hume's critique of inductivism without endorsing associationism, effectively updating Hume's psychology to the 20th century. Thus Hayek (1952b) rejects empiricism by a consistent application of its basic idea:

Precisely because all our knowledge, including the initial order of our different sensory experiences of the world, is due to experience, it must contain elements which cannot be contradicted by experience. It must always refer to classes of elements which are defined by certain relations to other elements, and it is valid only on the assumption that these relations actually exist. Generalization based upon experience must refer to classes of objects or events and can have relevance to the world only insofar as these classes are regarded as given irrespective of the statement itself. Sensory experience presupposes, therefore, an order of experienced objects which precedes that experience and which cannot be contradicted by it, though it is itself due to other, earlier experience [p. 172].

Physiological a priorism and the tacit dimension of neural organization argue simultaneously against empiricism and for realism.

But what of Hume the social philosopher? The bankruptcy of 18th-century enlightenment not only refers to the myth of inductivism and surefire "method" in science but, more broadly, to the whole of rationalist constructivism. In arguing against the rationalist dream of a method of scientific inference, Hume was emphasizing the contructivist rationalist approach to science; in social philosophy, he argued that social conventions and moral rules are not the end products of conscious rationality—that society is, in Adam Ferguson's phrase, the result of human action but not of human design. The "enlightenment" that Hume saw as bankrupt was epitomized in the French tradition, stemming from Descartes, that culminated in the constructivist ideal that society would be rational only if it was the product of conscious design and was entered into with full awareness of its rules (Rousseau's idea of the "social contract"). His attempt, in other words, was to whittle down the claims of reason by rational analysis, by showing that a spontaneously formed order ("artifacts"), neither "natural" in the sense of innate nor "artificial" in the sense of consciously planned, led to the social and moral structure that "rationalists" had assumed to be the glory of conscious rational planning. As "The Legal and Political Philosophy of David Hume" put it (Hayek, 1967):

It is no accident that Hume develops his political and legal ideas in his philosophical work. They are most intimately connected with his general philosophical conceptions, especially with his skeptical views on the "narrow bounds of human understanding". His concern was human nature in general, and his theory of knowledge was intended mainly as a step towards an understanding of the conduct of man as a moral being and as a member of society. What he produced was above all a theory of the growth of human institutions which became the basis of his case for liberty and the foundation of the work of the great Scottish moral philosophers [pp. 110-111].

Hume's skepticism, exemplified in his trenchant criticisms of received-view doctrines, is not solely directed at justificationist epistemology and philosophy;

the target includes those and other aspects of constructivist rationalism. By stressing the limits of explicit rationality; the unavailability of conclusive method in knowledge acquisition; and the psychological basis of knowledge, inference, and expectation, Hume was able to account for the appearance of rational social phenomena by emphasizing the notions of the evolution of social systems over time and the spontaneous formation of an order. As Hayek notes (1978): "In the moral and political sphere Mandeville and Hume did show that the sense of justice and probity on which the order in this sphere rested, was not originally implanted in man's mind but had, like that mind itself, grown in a process of gradual evolution which at least in principle we might learn to understand [p. 265]."

If one can fault Hume with historical hindsight, it would be on two points: first, the inadequacy of his psychology to account for the competences of the tacit and explicit mind; second, the failure to provide a consistently worked out nonjustificational philosophy in which the "positive" merit of his "negative" conclusions could be seen. We are just beginning, with the aid of *The Sensory Order,* to tackle the first problem. The second, I believe, is in principle resolved with positive but nonjustificational epistemologies, as I have outlined in Weimer (1979). But the integrity of Hume's thought and the relevance of his social and political views will only be clear if one abandons the rationalist constructivism and justificationism that permeates accounts such as Russell's.

Evolution of Society and Spontaneous Order

Hayek (1967) notes one further important reason why Hume's views were misunderstood and have not been acted upon. "The explanation lies largely in an accusation which with some justice has often been leveled against Hume, the accusation that his philosophy was essentially negative. The great skeptic, with his profound conviction of the imperfection of all human reason and knowledge, did not expect much positive good from political organization [p.120]." It is a truism in the history of science and philosophy that a "paradigm" will not be abandoned unless there is an alternative that can address the domain at least as successfully and can also provide new insights. Destructive criticism alone, no matter how devastating, fails to overthrow an entrenched view. Hume's skepticism is universally recognized as devastating, but few have seen any positive program in it.

Hayek argues that there is a positive program in the "negatives" and that the abstract ideals that we desire, such as liberty and justice, are essentially negative constraints upon our conduct rather than positive goals to be achieved. When one understands the primacy of the abstract within—and the evolutionary nature of—social organization, it becomes clearer why prohibitions to action and the absence of prescribed goals can specify a positive program, in the sense that what is important is a framework that allows certain possibilities to occur in unforeseen circumstances. We presaged this argument earlier in the discussion of freedom as bound to abstract rules rather than enforcement of specifics; let us now consider it in the context of the twin notions, stemming from Mandeville and Hume, of the evolution of society and the development of spontaneous order.

The evolution of society is historically obvious but virtually invisible in the present. The evolutionary selection of rules of conduct operates through the viability of the social order that it produces; if the resultant order is stable and productive, the rules will be selected for survival. Thus the system of rules of conduct must develop as a whole, and a given individual in a society will have little knowledge of anything beyond the particulars with which he or she is acquainted. At each stage of development, the overall prevailing order determines what effect, if any, changes in the individual's conduct will produce. We can judge and modify our conduct only within a framework that, although the product of gradual evolution, remains for us a relatively fixed result of evolution. This framework becomes, very literally, a context of constraints. Thus in summarizing to ourselves the effects of the social system upon individual conduct, we arrive at a set of particular descriptions of conduct—largely in terms of prohibitions to action—that instantiate abstract rules whose formulation, effect, and survival value we are unaware of. As "Notes on the Evolution of Systems of Rules of Conduct" (Hayek, 1967) indicates, we are like the "primitive" studied by the anthropologist:

> The individual may have no idea what this overall order is that results from his observing such rules as those concerning kinship and intermarriage, or the succession to property, or which function this overall order serves. Yet, all the individuals of the species which exist will behave in that manner because groups of individuals which have thus behaved have displaced those which did not do so [p. 70].

This leads to an inversion of the cause and effect relationship between the society as a whole and the individual. The complex social structure will exist because the individuals, who were selected by an earlier stage in the complex structure, do what is necessary to secure its continuation. The system is avowedly teleological, even though there is no single creator or central planning board for whom the system exists. This is the sense in which Adam Smith's famous remark, in *The Wealth of Nations,* that individuals are led to promote an end that is not part of their intentions, must be understood. There is no "invisible hand" of a creator (or surrogate such as a sovereign) involved: One must not assume, as did subsequent writers, that someone who does not promote his or her own individual ends must promote those of another agent or planner. One must not interpret the social rules of conduct that result from our actions but not our designs either anthropomorphically or animistically.

The development of a spontaneous social order will depend in large part upon taboos and prohibitions to individual action. This is so not simply because it is easier to state particular "thou shalt nots" than abstract "thou shalts." Such prohibitions to action are also the result of our partial knowledge of our world in combination with a fear of the unknown. Norms appear to be an adaptation to factual regularities that are relatively dependable only when we obey those norms. (Once deliberately taught, it is almost always in animistic terms, associated with the will of a particular mentor or some supernatural agency—such as the blindfolded "Justice" with "her" scales.) We tend to choose between alternatives on the basis of our knowledge of their consequences, preferring those that are known and relatively predictable to those that are unknown, unpredictable, and thus frightening (Hayek, 1967):

> Taboos or negative rules acting through the paralyzing action of fear will, as a kind of knowledge of what *not* to do, constitute just as significant information about the environment as any positive knowledge of the attitudes of the objects of this environment. While the latter enables us to predict the consequences of particular actions, the former just warns us not to take certain kinds of action. At least so long as the normative rules consist of prohibitions, as most of them probably did before they were interpreted as commands of another will, the 'thou shalt not' kind of rule may after all not be so very different from the rules giving us information about what is [p. 81].

Thus to the extent that our world is not completely known to us (and therefore predictable), the culturally transmitted prohibitions to action have considerable survival value both for the individual and society. It would appear that we should attempt to increase our tolerance for ambiguity rather than attempt the replacement of prohibitions merely because we do not understand how they arose or what function they serve. Like the British, we should be more willing to "make do" with what we have available. The "make do" attitude that the British tradition represents is not a return to concern with only the specifics of a given case, but rather a firm grasp of general principles; so that the English (having a context of constraint firmly in mind) are aware of what can and can't be done in particular cases without discussion of abstract ideas. It is not because they are indifferent to abstract principles that the British can "muddle through," but because they have them so firmly in mind. Their freedom is a matter of everyone being bound equally by the abstract rule of law and a refusal to legislate specifics or decide a case "solely on its merits." Such a position enables a society to cope with novel occurrences, to venture into the unknown and unexplored, because the reliance upon abstract principles encompasses the *possible* as well as the *particular* and is not limited to what has already been experienced. The problem of productivity or creativity in conduct, which is above all the possibility of new development and learning for the future, requires the primacy of the abstract over the particular.

Having realized this in social philosophy and economic theory, Hayek returned to the problem of developing a theoretical psychology to account for how the mind could exhibit such skills. The results of his investigation are in *The Sensory Order* and in more recent essays, such as "The Primacy of the Abstract" and "Rules, Perception, and Intelligibility." But before examining that psychology, let us tie up one loose end relating to the folklore of "18th-century enlightenment." Since Hayek represents an older British tradition against rationalist constructivist doctrines such as socialism, one might assume that he is a conservative. Let us see why this is not so.

Excursus: Liberalism or Conservatism?

The front cover of the paperback edition of *Capitalism and the Historians* (1954) says that it is "a defense of the early factory system and its social and economic consequences by a group of distinguished conservative historians." Although we rarely attach much importance to the "pap for the masses" that publishers plaster on dust jackets to increase sales, the folk knowledge it represents is often quite entrenched. Since Hayek is not a socialist, it is folk knowledge that he must be a conservative—just as it is folk knowledge that anyone who would defend capitalism must be a reactionary conservative. This folk knowledge persists despite Hayek's criticism of both conservatism and socialism and his defense of liberalism and the English Whig tradition. Let us pause to examine some of the issues to see why Hayek is not a conservative.

The socialist view of history has become a folklore of its own, and Hayek's (1954) defense of capitalism is largely an attempt to discredit one widespread socialist myth:

> The remarkable thing about this view (socialist political history) is that most of the assertions to which it has given the status of "facts which everybody knows" have long been proved not to have been facts at all; yet they still continue, outside the circle of professional economic historians, to be almost universally accepted. . . . Certain beliefs, for instance, about the evolution and effects of tradeunions, the alleged progressive growth of monopoly, the deliberate destruction of commodity stock as a result of competition. . . , about the suppression of beneficial inventions, the causes and effects of "imperialism," and the role of the armament industries or of "capitalists" in general in causing war, have become part of the folklore of our time [pp. 7–9].

The particular myth Hayek seeks to rebut in the essay "History and Politics" (1954) is:

> The legend of the deterioration of the position of the working classes in consequence of the rise of "capitalism" (or of the "manufacturing" or the "industrial system"). Who has not heard of the horrors of early capitalism and gained the impression that the advent of this system brought untold new suffering to large classes who before were tolerably content and comfortable [pp. 9–10]?

In defending capitalism on this account, Hayek is not being a conservative in the sense that conservatism defends the status quo against change. Rather, Hayek argues that the Whig tradition and that of capitalism contain within themselves the means for their own gradual improvement: Progress results from the capacity of the system to remedy errors that it itself uncovers. In this regard Hayek's approach to the economic and sociopolitical "system" is strikingly parallel to Popper's conception of the growth of knowledge resulting from a feedback process in which error is detected and eliminated. But whereas Popper sees the growth of knowledge resulting from self-conscious criticism in the attempt to refute erroneous theories, Hayek sees the growth and progress of society as much more tacit, resulting from strict adherence to abstract and impersonal principles that transcend any individuals or special groups within the society. The abstract principles constitute the rule of law, and it is as a result of strict adherence to the rule of law that we can have both individual freedom and liberty. Hayek's constant theme is that only by internalizing or making tacit the rule of law can we be free and progress to new achievements, even though we may not know in advance, or be able to predict, what form that progress will take. Conservatism, on the other hand, merely opposes change—it has no positive program for growth and change at all. Hayek (1960) wrote:

> The decisive objection to any conservatism . . . is that by its very nature it cannot offer an alternative to the direction in which we are moving. . . . It has, for this reason, invariably been the fate of conservatism to be dragged along a path not of its own choosing. The tug of war between conservatives and progressives can only affect the speed, not the direction of contemporary developments [p. 398].

THE PSYCHOLOGY OF *THE SENSORY ORDER*

Hayek is at all times an epistemologist, especially when doing technical economics, and even in his historical and popular writings. The subject matter of epistemology is the theory of knowledge—its nature, manner of acquisition, and how it is embodied. Hayek's constant concern is how knowledge is manifested in phenomena of organized complexity, and his analysis often centers on the tacit dimension of that manifestation and on the primacy of abstract rules of determination over particulars at the surface level of analysis. Those themes have already been developed above in social and cultural terms; we have not often needed to consider the nature of the individual as a phenomenon of organized complexity. Now we must explore the nature of the psychological subject, the individual who acquires knowledge and participates in complex social phenomena, to complement the sociocultural account. We begin by exploring the primacy of the abstract in what we call "mind."

What Is Mind?

Consider these passages from "The Primacy of the Abstract" (1978):

> We ought to regard what we call mind as a system of abstract rules of action (each "rule" defining a class of actions) which determines each action by a combination of several such rules; while every appearance of a new rule (or abstraction) constitutes a change in that system, something which its own operations cannot produce but which is brought about by extraneous factors.
>
> This implies that the richness of the sensory world in which we live, and which defies exhaustive analysis by our mind, is not the starting point from which the mind derives abstractions, but the product of a great range of abstractions which the mind must posess in order to be capable of experiencing that richness of the particular [pp. 43–44].

The emphasis upon abstraction and rules of order should be familiar by now; what is less familiar is the application of such notions to the phenomenal order of our experiences. Let us develop the line of reasoning that leads to the conclusions in that quotation.

Hayek begins by formulating the central problem for theoretical psychology in epistemic terms: There is a discrepancy between the order of appearances in phenomenal experience and what physical science indicates to be the physical order in the realm external to our senses. Psychology must start with stimulation, defined in physical terms, and show why and how our senses classify physically similar stimuli as alike in certain circumstances and as different in others. This is the classic problem of stimulus equivalence under disparate circumstances and stimulus disequivalence under similar circumstances. As *The Sensory Order* puts it (1952b):

> What psychology has to explain is . . . something which we experience whenever we learn anything about the external world and through which indeed we know about the external word; and which yet has no place in our scientific picture of the external world and is in no way explained by the sciences dealing with the external world: Qualities. Whenever we study qualitative differences between experiences we are studying mental and not physical events, and much that we believe to know about the external world is, in fact, knowledge about ourselves [pp. 6–7].

Structural Realism and the Nature of Scientific Knowledge

This epistemic inquiry requires that we be very clear about the nature of the knowledge that science may be said to disclose. Here Hayek's views are virtually identical with those of (the later) Bertrand Russell (1948), with both theorists formulating what has come to be called structural realism. Russell's thesis (especially as developed by Maxwell, 1968, 1970) is that all that we are directly acquainted with is our own phenomenal experience, whereas all our knowledge of the nonmental realm (including our physical bodies) is in terms of description of properties that we are never directly acquainted with. Our physical knowledge is of the structural (rather than intrinsic) properties of nonmental objects known by description in relational terms rather than intrinsic properties known by acquaintance. All nonexperiential knowledge (theoretical, conceptual, commonsensical, etc.) is inferential and relational and is never absolute or intrinsic. The undergoing of experience is one thing; our descriptive knowledge of experience is another. The latter is, like all theoretical knowledge, a description of relations. We can never know the absolute properties of experience: The moment we pass from undergoing experience to classifying, describing, theorizing about, etc., it, we have moved from acquaintance to description. Thus, although experience is infinitely rich phenomenally, a blind man can know all of physics and even perceptual psychology. As Hayek (1952b) said:

> There are no questions which we can intelligibly ask about sensory qualities which could not also conceivably become a problem to a person who has not himself experienced the particular qualities but knows of them only from the descriptions given to him by others. . . . Nothing can become a problem about sensory qualities which cannot in principle also be described in words; and such a description in words will always have to be a description in terms of the relation of the quality in question to other sensory qualities [p. 31].

From this it becomes obvious that what we call mind is actually an order of events, and that all attributes of mental events are a complex of relations. If the attributes of sensory qualities are relations (to other qualities) and the totality of such relations exhausts the mental realm, then mind is a relational ordering of events. It is a short step from this to mind as a system of abstract rules of action (to produce either experience or behavior), as in the quotation with which we began.

The Nervous System as an Instrument of Classification

If the mental realm is a relational order, then the central nervous system—as the physiological substrate of that order—must be capable of differentiating and comparing relational structurings of events. The functioning of the nervous system must effect a classification of the objects comprising the mental realm in the course of its activity. This is not only how the phenomenal order of sensation arises but also the mechanism underlying "higher" cognitive phenomena such as perception and conception. All our knowledge thus arises because of the nervous system's ability to classify and reclassify its own activity. The classificatory activity of the nervous system *results* in our perceptual experience of the richness of phenomena: The *memory* of the nervous system *creates* such phenomena. As

Hayek (1952b) put it: "We do not first have sensations which are then preserved by memory, but it is as a result of physiological memory that the physiological impulses are converted into sensations. The connexions between the physiological elements are thus the primary phenomenon which creates the mental phenomena [p. 53]."

This means that abstract (conceptual) organization always precedes and determines the characteristics of sensation. The primacy of the abstract is, in essence, that particulars in experience can only become the particulars that they are in virtue of the prior organization and classificatory ability of the nervous system. Classification of information as sensory is the result of complicated neural activity rather than the beginning of it. Hayek (1952b) wrote:

> It is only insofar as the nervous system has learnt . . . to treat a particular stimulus as a member of a certain class of events, determined by the connexions which all the corresponding impulses possess with the same impulses representing other classes of events, that an event can be perceived at all, i.e., that it can obtain a distinct position in the system of sensory qualities [p. 166].

This conception has important philosophical consequences. Consider first the impossibility of achieving unique perceptions. If perception is classification, we can never perceive unique properties of individual objects; we rather perceive only those properties that the objects have in common with other objects. Perception as classification is always interpretation, putting a pattern of impulses into one or another category. As Hayek (1952b) put it, more strongly: "An event of an entirely new kind which has never occurred before, and which sets up impulses which arrive in the brain for the first time, could not be perceived at all [p. 142]." This point is long familiar to nativistic and "relativistic" philosophers, and is well embodied in Goethe's famous dictum that were the eye not attuned to see it, the sun could not be seen by it. This provides a physiological correlate to the philosophical doctrine of factual relativity, which argues that facts are theoretically specified rather than given in advance of experience.

As a second consequence, all specification of particulars becomes a consequence of abstraction. The particular qualities that we attributed to objects in our experience are (Hayek, 1952b) "strictly speaking not properties of that object at all, but a set of relations by which our nervous system classifies them [p. 143]." This is structural realism again, once one realizes that the patternings of neural impulses provide knowledge by description (only) of nonmental objects. Perception as classification is always interpretation, which is always abstraction, which is always knowledge by description.

As a third consequence, the surface-deep distinction, recently reemphasized (and forced back into psychology) by transformational linguistics stemming from Chomsky, follows automatically. The particular ingredients in phenomenal experience are the product of deep conceptual structures (patterns of neural activity) that are generative or productive as the linguist uses the term. Further, those deep conceptual structures are always tacit: Although they provide the framework for our experience, they never occur within it. That is why Hayek (1952b) argues that "sensory experience presupposes . . . an order of experienced objects which precedes that experience and which cannot be contradicted by it, though it is itself due to other, earlier experience [p. 172]."

Mapping and Modeling

With this account of the nature of neural activity, one must still provide an account of an organism's adaptation to its environment. This is the traditional psychological problem of learning. Hayek treats it analogously to the marketplace, asking how knowledge is achieved by a distributed information-gathering system that has evolved during a long evolutionary history. His answer is found in the concepts of mapping and modeling.

As a result of the successive classification of impulses at different levels of CNS activity, it becomes obvious that the "signals reaching the higher and more comprehensive centres will often not represent individual stimuli, but may stand for classes or groups [p. 109]." These groupings of impulses will thus represent, rather than directly reflect, their external sources. The form of representation will be structural, or topological, and Hayek employs the simile of a map to characterize this. Mapping is thus the process (or apparatus) of classification, and the topological ordering of information that it provides "represents the kind of world in which the organism has existed in the past, or the different *kinds* of stimuli which have acquired significance for it, but it provides by itself no information about the particular environment in which the organism is placed at the moment [p. 115]." The map provides a semipermanent structure that is the framework within which further impulses are classified. Such further classification against the relatively static background of the map results in a model. The model represents the particular environment in which the organism finds itself, and it is much more fluid or dynamic than the map.

The adaptation of an organism to its environment is effected by the continually ongoing and constantly changing processes of mapping and modeling. If the organism had to learn new classifications of stimuli all the time, it would be a hopeless task:

> If [the organism] had to cope with the complexity of its environment solely by classifying individual events and learning separately for every combination of events how to respond, both the complexity of the model required and the time needed for building it up would be so great that the extent to which any given structure could learn to adapt itself to varying circumstances would be very limited [p. 130].

It is the process of multiple classification, the hierarchical structuring of the nervous system, that provides for adaptation within "realtime" constraints. This, rather than any associationistic linkages, is the basis of learning.

Knowledge and Action

Traditionally there is a sharp separation between learning (as a mechanism), motivation, and reinforcement. Similarly, knowing, doing, and valuing are discussed in relative isolation, as though they were related only after the fact. Hayek rejects these separations, for reasons similar to those admirably stated by C. I. Lewis (1946):

> The primary and pervasive significance of knowledge lies in its guidance of action: knowing is for the sake of doing. And action, obviously, is rooted in evaluation. For a being which did not assign comparative values, deliberate action would be pointless; and for one which did not know, it would be impossible [p. 1].

The process of classification, since it results from previous patternings of neural activity, will always anticipate changes, both in the environment and in the organism's actions. Representation will tend to run ahead of the actual developments, to be constantly checked by newly arriving information, which in turn will be evaluated against the background of expectations set up by previous patterns. Knowledge occurs for action as a result of evaluation (Hayek, 1952b):

> The representation of the existing situation in fact cannot be separated from, and has no significance apart from, the representation of the consequences to which it is likely to lead. Even on a pre-conscious level the organism must live as much in a world of expectation as in a world of "fact", and most responses to a given stimulus are probably determined only *via* fairly complex processes of "trying out" on the model the effects to be expected from alternative courses of action [p. 121].

This relates to attention as well. Because neural patterning is directed forward, in anticipation of expectation, a facilitation of certain patterns will occur. As Hayek (1952b) put it:

> Anticipatory excitation of parts of the following of certain kinds of sensory impulses will mean that we shall not only be more ready to perceive the corresponding stimulus, but also that we shall perceive them from a certain angle or a certain "point of view;" we shall discriminate them more fully with respect to certain types of responses towards which the whole organism is disposed at the moment [p. 140].

This is an unconscious mechanism by which attention can be generated (or, perhaps, focused). If we knew what consciousness was we would likely find that awareness (conscious attention) depends upon the same principles.

Thought and Classification

The nervous system as a hierarchically organized instrument of classification leads to the conception of conscious thought as an evolutionarily programmed fail-safe device for reclassification. The classification of the environment provided by the model will often be incorrect—that is, will give rise to expectations that are not borne out by subsequent actions or events. The mind will (according to Hayek, 1952b) "perform on the initial sensory experiences a process of reclassification, the objects of which are no longer the original stimuli but the elements of the classes formed [by preconscious classification] [p. 145]." Thus the experience in consciousness of elements classed at a "lower" level will provide the basis for a revision of the classification from which it begins.

The problems of stimulus equivalence and generalization—that similar-appearing objects behave differently and dissimilar-appearing objects behave similarly—will lead to the formation of new classes determined by the relationships elements exhibit in conscious thought. In this way what we call abstract concepts, which do not refer to the sensory properties of objects, will be formed. Abstract thought is thus a repetition, at a higher level of neural organization, of processes that operate at all levels of neural activity. As Hayek (1952b) put it: "This continuous process of reclassification is forced on us because we find that the classification of objects and events which our senses effect is only a rough and imperfect approximation . . . of the differences between the physical objects which would enable us correctly to predict their behaviour [pp. 145-146]." The approximate reproduction of differences that our senses effect is an accident of our evolutionary history, the result of "physiological capacities and the pragmatic needs of the individual and the species [p. 146]." The classificatory processes of neural activity determine not only the physiological modalities of experience, the sensory order, but also the unconscious mapping and modeling of the environment, as well as abstract and conceptual thought.

CONSEQUENCES FOR PSYCHOLOGY

The theory of the nervous system proposed in *The Sensory Order* has numerous consequences for philosophy, psychology, and all the "moral sciences." Let us mention some that seem relevant to current discussion in epistemology and cognitive psychology: The limits of empiricism, the futility of mysticism as an alternative, and the inadequacy of phenomenalism (as three epistemological consequences); the nature and limits of explanation; and the errors of rationalist constructivist engineering as more psychological consequences.

The Limits of Empiricism

We have discussed this earlier in connection with Hume's bankruptcy of the rationalist constructivist account of rationality, quoting Hayek to the effect that a consistent application of empiricism points to physiological a priorism with regard to the nervous system. Empiricism, consistently applied, leads to its own refutation; the principles determining the initial classification of stimuli, although themselves the products of experience in the evolutionary history of the species, are always a priori within the organization of the CNS of a given organism. As Hayek (1952b) put it:

> Sense experience therefore presupposes the existence of a sort of accumulated "knowledge," of an acquired order of the sensory impulses based on their past co-occurrence; and this knowledge, although based on (pre-sensory) experience, can never be contradicted by sense experiences and will determine the forms of such experiences which are possible [p. 167].

The Futility of Mystical Intuition

An extreme rationalist response to the failure of empiricism to account for the genesis of knowledge occurs in the currently popular mysticism and intuitionism that has pervaded "California cult" psychology and some forms of therapy. Part of this trend is perfectly reasonable and tenable, consisting in the admonition to take account of the tacit dimension in cognition and behavior. Unfortunately, proponents of these views neither know nor cite Hayek and Polanyi in support of what is defensible in their claims. Instead, they tend to propose mystical intuition or revelation as a source of knowledge that is far superior to experience (and experiment) and conceptual thought. In doing so, they fail to take account of the epistemic gulf between acquaintance and description, attributing to acquaintance, knowledge that can only be achieved by description. No matter how revelatory an experience one might undergo (as a result of drugs or esoteric training procedures), the experience per se is not knowledge. To move from the experience to knowledge of it is to cross the acquaintance–description boundary, and it becomes theoretically possible for one to know by description as much of the mystic's experience as he or she can describe. Indeed, unless he or she can describe it, no one has knowledge of the experience. Undergoing experience is one thing (acquaintance), but knowledge of it (description) is another. This is what Hayek emphasized in stating that a blind man could know all of physics, because all that can be communicated (to others *and* to oneself) are the differences between sensory qualities rather than their absolute nature. Our knowledge is a matter of relations structured by description rather than intuition of experience.

The Failure of Phenomenalism

Phenomenalism attempts to put a firm foundation under knowledge by arguing that sensory experience is more real, certain, and basic than the abstract constructions of reflective thought (science). The claim is that experience is indubitable, at least as to its occurrence, and that the certainty of phenomenal experience can somehow serve as a basis for human knowledge. Ernst Mach, whose *Analysis of Sensations* (1902/1959) greatly influenced Hayek, argued for phenomenalism, proposing certain elements of experience as both epistemically and ontologically basic.

The epistemic argument against phenomenalistic approaches has remained (since Descartes' *cogito* was advanced) that there is not enough "given" in experience to be "taken" as a foundation for anything, let alone all knowledge. Hayek (1952b) makes this point by noting that a purely phenomenalistic picture is inconsistent in the same way that stimulus equivalence is problematic: "Our knowledge of the phenomenal world raises problems which can be answered only by altering the picture which our senses give us of that world, i.e., by altering our classification of the elements of which it consists [p. 173]." Once one understands this, it is clear that reflective knowledge refutes phenomenalism and thus cannot be built upon it.

Explanation as Modeling

The nature of explanation is clearly a philosophical topic, but a consequence of Hayek's views makes it equally a psychological phenomenon. As a mental process, it is often suggested (very clearly by Kenneth Craik, *The Nature of Explanation,* 1943) that explanation is the brain's modeling of the complex of events to be explained. Hayek (1952b) agrees with this but cautions:

> The weakness of the ordinary use of the concept of the model as an account of the process of explanation consists in the fact that this conception presupposes, but does not explain, the existence of the different mental entities from which such a model could be built. . . . The concept of a model that is being formed in the brain is helpful only after we have succeeded in accounting for the different properties of the parts from which it is built [p. 180].

The Sensory Order provides such an account in the thesis that the CNS is an instrument of classification from which arises the determination of sensory qualities, mapping and modeling, and abstract thought. As Hayek (1952b) notes: "The formation of the model appears thus merely a particular case of that process of joint or simultaneous classification of a group of impulses of which each has its determined significance apart from the particular combination or model in which it now occurs [pp. 180–181]."

The Limits of Explanation: Complexity and Explanation of the Principle

If explanation is modeling, there are abstract constraints that apply to all systems that create models. One very important constraint will be the limit of explanatory capability that a given modeling system possesses: It will be beyond the capacity of systems to explain or model phenomena that are more complex than the systems themselves. An obvious limitation is reached in self-explanation: A system can only be itself; it can never model itself. An explaining system must therefore be more complexly organized than the thing it models. Hayek (1952b) put it this way:

> Any apparatus of classification must possess a structure of a higher degree of complexity than is possessed by the objects which it classifies; . . . therefore, the capacity of any explaining agent must be limited to objects with a structure possessing a degree of complexity lower than its own. If this is correct, it means that no explaining agent can ever explain objects of its own kind, or of its own degree of complexity, and, therefore, that the human brain can never fully explain its own operations [p. 185].

This logical point is independent of our earlier discussion of explanation of the particular and the principle but is related directly to that distinction. If the phenomena of interest are those of "organized complexity," such as our brains, market systems, social structures, etc., it follows that all our understanding can hope to achieve is explanation of the abstract principles according to which the system operates. We will never be able to model such systems completely, nor will we be able to confirm the adequacy of our models. Instead, our knowledge of a model's adequacy will be determined by falsification, and a "good" model will be one that, as Popper suggested, has thus far survived our sincere attempts to refute it.

This limitation on the possibility of explanation is analogous to the limit of empiricism. Just as empiricism points beyond itself to the principles of classification according to which sense experience is generated, explanation points beyond itself to the structure of rules that determines explanation but cannot be explained by it. The extent to which this limitation affects our understanding is far from devastating. As "Rules, Perception and Intelligibility" put it (Hayek, 1967):

> It is important not to confuse the contention that any . . . system must always act on some rules which it cannot communicate with the contention that there are particular rules which no such system could ever state. All the former contention means is that there will always be some rules governing a mind which that mind in its then prevailing state cannot communicate, and that, if it ever were to acquire the capacity of communicating these rules, this would presuppose that it had acquired further higher rules which make the communication of the former possible but which themselves will still be incommunicable [p. 62].

Precisely because we cannot model particulars in complex phenomena, we must concentrate upon what is attainable:—explanation of the principle.

The moral of this point refers back to complexity, as definitive of social and cognitive phenomena, and the danger of scientism. We would not be upset by the limit of explanation if a strong scientistic prejudice, that we should be able to deal with mental phenomena in the same manner as physical phenomena, were not so well entrenched. But as Hayek (1952b) reminds us: "The whole idea of the mind explaining itself is a logical contradiction—nonsense in the literal meaning of the word—and a result of the prejudice that we must be able to deal with mental events in the same manner as we deal with physical events [p. 192]."

RATIONALIST CONSTRUCTIVISM IN PSYCHOLOGY: ANOTHER ROAD TO SERFDOM

Hayek published *The Road to Serfdom* during World War II, as a tract for the times to expose the ideas underlying totalitarian regimes. When the examples are removed, the tract for the times becomes a timeless argument against collectivism in all its forms (e.g., Fascism, Nazism, Socialism, The New Deal, etc.) and in favor of individualism. His point is that the "unforseen but inevitable consequences of socialist planning create a state of affairs in which, if the policy is to be pursued, totalitarian forces will get the upperhand" (Hayek 1944, p. xiv). The book (and others, such as Popper's (1962) monumental *Open Society and Its Enemies*) was perhaps so successful that socialism changed its course from a "hot" version to a "cold" or moderate position that is now common. The new views are collectivist but much less avowedly socialist, and knee-jerk "progressives" endorse them with no appreciation of their pedigree, self-contradictory nature, or ultimate result. Since one young economist who attended this conference seriously argued that socialism is a "purely" political view that has no bearing upon economics, a slight detour through some ideas in *The Road to Serfdom,* is worthwhile, as well as a look at similar rationalist constructivist doctrines in psychology.

Liberty versus Central Planning

The essence of *The Road to Serfdom* is an elaboration of this quotation from Alexis de Tocqueville (in Hayek, 1944):

> Democracy extends the sphere of individual freedom, socialism restricts it. Democracy attaches all possible value to each man; socialism makes each man a mere agent, a mere number. Democracy and socialism have nothing in common but one word: equality. But notice the difference: While democracy seeks equality in liberty, socialism seeks equality in restraint and servitude [p. 25].

The "democracy" Hayek admires is built upon the classic, or British Whig, thesis of liberalism. The fundamental principle of liberalism is that we should make as much use as possible of the spontaneous forces of society in the ordering of our affairs. The attitude of liberalism toward society (Hayek, 1944) "is like that of the gardener who tends a plant and, in order to create the conditions most favorable to its growth, must know as much as possible about its structure and the way it functions [p. 18]." Liberalism is thus negative in character: In favoring individualism over (collectivist) interventionism, one fights proposals that limit freedom rather than proposing ways to tamper with (speed up) the evolution of society. Liberalism is a doctrine of cultural evolution (fully articulated long before Darwin applied its ideas to biology) according to the spontaneously generated forces in complex social phenomena, and it opposes the rationalist constructivist notion that "scientific progress" can only be achieved when people redesign society to their own choosing.

Socialism (or, more correctly, collectivism) is the road to serfdom precisely because the achievement of its goals requires the abolition of liberty in favor of the restraint of the members of the society upon which it is imposed. Socialists attempt to sidestep this issue by arguing for a "new" freedom: Whereas for the liberal, political freedom entails freedom from coercion, the socialist promises to achieve freedom from want or necessity. At this point, socialism becomes more obviously economic in tone, to the extent that contemporary socialism is chiefly concerned with the "redistribution" of wealth and the achievement of "equality" in "social justice" for all. Sophisticated socialists make no bones about the need for coercion to achieve their "new freedom"; naive ones (like our conference economist) are unaware of its necessity.

Against this, Hayek argues that personal and political freedom have in the past only occurred when there was economic freedom. Further, he argues that the superiority of "capitalism" (which, as an economic doctrine, entails freedom from coercion in the marketplace) is due to the presence of that freedom, because competition in the market place (analogous to the struggle for survival in Darwin) allows for progress. But that progress cannot be planned in advance; growth in the marketplace is largely a matter of taking advantage of unanticipated consequences, genuinely novel occurrences that arise because individuals make use of information that was not available (or could not be conveyed in time) to a central authority.

But the slow, unpredictable progress of the marketplace is vexing to contemporary authors who delight in making everything more urgent than anything else. This "engineering mentality" will argue that we have come to the limit of growth under the liberal ideal. The engineers want their aims achieved now, at the expense of all others. As Hayek (1944) noted: "According to the modern planners, . . . it is not sufficient to design the most rational permanent framework within which the various activities would be conducted by different persons according to their individual plans. This liberal plan, according to them, is no plan [p. 35]." What unites all collectivists is their hatred for competition and their common desire to replace it by directed planning, not only in politics but in economics and psychological adjustment as well. Not surprisingly, it is often the educated, technically competent who cry loudest for socialism, because they see it as furthering their particular individual aims. As Hayek (1944) wrote:

> There is little question that almost every one of the technical ideals of our experts could be realized within a comparatively short time if to achieve them were made the sole aim of humanity. . . . It is the frustrating of his ambitions in his own field which makes the specialist revolt against the existing order. We all find it difficult to bear to see things left undone which everybody must admit are both desirable and possible. . . . [This] creates enthusiasts for planning who feel confident that they will be able to instil into the directors of such a society their sense of the value of the particular objective [p. 53].

At this point, two things must be stressed. First, collectivist planning becomes logically self-stultifying; second, this is the means by which the worst rise to the top. Consider the latter point first. The movement for planning "unites almost all the single-minded idealists, all the men and women who have devoted their lives to a single task [p. 55]." This is precisely the group that should never be given coercive power over others: "It would make the very men who are most anxious to plan society the most dangerous if they were allowed to do so—and the most intolerant of the planning of others. From the saintly and single-minded idealist to the fanatic is often but a step [p. 55]."

The futility of directed planning for the achievement of social advancement should be obvious now. Planning would work only if there were a common goal shared by the society. But so long as individuals value different goals, no consensus of directed action can ever favor them all equally. Thus, inevitably, the proponents of the "majority" view must coerce the minority to go along with their views, advancing one special-interest group at the expense of others. This is why socialists always propose programs for "the common good," or "general welfare"; such various terms prevent the population from seeing that there is no single "good" or "welfare," but rather a welter of conflicting and often incompatible goals that cannot be advanced toward at all. Common action is limited to fields where everyone agrees on common ends to achieve; debate is then only about how to achieve them.

But surely everyone agrees that we should rationally plan our future. Don't we agree that we should always delegate that responsibility to experts and follow their recommendations? Something like this sentiment is now common, and it leads to the argument that democratic procedures are inadequate for our "unsettled" times. Hayek (1944) wrote:

> The effect of the people's agreeing that there must be central planning, without agreeing on the ends, will be rather as if a group of people were to commit themselves to take a journey together without agreeing where they want to go. . . . The inability of democratic assemblies to carry out what seems to be a clear mandate of the people will inevitably cause dissatisfaction with democratic institu-

tions. Parliaments come to be regarded as ineffective "talking shops," unable or incompetent to carry out the tasks for which they have been chosen [p. 62].

At this point, delegation of authority to a separate body occurs, in order to exercise discretion over particular cases. "In these instances delegation means that some authority is given power to make with the force of law what to all intents and purposes are arbitrary decisions (usually described as "judging the case on its merits") [p. 66]." The result now appears to be all but inevitable: Substitute a dictator for democracy. According to Hayek (1944):

> Agreement that planning is necessary, together with the inability of democratic assemblies to produce a plan, will evoke stronger and stronger demands that the government or some single individual should be given powers to act on their own responsibility. The belief is becoming more and more widespread that, if things are to get done, the responsible authorities must be freed from the fetters of democratic procedure [p. 67].

Thus arises the cry for an economic and then a political dictator. Planning leads to a dictatorship because that is the most effective form of coercion. Dictatorship is essential if central planning on a large scale is to be achieved.

The way to avoid this result should be obvious; it is also obvious that what is required on our part is the very painful admission that we were wrong in holding some of this century's most firmly held beliefs. "We are ready to accept almost any explanation of the present crisis of our civilization except one: That the present state of the world may be the result of genuine error on our own part and that the pursuit of some of our most cherished ideals has apparently produced results utterly different from those which we expected [pp. 10-11]." We must recognize today, as when Hayek wrote *The Road to Serfdom*, that it is now just as important to clear away the "obstacles with which human folly has encumbered our path and to release the creative energy of individuals than to devise further machinery for 'guiding' and 'directing' them—to create conditions favorable to progress rather than to 'plan progress' [p. 239]."

Psychology and the New Serfdom

In 1944 the danger of serfdom resulted from collectivism leading to the abandonment of liberty for central planning of economic and political life. In the present, that danger results more from the abandonment of the individual (and his or her individual differences) and the heritage of culture for social activism and "equality." This danger is prevalent in contemporary psychology from both the inheritance of rationalist constructivist ideals of planning and intervention, and the scientism of the engineering outlook pervading most "hardheaded" schools of thought. The social and behavioral engineers among us regularly call for the construction of one or another "new order" based upon what they perceive to be the "scientifically verified" position that they endorse.

The approach is not new. Consider John B. Watson (1928): "The cry of the behaviorist is, 'Give me the baby and my world to bring it up in and I'll make it crawl and walk; I'll make it a thief, a gunman, or a dope fiend.' The possibility of shaping in any direction is almost endless [pp. 31–32]." Although it is now fashionable to snicker at Watson's pompous naiveté, we nonetheless give rapt attention and credibility to B. F. Skinner, perhaps the epitome of scientistic psychology, when he (1959) makes remarks such as "Man is able, and now as never before, to lift himself up by his own bootstraps [p. 4]." Anyone familiar with *Beyond Freedom and Dignity* (1971) and his recent writings for the popular press can think of Skinnerian examples that carry this theme of explicit control and conscious planning of humanity and society into areas that George Orwell never dreamed of. When it is remembered that pollsters tell us that Skinner is the most famous living psychologist (and perhaps the most admired), it is time to consider whether psychology should follow the path of rationalist constructivism to serfdom, or embark on a new direction. But one does not have to be a scientistic Skinnerian to call for planning. Consider Kenneth B. Clark (1971), whose highly regarded APA presidential address called for psychology to live up to the ideal of constructivist rationalism by creating a crash program to develop "that kind of scientific, biochemical intervention which could stabilize and make dominant the moral and ethical propensities of man and subordinate, if not eliminate, his negative and primitive behavioral tendencies [p. 1048]." Clark's motivation would appear to be the desire for social justice to undo our previous transgressions against minorities, a goal with which hardly anyone would find fault. Similarly, one could cite the impact of the women's liberation movement upon psychology, where the drive for "equality" has gone so far as to introduce neologisms into the language (e.g., *chairperson*) in an effort to legislate the end of discrimination.

But what sort of "equality" will result if the social engineer's policies are pursued? Will it lead to freedom or serfdom? Is it equality under the rule of abstract and impersonal law, as the liberal tradition envisages, or equality in the sense of equal enslavement under the will of a centralized planning scheme? Perhaps we should reflect upon the epigram from Lord Acton that Hayek used to introduce a chapter in *The Road to Serfdom* (1944): "The finest opportunity ever given to the world was thrown away because the passion for equality made vain the hope for freedom [p. 101]."

The liberal tradition defines equality and freedom by subsuming both to the rule of law. One is free so long as one is constrained only by the same laws that apply to all members of the society; freedom requires the equal enforcement of abstract, general laws at all times and places. The equality that results from the rule of law is an equality of opportunity—the opportunity to make the most of one's particular talents and knowledge within a competitive marketplace. This equality is in a real sense negative—it is the absence of definite prescriptions for achieving a goal. The concern is for equal treatment in all circumstances, rather than the advancement of one or another special interest. Advancing special interest is perfectly permissible, but only on an individual basis—and the individual is free to do so only to the extent that everyone is bound by the common framework of law. Individualism creates conditions favorable to progress in this manner, whereas collectivism trys to legislate its occurrence by giving specific programs the force of law, and thereby destroys freedom.

Social engineering emphasizes another form of equality: Each individual is equally subject to the direction of planning. In this form of equality, freedom is impossible, and thus we are urged—always "for our own benefit"—to move beyond freedom and dignity into a "brave new world" in which we sacrifice our autistic, individual (and therefore selfish) goals for the "general welfare." The equally restrained society is then promised the "new" freedom from want as a sort of consolation prize. Should anyone resist, therapy (or another form of intervention) is in order, always under the guise of (re)education.

Consider the matter of reeducation and therapy in more detail. Begin with these remarks by the psychiatrist Brock Chisholm (1946), a Secretary-General of the World Health Organization and later President of the World Federation of Mental Health:

> The re-interpretation and eventual eradication of the concept of right and wrong which has been the basis of child training, the substitution of intelligent and rational thinking for faith in the certainties of the old people, these are the belated objectives of practically all effective psychotherapy. . . . The pretence is made, as it has been made in relation to the finding of any extension of truth, that to do away with right and wrong would produce uncivilized people, immorality, lawlessness and social chaos. The fact is that most psychiatrists and psychologists and many other respectable people have escaped from these moral chains and are able to observe and think freely. . . . If the race is to be freed from its crippling burden of good and evil it must be psychiatrists who take the original responsibility. . . . With the other human sciences, psychiatry must now decide what is to be the immediate future of the human race [pp. 9–11].

I quote Chisholm at length not only because this is one of the most blatant examples of self-serving scientism one could imagine but also to indicate the widespread influence of rationalist constructivism in therapy and clinical practice. Our profession tends to regard the therapeutic process as a matter of intervention (with an algorithmic formula) to change a client so that he or she fits the therapist's preformed idea of correct adjustment. This collectivist interpretation, in which the therapist assumes the role of planning commission, makes therapy a matter of legislation of particulars to restrain the client to a predetermined path; correct adjustment becomes acceptance of serfdom. For this interpretation, neither Chisholm nor Watson nor Skinner is responsible—the blame rests squarely upon Sigmund Freud.

Civilization and Its Discontents: The Freudian Attitude Toward Therapy

It is a commonplace that therapy for Freud was to free humanity from the burden of culture—that is, our culturally acquired repression, inhibition, and guilt— and thus to release the culturally blocked "natural" drives. Freud impressed upon all therapy an implicit rationalist constructivism that has been accepted as the raison dêtre of therapy since his time—the idea that the spontaneously developed models of adjustment that incorporate cultural and social rules and wisdom learned through the rise of civilization must be replaced by "rationally determined" patterns of behavior that the therapist, through his or her midwifery, is to instill upon the client. For the Freudian, the preferred "rational" behavior consists in the direct expression of innate needs and drives; for the behavior modifier, it consists in bits of behavior that are easily quantified on clipboards and susceptible to available contingencies of reinforcement; for the literary mentality that writes Utopian blueprints for the equally enslaved society, it lies in whatever fanciful notions are beyond freedom and dignity in the divine illumination of the central planner in the sky. In all cases it is assumed that an omniscient modern individual (at least one—the author in point) can rationally construct a new social order and individuals who are better adjusted to it than could ever be done by traditional means, such as old-fashioned moral values, outmoded concepts like liberty and justice, etc., that require the *discipline* of cultural and social interaction. Therapy thus assumes that it is not necessary to pass the *burden* of culture to a client in order to render him or her well adjusted, that one can consciously plan and direct the attunement of the social milieu in which humanity has arisen. Civilization is thus a burden to be overcome, rather than the source of human powers and the hope for our future.

In contrast to this, it should by now be apparent that social and cultural phenomena, which represent those factors that separate man from the other animals, cannot be either disregarded or reduced to explicit factors subject to conscious control and change. Insofar as a client's problems are even considered for treatment, they are inevitably social rather than individual, and thus fit into a complex system that has originated in human action but not human design. We have as yet done virtually nothing to study the social and cultural nature of the attunement of humanity to its environment, and as a result psychology is in danger of contributing to the breakdown of modern society rather than the evolution of it. If we are ever to do otherwise, it will be necessary to abandon the rationalist constructivist's positivistic approach to social structures and to study seriously those complex systems whose spontaneous development has shaped us into what we are today. We must learn to evolve within the framework of spontaneously developed features, the exact nature of which we may never know or anticipate completely. Therapy cannot go against the grain of those spontaneous factors on pain of disrupting the client's adjustment in directions that the therapist will likely never have considered, nor be able to cope with.

The problem of novelty or creativity is as much a factor in therapy as it is in cognition, language, or social phenomena. Since our lives consist in the main of unanticipated occurrences (and we would be incapable of learning anything new if they did not), it is clear that we must adapt to those occurrences by following, as consistently as we are able, abstract rules of conduct. As Hayek noted (1967): "Our actions form a coherent and a rational pattern, not because they have been decided upon as part of a single plan thought out beforehand, but because in each successive decision we limit our range of choice by the same abstract rules [p. 90]." We cannot hope to control the particular in therapy any more than we can explain the details of their occurrence. If we construe therapy as the application of algorithms thought out in advance, then the result must inevitably be frustrated, depressed therapists who regard every case as (at least in part) a failure.

In contrast to the constructivist approach, therapy ought to be directed toward creating conditions that allow the client to learn to cope with unexpected events. Rather than therapy as intervention with an algorithm to change behavior to preconceived ends, it would be far more effective to create conditions in which the client can educate him- or herself according to very general, abstract principles that can be applied to an indefinite number of particular problems. Doing so will, of course, require utilizing all those burdens of culture that the engineering mentality wishes to dispense with. If we were to dispense with them, we would not only lose freedom, which is an artifact of civilization and culture, but we would also prevent those unexpected occurrences upon which we learn everything that is new. Following the constructivist path suppresses those differences upon which all novelty, and therefore progress, (social and intellectual), rests.

Not following that path will require that we dismiss as a superstition the collectivist and constructivist views of the Freuds and Skinners. In this regard, consider these remarks at the conclusion of the postscript to Hayek's (1979) third volume of *Law, Legislation, and Liberty:*

> The most widely held ideas which dominated the twentieth century, of a just distribution, a freeing ourselves from repressions and conventional morals, of permissive education as a way to freedom, and the replacement of the market by a rational arrangement of a body with coercive powers, were all based on superstitions in the strict sense of the word. An age of superstition is a time when people imagine that they know more than they do. In this sense the twentieth century was certainly an outstanding age of superstition, and the cause of this is an overestimation of what science has achieved—not in the field of the comparatively simple phenomena, where it has, of course, been extraordinarily successful, but in the

field of complex phenomena, where the application of the techniques which prove so helpful with essentially simple phenomena has proved to be very misleading. . . . We are discovering that the task which our age is assigning to rational constructions of new institutions is far too big. What the age of rationalism—and of modern positivism—has taught us to regard as senseless and meaningless formations due to accident or human caprice, turn in many instances out to be the foundations on which our capacity for rational thought rests. *Man is not and never will be the master of his fate: His very reason always progresses him by leading him into the unknown and unforeseen where he learns new things* [p. 176].

REVISION AND REFORMULATION

It is manifestly obvious that I have been not only outlining Hayek's views but also advocating them. I know of no theorist in psychology, social and political philosophy, or methodology of science with whose views I am in comparable agreement. In virtually every direction I have pursued his thought, I have found Hayek stating clearly, and arguing cogently for, positions that I had been aware of only dimly and intuitively or, at best, from a one-sided perspective. Studying his work has forced me to further my appreciation of the extent to which the problems of complexity that surround us (in our nature and interpersonal interaction) are all of one piece, requiring a truly interdisciplinary perspective for their study. Although I had long recognized that the theoretical psychology of *The Sensory Order* is compatible with and serves to further and explain the resurgence of cognitive psychology (post-Chomsky and psycholinguistics), as well as the methodological views of science advanced by Karl Popper and Thomas Kuhn, I had failed to realize that Hayek's arguments against scientism and rationalist constructivism in all the "moral sciences" were an extension of his analysis of the nature of knowledge and its acquisition in phenomena of organized complexity, as well as the full extent to which those arguments ramify back into psychology. With that realization, it became obvious that Hayek's views, like those of David Hume, have an essential unity that is vastly more important than the fragmented views one gets from the perspective of any single discipline in which their thought is studied. Thus my appreciation and advocacy of Hayek: The unity and coherence of his views on humanity as a phenomenon of organized complexity ring true from every vantage point from which I study them.

But one should not conclude that Hayek's views are either essentially complete or not subject to critical revision. There are several areas in which recent developments suggest changes in the psychological model (as well as one weakness in the initial account) and methodological developments that distantiate Hayek from Popper, bringing him closer to Kuhn. Let us consider these points briefly.

Insufficiency of a Uniprocess Neural Model

The Sensory Order considers only one form of information transmission in the nervous system—the all-or-none spike potential characterized by Bernstein at the turn of the century (see Boring, 1950) as a wave of electrical depolarization. Contemporary accounts add to this the slow, graded potential activity of the junctional microstructure. Thus a two-process model of information transmission consisting of all-or-none impulses and the graded, slow potential interactions has supplemented the uniprocess model Hayek used in *The Sensory Order*. One model for the slow potential activity, developed from Lashley's interference ideas, is the holographic hypothesis of Karl Pribram (1971). Perhaps the central feature of Pribram's holographic model is that it provides a direct account of distributed information processing and thus a decentralization of control (and record keeping) in its interference patterns. Thus the two-process model (especially in Pribram's holographic model) supplements and strengthens Hayek's classificatory model of spike potential activity and provides a much more adequate account of the distributed information-processing capabilities of the CNS.

Hierarchical Control?

In contrast to associationistic linkage models, Hayek emphasized the hierarchical structure of control in classificatory activity. Although this was a distinct improvement over behavioristic doctrines then available, it is likely that an even more powerful and decentralized control structure guides the brain in its multitude of operations. Robert Shaw (Shaw & McIntyre, 1974) referred to such structures as coalitions, and the distributed information processing and control that they exhibit (in contrast to the centralization of control in hierarchical structuring) are two of their defining characteristics. Here is another case where Hayek's nonpsychological writings, which emphasize the distributed information processing and decentralization of control in complex phenomena, appear to be more compatible with contemporary developments than the models available when *The Sensory Order* was written.

Consciousness

One outright weakness in *The Sensory Order* is the account of consciousness. All that Hayek notes about consciousness is that there must be a "highest and most comprehensive" functionally specified center that can evaluate only a limited number of impulse followings at a given time, and that this functional mechanism is somehow intimately related to speech and communication. Although such a functional account of the role of consciousness in the adaptation of humanity to its environment (and the creation of the sociocultural milieu) is correct so far as it goes, it is uninformative as to the exact nature of this evolutionary fail-safe device and as to the self that ''has'' consciousness. Specification of the nature of consciousness, as well as how attention can be directed by it (and upon itself) is beyond *The Sensory Order*. Whereas one merit of Hayek's account is to specify clearly the nature of ''mental'' events that are not conscious (thus breaking previous definitional fusions of ''mental'' with ''conscious'') there is no comparable clear specification of which mental events are conscious.

The Tacit Dimension of Rationality

Because of his long-standing familiarity with Karl Popper's philosophy, Hayek characterizes the conception of rationality that he endorses as Popper's critical rationalism. This may have been correct several decades ago but Popper's views have, first, taken a new direction in opposition to theorists such as Polanyi and Kuhn; second, they have been criticized and improved by W. W. Bartley III (1962). Although his respect for Popper is not unwarranted on other matters, I think it clear that Hayek's conception of rationality is actually Bartley's comprehensively critical rationalism, and that its emphasis upon the tacit dimension of the growth of knowledge puts Hayek in the camp of Kuhn against Popper in current methodological debates. For Popper, rationality must be explicit; scientific progress is rational, for example, only if we consciously and continually attempt to weed out erroneous theories by attempting their refutation. Popper sees what Polanyi called the authoritarian structure of science (as well as its tacit dimension), and what Kuhn (1970) called normal science research, as uncritical, largely unconscious, and therefore irrational (see Weimer, 1979, for discussion and references). The Kuhn–Popper methodological controversy is largely about whether or not science can be rational if it is often (and indispensably) tacit and seemingly uncritical. Hayek's defense of liberalism and emphasis upon the tacit nature of decentralized control in the marketplace puts him squarely with Kuhn (and myself), since his arguments show precisely how complex phenomena can be rational (and how growth and progress can occur) in the absence of any centralized or conscious control. Science, as a complex phenomenon, can be perfectly rational even though the individuals who practice it remain unaware not only of the full details of its procedures but also of the import of the abstract rules that they in fact follow; Hayek's methodological individualism tells us clearly how and why this is so. Indeed, the tacit dimension of rational practice in research, to which Kuhn and Polanyi (and I) repeatedly refer, is given its fullest explication in Hayek's views on liberalism, the primacy of the abstract, and individualism in the economic order.

Granting that Hayek's work unpacks Kuhnian notions, one can still ask whether or not it is a critical rationalism that rests, in the last analysis, upon a faith in one or another presupposition that cannot be subjected to criticism. If such a retreat to commitment is made, then Hayek's rationalism would not be the comprehensively critical position of Bartley, but a variant of critical rationalism. Consider Bartley (1962) on this point:

> A comprehensively critical rationalist, like other men, holds countless unexamined presuppositions and assumptions, many of which may be false. His rationality consists in his willingness to submit these to critical consideration when he discovers them or when they are pointed out to him. When one belief is subjected to criticism, many others have to be taken for granted—including those with which the criticism is being carried out. The latter are used as the basis of criticism not because they are themselves justified or beyond criticism, but because they are unproblematic at present [pp. 151-152].

One can find numerous similar passages in Hayek's writing, such as this (1978):

> Though the liberal must claim the right critically to examine every single value or moral rule of his society, he knows that he can and must do this while accepting as given for that purpose most of the other moral values of this society, and examine that about which he has doubts in terms of its compatibility with the rest of the dominant system of values [p. 298].

Thus my interpretation of Hayek assumes that he is a comprehensively critical rationalist, as Bartley uses the term, and that the key feature of his view is an analysis of the tacit, decentralized, and therefore unconscious nature of the rationality of complex phenomena. That this means that Hayek cannot be a doctrinaire Popperian on this matter is of little consequence: The superiority of Hayek's account is what is important, especially to those of us in the "moral sciences."

REFERENCES

Bartley, W. W. III. *The retreat to commitment*. New York: Knopf, 1962.

Boring, E. G. *A history of experimental psychology* (2nd ed.). New York: Appleton-Century-Crofts, 1950.

Burkes, A. W. (Ed.). *Theory of self-reproducing automata*. Urbana, Ill.: University of Illinois Press, 1966.

Chisholm, G. B. The re-establishment of peace-time society. *Psychiatry*, 1946, *ix* 3-11.

Clark, K. B. The pathos of power: A psychological perspective. *American Psychologist*, 1971, *26*, 1047-1057.

Craik, K. *The nature of explanation*. Cambridge: Cambridge University Press, 1943.

Fuller, B. A. G., & McMurrin, S. *A history of philosophy*. New York: Henry Holt, 1955.

Hayek, F. A. *The road to serfdom*. Chicago: University of Chicago Press, 1944.

Hayek, F. A. *Individualism and economic order*. Chicago: University of Chicago Press, 1948.

Hayek, F. A. *The counter-revolution of science*. Glencoe, Ill.: Free Press, 1952. (a)

Hayek, F. A. *The sensory order*. Chicago: University of Chicago Press, 1952. (b)

Hayek, F. A. (Ed.). *Capitalism and the historians*. Chicago: University of Chicago Press, 1954.

Hayek, F. A. *The constitution of liberty*. Chicago: University of Chicago Press, 1960.

Hayek, F. A. *Studies in philosophy, politics, and economics.* New York: Simon & Schuster, 1967.

Hayek, F. A. *New studies in philosophy, politics, economics, and the history of ideas.* Chicago: University of Chicago Press, 1978.

Hayek, F. A. *Law, Legislation, and liberty.* (Vol. 3). Chicago: University of Chicago Press, 1979.

Kuhn, T. S. *The structure of scientific revolutions* (2nd Ed.). Chicago: University of Chicago Press, 1970.

Lewis, C. I. *An analysis of knowledge and valuation.* LaSalle, Ill.: Open Court, 1946.

Mach, E. *The analysis of sensations.* New York: Dover, (Originally published in 1902 by Open Court, Chicago.)

Maxwell, G. Scientific methodology and the causal theory of perception. In I. Lakatos & A. Musgrave (Eds.), *Problems in the philosophy of science.* Amsterdam: North-Holland, 1968.

Maxwell, G. Theories, perception, and structural realism. In R. Colodny (Ed.), *The nature and function of scientific theories.* Pittsburgh, PA: University of Pittsburgh Press, 1970.

Polanyi, M. *Personal knowledge.* New York: Harper & Row, 1958.

Polanyi, M. *The tacit dimension.* Garden City, N.Y.: Doubleday, 1966.

Popper, K. R. *The poverty of historicism.* London: Routledge & Kegan Paul, 1957.

Popper, K. R. *The logic of scientific discovery.* New York: Harper & Row, 1959.

Popper, K. R. *The open society and its enemies* (Rev. ed.). New York: Harper & Row, 1962.

Popper, K. R. *Conjectures and refutations.* New York: Harper & Row, 1963.

Pribram, K. H. *Languages of the brain.* Englewood Cliffs, N.J.: Prentice-Hall, 1971.

Russell, B. *The scientific outlook.* New York: Norton, 1931.

Russell, B. *A history of western philosophy.* New York: Simon & Schuster, 1945.

Russell, B. *Human knowledge: Its scope and limits.* New York: Simon & Schuster, 1948.

Shaw, R. E., & McIntyre, M. Algoristic foundations to cognitive psychology. In W. B. Weimer & D. S. Palermo (Eds.), *Cognition and the symbolic processes.* Hillsdale, N.J.: Lawrence Erlbaum Associates, 1974.

Skinner, B. F. Freedom and the control of men. In B. F. Skinner, *Cumulative Record* New York: Appleton-Century-Crofts, 1959, 3-18. Originally published in *The American Scholar,* 1955-56.

Skinner, B. F. *Beyond freedom and dignity.* New York: Knopf, 1971.

Watson, J. B. *The ways of behaviorism.* New York: Harper & Brothers, 1928.

Weimer, W. B. *Notes on the methodology of scientific research.* Hillsdale, N.J.: Lawrence Erlbaum Associates, 1979.

13 The Sensory Order After 25 Years

F. A. Hayek
University of Freiburg

I appear here not just as an old man. So far as psychology is concerned, I am really a ghost from the 19th century. By this I do not refer to the irrelevant fact that I was born in that century. This also does not go back far enough. What I have in mind is that even nearly sixty years ago, when I conceived my psychological ideas, I never had a live teacher in psychology. For a young man returning from World War I to enter the University of Vienna, with his interests having been drawn by those events from the family background of biology to social and philosophical issues, there was at the moment just no teaching in psychology available. To teach the subject was then still part of the duties of some of the professors of philosophy—not an altogether bad arrangement; but one of them (Friedrich Jodl) had recently died, and the other[1] was clearly dying and the few of his lectures I heard, as painful for him to give as for the students to listen to. So I had to get my knowledge of psychology from the books of men long out of fashion, such as Wilhelm Wundt, or long dead, such as William James, Johannes Müller, and Hermann von Helmholtz—the latter, in my opinion, the greatest of them all. But the decisive stimulus for taking up the problem on which I soon started to work came from Ernst Mach and particularly his *Analysis of Sensations* (1902/1959)—the work of an only recently dead physicist to whose writings turned most of the young scientists, who then arrogantly regarded all non-positivist philosophy as absurd nonsense.

Mach's acute analysis of how what he regarded as the elementary pure sensations corresponding to the individual sensory stimuli came to be further organized by such acquired properties as local signs as a result of experience made me, in a sudden flash of insight, perceive that the presumed pure core of sensation originally attached to the afferent impulse was a superfluous assumption,

287

and that all attributes of sense experience (and soon after that, *all* mental qualities) might be explained in some way by their place in a system of connections. I began to see that there were two orders in which we could conceive of the same set of events—two orders that were in some respects similar but yet differed in exactly that way in which our sensory picture of the world and our scientific conception of it differed from each other.

The conclusion that the world of our mental qualities provided us with an imperfect generic map with its own units existing only in that mental universe, yet serving to guide us more or less successfully in our environment, led me to a philosophical view of the relation between the physical and the sensory world that then had been recently revived by the physicist Max Planck, but that really goes back to Galileo Galilei, who in 1623 had written (1960):

> I think that these tastes, odors, colors, etc. . . . . are nothing else than mere names, but hold their residence solely in the sensitive body, so that, if the animal were removed, any such quality would be abolished and anihilated [p. 27].

My conclusion at an early stage was thus that mental events are a particular order of physical events within a subsystem of the physical world that relates the larger subsystem of the world that we call an organism (and of which they are a part) with the whole system so as to enable that organism to survive. Although I did soon see my problem as one raised by the qualitative character of *all* the different kinds of mental events, and was soon aiming at a general theoretical psychology, I thought that I could best demonstrate my conclusions by a closer analysis of the determination of the system of sense qualities only—or what I later called the sensory order. In the final version in the book, of course, I tried to make this fully clear and claimed that in this manner, it should be possible to provide an adequate explanation of all the events that took place between the input of (external and internal) stimuli and the output of actions. But the basic idea was on paper, though in a very amateurish fashion, by 1920.

After I got my law degree in 1921, after 3 years at the university devoted mostly to psychology and economics, I had to think about earning a living and to confine my extracurricular activities to one of those two subjects. I chose economics, perhaps wrongly; the fascination of physiological psychology never quite left me, though for the next 25 years—struggling to get on as an economist (and rapidly forgetting my law)—I could devote no time to following the development of psychology. Only after I had taught for 15 years as professor at the London School of Economics, and had established a certain reputation as an economist—and had made myself thoroughly unpopular with the majority of my fellow economists through an attack on socialism (incidentally, as a result of my recognition of the market as a mechanism for communicating information)—did I feel that I could afford to take out the old manuscript and see what I could do with it.

When I then, about 1946, began looking at the current psychological literature, I found to my amazement that my problem seemed to be in exactly the same
state in which I had left it 25 years before. Helpful factual information had of
course been accumulated, but on the purely theoretical issue, the muddle seemed
to me at least as great as before. Only in the course of the next 3 years—while
using what time I could spare from my teaching and work in economics to put a
fuller statement of my views on paper—did there seem to occur some revival of
interest in my problem, and some suggestive contributions to it appeared. The
point from which I could then start was the conviction that the different attributes
of mental entities—conscious or not—could be reduced to differences in effects
as guides to human action. But the crudities of behaviorism (which I had in the
meantime encountered in the social sciences) had too much repelled me (particularly in the person of the social science specialist of the Vienna Circle of logical
positivists) to make the effect on observable conduct more than a final visible
outcome of a complex process we had to reconstruct.

In the early 1940s, I had done a study of what I christened "scientism"—that
is, an examination of the harmful effects that the physics model had had on the
methodology of the social sciences—and in this work had been driven both to
rely in some measure on the results of my unpublished work in psychology and to
think further about some of the problems with which I had dealt in it.[2] Having
through this become somewhat clearer about the underlying philosophy, I felt
that I could at last state more precisely the problem that I had tried to solve in my
juvenile attempt. I had also learned to see what, in the case of really complex
phenomena, explanation ought to achieve and could achieve.

What I had from the beginning been unable to swallow was the conception
that a sensory fiber could carry, or a nerve cell store, those distinctive attributes
that we know mental phenomena to possess—know not only by introspection but
equally from our observation of other people's behavior. The result of my earlier
studies had been a clear perception of the fact that these mental properties could
be determined by the place of the impulse in a system of relations between all the
neurons through which impulses were passed. This led me to interpret the central
nervous system as an apparatus of multiple classification or, better, as a process
of continuous and simultaneous classification and constant reclassification on
many levels (of the legion of impulses proceeding in it at any moment), applied
in the first instance to all sensory perception but in principle to all the kinds of
mental entities, such as emotions, concepts, images, drives, etc., that we find
to occur in the mental universe. But the only thing I tried fully to show was that
the whole order of sensory qualities, all the differences in the effects of their
occurrence, could be exhaustively accounted for by a complete account of all
their effects in different combinations and circumstances, and that if we suc-
ceeded in this, nothing would be left to explain about them.

As I remembered my exposition after 25 years, the central conception in the
argument was the concept of "disposition." But as I discovered to my disap-

pointment when during the last few days I reread my book (I believe for the first time since I had received a finished copy)—and although in general, I was very much pleased with what I found in it—in that exposition, I actually use the term *disposition* only a few times in connection with my discussion of purpose and intention. Evidently my ideas have unconsciously further developed since; or perhaps while, in the first few years after I had finished the text of the book, I made an effort to complete its formulations of the theory in one respect. I had then endeavored to elaborate the crucial concept of "systems within systems" but found it so excruciatingly difficult that in the end, I abandoned the longish but unfinished paper that apparently nobody I tried it upon could understand.

It seems to me now that I could have greatly simplified my exposition in the book if I had throughout used the term *disposition*. Perhaps I refrained from doing so because I feared then that it would be understood as referring primarily to dispositions to act or to move, whereas of course what I had in mind were as much dispositions to interpret further stimuli and dispositions to change dispositions and also various long chains where dispositions succeed other dispositions, with actions coming in at a very late stage only as potential events that might have been produced if certain other stimuli had occurred.

In these terms the mental significance of any impulse (and group of impulses) proceeding anywhere in the central nervous system is determined by the "following" it evokes through "linkages" created by former simultaneous occurrence of these impulses at particular points. I deliberately avoided the term *field* in this connection, because it had been used in other somewhat vague senses; and I used "linkages" rather than "associations" because I wanted to stress that I was speaking of purely physiological connections between impulses and not of associations between mental events, which seemed to me to be produced by large numbers of such linkages. Indeed my "linkages" were assumed to create or determine the content of those mental events on which associations were supposed to operate.

The "followings" of all the impulses proceeding in the central nervous system at any one time are thus assumed to determine the potential or readiness of the system to do new things—internally or externally. Which of these potential neural events (toward which the system is inclined at any particular moment) eventuates would be decided by the partial overlapping of these followings through which, by summation, the potential effects of those linkages would be made actual. Only where a sufficient number of impulses converged on any one neuron would it be made to "fire" and to send out impulses to hundreds or thousands of other neurons.

It is very tempting to represent this graphically by showing a bunched tail of other neurons being affected by the excitation of any one particular neuron, with the overlapping of these tails determining where the impulses are to be passed on further. But any such graphic representation is apt to suggest a local grouping, whereas of course the streams of impulses being sent out by one firing neuron may be spread over the whole cortex, with the ramifications of the impulses spreading from the different neurons being completely interlaced. What perhaps deserves to be spelled out is that in this process, though each neuron may, by the impulses it sends on, "tend" to evoke further impulses in exceedingly large numbers of other neurons (the effectiveness of this depending on the summation of perhaps as many separate impulses arriving at more or less the same time), this process of a dispersion of individual impulses need not lead to a continuous increase of the number of excited neurons, but may be compatible with this number remaining approximately constant and, perhaps, if no new impulses were brought in by afferent nerves, even more or less the same assembly of impulses in particular neurons being evoked and reevoked for some time.

Mind thus becomes to me a continuous stream of impulses, the significance of each and every contribution of which is determined by the place in the pattern of channels through which they flow within the pattern of all available channels—with newly arriving afferent impulses, set up by external or internal stimuli, merely diverting this flow into whatever direction the whole flow is disposed to move. Stimuli and responses thus become merely the input and output of an ongoing process in which the state of the organism constantly changes from one set of dispositions to interpret and respond to what is acting upon it and in it, to another such set of dispositions. In my own mind—perhaps naturally, since not long before I wrote *The Sensory Order* (1952b), I published the results of many years' work on *The Pure Theory of Capital* (1941)—I liked to compare this flow of "representative" neural impulses, largely reflecting the structure of the world in which the central nervous system lives, to a stock of capital being nourished by inputs and giving a continuous stream of outputs—only fortunately, the stock of this capital cannot be used up.

I leave it at that, so far as psychology proper is concerned. But I would like to add a few words about philosophical implications concerning the relations of our experiential picture of the world, and that picture of the "real" world that the physical sciences elaborate, and about the nature and limits of explanation.

Perhaps the most basic contention in my book—not original but at the time of its publication, certainly not generally accepted—is that which occurs in the first chapter (Section 1.13), saying:

> The task of the physical sciences is to replace that classification of events which our senses perform but which proves inadequate to explain regularities of these events, by a classification which will put us in a better position to do so. The task of theoretical psychology is the converse one of explaining why these events, which on the basis of their relations to each other can be arranged in a certain (physical) order, manifest a different order in their effects on our senses [p. 5].

The relation between these two orders, one of which is a part of the other, is still one of the most intriguing problems of philosophy. I believe that this is a relationship that, in the nature of the case, and forever, we can explain only "in principle" and never in full or in detail. But I believe also that the question of whether there exist "objectively" two different worlds is really unanswerable or perhaps meaningless. The word *exist* loses all definite meaning in this context.

It is a different thing if we assert, as I believe to be true, that it is permanently impossible—because it would involve a logical contradiction—that we should ever be able *fully* to reduce the mental world to physical events. This, however, does not preclude, or make meaningless, the assertion that to a brain of a very much higher order than that which we possess, what our brain does might be capable of explanation in physical or physiological terms. But this suggests to me that the categorical questions of whether there *are* or *are not* two (or three) different worlds really do not have much meaning—at least if we impose upon ourselves the discipline of not talking about what we cannot know. Perhaps it would be sensible to agree not to use in this context the expressions "there is" or "there is not" in any absolute sense, and to understand any use of the term *exist* as meaning "exists for us"—that is, having a definable place in our system of thought.

The proof I have attempted in my book that any explanation—which always rests on classification—is limited by the fact that any apparatus of classification must be of a higher degree of complexity than what it classifies, and that therefore the human brain can never fully explain itself, may be inadequate. To prove it strictly is probably of a degree of difficulty comparable to that of the famous Goedel theorem in mathematics, which indeed seems to me to deal with a special case of the more general proposition that the mind can never fully explain itself. But the conclusion about the absolute limit to our powers of explanation seems to me of considerable importance for some of the basic problems of what used to be called the mind-body relationship and the tasks of the mental and moral sciences generally.

It would take too long, and would probably also exceed my powers of lucid oral explanation, to justify this contention abstractly. But I have recently thought of an illustration, or a fictitious case, that exhibits the essential points.

Assume I could construct a rat—that is, a mechanical model that can do all a rat does. To be a really true model, it would clearly have to do also a great many things we could not predict, even though we know precisely how the mechanism we have built works. It would both occasionally have to respond to external stimuli in a manner that we cannot predict, but also have to act "spontaneously" in response to internal processes that we cannot observe. The reason for our inability to predict, in spite of our precise knowledge of the mechanism that moves it, would be that our mind is not capable of perceiving and digesting, in the same manner as the mechanical rat does, all the particular stimuli that operate upon it and all the processes of classification that proceed in it. The only means by which we could achieve predictions would be to build a computer that imitates all that the mechanism of the rat performs; or, in other words, to build another rat identical in structure with the first one and making it live from the beginning in exactly the same environmental conditions, so that it would perceive and learn exactly what the first rat does. That is, in order to understand what a rat will do and why it does it, we would in effect have to become another rat. Need I spell out the consequences that follow from this for our understanding of other human beings?

In conclusion, let me just say how grateful I am for having been permitted to listen to your discussions. Although my book had at first a few sensible and sympathetic reviews, especially one by E. G. Boring, I have since had practically no indication of any response to my thesis by the psychological profession. All that showed me that some people must be reading it was that it had gone into a third printing. But I had no idea whether its basic approach was accepted or used by anybody else. I need hardly say how gratified I now am to discover how much active work is being conducted on the general lines I then indicated—irrespective of whether it was suggested by my early efforts or not. And I hope some of you may still discover in my books some hints you may find useful.

It seems to me that the young discipline of cognitive psychology is succeeding in showing that "meaning" can be given a meaningful place in our picture of the physical world.

CHAPTER NOTES

[1] Adolf Stöhr, a very profound thinker who, although I had barely looked in at his lectures, was prepared to read my first rough manuscript and encouraged me to go on.

[2] In three essays on "Scientism and the Study of Society," published in the journal *Economica* (1942–1944) and reprinted in a volume entitled *The Counter-Revolution of Science* (1952a) which appeared in the same year as *The Sensory Order* (1952b).

REFERENCES

Galilei, Galileo. Two kinds of properties. In A. Danto & S. Morgenbesser (Eds.), *Philosophy of science*. New York: Meridian Books, 1960. (Selection from *Il Saggitore* [*The Assayer*] translated by A. C. Danto.)

Hayek, F. A. *The pure theory of capital*. Chicago: University of Chicago Press, 1941.

Hayek, F. A. *The counter-revolution of science*. Glencoe, Ill.: The Free Press, 1952. (a)

Hayek, F. A. *The sensory order*. Chicago: University of Chicago Press, 1952. (b)

Mach, E. *The analysis of sensations*. New York: Dover, 1959. (Originally published in German, 1902.)

14 Categorical Perception: A Contractual Approach

Dennis R. Proffit
University of Virginia

Terry Halwes
Haskins Laboratory, New Haven, Connecticut

CATEGORICAL PERCEPTION: A CONTRACTUAL APPROACH

J. J. Gibson (1977, 1979) has argued that psychology, and specifically the study of perception, should adopt an ecological approach. By this he means we should attempt to understand how the perceptual systems of a given organism operate in the ordinary life of the organism, living in the ecological niche to which it is adapted, relative to stimulation naturally arising in that niche. Unfortunately, Gibson has left culture outside of his description. This chapter argues for the inclusion of cultural considerations in ecological theories of perception and, although much of our discussion is theoretical, we have grounded our arguments in research on categorical perception.

Hayek (1952) gives this description of the problem of categorical perception:

> The fact that the problem of psychology is the converse of the problem of the physical sciences means that while for the latter the facts of the phenomenal world are the data and the order of the physical world the *quaesitum*, psychology must take the physical world as represented by modern physics as given and try to reconstruct the process by which the organism classifies the physical events in the manner which is familiar to us as the order of sensory qualities. In other words: psychology must start from stimuli defined in physical terms and proceed to show why and how the senses classify similar physical stimuli sometimes as different, and why different physical stimuli will sometimes appear as similar and sometimes as different [p. 7].

Speech is perceived categorically. The same physical stimuli are sometimes classified together and sometimes separately. Physically different acoustic patterns are sometimes classified as similar and sometimes as different. Historically the generic problems of classification constitute the problems of stimulus equivalence. The problem of categorical perception is a specific application of stimulus equivalence to speech perception.

Speech perception is culturally constrained. The categories perceived as phonemes are defined within the structure of languages. Phonetic differences not used phonemically in one's native language are often very hard to hear and produce. At the turn of the century, Franz Boas argued that members of different cultures hear speech sounds differently.

CATEGORICAL PERCEPTION AND CULTURAL ANTHROPOLOGY

In the late 19th-century, philologists and anthropologists studying certain American Indian languages noticed a most peculiar phenomenon: Their native informants produced some of the sounds of their language inconsistently. The same speaker would utter a word differently on different occasions, with no change in meaning or linguistic context. The field worker might ask a speaker to utter a word several times in a session, and the informant might sometimes say it one way and at other times say it another way.

Anthropologists explained this apparent aberration in the phonology of American Indian languages by suggesting that these languages and their speakers were at a *primitive stage* in developing speech, a stage wherein phonological categories are not specific, as they are in more advanced languages, but merely define a general range of sounds that a speaker can use if he intends to utter a particular word.

Boas rejected this analysis. He argued that the alternation of sounds was not caused by inconsistency in production by Indian speakers, but rather by an inconsistency of anthropologists in hearing them. Boas (1889) described the problem as related to what was then known as "sound blindness,"—a condition of certain individuals who could not "distinguish differences in key and timbre of sounds which are easily discerned by ordinary ears... The characteristic feature of sound blindness is the inability to perceive the essential features of certain sounds" [p. 47].

The "sound blindness" of anthropologists is no malady of auditory physiology. As an adult member of a certain culture, an anthropologist hears speech through the phonologic categories specified by that culture. Boas wrote:

> [In their field notes, philologists] reduce to writing a language which they hear for the first time and of the structure of which they have no knowledge whatever. In this case men thoroughly trained in the science of phonology attempt to render by

writing combinations of sounds to them without any meaning. The study of their misspellings cannot fail to be instructive.

The first phenomenon that strikes us is that the nationality even of well-trained observers may readily be recognized. H. Rink had demonstrated this very clearly in regard to Eskimo vocabularies, and proofs are so abundant that I may well refrain from giving examples. It is found that the vocabularies of collectors, although they may apply diacritical marks or special alphabets, bear evidence of the phonetics of their own language. This can be explained only by the fact that each apperceives the unknown sound by means of the sounds of his own language [p. 51].

Speech perception is constrained by the phonology of one's native language. The philologist is automatically biased by his familiarity with the phonology of his own language, even when trying to accurately record the sounds of another. Boas reported results from two tests of the assertions: First, that sounds that are similar to one familiar sound should often be heard as the same, even though actually different, (the inverse of the alternating sound phenomenon); and second, that native speakers of languages containing the so-called alternating sounds should hear some of our sounds as alternating. Both assertions were confirmed by his experiments.

What Boas discussed in his article as "alternating apperception" is the phenomenon now known as categorical perception (Liberman, Cooper, Shankweiller, and Studdert-Kennedy, 1967). Two aspects of the phenomenon may be noted: First, the perception of speech is categorical; that is, speech sounds classified as the same by one's language are very hard to hear as different. Sounds which fall on the borderline between two phonemic categories alternate in perception between the two categories. Second, phonemic category boundaries differ from language to language, and categorical perception differs accordingly. Two sounds that are easy for speakers of one language to distinguish may be difficult for speakers of another. These are the basic aspects of the phenomenon. We will consider them in more detail later.

Our chapter is organized into three parts. The next section discusses the distinction between rules of individual behavior and cultural patterns of action. In the following sections we discuss the form of cultural constraints on perception, and evidence suggesting that categorical perception is of the proposed form.

THE CONSTRAINING INFLUENCE OF CULTURE

The Evolution of Culture

Much of the following discussion was taken from Hayek's (1967) collection of essays, in which he draws a distinction between the rules of individual conduct and the resulting social order of actions. We feel that this distinction is of enormous significance for psychologists who wish to study the co-constraining interplay between individuals and their culture.

Rules of Individual Conduct.   To the degree that behavior is regular, we may state that it is rule governed. That is, whenever we recognize some regularity in behavior we call that behavior rule governed regardless of whether the individuals involved are aware of the rule or not. Hayek stated, "It should be clearly understood that the term 'rule' is used for a statement by which a regularity of the conduct of individuals can be described, irrespective of whether such a rule is 'known' to the individuals in any other sense than that they normally act in accordance with it" (p. 67).

Behavior is rule governed because individuals are constrained in the possible actions that they can take in pursuing purposes. When, for example, we walk from here to there, our "walking" can be described as rule governed to the extent that the regularities in "walking" can be described. Since we are constrained by our physiology to walk in a manner characteristic of human beings, a description of "walking" in general should serve to adequately describe our walking *skill*. Other rules might describe individual *style*. *Rules of individual conduct describe the regularities of skilled activities.* The rules of conduct for speech production are specified by describing the constraints of the speech organs; thus, the distinctive features of phonemes are specifications of the configurations of the vocal tract (Chomsky & Halle, 1968).

Not only is speech production constrained by physiological structures, but by cultural factors as well. The phonological regularities of, for example, English are not those of Japanese. Language-specific rules specify a subset of humanly possible articulatory configurations and sequences of configurations. Just as the biological constraints of the range of possible positions of human speech organs differ from the constraints of non-human vocal tracts (Lieberman, 1968), so the linguistic constraints on speakers of English differ from those on speakers of other languages.

Cultural Patterns of Action.   Individuals acting according to rules of conduct will produce a pattern of actions for the group as a whole. The rules of individual conduct and the resulting social pattern of actions are distinct orders. Hayek states:

> That the system of rules of individual conduct and the order of actions which results from the individuals acting in accordance with them are not the same thing should be obvious as soon as it is stated, although the two are in fact frequently confused. (Lawyers are particularly prone to do so by using the term "order of law" for both.) Not every system of rules of individual conduct will produce an overall order of the actions of a group of individuals; and whether a given system of rules of individual conduct will produce an order of actions, and what kind or order, will

depend on the circumstances in which the individuals act. The classical instance in which the very regularity of the behavior of the elements produces ''perfect disorder'' is the second law of thermodynamics, the entropy principle. It is evident that in a group of living beings many possible rules of individual conduct would also produce only disorder or make the existence of the group as such impossible. A society of animals or men is always a number of individuals observing such common rules of conduct as, in the circumstances in which they live, will produce an order of actions [p. 67].

Individuals acting in regular ways cause an order of actions to result for the group as a whole and in human groups we call this order culture. More must be said about the evolution of culture.

Hayek (1966) traced the history of evolutionary thought back to Bernard Mandeville, an 18th-century philosopher of morals and society. Hayek attributes to Mandeville the breakthrough into modern thought of the *twin ideas of evolution and the spontaneous formation of an order*. It was Mandeville's insight that the pattern of actions that results from individuals acting in accordance with rules of conduct is no part of the intentions of the individuals. Cultural patterns of action are formed spontaneously and are neither a part of individual intentions nor the result of rational planning. *Cultural patterns are evolved structures that are advantageous for the group as a whole*. Hayek (1966) wrote of Mandeville:

His main contention became simply that in the complex order of society the results of men's actions were very different from what they had intended, and that the individuals, in pursuing their own ends, whether selfish or altruistic, produced useful results for others which they did not anticipate or perhaps even know; and, finally, that the whole order of society, and even all that we call culture, was the result of individual strivings which had no such end in view, but which were channelled to serve such ends by institutions, practices, and rules which also had never been deliberately invented but had grown up by the survival of what proved successful.

It was in the elaboration of this wider thesis that Mandeville for the first time developed all the classical paradigmata of the spontaneous growth of orderly social structures: of law and morals, of language, the market, and of money, and also of the growth of technological knowledge [p. 129].

Tracing the development of Mandeville's ideas as they influenced David Hume, Adam Ferguson, and Adam Smith, Hayek suggests that, although Mandeville had no direct influence on the thinking of Charles Darwin, Hume probably did through Darwin's grandfather, Erasmus Darwin. Darwin's theory of evolution through natural selection is consistent with Mandeville's ideas.

Within the sphere of social and economic philosophy of the 18th-century, there grew in England and Scotland an awareness that cultural patterns of action were distinct from individual rules of conduct. From among the many delightful quotes representative of this position we have chosen the following from Adam Ferguson (1767):

> Every step and every movement of the multitude, even in what are termed enlightened ages, are made with equal blindness to the future; and nations stumble upon establishments, which are indeed the result of human action, but not the execution of any human design [p. 183].

What was being suggested by this school of thought was that all that we call culture results from evolutionary processes. Societal systems such as markets and languages are emergent phenomena that no mind had designed. The spontaneous creation of such orders is due to the regular actions of individuals pursuing their purposes. However, the cultural patterns of action which emerge are not part of the intentions, purposes, or plans of individuals. Societal systems are *constructed* only in the sense that they are the *product of human action*. They are *not the result of human design*.

The evolutionary account of the genesis of culture may be contrasted with what may be called, following Hayek, Constructivist Rationalism. Historically this is the position of Francis Bacon, Thomas Hobbes, and Rene Descartes, characterized by their assumption that all societal systems are the invention of rational planning. The inadequacies of Constructive Rationalism, and the dangers that arise when authorities in positions to effect changes in societal systems believe in its assumptions, have been a continuing theme throughout Hayek's writings. (See Hayek's [1975] Nobel Memorial Lecture as well as his [1945] article and [1967] collection of studies.) Hayek's argument rests on his theory of complex phenomena which asserts that due to the degree of complexity found in societal systems, no single mind could ever obtain the information necessary to efficiently plan or regulate such systems (see chapter 12, this volume). Constructive Rationalists described societal systems as constructed since, for them, there were but two categories of phenomena: the natural order and the man-made or conventional order. They chose to place culture in the man-made order. It was the revolutionary ideas of evolution and the spontaneous formation of an order, proposed as an alternative to Constructive Rationalism, that allowed for the possibility that cultures have evolved from human activity but not human planning. Hayek (1967) wrote:

> It was finally in reaction to this Cartesian rationalism that the British moral philosophers of the eighteenth century, starting from the theory of the common law as much as from the law of nature, built up a theory which made the undesigned results of individual action its central object, and in particular provided a comprehensive theory of the spontaneous order of the market [p. 99].

The social sciences have taken on the task of studying emergent societal systems. Economists have found their object of study in markets just as linguists have in language, and within both disciplines the cultural patterns of action are often described without reference to individual intentions. It is the task of these social sciences to describe the overall order of action that defines markets and languages and in so doing ignores the purposes, motives, and intentions of individuals.

Cultural Behavior.   Individuals are constrained when acting within societal systems by the patterns of action that define such systems. When engaging in market behavior, for example, we are constrained to follow those rules of conduct appropriate for the market place. Likewise, when engaged in linguistic behavior, we are constrained to follow those rules appropriate to the language we speak.

The constraints on social behaviors vary enormously in the degree to which they are explicitly known. Judicial laws have been codified and, in free societies, are available to all. Grammatical rules have likewise been written down. It should be noted that both judicial laws and grammatical rules were expressed in words with varying degrees of adequacy long after they had evolved as the systems of common law and language. Taboos are known by the members of the culture to which they apply, though often they are never written down nor differentiated from the larger systems of myth. Most societal constraints are not explicitly known, and it may well be that this degree of explicitness is directly proportional to society's desire to enforce the constraints in question.

Whenever they are engaged in a cultural behavior, individuals are constrained by the structure of the societal system in which they are acting. Consider an example of market behavior: Suppose that you walk into a store in order to purchase an apple. Apples are displayed in the store along with their price. In order to obtain the apple of your choice you must engage in market behavior. That is, you must furnish the store clerk with an amount of money equivalent to the price of the apple. Your purpose of buying an apple is constrained by the structure of the price system. The price system is a part of the emergent market system; it is not a part of your immediate intentions. In order to behave appropriately in markets, individuals must have a knowledge of how to conform to the constraints of market systems. They must have a knowledge of the price system in order to utilize the information symbolically presented in prices.

When engaged in linguistic behavior, individuals are likewise constrained by the structure of that cultural pattern of actions. Participation in linguistic behavior requires a knowledge of how to utilize the language system. In phonology, for instance, the structure of each language includes a specification of the classes of sounds defining the phonological system. Individuals engaged in linguistic behavior are constrained by these rules prescribed by the phonology of their language. Phonological systems are part of language, and yet are not related to individual intentions.

Gibson and Cultural Systems.   Gibson seems to have ignored the distinction between cultural systems and the intentions of individuals. By not considering the constraints that culture places on behavior, he has misrepresented our ecological niche. The theory of affordances attempts an "explanation of how the 'values' or 'meanings' of things in the environment could be directly perceived" (Gibson, 1977, p. 67). An affordance is the functional value of an object or event for an individual. For example, "If a substance is fairly rigid instead of fluid; if its surface in nearly horizontal instead of slanted; if the latter is relatively flat instead of convex or concave; and if it is sufficiently extended, that is, large enough, then it affords support" (Gibson, 1977, p. 70). Functional accounts of meaning, such as Gibson's, relate the structural properties of objects and events to the purposive activities of organisms as these activities are constrained by individual rules of conduct. For example, the affordances of an object could include "graspability" if a person following the rules of conduct for the intentional activity of grasping, is able to grasp the object. Since affordance structures are always directly related to the intentional activities of individuals, these structures cannot account for emergent cultural patterns of action which are not so related. Gibson's affordance theory of meaning is thus limited in scope to those perceptual events not influenced by culture. We are at a loss to imagine just what those events might be. When viewing a surface which affords support, one sees a floor, lawn, field, road, or some other culturally defined surface. Floors, lawns, etc., do certainly afford support; however, these *concepts* are also part of culture.

Try to answer the question: *What does a phoneme afford?* Only one answer is possible. *A phoneme affords itself for an individual engaged in linguistic behavior.* The value of phonemes is defined by the role they play in language. They are wonderously independent of the intentions of individuals. Thus, in considering speech perception we must place the individual in the appropriate ecological niche, i.e., the linguistic community. The language shared by a linguistic community is a culturally emergent pattern of actions constraining the linguistic behavior of the individual members. Gibson's approach gains its plausability only by begging the questions and issues posed by cultural constraints.

To reiterate, individuals acting within culture are constrained by the structure of societal systems. Cultural patterns of action are constructed in the sense that they are the result of human action, although it is not necessary to assume that they are the result of human planning. Societal systems are evolved structures constraining the rules of conduct of individuals acting within them. In discussing the interplay between cultural patterns of actions and the activities of individuals, Adam Smith (1776) wrote that man was "led by an invisible hand to promote an end which was not part of his intention" (p. 400).

The Cultural Relativity of Symbolic Forms

Shaw and his colleagues (see chapter 10, this volume) speak of an affordance as a relationship involving three terms: X affords Y for Z. For the affordance relation to hold, X and Z must be *compatible* with respect to Y. Whether a surface actually affords support for a person depends on physical aspects of the surface and of the person (e.g., What is the strength of the surface? What is the weight of the person?). Affordances also depend on psychological factors in the person (e.g., Thin ice may afford support for a person *if* the person *knows* to lie down and crawl rather than to walk upright across it.) as they condition the specific form of the relationship between the surface and the person. Why should cultural aspects of the adaptive strategy be treated differently? Surely money affords eating for someone who knows how to use it. Why should there be any problem in extending the affordance analysis to cultural forms?

The problem arises because of the introduction of two new terms in the expression of the compatibility relationship: other people and culture. For money to afford eating to a person requires more than that the person and the money be compatible with respect to eating. Another person must be present, who also knows the use of money, and who views himself as more in need of money than of food (which he already has) at the time of the transaction.

Affordances relate invariant properties of objects to functional activities of individuals. In social situations, individuals trade commodities and information through the use of cultural mediums of exchange, such as money and phonemes. These symbolic mediums lose their meaning when related solely to a person *outside* of culture. In order to understand, for example, the affordance relationships of water for finned organisms adapted to living in water, we must understand the physics of the relationship between fins and water. But the natural order that constrains the relationship between money and eating is not solely a physical order. Knowing the cultural order of the market is as essential to our understanding of the man–money–eating system as knowing the physics of solid bodies in water is to our understanding of the fish–fin–locomotion system.

The compatibility relationships involved in using money are largely cultural. The physical properties of the money itself are important too, of course, but there is hardly any difference between a twenty dollar bill and a piece of green scrap paper at the level of physical compatibility and affordance. Both are easy to grasp, can be seen easily in ordinary illumination, and so on. Money is a *symbol* having culturally given value. Give a twelve year old child a piece of scrap paper and on another occasion a ticket to Disneyland, and compare. What about the physical difference between the two pieces of paper accounts for the difference in reactions? The patterns of ink? The pattern of ink on the ticket *supports* perception of the ticket as a ticket, with its cultural value.

Language forms are also objects whose value is mostly cultural. Consider naming: One function of verbal naming is to allow communication without visual contact. Suppose we are in the woods and it is dark and someone yells "Bring the flashlight, quick!" They do not have to wait until the sun comes up so they can point at the flashlight. The sound of "flashlight" has a culturally given value about which we agree.

Objects differ in how much their values are determined by culture. At one extreme, an apple is intrinsically valuable, as food, even to a chipmunk or a slime mold. Its nutritive value is not culturally given. Though this particular apple is in part a product of culture (see how much larger it is than a wild apple), its value to a human does not depend on culture. But a word or a syllable is a purely cultural form. Although each is physically embodied, the *physical* form has little or no value at all save to bear the cultural form. The sound of the word "flashlight" is useless except as a culturally conditioned symbol. Inasmuch as the value an object has for a person is cultural value, the name indicating this value can stand for the presence of the object and is a *symbol* of it.

Let us consider the form of cultural constraints on compatibility relationships involving people, their individual purposes, and the culturally valued objects they use. Cultural constraints take the form of *agreements* made between individuals. The form of agreements is specified by *contracts*.

THE CONTRACTUAL SPECIFICATION OF MEANING

Concepts define classes of objects relative to cultural patterns of action. The meaning of every "thing kind" is relative to a cultural niche of human activity. For example, the functional activities which a "book" affords are culturally constrained by the societal systems of language, writing, reading, etc. Cassirer (1955) wrote:

> We see, then, that in order to characterize a given form of relation in its concrete application and concrete meaning, we must not only state its qualitative attributes as such, but also define the system in which it stands. If we designate the various kinds of relation—such as relation of space, time, causality, etc.—as R_1, R_2, R_3, we must assign to each one a special "index of modality," μ^1, μ^2, μ^3, denoting the context of function and meaning in which it is to be taken. For each of these contexts, language as well as scientific cognition, art as well as myth, possesses its own constitutive principle which sets its stamp, as it were, on all the particular forms within it. The result is an extraordinary diversity of formal relations, whose richness and inner involvements, however, can be apprehended only through a rigorous analysis of each fundamental form. But even aside from such an analysis, the most general survey of consciousness as a whole reveals certain fundamental conditions of unity, prerequisites for synthesis, combination, and statement. It lies in the very nature of consciousness that it cannot posit any content without, by this simple act, positing a complex of other contents. Kant—in his treatise on negative quantities—once formulated the problem of causality as the endeavor to understand why because *something* is, *something else,* of a totally different nature, ought to be and is [p. 97].

Each cultural pattern of action defines an order in which concepts derive relative meanings. Consider the market system and the concepts related to it. The meaning of "price" is relative to the functional contexts provided by markets. The term literally loses its meaning if an attempt is made to define it without reference to the market system or metaphorical expressions of it. Price systems are specified relative to market systems, currency systems are defined relative to price systems, "dollar" is defined relative to a particular currency system, and so on. The language system and its constituents are likewise interrelated. The value of phonemes is relative to phonological and language systems of which they are a part. Cassirer noted that cultural patterns of action constrain the functional contexts appropriate for the concepts defined within them. Since "price," for example, is defined relative to the market system, the meaning of "price" is specified within those functional contexts appropriate to markets. The significance of market terms is defined within those functional contexts prescribed by the market system.

Let us consider further the relationship between concepts and contexts. To this end we present the following demonstration:

> A subject enters our laboratory and an object is held before him which he is asked to name.
> "The object is a pencil," he replies.
> "Why is this object a pencil?" we ask.
> The subject's reply includes a description of the object in terms of the properties which most pencils have. For example:
> "It looks like a pencil. It is a six-sided cylinder-like wooden object and is about six inches long. It is painted yellow and has No. 2 Pencil written on its side. One end is sharpened revealing a thin black cylinder which comprises the center of this object. It has an eraser on the other end. I may continue indefinitely to describe this object and all of these descriptions refer to what I take to be a pencil."
> We now ask the subject to write with the object, and he discovers that this object will not write. The center of the object is not made of graphite but rather of rubber.
> "It is not a pencil after all," he replies. "You *tricked* me."
> Now we ask, "How was it that we were able to trick you?"

When we held the object before the subject, he *took it to be* a pencil as surely as if it had not been a fake. So long as we can obtain a fake pencil that looks like the real thing, no one will suggest that it is anything other than what it appears to be. This is true, of course, only so long as our subjects do not suspect that we are intentionally deceiving them.

Suppose, however, that subjects have prior knowledge of our experiments and suspect that the objects presented are not what they appear to be. In these cases the subjects would state that the object to be identified looks like a pencil but might not actually be one. These subjects are skeptical of this experimental situation and are, thus, not willing to accept appearances for the truth. Their experience is meaningful, but they doubt that these meanings are necessarily true. These subjects demonstrate that they are aware of a possible difference between their meaningful experiences and a correct or true interpretation of that experience. Since deception always is a possibility, we may question the truth of any perception. When a meaningful experience has occurred, we may question the assumptions upon which the interpretation was based. That is, we may doubt the validity of those assumptions presupposed by the rules defining the interpretation; but we cannot doubt that the experience was interpreted as it had been.

Within our demonstration the subject decided that the object was not a pencil because pencils *ought* to write. If the object had been capable of being written with as expected, then the subject would have reaffirmed that this object was a pencil. The core of a pencil ought to be made out of a substance suitable for writing and since this object's core was not, it could not possibly be a pencil. If an object is defined in such a way that it has certain culturally agreed upon characteristics (such as writability) then when the object is perceived in appropriate contexts, it ought to have those characteristics applicable to that context.

Context sensitive rules used to specify meaning define not what "is" the case but rather what "ought to be" the case. When an object is taken at a glance to be a pencil, the rules which are used do not specify what a pencil "is," but rather, they define how a pencil "ought" to appear in that context. Context sensitive rules define what an object ought to be with respect to the functional context in which it is presented.

When one perceives an object in a particular context as an instance of a particular "thing kind," then one is also asserting that the object ought to have those properties *in other contexts* that the particular "thing kind" must have. The rules defining the meaning of the object in the first context, however, are no different in kind than the rules specifying the meaning of the object in other contexts. Let us specify the form of these rules in as simple a manner as possible.

Let (G) be the set of perceptual "grounds" from which in a particular context (C) the object (O) is taken to be an instance of the "thing kind" (K). Let $(G', G'', \dots)$ and $(C', C'', \dots)$ represent additional grounds and contexts in which the object (O) may be construed as an instance of (K). The rules specifying the meaning of (O) as an instance of (K) are then:

1. Given that (O) is (G) within (C), then (O) is an instance of (K) if and only if (K) ought to be (G) within (C).
2. If (O) is taken to be an instance of (K), then (O) ought to be $(G', G'', \dots)$ within $(C', C'', \dots)$ if (K) ought to be $(G', G'', \dots)$ within $(C', C'', \dots)$.

Rules such as these may be described as contracts (Proffitt, 1976). *Contracts specify mutual obligations. An obligation is a prescription of what ought to be the case.* The appearance of a meaningful entity is contractually defined for all contexts in which it could possibly be perceived. For example, an object taken to be a pencil, based upon certain characteristics, ought to have additional characteristics such as writability when it is construed in the appropriate context. The rules defining meaning in the perceived context are also contractual. Rule 1 specifies that an object is taken to be an instance of a particular "thing kind" if and only if it has those characteristics which the "thing kind" ought to have in that context. Furthermore, if it manifests those characteristics then it ought to have additional characteristics in other contexts which the "thing kind" ought to have.

It may be objected that meaningful experience is immediate, and that the sense of the "ought" relationship is not to be found in introspection. This objection is that meaningful experience occurs without qualification. We may counter this objection by examining the interrelationship between contracts and beliefs. If one assumes that he or she is not being deceived, then one will believe that what is being perceived "is" what it "ought to be." The conclusions of a contractual inference are believed when the conditions of the contract are met. Contractual rules of inference may be related to beliefs as follows:

3. (O) is believed to be an instance of (K), given that (O) is (G) within (C) and (K) ought to be (G) within (C).
4. If (O) is believed to be an instance of (K), then (O) will be believed to be $(G', G'', \dots)$ within $(C', C'', \dots)$ if (K) ought to be $(G', G'', \dots)$ within $(C', C'', \dots)$.

The meaning of everyday experience comes to us as the conclusion of a contractual process. Our immediate awareness is of the conclusions and not the process of inference itself. When the conditions of a contractual inference are met, the conclusions of that inference are perceptions believed to be statements of what really is the case.

Although the contractual nature of meaning does not come into awareness in ordinary perception, it does enter awareness when we make an error in our inferences or are deceived and recognize such errors as having occurred. *We become aware of contracts when after having construed an event in one context, we perceive it in another and discover that the event is not what it ought to be.* When we attempt to write with an object believed to be a pencil and discover that the object will not write, our awareness is focused on a contractual obligation of the class of pencils: to have the characteristic of writability. Likewise, should we construe an object to be a brick after visual inspection in a particular context, we would become very much aware of the contractural obligations of the class of objects called "bricks" should a small gust of wind be found to blow the object away.

To reiterate, a contractual inference in a particular context may be sufficient to establish a belief in the conclusions of that inference. The belief in question, however, is not the same as the contract that established it. Each contractual inference is specific to a particular functional context. Beliefs transcend contextual relativity. If an object is believed to be an instance of a particular "thing kind" then its appearance will be contractually specified for all possible contexts. *Contracts relate perceptual grounds to concepts. Beliefs relate contracts to other contracts.* Thus we have a mechanism of what may be called "conceptual transcendence" to account for the "absolute" nature of generic terms. We believe that it is this conceptual transcendence that Cassirer (1955) was alluding to when, discussing Kant, he wrote "because *something* is, *something else* of a totally different nature, ought to be and is" (p. 97).

CATEGORICAL PERCEPTION AS A CONTRACTUAL FORM

What can we learn about categorical perception, by considering it as the result of a contractual process? What can we learn about contracts, by considering categorical perception as a specific example? To answer these questions, we consider experimental work done at Haskins Laboratories, though the same conclusions could be drawn from Boas' work.

Categorical Perception at Haskins Laboratories

Since 1950, investigators at Haskins have studied the perception of speech, using speech synthesizers to create precisely controlled acoustic signals with known properties. We discuss two landmark Haskins experiments which have shaped our basic understanding of speech.

Imagine a series of sounds. The sounds gradually change in their acoustic properties as we go through the series. Suppose we hear the first sound as "beh" (as in "better") and the last as "geh." Somewhere in the middle of the series we hear "deh." Such a series is called an acoustic continuum. This one is a "beh–geh" continuum. With a speech synthesizer we can create acoustic continua. If we have a pattern that gives a good "ba," and another that gives a good "pa," we can create a "ba–pa" continuum by producing a series of stimuli which change gradually from the "ba" pattern to the "pa" pattern.

Liberman, Harris, Hoffman, and Griffith (1957) used a synthetic "beh–geh" continuum to study how people divide sounds into phoneme categories. Each listener in their experiment took two different tests. One was a simple labeling test—the stimuli on the continuum were presented in random order and the listener was to judge each as *b*, *d*, or *g*. On this test most listeners divided the stimulus continuum neatly into three categories. Figure 14.1a shows how one of their listeners divided the continuum.

The other test was a discrimination test, a test of the listener's ability to tell the stimuli apart. A pair of stimuli were presented, followed by repetition of one or the other (the *ABX* format). The listener was to judge which of the first two (*A* or *B*) was identical to the last (*X*). It was always true that either the *A* stimulus or the *B* stimulus was identical to the *X* stimulus and that the other was different.

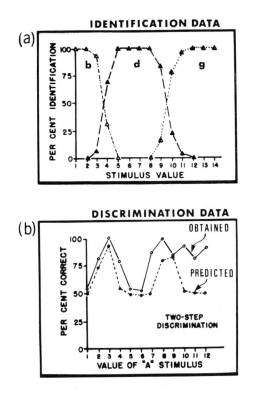

FIG. 14.1. Evidence of categorical perception of the beh–geh continuum. (a) Labeling performance for a single listener; (b) discrimination performance for the same listener. The "predicted" function is computed from the labeling data, and represents the results that would be obtained if discrimination performance were entirely based on labeling differences. (From Liberman, Harris, Hoffman & Griffith, 1957, p. 361).

The stimuli were combined in this way with each of their neighbors (stimuli one, two, and three steps away on the continuum) on both sides. With this test, Liberman et al. got very surprising results. Listeners could distinguish stimuli falling on opposite sides of a phoneme boundary better than they could distinguish stimuli which fell into the same phoneme category. These were large differences. When stimuli are paired across a phoneme boundary, discriminability is nearly perfect. When the stimuli paired are both well within the same phoneme category, discriminability is near chance. Figure 14.1b shows discrimination performance for the listener superimposed upon the labeling results from Figure 14.1a.

This pattern—a sharp division of the acoustic continuum on the labeling test, combined with peaks of discriminability at the points on the continuum where labeling changes from one category to another—is a symptom of the presence of categorical perception. Similar results have been obtained by various experimenters with hundreds of listeners on many different acoustic continua.

That a listener can distinguish two sounds, one heard as "beh" and the other as "deh," is no surprise. Of course, they are discriminable. What is surprising is that a listener who labels two stimuli as members of the same phoneme category will have trouble telling them apart; so much trouble that scores on the discrimination test are little better than would be expected if the listener had been guessing. In fact, if one asks one often finds that the listener *was* guessing. This result is surprising. The within–category stimulus pairs, which listeners fail to distinguish, are just as different, physically, as the between–category pairs which they do distinguish correctly.

Along with the discrimination and labeling results go several other symtoms of categorical perception. Listeners are *more confident* of their discriminations of pairs which straddle a boundary. Their judgments of such pairs are also *faster.* We also have the alternating sounds phenomenon. All of these results, taken together, are what we mean when we say that people perceive speech categorically.

The alternating sounds phenomenon occurs at the phoneme boundary. In Fig. 14.1a, stimulus No. 4 is heard (by this listener) as "beh" a third of the time, and as "deh" two-thirds of the time. Experimentally, on each presentation of this stimulus the listener hears one or the other. There is no change in the stimulus from one occasion to the next. What changes is the assignment of the stimulus to the phonological categories. The perceptual change, where no stimulus change has occurred, shows that the listener's assignment of the stimulus to the linguistically specified phonological categories must be quite active. From the perspective of the experimenter we can see that the stimulus remains constant. But since human beings have evolved to hear speech *as speech,* the rules constraining individual perception have no place for a mediocre "33% beh, 66% deh." Instead, this stimulus is heard clearly as "beh" on one occasion and as "deh" on another. This pattern of alternating perception is familiar from many other contexts. In vision, many well known ambiguous stimuli give first one meaning, then another (The Necker Cube, the Rat-man, etc.). In language, we have ambiguous sentences which alternate in meaning. Whenever this pattern is found, we may suspect that categorical perception is present.

People who speak different languages have different patterns of categorical perception. The work of Boas cited earlier established this fact; it is confirmed by the experience of anyone who tries to learn to converse in another language. Liberman et al. (1957) recognized this immediately:

> [It is a common experience that] in learning a new language one often has difficulty in making all the appropriate sound discriminations. The evidence for this is impressionistic in the extreme, and there is little information that would permit a defintion of the more specific aspects of the difficulty. In whatever degree this difficulty exists, however, a reasonable assumption is that some part of it arises

from the fact that a person who is newly exposed to the sounds of a strange language finds it necessary to categorize familiar acoustic continua in unfamiliar ways. If his discriminations have, by previous training, been sharpened and dulled according to the position of the phoneme boundaries of his native language, and if the acoustic continua of the old language are categorized differently by the new one, then the learner might be expected to have difficulty perceiving the sounds of the new language until he had mastered some new discriminations and, perhaps, unlearned some old ones [p. 358].

Experimentally, the cultural dependence of categorical perception was established by Lisker and Abramson's (1970) work on the Voice Onset Time (VOT) continuum. Voice Onset Time is the primary acoustic difference supporting the distinction between voice and voiceless stops ("ba"-"pa") in English. Other languages use this same acoustic dimension but use it differently. Thai, for example, has three phonemic categories on the VOT continuum, where English has only two. Spanish has two categories, but the boundary is located at a different point on the acoustic continuum than for English. Abramson and Lisker measured VOT values of natural syllables uttered by natives of these and other languages. Native listeners also took labeling and discrimination tests made up from a synthetic VOT continuum. Individuals differ in the position of the phoneme boundary. For any individual, the region where the labeling change occurs is the discriminable region. When two individuals differ in boundary position, both labeling and discrimination testing will indicate this fact, and the results of the two tests will agree. The boundary position for a certain culturally defined population is determined by testing a sample of natives of that culture, and finding the averages of the individual boundary positions. Figure 14.2 shows results obtained by Lisker and Abramson (Lisker and Abramson, 1970; Abramson and Lisker, 1970) using the same stimulus continuum with members of different cultures. The basic pattern of categorical perception is present in each case. What differs, from culture to culture, is the *number* and *position* of the category boundaries. Each listener hears according to contractual rules appropriate to a particular culture.

We can now understand why sounds which are heard consistently by members of one culture may alternate for members of another. Whenever a phoneme boundary, as defined by one culture, falls in the middle of a phoneme category, as defined by another culture, the alternating sound phenomenon can occur. We can also understand why adults have such difficulty learning to use foreign phonetic distinctions appropriately. If the foreign phoneme boundary falls in the middle of one of our phoneme categories, we may not be able to *hear* the difference.

Of course, some people do seem to learn to use foreign languages well. What happens to categorical perception during this learning?

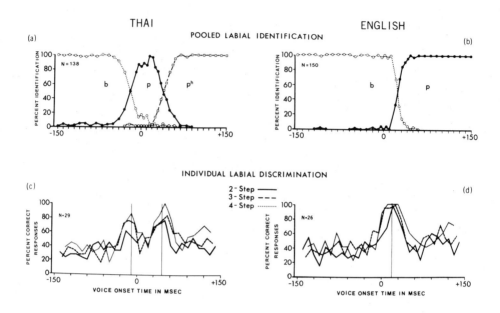

FIG. 14.2. Evidence of cross-cultural differences in perception of the labial voice onset time continuum. (a & b) Labeling performance for two groups of listeners: (a) Averages for eight Thai speakers; (b) averages for twelve American speakers. (After Lisker & Abramson, 1970, pp. 556 & 567.) (c & d) Discrimination performance for two individual listeners: (c) Data from a single Thai speaker; (d) Data from a single American English speaker. Vertical lines indicate labeling boundaries for these individuals. (From Abramson & Lisker, 1970, pp. 571 & 572.)

Categorical Perception in Bilinguals

An especially interesting case is that of bilinguals. How do bilinguals deal with these differences between languages in the positions of phoneme boundaries on acoustic continua? One possibility, which seems to be well supported by evidence, is that bilinguals develop a single boundary for a given phonemic contrast, that boundary being intermediate between the monolingual boundaries for the two languages. This would allow the listener's perceptual system to be organized without reference to information about different languages. The domain of acoustic possibilities could be simply divided into a single set of phoneme categories—some from one language, some from the other, and some from both.

Alternatively, the bilingual could have different phoneme boundaries—one for each language—switching from one to the other as he switched languages.

This would seem to provide more accurate information about what was said, since no compromise would be necessary. Phoneme boundaries could be as precise as those of monolinguals. Such precision could be expensive, however, requiring a more complicated organization of the perceptual system.

Experimental evidence from a study by Caramazza, Yeni-Komshian, Zurif, and Carbone (1973) supported the fixed boundary hypothesis in perception, but not in production. They tested monolingual French (Canadian) and English speakers, and French-English bilinguals on the VOT continuum. Data from the monolinguals agreed with that of Abramson and Lisker. The French boundary was earlier than the English boundary. The bilingual data indicated a boundary intermediate between the French and English boundaries, which did not shift as a function of the language used in the testing session. However, measurements of syllables produced by the same subjects showed clear shifts; bilinguals speaking English spoke similarly to monolingual English speakers—when speaking French the bilinguals spoke similarly to monoloingual French speakers. Similar results were reported by Williams (1977), who tested Spanish-English bilinguals. She reported no systematic change in either the identification crossover point or the position of the discrimination peak as a function of the language in which the experiment was conducted (including ten minutes of conversation before the testing). However, she too found clear shifts in production. If we were to take these results at face value, we might conclude that bilinguals can change their speech to correspond to the monolingual norms for the target language; but that in hearing speech, each bilingual has a single phoneme boundary which is used for both languages.

Elman, Diehl, and Buchwald (1977) however, suspected that the procedures used in the perceptual portions of these studies might not have been sufficient to sustain a given language set throughout the period of testing. In both earlier experiments the language context was determined by events which occurred before the testing. As the test progressed the language set might well have diminished. Further, both experiments had used synthetic speech stimuli—the same ones used by Abramson and Lisker—which might tend to disrupt a particular language set. Thus, to improve the chances that a particular language set would be in effect throughout the testing session, Elman and his colleagues used a precursor phrase ("Write the word" in English, "Escriba la palabra" in Spanish) before each test item. Also, filler words in the language of the particular testing session were included among the nonsense syllables as test items. And the VOT test syllables used were natural speech (VOT values selected by analyzing a large number of recorded syllables).

The results of this preparation were gratifying. They clearly showed that strong bilinguals shift the VOT boundary as a function of the particular language in use. Weaker bilinguals (those whose fluency in the second language was low) showed smaller shifts. Notably, even the strongest bilinguals did not shift the boundary all the way to the positions of the monolingual boundaries. Perhaps this

accurately reflects the perceptual organization of these listeners; but further re-
finements of the experimental set-up, such as using actual words in the particular
language, rather than nonsense, might yield still larger shifts.

The bilingual has more than one contractual framework for perceiving speech,
and can shift from one set of contracts to another as the situation warrants. The
English-Spanish bilingual *hears* differences when she is set for English that she
does *not* hear when she is set for Spanish. Here we have also learned something
about our own experiments. Some aspect of the way these bilingual listeners
ordinarily react to speech stimuli is missing from their reaction to the stimuli in
earlier experiments. The result from the earlier experiments was that bilinguals
have a single perceptual boundary, intermediate between those appropriate for
the two languages. Thus, in all, we have *three* patterns: one contractual
framework for listening to English, one for Spanish, and one for stimuli in
psychology experiments!

The conditions of the earlier experiments, which used standard procedures,
failed to elicit in listeners the contracts they actually use in conversation. Is this
also true for listeners who are monolingual? Do listeners generally use different
contracts in our laboratories than in ordinary situations?

Attentional Factors in Categorical Perception

The effects noted earlier for laboratory contexts are reminiscent of research on
"demand characteristics of experiments" (Orne; 1962, 1969), in which such
factors were explicitly studied by observing the effects of subjects' beliefs about
an experiment on the results obtained. Listeners develop special contracts to meet
the explicit and implicit social demands of the experimental set up.

Normally such factors are background considerations leading to a particular
choice of experimental conditions. We know that the listener must be led to adopt
a particular attitude toward the stimuli to be presented, that is, a particular
perceptual set must be established. The stimuli must be heard as speech but not as
meaningful words. The listener must not expect any feedback. The listener may
be told what syllables to expect. Results from any who hear something else may
be excluded from the analysis. Reasons exist for all these constraints, reasons
that are rediscovered by each new generation of experimenters as they begin to
move in new directions. How much of the "real" world can we let into our
laboratory without losing our grip on the phenomena we intend to study?

The largest difference between the contracts used in ordinary conversation and
those called forth by the standard speech perception testing situation seems to lie
in the area of *attention*. Listeners in experiments have to pay attention, of course,
but what they pay attention to is very different in the laboratory than in the
kitchen.

Perceptual contracts are always embedded within functional contexts. The
"functional context" is a name for what the person is "up to" at the moment,

i.e., what he or she is doing or trying to do, and all the situational factors involved in determining what actions and perceptions are relevant. If someone is trying to put out a grease fire on their stove, they are not interested in the picture on the box of baking soda, except as support for the belief that it *is* baking soda.

That the functional contexts of our experiments differ from those involved in communication was made clear by Spencer (1980). She was interested in such difficult contrasts as that in "a name"–"an aim." Textbooks of elocution sometimes use such pairs as examples for practice, but linguists question whether people normally distinguish them in ordinary speech. She wanted to see if people could hear the difference when these words were cut out of a tape recording and presented out of context. Spencer had trouble with her experiments. When listeners were told nothing about what they were going to hear, they almost always heard one of the two. Each pair has a preferred member. In the example above, "a name" was almost always heard, no matter which had been the original intent of the speaker. People heard "an aim" only when they were told before the experiment what the possibilities were. In this latter condition they always heard whatever the speaker intended. This phenomenon has been studied for many years and is called the familiarity effect or the word-frequency effect. The more familiar the word, the easier it is to hear and the easier it is to read. When words are made hard to hear by noise or whatever, the rare words are lost first, and the errors of commission which are made when rare words are misheard are mostly more common words. These effects disappear if listeners know in advance that they are to listen to one of a small set of words announced by the experimenter before the testing session. Spencer used materials in which acoustic support for the rare form was present. Her subjects accurately heard this form only when they knew the alternatives in advance. When they were told nothing about the possibilities, the word frequency effect took over and determined the perceptual experience. The listeners discarded acoustic information which was available to support perception of the rare form, in order to hear something more likely. These phenomena occur all the time in real speech, but we systematically exclude them from our laboratories when we tell the listener the possibilities before presenting our stimuli.

When, in a speech experiment, we give the listener a list of words, the fundamental contract governing the listening situation changes. The listener knows that we are not asking him to report on what the speaker meant. We are after what the speaker said, in the literal sense. We want a quote; not a paraphrase. The listener is obviously aware of this. If he hears a word which is not on our list, that is too bad. There is no alternative on the answer sheet for "innane." A or B: a name or an aim. The listener is not being paid to be creative.

Elman, et al. (1977) demonstrated that bilinguals have perceptual skills which they presumably apply in normal conversation but which are not applied in the typical speech perception testing situation. The contractual constraints on speech perception in bilinguals are flexible and are adjusted to fit the current situation.

However, the perceptual testing situation calls up neither the English nor the Spanish contract. Spencer has now shown that monolingual listeners also adjust their perceptual contracts to fit the demands of the testing situation.

Speech therapists encounter a similar problem in practical work with cultural differences in categorical perception. The client at a university speech clinic is often a foreign-born student who has come in for help with spoken English. Many of these students, after a period of therapy which may last months, are able to hear and produce appropriate phonetic distinctions for American English. However, skills which have been learned in the clinic may fail in the world outside. This is true as well in work with children who have speech development problems. Here too, the problem seems to be one of attentional focus. Speech therapists recognize that phonetic skills developed in deliberate drills regress when the speaker concentrates on the meaning. Gerber (1966) writes:

> Speech therapy cannot be judged to be effective unless the newly acquired patterns of articulation or vocalization become the habitual method of production in automatic, spontaneous utterance. Even after competent clinical techniques have resulted in a high degree of stability in the production of either corrected or improved speech sounds on the conscious, deliberate level, the formidable task of achieving consistency in carryover frequently continues, for relatively lengthy periods of time, to frustrate both client and clinician. A survey of 176 speech clinicians in Pennsylvania, functioning in the public schools and in hospital and university clinics, revealed that more than seventy-five per cent of the respondents ranked carryover of corrected speech sounds into spontaneous speech as the problem presenting the greatest difficulty in therapy.
>
> This is not difficult to understand when one considers the dual nature of the speech act: a physical manipulation, with great speed and complexity, of the speech mechanism concurrent with the communication of ideas, needs, and emotions. What can, therefore, be achieved at the conscious, deliberate level cannot be accomplished to the same degree at a level sufficiently automatic to permit the major focus of attention on the content without detriment to the successful mechanics of the utterance [p. 4].

It seems that skills learned and practiced in a laboratory or clinic situation, where attention is on pronunciation and perception of speech rather than on meaning, are very different from those involved in our ordinary lives. These skills are so different that they do not transfer well. If the situation in which we study the perception of speech excludes some factors which are involved in ordinary speech perception, we will not be able to study the influence of those factors on perception.

Speech involves meaning, or at least communicating with speech involves meaning, and the meaning is what the listener is focusing on. When we have the listener focusing instead on the speech itself, she is doing something with the speech which she does not ordinarily do. She is ignoring meaning and focusing on speech sounds. With this shift of attentional focus comes a definite change in the contractual rules which are being applied to perception. When meaning is attended, considerations of meaning enter into the decision about what we ought to hear. Thus, the range of acoustic patterns which may be heard as a given syllable increases tremendously. Categorical perception in ordinary situations is even stronger than its cousins in the laboratory. People are constantly mishearing things said to them, and often remain entirely oblivious of the error unless they are tipped off by some consequence of their mishearing. "I know that you believe you understand what you think I said, but I'm not sure you realize that what you heard is not what I meant."

Garnes and Bond (1977a) have studied this phenomenon experimentally, by embedding a synthetic continuum in different sentence contexts. For example, they embedded a "bait"—"date"—"gate" continuum in sentences such as "Check the time and the   ," or "Paint the fence and the   ." They found that the phoneme boundaries were shifted by the carrier sentence. This design suffers from a flaw discussed earlier. The test word always come at the end of the sentence, and it is always a contrast among bait–date–gate. For this reason they ran another version of the experiment in which several different contrasts were used and the test word was varied in its position in the sentence. In this set-up, the shifts obtained were stronger. Not only stimuli near the boundary, but stimuli formerly heard as clear instances of the other categories were now heard as the preferred form (Garnes and Bond, 1977b).

As we first introduce a semantic context to our testing situation, and then arrange for the listener to pay more and more attention to the meaning of the utterance, we find that the range of acoustic patterns which are heard as a particular word is increased. Thus, we conclude that perception in ordinary situations is much more categorical than what we normally see in the laboratory, and this stronger form of categoricity can be studied experimentally.

CONCLUDING REMARKS

When hearing a syllable such as "ba," one hears what ought to have been said, given the perceptual grounds revealed by the senses, the culturally given contract relating sensory grounds to syllables in a particular language, and the functional context in which all this is occurring. Categorical perception varies in its influence on a person's perceptual world according to culture. An individual's conceptual categories are social and cultural constraints that are manifested in perception. Perceptual boundaries enhance the contrast between conceptual categories having value within societal systems.

Categorical perception arises when sounds are heard as speech. The phoneme exists as a conceptual form and not as a part of the acoustic signal. "Ba" is *supported* by many different combinations of acoustic information in different contexts. The acoustic signal is taken as indicative of the presence of "ba" if the signal is what "ba" *ought to be* in that context. Even if the signal is not what "ba" ought to be in a particular context, we may hear "ba" anyway, if other factors are present which *prescribe* the presence of "ba," and are more heavily weighted. Presumably not any acoustic signal will permit the perception of "ba," but we can be sure that no acoustic form or combination of forms or aspects (features) of acoustic signals is common to all hearings of "ba."

We cannot define the invariant properties of "ba" solely in terms of the properties of acoustic signals. Such simplified descriptions work only when other influences are excluded from the experimental set-up. On the other hand, there must be some limit to the range of possible acoustic signals compatible with the perception of "ba" in any given context. We hope that a contractual approach to categorical perception will help in the search for these limits.

REFERENCES

Abramson, A. S. & Lisker, L. Discriminability along the voicing continuum: Cross-language tests. *Proceedings of the Sixth International Congress of Phonetic Sciences.* Prague: Academia, 1970, 569–573.

Boas, F. On alternating sounds. *American Anthropologist,* 1889, *2,* 47–53. Reprinted in G. W. Stocking, Jr. (Ed.), *The Shaping of American Anthropology 1883–1911: A Franz Boas Reader.* New York: Basic Books, 1973.

Caramazza, A., Yeni-Komshian, G., Zurif, E., & Carbone, E. The acquisition of a new phonological contrast: The case of stop consonant, in French-English bilinguals. *Journal of the Acoustical Society of America,* 1973, *54,* 421–428.

Cassirer, E. *The philosophy of symbolic forms, Volume 1: Language.* New Haven: Yale University Press, 1955.

Chomsky, N. & Halle, M. *The sound pattern of English.* New York: Harper and Row, 1968.

Elman, J. L., Diehl, R. L., & Buchwald, S. E. Perceptual switching in bilinguals. *Journal of the Acoustical Society of America,* 1977, *62,* 971–974.

Ferguson, A. *An essay on the history of civil society.* Dublin: Boulter Grierson, 1767.

Garnes, S. & Bond, Z. S. The relationship between semantic expectation and acoustic information. *Proceedings of the Third International Phonology Meeting,* 1977(a).

Garnes, S. & Bond, Z. S. The influence of semantics on speech perceptions. *Journal of the Acoustical Society of America,* (supplement), 1977(b), *61,* S65.

Gerber, A. J. The achievement of /r/ carryover through intensification of simultaneous auditory feedback. *Pennsylvania Speech and Hearing Association Newsletter,* Feb., 1966.

Gibson, J. J. The theory of affordances. In R. Shaw and J. Bransford (Eds.), *Perceiving, acting, and knowing.* Hillsdale, N.J.: Erlbaum, 1977.

Gibson, J. J. *The ecological approach to visual perception.* Boston: Houghton Mifflin, 1979.

Hayek, F. A. The price system as a mechanism for using knowledge. *American Economic Review,* 1945, *35,* 21–32.

Hayek, F. A. *The sensory order.* Chicago: University of Chicago Press, 1952.

Hayek, F. A. Dr. Bernard Mandeville. *Proceedings of the British Academy,* 1966, *52,* 125–141.

Hayek, F. A. *Studies in philosophy, politics, and economics.* New York: Simon and Schuster, 1967.

Hayek, F. A. The pretence of knowledge. *Swedish Journal of Economics,* 1975, *77,* 433–442.

Liberman, A. M., Cooper, F. S., Shankweiller, D. P. & Studdert-Kennedy, M. Perception of the speech code. *Psychological Review,* 1967, *74,* 431–461.

Liberman, A. M., Harris, K. A., Hoffman, H. S. & Griffith, B. C. The discrimination of speech sounds within and across phoneme boundaries. *Journal of Experimental Psychology,* 1957, *54,* 358–368.

Lieberman, P. Primate vocalizations and human linguistic ability. *Journal of the Acoustical Society of America,* 1968, *44,* 1574–1584.

Lisker, L. & Abramson, A. S. The voicing dimension: Some experiments in comparative phonetics. *Proceedings of the Sixth International Congress of Phonetic Sciences,* Prague: Academia, 1970, 563–567.

Orne, M. T. On the social psychology of the psychological experiment: With particular reference to demand characteristics and their implications *American Psychologist,* 1962, *17,* 776–783.

Orne, M. T. Demand characteristics and the concept of quasi-controls. In R. Rosenthal & R. L. Rosnow (Eds.), *Artifact in behavioral research.* New York: Academic Press, 1969.

Proffitt, D. R. *Demonstrations to investigate the meaning of everyday experience.* Unpublished doctoral dissertation, Pennsylvania State University, 1976.

Smith, A. *The wealth of nations.* London, J. M. Dent & Sons, 1776.

Spencer, N. J. & Wollman, N. Lexical access for phonetics ambiguities. *Language and Speech,* 1980, *23,* 171–198.

Williams, L. The perception of stop consonant voicing by Spanish-English bilinguals. *Perception and Psychophysics,* 1977, *21,* 289–297.

15 Weimer–Hayek Discussion

Member of Audience: Is the difference between simple and complex phenomena one of degree or of kind?

Hayek: It is certainly one of degree. But it is not at all easy to define what complexity means. Some philosophers deny that it can be defined. I think the essential point is that the degree of complexity of phenomena is measured by the number of variables that an explanatory theory must contain. That makes quite a difference when we move from the physical sciences to the social sciences. One can easily test this by looking in a textbook of physics or mechanics at the formulas in the appendix. One finds there are very few formulas that contain more than three variables. Now when we turn from physics to biology, we find that in a theory explaining any phenomenon, the minimum model that must be formed in order to explain it will contain a large number of variables. My understanding of complex phenomena comes from economics, where free competition operates in an open marketplace. Here the models we use are even more complex than in biology, and there is a real danger in oversimplifying our theories or making them deal with artificially restricted situations.

Turvey: Polanyi makes the distinction between subsidiary and focal control vis-à-vis complex biological systems, and I'm wondering if Hayek makes a similar distinction concerning complex phenomena.

Hayek: Yes, and of course my presentation left out all the hierarchical levels of control that are involved in complex phenomena. If you talk about the perception of my sentence, you have it all on one level; but in fact, we have a hierarchy of coordinated structures involved in classifying and understanding the sentence.

Weimer: Let me ask one question with regard to the theory of complexity. In 1948 the Hixton symposium included a large number of what, with hindsight, are very important papers—one by Lashley on the problem of serial order in behavior; and John Von Neumann presented, I think for the first time, the basic outline of the theory of self-reproducing automata. In Von Neumann's thought there is considerable similarity to your approach to complexity. Were you aware of Von Neumann's work, or did you develop your ideas independently?

Hayek: No, I wasn't aware of his work, which stemmed from his involvement with the first computers. But when I was writing *The Sensory Order,* I reasoned that I could explain to people what I was doing. Usually I found it very difficult to make them understand. And then I met John Von Neumann at a party, and to my amazement and delight, he immediately understood what I was doing and said that he was working on the same problem from the same angle. At the time his research on automata came out, it was too abstract for me to relate it to psychology, so I really couldn't profit from it; but I did see that we had been thinking on very similar lines.

Mishkin: I thought I heard Weimer say that one could throw overboard, or discard, a number of proposals Hayek makes and not do injustice to his system—one could discard his mediationalism, his associationism, perhaps even his representationalism—but I didn't hear Professor Hayek discard them. I heard him affirm them, and in fact quite strongly. Do I misunderstand him?

Weimer: My comment was that due to the era, the historical epoch, when Professor Hayek was writing, the only terminology available was associationistic and was formulated in terms of connections between stimuli and responses. What I tried to point out was that that does not mean Hayek was an S–R theorist in the 1950's, or that he was then or is now an associationistic learning theorist (to take, for instance, two types of theorists who would utilize the same terminology). My point was that you can translate Hayek into contemporary terminology without any real loss of content.

Hayek: I would agree. In fact, I have said so in the preface of my book. The book consists of three major portions. The first two chapters state the problem. The two final chapters state philosophical consequences. The second part attempts to spell out my theory in terms of the then-available physical mechanisms. In the preface I say I am not sure it was right to attempt such an explication at all, but I wanted to attempt a statement of the problem and outline what sort of statement would be a solution without trying to elaborate the solution in any detail. Then I concluded by drawing some philosophical consequences. But I think that the theme was not to provide a true explanation, but to show what an account would need to look like to be an explanation. It didn't really matter who I got my facts from, or what terminology was used, or even which neurophysiological model was employed.

Member of Audience: But the terms *association, mediation,* and *representation* do not presuppose any particular physiological mechanism.

Weimer: That is correct, but if I may answer that, precisely what this conference is about—or ought to be about—is the exploration in detail of what those terms really ought to mean. And in that sense, despite the fact that our problems and terms are age-old, what those problems mean is a function of—to use Shaw's terminology—the context of constraint in terms of which they are cast.

Pribram: I have a question that is related to this but may not seem to be. What is the relationship between heterarchy and hierarchy? And in the terms of this morning's discussion of the Gibsonians, how can the complement be part of that which it complements?

Hayek: I would really have to think about that. I have no ready answer.

Member of Audience: One of the most complex phenomena that science has had to deal with recently is the nature of scientific revolutions. There's been considerable debate between the Popperians and the Kuhnians as to whether science can be reconstructed from a logical-philosophical point of view or from a psychological–sociological point of view. Would your book *The Sensory Order* put you more with the Kuhnians or more with the Popperians?

Hayek: I was so much a Popperian long before Kuhn appeared that I've never been able to see that Kuhn "refuted" much of Popper. But so far as the pure theory of knowledge is concerned, I have reservations. Not only Kuhn but Lakatos and Feyerabend have made the field perhaps a little more difficult than Popper ever acknowledged. But basically, I am still a Popperian. Indeed, I should tell you that in a way, I was a Popperian before he published *The Logic of Scientific Discovery*. We were both, in the 1920s, constantly arguing with two types of people—Marxists and Freudians—who both claimed that their theories were, in their nature, irrefutable. Now the claim that a scientific theory should be beyond the possibility of refutation is of course, very irritating. This led Popper to the conclusion that a theory that cannot be refuted is, by definition, not scientific. When Popper stated that in detail, I just embraced his views as a statement of what I was feeling. And that is why ever since his *Logik der Forschung* first came out in 1934, I have been a complete adherent to his general theory of methodology. And since I respect his early views, I am prepared to be convinced about his later development—such as his neutral epistemology and use of Plato's three worlds—but he has not yet convinced me about that.

Weimer: May I try to sharpen the question to a particular issue? One way of looking at the difference between Kuhn and Popper is that Kuhn argues that an adequate understanding of the rationality of science requires psychological as well as philosophical explanation. Popper, on the other hand, prefers a more purely philosophical analysis. Do you see a real difference there, or would you prefer to side with Popper?

Hayek: I doubt whether there is much of a difference. I am aware that the use of terms seems different, but whether there really is a difference I am not sure.

Turvey: Hayek said something like "Sensations are not interpreted by memory, but sensations are yielded by physiological memory." Is that correct?

Weimer: Yes, it's only as a result of the fact that the nervous system is organized in terms of, if you will, the racial experience and memory of the species that we have sensations at all. *The Sensory Order* spells it out exactly on page 53.

Hayek: I didn't hear the question, but I agree with your answer.

Member of Audience: I'd like to follow up on Dr. Mishkin's comment and ask Weimer if he would say that one could remove contiguity from Dr. Hayek's model. Did you mean by associationism the notion of contiguity? Contiguity is central to *The Sensory Order.* One way of looking at the book is as a development of that one idea—contiguity.

Weimer: The question I would ask in return is, what are you packing into the term *contiguity?* If you are talking about contiguity as simply the contiguity of events in the space–time manifold, the answer is obviously no, you cannot discard the notion. If, on the other hand, one interprets contiguity as "the mechanism of learning" in terms of, for instance, some of the associationistic learning theorists of the thirties, I would say one can divorce that from his views. But contiguity in space–time or in terms of a descriptive account of the nervous system is essential to any theory.

Member of Audience: One implication of the talk that I found disturbing was that psychology is, in principle, impossible. What I heard being said was that we need a more complex classificatory system—a system of greater complexity than the system that we are working with—and that therefore I couldn't understand myself. Not only that, but then with Hayek's rat example, it seemed that not only could we not understand ourselves, but we could not understand lower organisms—even lower organisms we had created—if we didn't have access to their experience. That leaves me with the impression that psychology not only can't understand human beings but can't understand lower animals either, so therefore there is no such thing as psychology. Is that what you mean?

Weimer: No. That conclusion neglects Hayek's distinction between explanation of the particular and explanation of the principle.

Hayek: It depends on what you mean by possibility. I don't think psychology, or any of the sciences of complex phenomena, will ever be able to make the same kinds of specific predictions—in that particular moment, in that particular place, such and such an event will happen—as can be made by the physical sciences. It will only be able to make what, in my (1967) essay "The Primacy of the Abstract," I called pattern prediction—that a structure of a certain character will appear, the details of which we cannot predict. The more complex the phenomena, the more our predictions are in this sense limited to very general statements—as, for example, are the type of statements in the theory of evolution. Now that must be adequate because it's all we can have; it is still a science, and as good a science as we can form of complex phenomena; but we must not imagine that we can ever have a specific prediction that, after enumeration of the easily ascertainable conditions, says that if a few ascertainable conditions are present, then such and such a unique result must happen.

varying data at a single point in time is an absurdity. But that's exactly what economists have been trying to do ever since. They have not found what the founders of economics had suggested—that mathematics is important just because mathematics is a method by which one can describe patterns without having information about the elements constituting the patterns—but most economists have thought mathematics justified only if we can insert the quantitative data into the formulae. And that's where the history, but not the mistake, ends. I have grave reservations about the use of these magnificent systems of equations where there is really no possibility of our being able to fill in the details. Indeed, I don't think complex systems ever reach a state of equilibrium—all we can know at any moment is the direction in which they move. But such patterns have great significance. But the idea that mathematics can take this abstract picture and compress it into a complex, quantitative statement is fundamentally mistaken—it cannot be done.

Member of Audience: Would you agree that in economic theory, the price of any given thing in its system theoretically gives you information about the whole system?

Hayek: The price of any one thing tells the user of that thing all he or she *needs to know* about the other users of it, which information is needed in order to use it efficiently. What is being communicated by the price is, on one hand, the cost in terms of all other users, who are using the thing for that particular purpose; and on the other hand, the equivalent value people might be prepared to give for the same, in a sense, information about the needs of persons the producer doesn't even know about—the producer doesn't even know they exist. Of course, *need* is a misleading term I have hesitantly employed; I think *demand* would be a better term, because it expresses what other people, whom the producers need not know at all, are willing to give in order to acquire the item in question. The division of labor of the market is made possible only by this communication of the relevant aspects of facts that supposedly are guided by the prices. We don't know the particular facts; we only know they have an effect upon the market. And a second point is that this type of analysis, leading to an understanding of the function of prices as guides, emerged in modern economics after Walras and Marshall, after Marx, when we learned to regard prices as indicators of what people ought to do, which is just the opposite of what Ricardo, Marx, and Mill believed. They thought that prices were determined by what people had done. They believed that prices were determined by how much people had, in the past, invested. And that blinded them to any understanding of the workings of the market. A Marxist cannot understand how the market functions or what functions it has in society.

Weimer: The question relates to the old issue of where the complete specification of price gets you if you are a Laplacean Demon. If there were a Laplacean Demon, possessing all relevant knowledge of prices, would that do him any good? Could he predict the future of the marketplace? The answer is, I think, clearly no, because complete specification of the needs of any one individual will never get you to the Laplacean Demon who can do something with that information beyond the individuals themselves.

Member of Audience: Weimer mentioned the influence of David Hume and the problem of induction, and one issue in this conference has been the rejection of *causality* as a term, but I haven't heard it defined yet. Would you care to give a definition of causality and comment on whether it has been rejected in Hayek's system?

Weimer: The common interpretation of causality, as I pointed out in "Manifestations of Mind: Some Conceptual and Empirical Issues" (Weimer, 1976), involves two crucial notions: linear and microdeterministic relationships between events, within a single phase of existence. The usual example is the linear, deterministic interaction of one billiard ball with another, through molecule-to-molecule transference of energy, "causing" it to move. Quantum physics has overthrown the deterministic half of the definition, and hierarchical (and coalitional) structures are not linear in their controlling relations. Hayek's nervous system, since it is (at least) hierarchically organized, is not causal in the traditional sense.

Member of Audience: I've noticed that in psychology, a process ontology is necessary to study the higher mental processes, and I was wondering about economics. There seems to be a static equilibrium ontology underlying economics. Would you recommend an ontological shift in economics from a static ontology to a process-type ontology?

Hayek: Yes, that is absolutely necessary.

Member of Audience: Shaw suggested this morning that one can never understand a system without coming to grips with the compatibilities that exist between that system and its environment. I wonder if Hayek agrees with that notion and if so, if he thinks it is applicable to the study of the market?

Hayek: I can only say it sounds plausible to me, and I would have to think about it.

Member of Audience: One commonsense notion about the growth of knowledge is that it is a matter of unpacking our intuitions and of moving from a tacit conception to a more explicit one. It would seem that what you indicated, and what Weimer indicated in his introduction, is that you conceive the growth of knowledge to be much more of a movement toward an enlightened intuition than toward explicit knowledge.

Hayek: It is a way of looking that gives enlightened intuition a place. It explains the behavior of complex phenomena by showing how local information is utilized, and I acknowledge that there is a great deal of implicit knowledge involved in habits, rules, and in traditional customs that, before we understood them, were regarded as completely irrational. We are now beginning to understand that such things may have persisted for generations because they were in fact rational and useful. So useful functions are often outside our understanding.

This in a sense applies to our earlier civilization as a matter of course, where every social and cultural interaction would be regarded as irrational by collectivist planners, because our ancestors did what they did without knowing why they did it; and yet in spite of this, they frequently survived. But similar considerations apply to us today: We are still to a very large extent in the situation that we owe our persistence and survival to observing practices and rules that we do not understand and would not have made consciously. It is obvious that it is not a reason for rejecting a pattern of behavior that we cannot explain why we do it unless we have, in theory, a way of showing that it is an ineffective procedure. In that sense, it is just an indication of respecting tradition, and of realizing that our intuitions are based upon our developmental history.

REFERENCES

Pribram, K., & Gill, M. *Freud's "project" reassessed.* New York: Basic Books, 1976.

Weimer, W. B. Manifestations of mind: Some conceptual and empirical issues. In G. G. Globus, I. Savodnik, & G. Maxwell (Eds.), *Consciousness and the brain.* New York: Plenum Press, 1976.

Hayek, F. A. The primacy of the abstract. In F. A. Hayek, *Studies in philosophy, politics, and economics.* New York: Simon & Schuster, 1967.

16 Ambiguity and the Future of Psychology: *Meditations Leibniziennes*[1]

Walter B. Weimer
The Pennsylvania State University

At least three fundamental problems stand between current research and an explanatorily adequate cognitive psychology. Unless the field comes to grips with them and provides a theoretically motivated account of their role in cognition and action, we shall at best have a technology (such as engineering) rather than an explanatory science. The first problem centers on the role of abstract entities, primarily in perception and conception: I have argued (Weimer, 1973) that this ancient problem of philosophers, the one and the many, forces us back to square 1 on issues such as nominalism–realism, environmentalism–nativism, and many others. Perception and comprehension force us to acknowledge that the relevant variables our theories must range over are far more abstract than has been acknowledged in the past. But knowing this has not yet helped; we are still far from a characterization of the psychological conception of information required to explain perception and concept formation. The second problem, productivity in acting and perceiving, is related to but distinct from the first. Both the pickup of information from the environment and the organism's ability to commerce effectively with the environment require a conception of the organism as an active generator, or producer, of indefinitely extended domains of sensory input and motor output. Here at least we may have a conceptual framework, in the motor metatheory of mind (Weimer, 1977), that can, for the first time in history, unite the heretofore disparate domains of action and perception. But the third problem, *ambiguity,* gives less cause for optimism. By ambiguity, I mean what the linguist refers to as surface- and deep-structural ambiguity, in which one object (such as a sentence) may have different interpretations or meanings, or in which two objects simultaneously are manifest in one common form. This chapter traces one way in which ambiguity (primarily deep-structural) enters into

331

science (in the epistemic problems of quantum physics) and, in so doing, into psychology. Then it considers what a science of cognition that acknowledges this *could* look like. The framework sketched owes much, in flavor and some details, to Leibniz. If it seems unfamiliar, draws upon areas of inquiry not usually regarded as relevant, or is incompatible with what passes for contemporary theoretical "psychology," the inference to be drawn is to the detriment of that congeries of largely incoherent positions. My claim is that psychology cannot possibly succeed unless it can address the issues discussed here, and that these issues require considerable expansion of the domain of psychological inquiry, as well as radical reformulation of what constitutes psychological science.

THE EPISTEMIC PROBLEM IN QUANTUM PHYSICS

When psychologists wish their discipline to be "scientific," they compare it to physics. Those who feel their approach is the "true" science of psychology point to similarities; those who disparage such "scientism" are equally adept at pointing to dissimilarities. Unfortunately, psychologists (of any persuasion) rarely know anything about physics firsthand; their "knowledge" is usually limited to what some methodologist told them about what that "true science" has to be like. This depressing state of affairs renders intelligible what is otherwise paradoxical: Psychologists, thinking themselves to be following the successes of physics in explaining the nonmental realm, conclude that a materialistic picture of the universe is the only acceptable one; whereas physicists, attempting to unravel the "physical" universe as cognizing subjects of theoretical inquiry, find themselves forced to be mentalists. Put another way, examination of the nature of the knowledge disclosed by physics leads to an epistemic dualism (consisting of acquaintance and structural knowledge by description) and an ontological agnosticism in which what really exists cannot be identified with traditional notions of either "matter" or "mind" (see Weimer, 1976). Indeed, if anything like the conventional interpretation of quantum mechanics is considered, it is simply not possible to formulate the laws of quantum physics in a consistent way without including reference to paradigms of the mental—intentionality and meaning. The problem of measurement in the description of quantum mechanical states leads to a deep-structural ambiguity in our knowledge and theory of reality that can be resolved only by integrating psychology and physics. Consider why this is so.

The Collapse of the State Vector

The problem, grossly oversimplified, is that a percipient observer (rather than an inanimate device) is necessary to determine which of several possible state configurations a quantum system is in. It is not the traditional problem of refining measurement, but rather that a cognizing subject must determine what a given measurement (or state description) *means* in describing a possible state of the real world. Wigner (1970) develops this succinctly, and we can easily paraphrase his account.

The only information available about the possible states of a system can be characterized, quantum mechanically, by state vectors that can change in only two ways. Due to temporal succession, they change continuously, according to Schrödinger's (1956) time-dependent equation (equations of motion). The state vector also changes discontinuously, in probabilistic fashion, as a result of measurement operations performed on the system. The problem of measurement *on the object* leads inevitably to the problem of observation *on the measuring apparatus*. This latter step is the epistemically problematic one, and it concerns what is known variously as "the reduction of the wave function" or "the collapse of the state vector." (It is worth parenthetical mention that the probabilistic aspect of the theory is located quite far from what "ordinary experience" would expect: One would assume probability laws to govern the change of the system over time, such that interactions of particles would be statistical. But the uncertainty of the system does not increase over time if it is undisturbed by measurement; in such a case, change in the state vector is "causal." Chance or probability enters when one observes the system to judge if it changed in the manner predicted by the equation of motion.)

Consider a simple situation in which there is an object, a light emission source, and someone present to indicate whether or not the light is visible. Assume that the object has only two possible states, ψ_1 and ψ_2. If the state is originally ψ_1, then the state of object plus observer will be $\psi_1 \times \chi_1$ after their interaction; if the state of the object is ψ_2, it will be $\psi_2 \times \chi_2$. The wave functions χ_1 and χ_2 give the state of the observer: In χ_1 he is in the state that responds to the question, "Have you seen the light?" with yes and in χ_2, with no.

Consider further an initial state of the system $\alpha\psi_1 + \beta\psi_2$, which is a linear combination of the two states ψ_1 and ψ_2. The state of the system after interaction with the observer is $\alpha(\psi_1 \times \chi_1) + \beta(\psi_2 \times \chi_2)$ (this follows from the equations of motion). Asking the observer whether he saw the light will be answered with yes, with a probability $|\alpha|^2$, and the wave function from the object will be ψ_1. Similarly, no will occur as the observer's answer with probability $|\beta|^2$, and the object's responses will correspond to the wave function ψ_2. The probability that the observer will say yes but the object give the function ψ_2 must be zero; the wave function $\alpha(\psi_1 \times \chi_1) + \beta(\psi_2 \times \chi_2)$ of the joint system has no $\psi_2 \times \chi_1$ component. The converse holds equally, because there is no $(\psi_1 \times \chi_2)$ component. So long as *we* maintain the privileged position of ultimate observers, no inconsistency develops.

But suppose the observer had been a friend (Wigner, 1970):

> If after having completed the whole experiment I ask my friend, "What did you feel about the flash before I asked you?" he will answer, "I told you already, I did

[did not] see a flash," as the case may be. In other words, the question whether he did or did not see the flash was already decided in his mind, before I asked him. If we accept this, we are driven to the conclusion that the proper wave function immediately after the interaction of friend and object was already either $\psi_1 \times \chi_1$ or $\psi_2 \times \chi_2$ and not the linear combination $\alpha(\psi_1 \times \chi_1) + \beta(\psi_2 \times \chi_2)$. This is a contradiction, because the state described by the wave function $\alpha(\psi_1 \times \chi_1) + \beta(\psi_2 \times \chi_2)$ describes a state that has properties which neither $\psi_1 \times \chi_1$ nor $\psi_2 \times \chi_2$ has. If we substitute for "friend" some simple physical apparatus, such as an atom which may or may not be excited by the light-flash, this difference has observable effects and *there is no doubt that* $\alpha(\psi_1 \times \chi_1) + \beta(\psi_2 \times \chi_2)$ *describes the properties of the joint system correctly, the assumption that the wave function is either* $\psi_1 \times \chi_1$ *or* $\psi_1 \times \chi_2$ *does not.* If the atom is replaced by a conscious being, the wave function $\alpha(\psi_1 \times \chi_1) + \beta(\psi_2 \times \chi_2)$ (which also follows from the linearity of the equations) appears absurd because it implies that my friend was in a state of suspended animation before he answered my question.

It follows that the being with a consciousness must have a different role in quantum mechanics than the inanimate measuring device [p. 179–180].

The point of this is that consciousness, which is indicative of sapience (the assignment of meaning), collapses the state vector from the joint function $\alpha(\psi_1 \times \chi_1) + \beta(\psi_2 \times \chi_2)$ to either $(\psi_1 \times \chi_1)$ or $(\psi_2 \times \chi_2)$. Taken at face value, this leaves two alternatives: (1) The laws of nature have a different form depending upon whether cognitive interpretation is present or absent; or (2) quantum mechanics is incomplete. Proponents of the Copenhagen orthodoxy, following Niels Bohr's interpretation of the principle of complementarity, argue that quantum mechanics is complete. Thus, they have only the first problem to worry about. Opponents of the orthodox interpretation deny that quantum mechanics is complete, often trying to find hidden variables at a subquantal level of analysis. Thus, they often cite the first alternative as a reason for challenging the orthodoxy. The result is that both interpretations are faced with explaining why the laws of nature should be ambiguous depending upon the presence or absence of meaning. As yet, none can do so.

Schrödinger's Cat

Another way to bring out the ambiguity involved in quantum measurement is to recast the situation as Erwin Schrödinger did in considering a hypothetical experiment in which a single photon passes through a half-silvered mirror. This photon will either be reflected or transmitted. If it is reflected, nothing happens. If it is transmitted, it activates a photo cell that fires a gun that kills a cat that has been placed in a small box. After this "experiment" is over, but *before anyone has looked,* the wave function that represents all the information that quantum mechanics can specify for the combined system is a linear combination of functions representing a dead cat and functions representing a live cat. Indeed, given all the information that is available to quantum mechanics, which is non-deterministic, it is impossible even to say that the cat is either dead or alive! When, however, an observer looks inside the box, she sees that the cat is alive or that it is dead—which adjusts the wave function accordingly.[2] The point is that cognitive intervention—in the form of the ultimate *interpretation of the meaning of the system*—is necessary to remove an intolerable ambiguity.[3]

Is Physics Ontology or Epistemology?

The problem is not that of the well-known Heisenberg indeterminacy relation: that one cannot simultaneously measure accurately the position and momentum of quantum entities. Rather, the problem is that someone—a cognizant, evaluating self—has to *interpret* the measurements performed by our inanimate measuring apparatus. As Wigner (1970) wrote:

> It is the entering of an impression into our consciousness which alters the wave function because it modifies our appraisal of the probabilities for different impressions which we expect to receive in the future. It is at this point that the consciousness enters the theory unavoidably and unalterably. If one speaks in terms of the wave function, its changes are coupled with the entering of impressions into our consciousness. If one formulates the laws of quantum mechanics in terms of probabilities of impressions, these are *ipso facto* the primary concepts with which one deals [p. 175–176].[4]

Furthermore, this problem exists regardless of whether one accepts the orthodox interpretation of quantum mechanics, the so-called Copenhagen interpretation, or any proposed alternative.[5] Consider this statement by Werner Heisenberg (1958):

> The laws of nature which we formulate mathematically in quantum theory deal no longer with the particles themselves but with our knowledge of the elementary particles. . . . The conception of objective reality . . . evaporated into the . . . mathematics that represents no longer the behavior of elementary particles but rather our knowledge of this behavior [p. 99].

With this admission, physics has lost its ontological character or, rather, has lost its claim to ontological specification until further developments transpire within epistemology. It is as if physics, in its quest to resolve more precisely the structure of reality, has constructed more and more powerful conceptual microscopes that, when we look through them, reflect ourselves more and more prominently within the physical entities. The quest for "the real" has bogged down until "the known" can be understood in relation to it. Thus, the best way to do physics appears to be to do that branch of psychology known as epistemology.

From Physics to Psychology: The Buck Stops Here

Given the problem of the interpretation of observation, it is easy to see that development of an adequate psychology is a necessary step toward further conceptual advance in physics. The buck stops here, in our dicipline. Whereas psychologists have been blissfully unware of this, theoretical physicists have not. They have anticipated a future state of science in which physics and psychology form an integrated, interdependent conceptual system. But physics is conceptually mature, and psychology is not; it cannot hold up its end of the bargain. Even cursory examination indicates that not only does the buck stop here, but it is presently counterfeit. Wigner (1970) put this point well:

> That a higher integration of science is needed is perhaps best demonstrated by the observation that the basic entities of intuitionistic mathematics are the physical objects, that the basic concept in the epistemological structure of physics is the concept of observation, and that psychology is not yet ready for providing concepts and idealizations of such precision as are expected in mathematics or even physics. Thus, this passing of responsibility from mathematics to physics, and hence to the science of cognition ends nowhere [p. 37].

Quantum theory, even in its presently incomplete form, has exposed the roots of ignorance in physics. As Wigner notes, they are psychology. But the roots of ignorance in psychology are also psychology. I can do little better than paraphrase Walt Kelley's character, Pogo: "We have met the enemy, and they are us."

REASONABLE EXPECTATIONS FOR A SCIENCE OF PSYCHOLOGY

It could be countered that I have been moving too fast, that the "doomsaying" quotations from the physicists carry no weight, because psychology should not be expected to solve such problems anyway. Against this, I reiterate that it has been physicists attempting to do physics who have concluded that psychology must provide the next decisive step; since this is so, the problem is of paramount importance at least for physics. Should it really be the same in psychology? This can only be addressed by considering what the reasonable expectations for a science of psychology might be. Consider some theoretical, methodological, and substantive issues that psychology as a science must face.

Psychology as a Theoretical Science

Perhaps their most distinguishing feature is that *mature* sciences are explanatory rather than descriptive. Explanation consists in rendering intelligible how and why the phenomena within a domain exhibit the properties that, descriptively, they do possess. Science explains by conjecturing theories (either tacitly or in explicit, after-the-fact construction) that tell why things must be as they are observed to be. Psychologists, in contrast, have limited their accounts to dispositional analysis of the psychological domain. Dispositional analysis is at best descriptive and cannot be considered explanatory.[6] It is thus incumbent upon psychology to develop the sort of explanatory theory that mature sciences possess—theories that will derive surface-structure appearances lawfully from an abstract, deep-structural realm that is causally productive of those appearances. The regularity and lawful intelligibility of reality is located by explanatory science at the deep conceptual level of analysis, rather than at the "irregular" (often contradictory) level of appearances. Science postulates an underlying level of reality responsible for the flux of events found in phenomenal experience, and its success is largely a matter of its ability to correct and refine the picture of reality that emerges in the manifest image of common sense (see Sellars, 1963, esp. Chap. 1).

It is worth remarking that science "explains" by subsuming the familiar to the unfamiliar, rather than vice versa. Science proceeds by placing the familiar and well known, our phenomenal experiences, in an ordering determined by the unfamiliar and the indirectly known—that is, the abstract principles postulated to be responsible for those experiences. Thus, we explain the known—for example, the agitation and warmth in hot coffee—by reference to the unfamiliar and abstract—in this case, the kinetic theory. This process of explanation gradually refines its familiar origin, the naive realist's conception of the world, off the center stage of science. Science continually explains irregularities and discrepancies at the molar level of phenomenal appearances in terms of abstract, underlying properties of a more rarified microlevel of analysis. Consider a typical naive realist statement such as "sugar is soluble." How, then, does one explain that this sample, in my coffee, did *not* dissolve? The explanations proffered (perhaps in terms of impurities in the water, or supersaturation of the solution) will invariably lead to a different level of analysis, involving the physicochemical properties of the molecules of mixtures involved. When the process is completed, the generalizations made in phenomenal terms will be shown to be either incorrect or incomplete. As Russell (1940) said: "Naive realism leads to physics, and physics, if true, shows naive realism to be false. Therefore, naive realism, if true, is false; therefore, it is false [p. 13]." This gradual refinement of naive realism has enormous consequences for psychology, for it has removed the qualitative dimension of phenomenal experience from the physical realm entirely. Thus, it gives psychology a unique subject matter that can be tackled by literally no other discipline (see following). But that process of refinement has also developed the pattern of explanatory conjecture that characterizes postulational science, that explains our everyday world as an appearance (usually deceiving) of a realm of entities interacting in a manner that, although known to reason in knowledge by description, can never be known to acquaintance. With this, our discipline is left in a doubly unpromising situation: on one hand, with a highly successful pattern of explanatory argumentation to apply for the first time; and on the other, with the realization that our unique subject matter is not known to be susceptible to such treatment. Thus arises another paradox if not quite an ambiguity: What we know by acquaintance is indispensable to the generation of scientific knowledge by description; yet it nowhere appears within it.[7]

The Primacy of Structural Analysis

Psychological concepts are, by their very nature, functionally specified. It is simply impossible to define a psychological concept, such as "writing your signature" or "believing a proposition," in extensional terms, because no finite physical specification can exhaust the ways in which functional concepts may be instantiated. There is an infinitude of "physical movements" that a rat can make in (to take a prosaic example) "leaping a barrier"; the only way to understand such a concept is intentionally, in terms of the *meaning* and *effects* of the movements rather than the movements themselves. Brentano's criterion of intentionality, usually assumed to delimit the mental realm from the physical, is what is involved here: Functional specification is the hallmark of psychological concepts.

But functional specification *alone* is inherently ambiguous: Without a concomitant *structural* analysis to show the derivational history of the "mere movements" comprising psychological behavior, one cannot tell which of many possible behaviors those movements instantiate. Structural analysis is always necessary to resolve the ambiguity of psychological concepts. To put the point another way, given any (exhaustive) analysis of the physical movements of a psychological subject, it is always necessary to ask, "What act did those movements instantiate?" Unless this question can be given a principled answer in terms of the structural derivation of the elements of "behavior" in question, physical movement per se remains ambiguous. To take a concrete example, without a structural analysis of the derivation of the behavior involved, the same sequence of physical movements could equally instantiate acts of "writing a check," "exhibiting latent hostility toward blue-eyed people," or "signaling the beginning of a holdup." Which (if any) of these actions is represented can only be specified by a structural analysis that disambiguates the movements in question.

What psychology must develop is a set of abstract explanatory entities comparable to the nonterminal vocabulary items available to linguists, so that we may begin to construct a grammar of behavior analogous to the generative grammars in linguistics. Faced with an ambiguous utterance, the linguist has no insurmountable trouble disambiguating it; all he or she must do is delineate its structural derivation. But in doing so, the linguist has recourse to abstract structural entities such as S, NP, det, aux, etc. As yet, psychology has nothing comparable to these concepts; we do not know what abstract structures are the constituents of behavioral acts.

But the point remains: It is obvious that psychology must provide a structural analysis of its domain instead of resting content with purely functional accounts that are at best "data summaries" (such as dispositional analyses). Until psychology becomes explanatory (rather than descriptive) and structural (rather than solely functional) there is no hope for any "science of cognition," no matter what we construe its subject matter to be.[8]

Substantive Issues for Theoretical Psychology: The Mind–Body Problems

The preceding points become constraints upon psychological theory imposed by the requirement that psychology be a science analogous to the physical sciences; now it is time to detail more substantive considerations. The primary concern for psychology *as a science* is not the analysis of either behavior or intentionality (even if an explanatory account is proffered) nor a phenomenology of mind (via introspection, intuition, or whatever). Such programs are quite worthwhile, but they only make sense as an adjunct to the central problem of psychology: resolution of the core cluster of mind–body problems. What psychology has to explain is precisely those aspects of our existence that find no place in the accounts of the other sciences and that hitherto have been dealt with in systematic fashion only by philosophy.

Perhaps the most central mind–body issues are sentience, sapience, and selfhood. The problems of *sentience* concern the nature and existence of phenomenal experience: the "sensory qualia," or "raw-feels" of experience, which we know by acquaintance as we (so to speak) undergo or live through them. These qualia are the mental existents that we know, and our acquaintance with them is far more direct than any knowledge by description of the physical (in either science or common sense). *Sapience* concerns knowledge and intelligence; the problems center around what sapience is, how we have it, and how the universe is such that it exists. Most psychologists have thought that this problem exhausted their domain, and one normal science research program (behavioristic learning theory) considered it all but solved. *Selfhood* refers to *who* has sapience and sentience, and how selves or persons can be both mental and physical, subject and object. Consider some of the ways in which these issues ramify into a psychology that aspires to explanatory status.

Sentience and the Problem of Qualities

Hayek (1952/1963) put the problem we face in attempting to deal with the qualitative dimension of phenomenal experience (better; acquaintance) in stark relief:

What psychology has to explain is not something known solely through that special technique known as "introspection," but something which we experience whenever we learn anything about the external world and through which indeed we know about the external world, and which yet has no place in our scientific picture of the external world and is in no way explained by the sciences dealing with the external world: qualities. Whenever we study qualitative differences between experiences we are studying mental and not physical events, and much that we believe to know about the external world is, in fact, knowledge about ourselves.

It is thus the existence of an order of sensory qualities and not a reproduction of qualities existing outside the perceiving mind which is the basic problem raised by all mental events. Psychology must concern itself, in other words, with those aspects of what we naively regard as the external world which find no place in the account of that world which the physical sciences give us [pp. 6–7].

Differentiating the sensory orders by studying the patterns of neural activity that are concomitant with them,—that is, providing a structural analysis of their generation,—ought to be an ultimate (but not the sole) aim of cognitive psychology and neuropsychology.[9] Whether it shall be or not depends in large part upon whether more psychologists come to understand Hayek on this issue.

Sapience

Psychologists spend a lot of time on intelligence and the manner in which knowledge manifests itself. Indeed, during the great age of learning theory initiated by behaviorism, it was assured that specification of the responses that organisms were disposed to make in response to stimulus configurations exhausted the domain of psychology. Despite the fact that few researchers continue to endorse such a position, the majority of our so-called theoretical terms are left over from this bygone era. Thus the character of much experimental research—studies constructed to accommodate easily a vocabulary whose familiarity is reassuring enough to make us neglect the theoretical bankruptcy of the framework that generated that vocabulary. It is then not surprising that the only behaviorists who have survived to this date are those willing to work with a theory of method (scientistically claimed to be the *true* method of *science*) rather than a substantive psychological theory; "thinking" behaviorists, those who desired to explain psychological phenomena rather than practice a method, are now ex-behaviorists.[10]

But the futility of behaviorism leads too far afield; what must be stressed is that considering what we know of the physical universe, the very existence of knowledge is miraculous. Psychologists, who take it as a humdrum datum, should think about what researchers in other fields have known for a long time. For example, the philosopher Karl Popper (1972): "The phenomenon of human knowledge is no doubt the greatest miracle in our universe. It constitutes a problem that will not soon be solved, and I am far from thinking that the present volume makes even a small contribution to its solution [preface].'' And the physicist Erwin Schrödinger (1956), speaking first of genetic coding:

That is a marvel—than which only one is greater; one that, if ultimately connected with it, yet lies on a different plane. I mean the fact that we, whose total being is entirely based on a marvellous interplay of this very kind, yet possess the power of acquiring considerable knowledge about it. I think it possible that this knowledge may advance to little short of a complete understanding—of the first marvel. The second may well be beyond human understanding [p. 32].

Selfhood, Subject, and Object

Selfhood is the most obvious problem of ambiguity, as it is manifested in science and psychology. We have traced the breakdown of traditional concepts in physics with reference to problems of measurement and have seen that physics, in a truly ''ambiguous'' sense, becomes psychology. This leads to the interesting question of the relation within science of the physical to the psychical, of subject to object. At one time or another, thinkers have given ontological primacy to each (Descartes, for instance, thought that his *''cogito, ergo sum''* gave primacy to the ego). It remained for Leibniz to bring out the relational character of subject and object, when he argued that from the standpoint of science, both arise in unison, linked by relations specifying invariance in appearances. Thus, the unique ''I'' of consciousness appears, from the perspective of objectivity, as but one of many of a kind. The ambiguity of perspective prevents determination of ontological priority.

But this happy indifference is not to be had in epistemology. Here the priority is undeniable: The absolute subject, I, remains unique in spite of the objective equivalence of all subjects. As mathematical physicist Hermann Weyl (1949) put it:

The postulation of the ego, of the ''thou,'' and of the external world is without influence upon the cognitive treatment of reality. It is a matter of metaphysics, not a judgment but an act of acknowledgement or belief. . . . Yet this belief is the soul of all knowledge. From the metaphysicorealistic viewpoint, however, egohood remains an enigma. Leibniz (Metaphysische Abhandlung, Philosophische Schriften, IV, pp. 454–455) believed that he had resolved the conflict of human freedom and divine predestination by letting God (for sufficient reasons) assign existence to certain of the infinitely many possibilities, for instance to the beings Judas and Peter, whose substantial nature determines their entire fate. This solution may objectively be sufficient, but it is shattered by the desperate outcry of Judas ''Why did I have to be Judas?'' The impossibility of an objective formulation of this question is apparent. Therefore no answer in the form of an objective insight can ensue. Knowledge is incapable of harmonizing the luminous ego with the dark erring human being that is cast out into an individual fate [p. 124–125].

Somewhere, somehow, psychology will have to come to grips with the mind–body problem of selfhood. I and thou must be reconciled (rather than explained away) in a conceptual framework that acknowledges their ontological relativity while retaining the epistemic primacy of the cognizing ego. The question of *who* it is that has knowledge, the absolute basis against which the relativity of scientific knowledge by description seems inevitably opposed, has simply not yet been considered within psychology. Indeed, it has not been considered by any science except particle physics, and then only to the extent that it is acknowledged as another perspective of the Necker cube of reality. The integration of physics and cognition to which Wigner looks forward will have to resolve this ambiguity so hauntingly portrayed by Weyl.

Methodology and the Subject Matter of Psychology

The subject matter of quantum physics leads to psychology; considering what psychology ought to be, in conjunction with what we know physics to be, leads to the question of how physical "science" got there in the first place. Thus, epistemology, concerning the nature of our knowledge and manner of its acquisition, ought to be one of the psychological sciences. A substantive component of the discipline should be concerned with explanation of the methods used by the sciences as generators of human knowledge.

This contrasts sharply with previous paradigmatic approaches to psychology. Recall that Wundt legislated the method for psychology as science to be *selbstbeobachtung*. Thus, structuralism secured its (self-appointed) scientific status by comparison and contrast to physics and arrived at a methodology that rendered the study of methodology outside of psychology.[11] The behavioristic revolution did nothing but change the purported scientific method; *selbstbeobachtung* made way for the "objective analysis of behavior." In both paradigms, methodology was considered an unproblematic issue, modeled upon what was assumed to be "the method" in the hard sciences.

But examination of the history of science falsifies every methodology yet proposed by philosopher or psychologist, and the questions of the growth of scientific knowledge are up for grabs (Weimer, 1975, 1979). I have argued at length that cognitive psychology, even in its present embryonic state, has much to say to methodology, and that ultimately, it will arbitrate among competing alternatives. It is clear that methodology must be consonant with what Campbell (1974) aptly called *evolutionary epistemology;* from such a biological, adaptive perspective, the organism becomes psychologically a theory of its environment (Weimer, 1973, 1975), and knowledge becomes a biological as well as psychological process (Piaget, 1971) resulting from the interaction of organism and environment via *The Senses Considered as Perceptual Systems* (Gibson, 1966).

Rather than continue what some will perceive as a polemical digression (and others as merely a rehashing of the obvious), let me simply point out a seeming paradox and once again the pervasive presence of ambiguity. The seeming paradox is this: Just as it can plausibly be maintained that given the present state of the art in both, the best way to do physics is to study psychology, so it is that the best way to do psychology is to study physics! That is, since the problems of the methodology of science and the epistemic problems of knowledge are part and parcel of psychology, serious study of the history of physical science and its present form and problems is an integral part of doing psychology. If we are to explain the nature of knowledge and its acquisition, we must be conversant with what knowledge consists of and how it has arisen in history. There is, of course, no real paradox here—just hard work: Although numerous physicists have studied the problems of psychology and are capable of staying at the forefront of our research, I daresay that the psychologists competent to discuss the history or methodology of, let alone contemporary developments in, physics can be counted on the digits of a rat's paws.

But still this is polemical and threatening—or equally obvious and welcome. How and why can this be so? Here we face the problem of ambiguity again, in the methodology of scientific research and the growth of knowledge: in what Hanson (1958), Kuhn (1970), and Feyerabend (1965, 1970) have referred to as the incommensurability of the conceptual systems (Kuhn's sociological paradigms) of science. Here we have one of the defining characteristics of scientific revolutions: Even though theorists who practice on opposite sides of the divide acknowledge that they are referring to the same domain of inquiry, and often to the same phenomena, the meanings or interpretations that they supply to/derive from those phenomena are incommensurably different. Alternatively, what one theorist sees as obvious and indispensable to the domain is not seen and is of no importance whatever to an antagonist. What mechanism—psychological, sociological, or philosophical—could explain this ubiquitous phenomenon in science, known personally to those psychologists who felt the revolution in linguistics due to Chomsky? Descriptively, the answer is relatively easy: It is not the indeterminacy of language translation proposed by Kuhn, but rather the deep-structural ambiguity of both the languages and perceptions of scientists (Weimer, 1979). Explanatorily, we have no answer at all: There is no cognitive theory of ambiguity even on the horizon. But there will have to be if we are ever to understand our knowledge and its growth.

LEIBNIZIAN INTERLUDE

Our problems are both ontological and epistemic—to understand reality, and to understand our understanding of reality. Natural philosophy, before it split into various sciences and technologies, undertook rational and empirical investigations of both sorts. But physics and psychology, products of the split, lost the rational metaphysics and metapsychology necessary for such work. Perhaps both disciplines could benefit from the ideas of past thinkers who, as natural philosophers, attempted to integrate physics and psychology. Consider some proposals of Leibniz in this regard; although fantastic to classical physicists and earlier psychologists, his ideas may yet provide enlightenment to the physicist wishing to push beyond quantum theory and to the psychologist who seeks a structural analysis.

The Great Chain of Being

Leibniz inherited the classic Western conception of the cosmos as a chain of being, complete and filled with everything that could coexist (see Lovejoy, 1936). The principles of plenitude, continuity, and gradation lie directly behind Leibniz' supreme principle of sufficient reason, which in turn determines the formulation of all his other principles. Although his major metaphysical principles can be reinterpreted as constraints that apply to all conceptual systems,[12] that is not our focus. Instead consider some ontological ideas that were intertwined with his epistemology.

For Leibniz, reality consists of monads, whose destinies are predetermined, in a form of primal regulation that is not causal in nature, from the beginning of time. Monads are not atoms but rather the ultimate constituents of atoms and other aggregates, and they come into existence and cease to exist (are annihilated) all at once rather than gradually. Further, every monad mirrors the universe, even though monads are not causally related. As the *Monadology* (Paragraphs 56, 61) put it (Loemker, 1956):

> This interconnection, relationship, or this adaptation of all things to each particular one, and of each one to all the rest, brings it about that every simple substance has relations which express all the others and that it is consequently a perpetual living mirror of the universe. . . . every body responds to all that happens in the universe, so that he who saw all could read in each one what is happening everywhere, and even what has happened and what will happen [p. 648–649].

Aside from a physics, Leibniz proposed a psychology. He postulated that monads, being the ultimate simples, possess qualities in common with mental phenomena, such as perception (Paragraph 14). Perception cannot be explained mechanically; were we to construct a giant perceiver that a person could enter like a mill, "we should find nothing within but parts which push upon each other; we should never see anything which would explain a perception (Loemker, 1956, p. 644)." Since this is so, mind and body[13] are to be distinguished by the types of causality that our reason imposes upon them, rather than by ultimate ontological differences. Mind and body work in parallel, according to the preestablished harmony between all substances (Paragraph 78), and "souls act in accordance with the laws of final causes through their desires, ends and means. Bodies act in accordance with the laws of efficient causes or of motion" (Loemker, 1956, p. 651). The two realms are in harmony, rather than causal relation; causal relations obtain within the realms, but not across them. Leibniz argued that memory, or record keeping, is a property of all substantial aggregates but that memory must be distinguished from reason (Paragraph 26). Reason, which is the rational soul or mind, requires knowledge of "eternal and necessary truths" (Paragraph 29). Further, our conception of selfhood results from reflection: "It is also through the knowledge of necessary truth and through abstractions from them that we come to perform *Reflective Acts,* which cause us to think of what is called the I" (Loemker, 1956, p. 646).

Physics and psychology for Leibniz are thus aspects of the great chain of being, and the task of reason is to understand them as aspects of a harmonious whole. That is, mind and body are compatible within a framework of compossible existents. Compossibility defines possible worlds that are internally consistent although mutually exclusive. That is, the actualization of some possible events is incompatible with that of others, and so the possibilities for the "real world" split into mutually exclusive systems of compossibles. Leibniz postulated that God (the only monad whose notion entails His existence) brought into being that "real world" that is the best of all possible worlds—thus leaving himself open to Voltaire's caricature, Dr. Pangloss, in *Candide.*

Leibniz in Contemporary Physics

One might wonder how this metaphysical fantasy could be of any relevance, so let us look at physics to see if there are any applications of Leibnizian thought. For background, recall that Einstein, in the special theory of relativity, generalized Leibniz' arguments against Newtonian conceptions of absolute space and time. "As the same city regarded from different sides appears entirely different, and is, as it were multiplied respectively, so, because of the infinite number of simple substances, there are a similar infinite number of universes which are, nevertheless, only the aspects of a single one as seen from the special point of view of each monad" (Loemker, 1956, p. 648). Then one may note that classic conceptions of causality were overthrown in quantum physics in favor of an analysis that is much like the "harmony of events." Our picture of subatomic entities, growing more complicated every day, begins to "mirror" more and more the conception of monads as coming into being and being annihilated as "simples" according to principles of primal regulation that are explicated by symmetry-theoretic analyses. The Ne' Mann Gell-Mann 8 fold way, and Chew's (1971) bootstrap hypothesis are applications of such symmetry analyses. Leibniz thought that God regulated the affairs of all monads (Paragraph 51); today, following a long tradition of identifying God with symmetry (Weyl, 1952 p. 5), we look upon symmetry as providing a context of constraint that regulates the basic features of existence. Perhaps even more striking is the congruence of Leibniz' plenum universe everywhere filled with monads and P.A.M. Dirac's (e.g., 1947) conception of matter swimming in a sea of infinitely densely packed antimatter (entities of opposite electrical charge). Dirac's ocean implies that positive and negative electrons (perhaps each one a type of monad) must always be "created" in pairs and that should a negative electron meet its positive counterpart, their mutual "annihilation" in a release of energy would result.

It might also be pointed out that Dirac's reasoning in postulating the existence of positrons (to say nothing of the magnetic monopole) was to save symmetry in the laws of nature. In the case of the monopole, the conception preceded the first tentative experimental corroboration in 1975 by 44 years. This should be pondered by anyone thinking that physics is "empirical" instead of "rational."

Related to Dirac's reinstatement of the "ether" hypothesis in a sea of monads is the issue of every monad mirroring the entire universe. Were this true, the problem for understanding would be to gain access to the information in our local environments rather than, say, traveling to the ends of the universe. And that is exactly what science attempts to do: Astronomy, which provides information concerning the distant past as well as the structure of the space–time manifold, is contained in electromagnetic radiation that impinges upon our bodies and instruments here and now. Thus we find it easy to comprehend the idea that information for events and processes far removed from us may be contained in things to which we have access. Until recently, our only model for how information was transmitted was, in the case of light, Newtonian optics. Here the model was the reflection of light from a source through a focusing device (a lens) and the projection of the information to an image plane (the eye or a recording device). Lens microscopes and telescopes are instances of magnifying the information to provide satisfactory image resolution for small and distant objects and events. The lens, as a focusing device for reflected light, allows access to things not immediately present, but it hardly provides information for "everything" when looking "anywhere." But thanks to Gabor's (1972) work in optical information processing, which led to the development of holography, we now have a model for understanding how all the information in a manifold can be represented in any part of it. The hologram, utilizing image reconstruction from interference waves, effectively retrieves "the whole image" from any part of itself. Gabor's development of optical holography has cashed in Leibniz' promissory note that every monad mirrors the remainder of the universe. Insofar as the universe contains interference patterns of the sort constitutive of holograms, it *is* a hologram; and the problem for science is to gain access to that infinite domain of information (and, of course, to render it intelligible).

Leibnizian Psychology

The preceding cursory remarks hardly indicate the extent to which Leibniz' ideas have found their way into physics, but they do indicate that those ideas should not be dismissed a priori as too fantastic. Consider the directions psychological inquiry would take if we began to take Leibniz as seriously as physics has done. In order to do psychology, of course, we should return to physics.

We can begin by considering the similarities and differences in *inter-* and *intra*phasic relationships. There are different phases, or modes of instantiation, of existence. Classical physics, for instance, deals with matter (neutrally construed) in what we can call the *ordinary* phase. Laws of nature for ordinary matter are the paradigm exemplars of causal relationships; the concept of causality had its first application in scientific analysis in explicating the relationships obtaining between entities within the ordinary phase of matter.[14] But the 20th century has seen the rise of a new physics, one that deals with the instantiation of "matter" in a new mode of existence: *plasma* physics. The laws of nature for plasma (ionized gases at high temperature and pressure) are not those of ordinary physics, since they depend upon quantum laws for their formulation. Quantum laws are not classical laws. Once again, within the phase boundaries of plasma, the relationships the natural laws explicate can, by stretching the traditional analysis, be called causal (but *not* microdeterministic). But no causal relations obtain *across* phase boundaries from ordinary to plasma physics. The laws relating ordinary and plasma physics are *invariance* principles rather than causal laws.[15] Invariance principles specify constancy of formal structure of entities with respect to permitted changes in the entities and can apply both within and across phase boundaries. Within phase domains, causality may be one type of invariance (see Lazlo & Margenau, 1972), but across phase boundaries, *that* type of invariance does not apply.

The different phases of plasma and ordinary matter are no longer questioned. More controversial is the contention that there is a *biotonic* phase of existence, which is the phase of living things. Eminent authors have argued for admitting the biotonic phase as irreducible to any inanimate phase, among them Elsasser (1958), Schrödinger (1956), Pattee (1971, 1972), Von Neumann (1966), and Wigner (1970). There is no space to argue the case here, and I simply assume the existence of this phase of existence. There are two important things about biotonic laws: First, they are emergent, in terms of complexity and organizational properties, with respect to inanimate laws of nature; second, they are likewise not causally related to the other phases. Once again, within the phase boundary, causal specification appears to be applicable (although the "billiard ball" model of ordinary matter causality is clearly inapplicable); but across the phase boundaries, causal specification does not hold. It does not make sense to say that physical systems "cause" life, despite the fact that it is both sensible and illuminating to speak of a physical substratum underlying a living system.

But what we know as the mental realm is not coextensive with the biotonic phase; not everything living is also psychological. One can be a panpsychist and hold that *life* is *not* an emergent property of the universe but rather is coextensive with the inanimate realm. But the mental is not just the living; attributes such as sentience, sapience, and selfhood are emergent with respect to living systems (and *ipso facto* to inanimate systems). Thus if a biotonic phase of existence be admitted, it is implausible to deny a *psychic* phase for the mental realm, despite its restricted localization (so far as we presently know) in the central nervous system of the highest primate(s). Again the same picture emerges: Within the phase boundary, causal specification is possible, but none is permissible across phase boundaries. As before, the type of causality that occurs within the psychic phase is neither the classical mechanical concept of ordinary matter physics nor the quantum mechanical concept. Following Semon (1923), Russell (1921) called the causality that occurs in the mental realm *mnemic* causality, in virtue of the central role of memory (which is more than physical record keeping—see Pattee, 1972) in all psychological processes. He defined ''mind'' as a group of events in space–time connected by mnemic causal laws. Wherever mnemic relations are found, attributes of the mental will be in evidence.

But Semon originally intended the mnemic domain to encompass all living phenomena (see Semon, 1923, p. 26), since record keeping of the type we call memory is not unique to psychic phenomena (see Pattee, 1971, for an excellent account of the biotonic nature of the mnemic realm and its separation from quantum physics). Russell subsequently (1927) adopted Semon's usage but continued to refer to the mental realm as mnemic. I prefer to follow Semon and Pattee (1971, 1972), restricting mnemic causality to the biotonic phase of existence. Intentionality and meaning are the keys to the psychic phase, not memory. Intentional causality or, if a new term be needed, *sememic* causality obtains in the psychic phase.

If mind has causal efficacy, it is only with regard to the entities of the *psychological* phase of "existence." And indeed, this fact is implicitly recognized in extant theorizing. Volition and intention are said to cause *behavior* or *action*. Behavior and action are *psychic* concepts; they cannot be reductively defined in terms of any of the other phases of being. As noted earlier, psychological behaviors are functionally rather than physically (or physiologically) specified; to attribute to a psychological subject the ability to "leap a barrier" or "write a signature" or any behavior whatever is to attribute to that subject the ability to execute an infinitude of physically specified movements. The mental realm in which intentionality is causal is simply not the same as, nor specifiable solely in terms of, anything except the psychological phase of existence.[16] As Leibniz argued, psychic relations are teleological, and final causes occur in no "lower" phase.

From this perspective, it becomes clearer what Russell meant when he said (1951): "An event is not rendered either mental or material by any intrinsic quality, but only by its causal relations [p. 164]." What we require at this point is a theory specifying the coimplication relations holding between events that exist simultaneously in more than one phase of existence. Mind and body are correlated in a context of constraint that Utopian invariance laws may specify. Perhaps we shall never know why the relations that obtain do so, but at least we may aspire to a specification of what those relations are. At present, it seems that these relations exemplify what Leibniz had in mind in talking about compatibility and existence. The framework in terms of which the phases of existence are related seems to be one of Leibnizian *compossibility* rather than causality. Descriptively, this is the sort of parallelism that the preestablished harmony envisaged.

The problem for science is to explicate that compatibility, literally the co-relations, obtaining between "monadic aggregates" within the various phases of existence. Following Leibniz and, more recently, Mach (1902), Einstein (see Clark, 1971), Weyl (1950, 1952), and Wigner (1970), I believe that symmetry theory considerations govern the relationships between phases. The invariance laws relating phases are invariably symmetry laws. If this is so, then the task of both psychological and physical science involves uncovering the coimplication relations obtaining among phases. The formal structure of causal laws within one phase will be mirrored, according to symmetry group theory principles, in the other phases. Thus there is a context of constraint supplied by the formal or structural properties within each phase, because those same formal characteristics must have their symmetry-theoretical counterparts in the other phases. If the compatibility of phases is correctly captured by this symmetry-theoretic analysis, then mind, body, and matter are coimplications of the compossible system that is the actual universe.

The Neural Hologram

Psychology has recently begun to incorporate holography, and Pribram (1971) postulated a neural holographic model utilizing the continuously graded potentials of the junctional microstructure to account for the brain's ability to "image." If the brain codes information in holographic fashion, then Pribram's account (or one similar) provides a model for how the nervous system could contain tremendous amounts of continuous or holistic information at a deep structural level. By utilizing the appropriate "reference beam" to reconstruct the images contained therein (a function, if Pribram is correct, of the limbic system), an indefinitely extended domain of "discrete" surface structure representations could be generated. In this regard, it is worth considering Penfield's results (Penfield, 1975; Penfield & Roberts, 1959), which indicate that the brain retains a record of virtually everything that one experiences, since under appropriate conditions (direct cortical stimulation), Penfield's patients could recall, in minute detail, long-"forgotten" experiences. Perhaps what Penfield's electrodes activated was circuits of the neural holographic machinery's reference beam; if so, the psychological problem of memory becomes analogous to that of scientific theory construction—all we need to do is gain access to the information that, instead of being all around us, is now all inside us.

In such a framework, development of (re)constructive memory, which isolates the "gist" of surface structures to which we are exposed, is the development of the ability to assimilate infinitely varied surface structures to deep conceptual structures. If we had direct recall of all the surface structures in our experience, we would be like Luria's (1968) subject S, who had to be taught how to forget so that he would not be buried in trivia. Evolutionary adaption apparently did this for us with constructive memory, which nevertheless allows us to utilize surface structures (such as images in *Loci et Res*) to reference vast amounts of information. The holographic model of record keeping in the CNS renders plausible why this is so.

Incidentally, Pribram's account provides an extremely strong argument against feature detector and neural network models of perception. Feature *detectors* (a natural suggestion on the lens model) are ruled out, but feature analysis is provided with a new mechanism. The holographic model rules out the initial encoding of information in terms of distinctive feature networks at the surface level; the information in the deep structure generates features but is not abstracted from them.

Implicate and Explicate Order

The reasoning behind Pribram's argument against feature detectors in favor of holographic analysis is analogous to David Bohm's (1971b, 1973) arguments in favor of implicate order in physics and a new conception of physical "analysis." Recall the quantum measurement problem as one of the sharp separation of measurement apparatus from events measured. Bohr's analysis is like a lens microscope examining a minute particle. What a lens does is form an image of an object in sharp relief in a focal plane. This furthers the tendency to think in terms of analysis and synthesis, in explicate order, of sharply defined and isolatable objects. But Bohm argues that the quantum measurement situation is more like a hologram than a lens analysis, because there can be no separation, for purposes of analysis, of instrumentation and object: Everything is in intimate interaction with everything else. Bohm (1973) urges that we "consider the possibility that physical law should refer primarily to an order of undivided wholeness of the content of a description similar to that indicated by the hologram rather than to an order of analysis of such content into separate parts indicated by a lens [p. 146]." The hologram implicates a total structure in each of its regions, and if the universe is holographic, then (Bohm, 1973):

> a *total order* is contained, in some *implicit* sense, in each region of space and time.... The word "electron" should be regarded as no more than a name by which we call attention to a certain aspect of the holomovement, an aspect that can be discussed only by taking into account the entire experimental situation and that cannot be specified in terms of localized objects moving autonomously through space. And, of course, every kind of "particle" which in current physics is said to be a basic constituent of matter will have to be discussed in the same sort of terms (so that such "particles" are no longer considered as autonomous and separately existent). Thus, we come to a new general physical description in which "everything implicates everything" in an order of undivided wholeness [pp. 147; 153].

In the *Monadology* (Paragraph 61), Leibniz quoted the phrase "all things conspire" from Hippocrates to catch this aspect of the great chain of being to which Bohm is referring. Conspiracy or not, the extent to which physics and psychology are proceeding apace cannot be ignored. The problem for both domains is to develop a conception of the processing of information (such as occurs in measurement and all perception) that transcends the limitations of the method of analysis underlying Newtonian optics. We need, in short, a new theory of vision that is capable of dealing with what Bohm calls implicate order. Holography, in which "all things conspire" in the interference patterns of wave fronts, may be the answer for the problems of memory and the initial encoding of information.

Memory Is Not the Rational Soul

The problems of perception and memory are more than problems of record keeping in physical systems—a record of a river is kept by the river bed. Regardless of how such information is kept in the CNS, two problems remain: *What* does it mean, and for *whom* does it have meaning? Leibniz was clear (Paragraphs 26–29) that memory is not comprehension—that is the business of the Rational Soul or mind. The problem of comprehension—part of the mind–body issue of sapience—remains, no matter what solution is provided for imaging and record keeping. This is why the "measurement problem" in physics remains; it is a problem of meaning, not memory. That is why the epistemic problem is not consciousness but cognition.

The goal of conceptual analysis is the ascription of meaning to two manifolds unique to the human situation—rational (purely conceptual) and empirical (or experiential) manifolds. What we mean by understanding simply is that ascription. To the extent that such ascription is ambiguous, we have no clear understanding. We need a theory of meaning and its manifestations before we can say more than this. Just as we need a new psychology of vision, we also need a theory of comprehension adequate to unlock deep-structural ambiguity. Holograms, in that they are one thing, are simultaneously many things at once; they are in that sense deep-structurally ambiguous. We know that they are ambiguous, but how we know that and what it means remain unknown.

Selfhood and Ontology

Before discussing selfhood in relation to knowledge, it is worth considering how a "self" could arise in the universe. Hayek's work on the "self"-originating organizational properties of phenomena of organized complexity (see Chapter 13 in this volume), Bohm's conception of the nonlocality or unbroken wholeness of the universe (see Bohm & Hiley, 1975), and some speculations of Leibniz about the necessity of existence in compossible systems are relevant here. Taken together, they imply that selfhood is a necessary consequence of structurally complex systems that satisfy certain constraints. That we know only selves as embodied by the highest primates is, in effect, due to local factors in this region of the universe; selves could be embodied quite differently.

Hayek's inquiry into the rationality of the marketplace stresses the distributed nature of the information that eventuates in buying and selling (the behavior of the market). There is no single locus of control that can possess sufficient information to duplicate consciously (or improve upon) the market as a "selfless" system. The organization of such systems is tacit, leading individuals to serve ends that are not their original intentions. Nonetheless, such self-originating complex systems behave analogously to individual selves; witness the confusion of rationalist constructivists in interpreting Adam Smith's analysis in teleological terms as due to the intervention of a deity. This skilled performance, so reminiscent of a self in conscious control, results from strict adherence to abstract rules of determination that have their origin in the evolutionary development of the system. The primacy of the abstract in complex systems accounts for the tacit substratum of "selves"—the self *is* a matter of organized complexity.

Bohm's notion of nonlocality proposes that the "inseparable quantum interconnectedness of the whole universe is the fundamental reality and that relatively independently behaving parts are merely particular and contingent forms within this whole" (Bohm & Hiley, 1975, p. 102). What this implies is that everything is systemic; there are no isolated entities except when we think of them in that fashion. If so, the self that we experience as utterly unique and isolated cannot be so: The locality of the self stands out "in relief" only in our understanding, not in ontology. In the order of being, the self is isolated only in the sense that it functions as a complexly organized system relative to more inclusive systems. Selves are thus dynamic rather than static entities; selfhood exists only when systems achieve a (presently unknown but perhaps specifiable) definite degree of complexity and organization.

This last point brings us to Leibniz and the relationship of compossibility and existence. In explaining why there should be a "preestablished harmony," Leibniz argued that existence pertains to systems of compossibles rather than to individual events (or, derivatively, entities). What exists is necessarily determined by systemic interconnectedness, and the choice of what will exist (and what will not) is in terms of mutual compatibility relationships obtaining within compossible systems. Thus if anything in a compossible system comes into existence, then everything else in the system must also come into existence, and nothing that is incompatible with that system of compossibles can come into existence. The possible blueprints for the universe include many that are incompatible; and if one does obtain, the others cannot. Which one does exist is a matter of contingence; reason can only establish necessary constraints upon contingency, not its nature.

But granted that there is our universe, and that it contains (our) selves, will it contain others? One would think the answer must be that selves will result in any existent system of organized complexity that meets certain requirements (as yet unknown) of relative systemic isolation, complexity, and organizational structure. Selfhood is a self-organizing property of systems of the requisite complexity and organization that must occur whenever such systems form. It is the result of the activity of its system's entities, but not their (or anyone else's) design.

Selfhood, Reference, and the Imaginary

Leibniz felt that our awareness of self arises as a product of reflection by the mind. What arises as a product of reflection is that we come to *refer* to our "selves." We comprehend in reference to the self—that is, in reference to a subject who has experience, knowledge, etc. When it came to characterizing the self, all Leibniz had to offer was the notion of a supreme monad with clearer perception than the others in a created monadic aggregate. This is no more illuminating than any other conception of selfhood and is, in this age, totally unsatisfactory—as are all other accounts. What would be required for an adequate account of selfhood as an epistemic locus?

It is hard to recognize what would constitute an answer. The problem is to explicate how there can be a self who, epistemically, is the absolute subject of psychic activity and that is, ontologically, one of many similar entities. This is a Kantian antinomy: The self is both subject and object at once, and that appears to be contradictory.[17] How could we resolve this antinomy? One model of a solution can be seen in some simple, yet profound, mathematical analogies.

Suppose we formulate the problem as one of solving, in Boolean algebra, the equation:

$$X^2 + 1 = 0$$

where we assumed that a number is either positive, zero, or negative, and that a nonzero number is negative if not positive, and vice versa. Transposition yields:

$$X^2 = -1.$$

Dividing by X yields:

$$X = \frac{-1}{X}$$

This statement, like "the subject is object," is self-referential: The root value of X must be put back into the expression from which we seek it. Let us try $+1$ and -1, since inspection discloses that our number must be unitary. Setting $X = +1$ gives:

$$+1 = \frac{-1}{+1} = -1,$$

which is antinomous. Likewise, setting $X = -1$, we get:

$$-1 = \frac{-1}{-1} = +1,$$

which is equally paradoxical.

But everyone knows we can solve such an equation and that the missing root is $\sqrt{-1}$. But this number is *not* a number according to our initial stipulations. This is a new kind of number—an *imaginary* number. Imaginary numbers are well known in ordinary algebra but were unknown in Boolean algebra until Spencer Brown (1972). By the simple expedient of introducing imaginary numbers to Boolean algebra, Spencer Brown was able to eliminate Russell's theory of types and cleared up centuries of confusion surrounding the ambiguity of self-referential statements.

Psychology could perhaps resolve some of its problems of selfhood in the same fashion—if we could figure out what constitutes the necessary analogue to imaginary numbers in the structural analysis of the psychic realm. Just as Bohm calls for a new order in physics, capable of addressing the undivided wholeness of the hologram in terms other than traditional analysis and synthesis into isolated parts, I want to call for a new order in psychology, capable of addressing selfhood in more fruitful terms than subject and object. Unless we succeed in constructing such a new order, we are at the end of the road and can do no better than recall Weyl (1949): "Thus the ultimate answer lies beyond all knowledge, in God alone; emanating from him, the light of consciousness, its own origin hidden from it, grasps itself in self-penetration, divided and suspended between subject and object, between meaning and being [p. 125]."

CHAPTER NOTES

[1]The feminine gender reflects my opinion on those who legislate equality with "new speak" words instead of achieving it through education.

[2]Opponents of the Copenhagen interpretation utilize situations such as the cat paradox to argue for the incompleteness of quantum mechanics. David Bohm (1951, 1957, 1965) and J.- P. Vigier (1957, 1970), perhaps the foremost exponents of the hidden variable approach, suggest that in addition to the wave function, there must be specified further parameters that tell what the actual state of a system is after interaction but before "looking." Such information, they propose, can only come from a subquantum level of analysis that would explain the observed effects at the quantum level (and more). If successful, such an approach would show that quantum theory is not a complete description of reality while at the same time leaving it a complete description at its own level of

analysis (as indicated by the famous "Von Neumann Proof"). Although I hope this approach is successful, and succeeds in replacing the orthodox approach by a more comprehensive account, it is necessary to point out that even if successful, the hidden variable approach must still explain why cognition has the effect that it does in observation. To do so, I see no alternative to including laws of cognition directly in that "hidden variable" account, along the lines of the integration of physics and psychology mentioned in the last part of this section.

[3] The problem for physics need not be framed solely in terms of the collapse of the state vector. The measurement situation may be looked upon as an instance of either surface- or deep structural ambiguity and the proposals for "disambiguation" treated accordingly. Bohr's reasoning, leading to the principle of complementarity, was that the only possible language for the unambiguous communication of the results of an experiment was that of "ordinary" or prequantum physics. In discussion of the measurement in such classical terms, the results permit inferences about an observed object that exists separately and independently, since it can be said to "have" those properties whether it interacts with anything else (the experimental apparatus) or not. This makes the situation one of surface structure ambiguity: One and the same entity is *described,* and therefore interpreted, differently depending upon the context of inquiry. In other words, as experimenters, we disambiguate the ambiguous meaning of the experimental operation by supplying a context that "parses" it in one manner or the other. This led to a dilemma concerning the context: Is physics about reality or the observer? Dirac argued that by *convention,* we studied a "choice" upon the part of nature; Heisenberg, that we studied a "choice " upon the part of the observer constructing the instruments and reading them (see Bohr, 1949, p. 223). Wigner's and Schrödinger's arguments are powerful support for Heisenberg's "choice" in this dilemma, and it was in those terms that we began discussion of the measurement problem.

But examination of the quantum nature of the apparatus forces a deep-structural interpretation of the ambiguity. The experimental conditions cannot be considered just a link in the chain of inferences; they remain an indissoluble part of the description of what is called the "observed" object. The quantum context calls for a new kind of description, which does not attempt a sharp separation of observer and observed object. As Bohm (1971b) has argued: "A centrally relevant change in descriptive order required in the quantum theory is thus the dropping of the notion of analysis of the world into relatively autonomous parts, separately existent but in interaction. Rather, the primary emphasis is now on *individual wholeness,* in which the observing instrument is not separable from what is observed [p. 377]. " This is a new step, not often taken by discussants of the measurement problem, quite likely because they are reluctant to admit what it does to our conception of scientific analysis. This makes the problem one of deep structural ambiguity, in which one "object" (a system that is literally a whole) is actually two systems, in the same way that one Necker cube is two cubes depending upon the perspective. According to Bohm (1971a): "In the quantum situation, terms like 'observed object', 'observing instrument', 'experimental conditions' and 'experimental results' are just aspects of a single overall 'pattern' that are, in effect, abstracted and 'pointed out' or 'made relevant' by our mode of discourse. Thus, it has no meaning to say, for example, that there is an 'observed object' that interacts with the 'observing instrument' [p. 38]. " Instead there is only reality, an undivided totality of events and their relationships, which is referentially unitary but intensionally ambiguous. The wave–particle duality that separates classical from quantum accounts represents this: What is at issue is whether "the same" phenomenon, which can alternatively be construed as a particle or a wave, is either a particle or a wave.

Bohr's proposal said that when it is "in" the apparatus, the wave must be treated as a particle. Consistent applications of quantum mechanical description yield only waves. The so-called completeness of quantum mechanics (as in Von Neumann's "proof") arguments say that no analysis of quantum phenomena can disclose other than waves. The hidden variable theorists, such as Einstein, Bohm, and Wigner, search for a deep structure underlying both relativity and quantum frameworks.

[4]Wigner's formulation is cast in terms of consciousness, but that is not central to the issue, it is the presence of a conceptual being that evaluates the meaning of information that is the key feature.

[5]Many theorists would disagree that quantum mechanics presents any problem of observation, perhaps none more vehemently than Karl Popper. In a series of papers, such as "Epistemology Without a Knowing Subject" (in Popper, 1972) and "Quantum Mechanics Without 'The Observer'" (Popper, 1967), he has continued to argue for a realistic and objective interpretation of physics without the subjectivism of the observer that was begun in 1934 (Popper, 1959). In outline, his contention is as follows:

  a. The "indeterminacy principle" of Heisenberg is a misinterpretation of formulae that assert *statistical scatter*.

  b. *These formulae do not* refer to measurements; therefore no measurements can be "forbidden" by them.

  c. What is instead peculiar to (but perhaps not ultimate within) quantum mechanics is the (phase-dependent) interference of probabilities.

  d. One must reinterpret the concept of probability in quantum mechanics in terms of *propensities* rather than either subjectivistically or in terms of relative frequencies. Probabilities in quantum formulations thus reflect physically real, although *indeterministic,* states of affairs rather than subjective states of the observer.

Discussing Schrödinger's cat paradox specifically, Popper has maintained for 40 years (1959, p. 235f.; 1974, p. 123f.) that interpreting the Heisenberg indeterminacy formulae as scatter relations, in conjunction with his propensity interpretation of probability, simply *dissolves* the paradox.

In reply, two points should be stressed. First, although I agree with Popper that the Heisenberg formulae are statistical scatter relations, that is *irrelevant* to the problem at issue, which concerns the particular relation that obtains in a situation given the presence or absence of an interpreting knower. Second, the propensity interpretation, in any extant formulation, is not superior to relative frequency and cannot bear the theoretical weight that Popperians place upon it (Bub, 1975).

[6]Limits of dispositional analyses have been discussed by several authors, perhaps most clearly by Pap (1959, 1962) and Sellars (1958). The limitation with regard to explanation is that dispositions, which are collections or "bunched" groupings of facts, are not sufficiently high in the hierarchy of scientific terms to be explanatory. Consider the following levels of constructs in science:

nonexplained explainers	theories
explained explainers	laws
explained nonexplainers	facts

Since dispositional analyses, such as those in terms of "habits" or "drives" in psychology, are at best bunched factual descriptions at the lower level, they cannot be explanatory analyses.

[7]Perhaps Democritus of Abdera was the first to notice that phenomenal qualia are unique to the percipient subject: "Color is by convention, sweet by convention, bitter by convention; in truth there are but atoms and the void." Plato argued the same way in the *Theaetetus* (156é), as did virtually every significant epistemologist since (and including) Descartes, such as Locke, Galileo (see Hayek's chapter [13] in this volume), Leibniz, and modern theorists. Bertrand Russell formulated the distinction in its contemporary form as that of acquaintance and description. Schrödinger (1956) exphasized the gulf between acquaintance and description in this passage:

> While all building stones for the world-picture are furnished by the senses qua organs of the mind, while the world-picture itself is and remains for everyone a construct of his mind and apart from it has no demonstrable existence, the mind itself remains a stranger in this picture, it has no place in it, it can nowhere be found in it.... Strange reality. Something seems to be missing from it [pp. 216-217].

[8]That "science" of psychology, since its domain includes phenomena of organized complexity, will employ what Hayek calls explanations of the principle rather than of the particular (see Chapter 12, this volume, my introductory essay to Hayek's thought). The explanatory principles it employs therefore will not, strictly speaking, be "laws" in the physical theory sense. For brevity, this essay refers to psychological "laws" without noting the distinction.

[9]Sigmund Freud was perhaps the first psychologist to attempt this, in his long-unpublished "Psychology for Neurologists," in 1895 (published in Strackey [1955] as *Project for a Scientific Psychology*). Consider Freud's formulation next to Hayek's:

> Every psychological theory, apart from what it achieves from the point of view of natural science, must fulfill yet another major requirement. It should explain to us what we are aware of, in the most puzzling fashion, through our "consciousness"; and, since this consciousness knows nothing of what we have so far been assuming—quantities and neurons—it should explain this lack of knowledge to us as well [pp. 307-308].

Pribram and Gill (1976) provide an excellent account of Freud's views, in the context of a structural analysis of the sort this chapter advocates.

[10]One need look no further than the exodus resulting from Chomsky's impact upon psycholinguistics to see this. Miller, Galanter, and Pribram (1960) led the way in *Plans and the Structure of Behavior*, but they bowed to the popularity of behaviorism by calling themselves "subjective behaviorists." By the end of the sixties, however, no such verbal magic was necessary; these authors and many others repudiated behaviorism in any form. This is not to deny that behavior is a legitimate problem for explanation by psychology—it certainly is—but the behaviorist "explanation" is no explanation at all.

[11]Recall Titchener's dismissal of this problem in the "stimulus error." If a psychologist thinks in terms of physical, theoretical, or commonsense constructs in describing his

experiences, the structural psychologist accuses him of committing the stimulus error of not describing them in Wundtian phenomenology. Likewise, were a physicist to describe her ammeter as a whitish, grayish expanse with darker blotches (the "correct" response for the psychologist), she would commit a stimulus error from the point of view of physics.

[12]For example, sufficient reason, formulated by Leibniz as "every true proposition is analytic," may be interpreted as requiring every theorem (consequence) of a system to be a deductive consequence of its axiom set. Leibniz is doing both epistemology and ontology, developing a context of constraint that relates both what is known and how it is known in one grand scheme.

[13]Leibniz was ambiguous in the usage of "monad" to refer: (a) to the ultimate "simples" of existence, and (b) to aggregates of monads such as in the bodies of human beings, which were referred to as created monads, or substantial aggregates.

[14]Classically, causality is a succession of events sufficient to permit microdeterministic state specification of a system. A system is causal if a linear sequence can be traced from event to event, leaving no "unfilled" gaps in the chain. Such interactions involve a direct transference of energy from one event to the next in the sequence.

[15]Only laws formulated in terms of the interaction of *events* could conceivably be linear and microdeterministic and, hence, causal. But interphasic invariance laws relate laws of nature, not the events themselves; they relate events only by relating laws of nature. Interphasic laws deal with entities that are not only separated in space–time but also in different phases of existence, and are thus nonlinear and nonmicrodeterministic; they have neither property that may be considered definitive of causal analysis.

[16]Physicists have acknowledged this all along. As Weyl (1949) wrote: "In our natural understanding of living beings *concepts of a teleological origin* play a part beside causal law and statistics. The hand is there to grasp, the eye to see. My body is my real existence in the world. No theory of life that disregards these simple facts can succeed [p. 211]." The only change I would make in Weyl's statement would be to substitute "psychology" for "life" in the last sentence.

[17]Weyl (1949) became pessimistic at this point.

> The real riddle, if I am not mistaken, lies in the double position of the ego; it is not merely an existing individual which carries out real psychic acts but also "vision", a self-penetrating light (sense-giving consciousness, knowledge, image or however you may call it); . . . But this secret, by its very nature, lies beyond the cognitive means of natural science [pp. 215–216].

Is this the end of analysis, or is there an alternative form of understanding?

ACKNOWLEDGEMENTS

A number of colleagues and students have sharpened points and corrected errors. I especially thank C. N. Cofer, David Bohm, H. H. Pattee, K. H. Pribram, Robert Shaw, and Jon Doner.

REFERENCES

Bohm, D. *Quantum theory*. Englewood Cliffs, N.J.: Prentice-Hall, 1951.

Bohm, D. A proposed explanation of quantum theory in terms of hidden variables at a sub-quantum-mechanical level. In S.Körner (Ed.), *Observation and interpretation in the philosophy of physics*. New York: Dover, 1957.

Bohm, D *The Special Theory of Relativity*. New York: Benjamin, 1965.

Bohm, D. On the role of hidden variables in the fundamental structure of physics. In T. Bastin (Ed.), *Quantum theory and beyond*. Cambridge: Cambridge University Press, 1971. (a)

Bohm, D. Quantum theory as an indication of a new order in physics. Part A. The development of new orders as shown through the history of physics. *Foundations of physics I*, 1971, 359-381. (b)

Bohm, D. Quantum theory as an indication of a new order in physics. Part B. Implicate and explicate order in physical law. *Foundations of physics 3*, 1973, 139-168.

Bohm, D. & Hiley, B. J. On the intuitive understanding of nonlocality as implied by quantum theory. *Foundations of Physics 5*, 1975, 93-109.

Bohr, N. Discussion with Einstein on epistemological problems in atomic physics. In P. A. Schilpp (Ed.), *Albert Einstein: Philosopher-scientist*. La Salle, Ill.: Open Court, 1949.

Bub, J. Popper's propensity interpretation of probability and quantum mechanics. In G. Maxwell & R. M. Anderson (Eds.), *Minnesota studies in the philosophy of science*, (Vol. VI). Minneapolis: University of Minnesota Press, 1975.

Campbell, D. T. Evolutionary epistemology. In P. A. Schilpp (Ed.), *The philosophy of Karl Popper*. La Salle, Ill.: Open Court, 1974.

Chew, G. F. The bootstrap idea and the foundations of quantum theory. In T. Bastin (Ed.), *Quantum theory and beyond*. Cambridge: Cambridge University Press, 1971.

Clark, R. W. *Einstein: The life and times*. New York: McGraw-Hill, 1971.

Dirac, P. A. M. *The principles of quantum mechanics*. Oxford: Oxford University Press, 1947.

Elsasser, W. *The physical foundations of biology*. New York: Pergamon Press, 1958.

Feyerabend, P. K. Problems of empiricism I. In R. Colodny (Ed.), *Beyond the edge of certainty*. Prentice-Hill, 1965.

Feyerabend, P. K. Problems of empiricism II. In R. Colodny (Ed.), *The nature and function of scientific theories*. Pittsburgh; Pa.: University of Pittsburgh Press, 1970.

Gabor, D. Holography, 1948-1971. *Science*, 28 July 1972, *177*, 299-313.

Gibson, J. J. *The senses considered as perceptual systems*. Boston: Houghton Mifflin, 1966.

Hanson, N. R. *Patterns of discovery*. Cambridge: Cambridge University Press, 1958.

Hayek, F. A. *The sensory order*. London: Routledge, 1952. (Reprinted by University of Chicago Press, 1963).

Heisenberg, W. *Physics and philosophy*. New York: Harper Torch Books, 1958.

Kuhn, T. S. *The structure of scientific revolutions* (2nd ed.). Chicago: University of Chicago Press, 1970.

Lazlo, E. & Margenau, H. The emergence of integrative concepts in contemporary science. *Philosophy of Science*, 1972, *39*, 252-259.

Loemker, L. *Leibniz: Philosophical papers and letters*. The Hague: Mouton, 1956.

Lovejoy, A. *The great chain of being*. Cambridge, Mass.: Harvard University Press, 1936.

Luria, A. R. *The mind of a mnemonist*. New York: Basic Books, 1968.

Mach, E. *Science of Mechanics: A critical and historical account of its development*. Chicago: Open Court, 1902.

Miller, G. A., Galanter, E., & Pribram, K. H. *Plans and the structure of behavior*. New York: Holt, Rinehart & Winston, 1960.

Pap, A. On the empirical interpretation of psychoanalytic concepts. In S. Hook (Ed.), *Psychoanalysis, scientific method, and philosophy*. New York: New York University Press, 1959.

Pap, A. *An introduction to the philosophy of science*. Glencoe, Ill.: Free Press, 1962.

Pattee, H. H. Can life explain quantum mechanics? In T. Bastin (Ed.), *Quantum theory and beyond*. Cambridge: Cambridge University Press, 1971.

Pattee, H. H. Physical problems of decision-making constraints. *International Journal of Neuroscience*, 1972, *3*, 99-106.

Penfield, W. *The Mystery of the Mind*. Princeton, N.J.: Princeton University Press, 1975.

Penfield, W., & Roberts, L. *Speech and brain mechanisms*. Princeton, N.J.: Princeton University Press, 1959.

Piaget, J. *Biology and knowledge*. Chicago: University of Chicago Press, 1971.

Popper, K. R. *The logic of scientific discovery*. New York: Harper, 1959.

Popper, K. R. *Objective knowledge: an evolutionary approach*. Oxford: Oxford University Press, 1972.

Popper, K. Z. Quantum mechanics without "the observer." In M. Bunge (Ed.), *Quantum theory and reality*. New York: Springer-Verlag, 1967.

Pribram, K. H. *Languages of the brain*. Englewood Cliffs, N.J.: Prentice-Hall, 1971.

Pribram, K. H., & Gill, M. *Freud's project reassessed*. New York: Basic Books, 1976.

Russell, B. A. W. *The analysis of mind*. London: Allen & Unwin, 1921.

Russell, B. A. W. *The analysis of matter*. London: Allen & Unwin, 1927.

Russell, B. A. W. *An inquiry into meaning and truth*. London: Allen & Unwin, 1940.

Russell, B. A. W. *Portraits from memory*. New York: Simon & Schuster, 1951.

Schrödinger, E. *What is life? & other scientific essays*. Garden City, N.Y.: Doubleday, 1956.

Sellars, W. Counterfactuals, dispositions, and the causal modalities. In H. Feigl, M. Scriven, & G. Maxwell (Eds.), *Concepts, theories, and the mind-body problem. Minnesota Studies in the Philosophy of Science*, (Vol. II). Minneapolis: University of Minnesota Press, 1958.

Sellars, W. *Science, perception and reality*. New York: Routledge & Kegan Paul, 1963.

Semon, R. *Mnemic psychology*. London: Allen & Unwin, 1923.

Spencer Brown, G. *Laws of form*. New York: Julian Press, 1972.

Strackey, J. (ed.). *The standard edition of the complete psychological works of Sigmund Freud* (Vol. 1). London: Hogarth Press, 1955.

Vigier, J.-P. The concept of probability in the frame of the probabilistic and the causal interpretation of quantum mechanics. In S. Körner (Ed.), *Observation and interpretation in the philosophy of physics*. New York: Dover, 1957.

Vigier, J.-P. Possible internal subquantum motions of elementary particles. In W. Yourgrau & A. D. Breck (Eds.), *Physics, logic, and history*. New York: Plenum Press, 1970.

Von Neumann, J. *Theory of self-reproducing automata* (A. W. Burks, Ed.). Urbana, Ill.: University of Illinois Press, 1966.

Weimer, W. B. Psycholinguistics and Plato's paradoxes of the *Meno. American Psychologist*, 1973, *28*, 15-33.

Weimer, W. B. The psychology of inference and expectation: Some preliminary remarks. In G. Maxwell & R. M. Anderson (Eds.), *Minnesota Studies in the Philosophy of Science* (Vol. VI). Minneapolis: University of Minnesota Press, 1975.

Weimer, W. B. Manifestations of mind: Some conceptual and empirical issues. In G. G. Globus, I. Savodnik, & G. Maxwell (Eds.), *Consciousness and the brain*. New York: Plenum Press, 1976.

Weimer, W. B. A conceptual framework for cognitive psychology: Motor theories of the mind. In R. Shaw & J. D. Bransford (Eds.), *Perceiving, acting, and knowing: Toward an ecological psychology*. Hillsdale, N.J.: Lawrence Erlbaum Associates, 1977.

Weimer, W. B. *Notes on the methodology of scientific research*. Hillsdale, N.J.: Lawrence Erlbaum Associates, 1979.

Weyl, H. *Philosophy of mathematics and natural science*. Princeton, N.J.: Princeton University Press, 1949.

Weyl, H. *The theory of groups and quantum mechanics*. New York: Dover Press, 1950.

Weyl, H. *Symmetry*. Princeton, N.J.: Princeton University Press, 1952.

Wigner, E. P. *Symmetries and reflections*. Cambridge, Mass.: MIT Press, 1970.

17 Reflections on the Place of Brain in the Ecology of Mind

Karl H. Pribram
Stanford University

There seems to be good evidence for the age-old belief that the brain has something to do with the mind. Or, to use less dualistic terms, when behavioral phenomena are carved at their joints, there will be some sense in which the analysis will correspond to the way the brain is put together. Psychological problems may not be solved by making measurements on the brain; but some more modest aim may be accomplished. A psychological analysis that can stand up to the neurological evidence is certainly better than one that can not. The catch, obviously, is in the phrase "stand up to," since considerable prejudice can be involved in its definition. In any case, each time there is a new idea in psychology, it suggests a corresponding insight in neurophysiology, and vice versa. The procedure of looking back and forth between the two fields is not only ancient and honorable—it is always fun and occasionally useful

[Miller, Galanter, & Pribram, 1960, p. 196].

INTRODUCTION

The issues I wish to address stem directly from the conference that generated this volume. During the conference, I was, and still am, disturbed by the almost complete disregard, in otherwise excellent presentations by psychologists, of the contributions the brain sciences can make to the problems under investigation. Some of this disturbance is purely personal: Why should my proposals be repeatedly and universally quoted when they appear devoid of their neurological skin, flesh, and bones in *Plans and the Structure of Behavior* (Miller et al., 1960), but be totally ignored when instantiated and substantiated in *Languages of the Brain* (Pribram, 1971)? Why is it that in this group of scientists, where communication is relatively easy because of mutual respect and trust, only the *philosopher* addresses the issues before us without regard to race (neuro vs. psycho)? Is psychology still so insecure, even here and at this late date, that it must (as Skinner and Freud both argued in that distant past) build on its own level without recourse to physiology? If that is the case, I asked myself, what am I doing here? It seems to matter little what I say; no one is listening anyway.

The answer to this question is, of course, the major contribution James Gibson has made to my understanding of phenomenal reality. But I want to insist that explorations of the issues he has raised can be enriched considerably by investigations of the nervous system. The question is whether in the long run any science can ignore its relationships with others without suffering obsolescence. Has the descriptive functionalism so dear to Gibson and other behaviorists outlived its usefulness?

I wish here to share my conference experiences, both the frustrating and the rewarding, and shall try for once to keep references to the nervous system at a minimum without the detail that might otherwise bring down those defensive gates that psychologists are apparently so prone to use. But to the brain, I do and must refer, for whether you believe it or not, that's where the action is, as the younger generation is wont to remark.

REPRESENTATION

The central issue before the conference turned on the question of the existence of *brain* representations and their nature. Surprisingly, *everyone*—and I mean *everyone*—agreed that representational mechanisms exist, though not everyone wanted to label them as such, and there was considerable range in attributing their importance. Thus, for Gibson "Sensations triggered by light, sound, pressure and chemicals are merely incidental,—*information* is available to a perceptual system and—the qualities of the world in relation to the needs of the observer are experienced directly [this volume]." But then Gibson goes on to suggest

> that when we view phenomena in terms of e.g., a special sense, the process of attention occurs at centers within the nervous system, whereas [when we view a phenomenon as a] case of a perceptual system attention pervades the whole input–output loop. In the first case attention is a consciousness that can be focused, in the second case it is a skill that can be educated. In the first case physiological metaphors are used such as the filtering of nervous impulses or the switching of impulses from one path to another. In the second case the metaphors used can be terms like resonating, extracting, optimizing or symmetricalizing, and acts like orienting, exploring, investigating or adjusting."

Let us examine these quotations closely (as examples of a wider range of pronouncements) with respect to the issue of representation. In the first case "sensations" appear although they are incidental. Just how are sensations constituted except by a match between the input to the senses (or even perceptual systems) and a brain mechanism ready to process this input? (See Pribram, [1971] Chaps. 3, 6, 12 for the gory—i.e., bloody—biological details.) Then, as an alternative comes "information" available to perceptual systems. Does "information" exist in the absence of an informed (uncertain) organism? Here I use the term in the strict (measurement) sense as well as in the more informal Gibsonian sense. To be informed is to be in-formed, literally formed within. Has Gibson really begged the question by equating external pattern, structure, and organization with information—much as those who insist that the perturbations produced by a falling tree make phenomenal sounds even in the absence of an acoustically sentient observer?

Figure 17.1 makes my point in brain terms. It diagrams the response of a cell in the visual cortex of a cat. The experiment was performed in my laboratory and reported by Erich Sutter (1975). The cell's responses were correlated with the appearance of points of light on an oscilloscope. However, the points of light were not arranged in an elongated fashion. They were displayed randomly with respect to place and time over the entire oscilloscope face. When the correlation encompassed approximately 30 msec, the elongated receptive field of the cell becomes apparent; at 40 msec of correlation, its inhibitory flank is demonstrated.

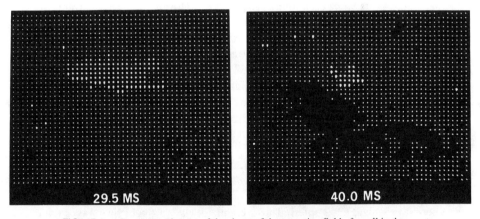

29.5 MS   40.0 MS

FIG. 17.1. Computer print-out of the shape of the receptive field of a cell in the visual cortex of a curarized cat responding to visual white noise on an oscilloscope face. Intensified spots indicate a correlation between the appearance of a spot on the oscilloscope face and the firing of the cell above baseline. Absent spots indicate that when a spot appeared on the oscilloscope face, the visual cortical cell's firing rate was depressed below baseline. A. The record obtained over 29.5 msec of correlation. B. The record obtained over 40 msec of correlation. Note that the generation of the inhibitory flank takes approximately 10 msec longer than the generation of the excitatory field, suggesting that inhibition is secondary to excitation (and probably produced intracortically). For complete report, see Sutter (1975).

These characteristics describe this cell's receptive field when ordinary techniques (such as presenting a line in a specific orientation) are used to demonstrate the cell's feature sensitivity. But the cell, by itself, cannot distinguish a line from the visual white noise presented to it on the oscilloscope. Gibson is correct that only the system's network properties can make this distinction. But how can Gibson and his colleagues, *ex cathedra,* be so certain that the relevant organization ("information") is "out there" when his (and their) own brain cells can't distinguish a line from visual noise? For unless it has a nonphysiological basis, it is the connections of these very brain cells that must be involved in constructing whatever "information" is being processed, and the information might just as well "reside" in these brain connectivities as in the environment. My own view, repeatedly documented with neurophysiological data (as noted earlier), is that the organization in the environment must match some "representational" organization in the organism. So let us return to the central issue of the conference and review some evidence once again in the context of Gibson's approach.

Consider Gibson's statement about qualities being perceived directly, but note that he adds the phrase "in relation to the needs of the observer." The term *needs* can refer to two types of states: (1) those "physiological" needs that we ordinarily conceive as being determined by physicochemical stimuli impinging on the homeostatic mechanisms of the brain stem; and (2) those that are more "psychological" in nature, such as the "need" to investigate due to uncertainty (used here in its strict definition) generated by information (strict definition) in the input. The homeostatic mechanisms are representational in that the quantities they control are being sensed by the controlling system. Note that sensing is here equated with a form of representation (more about the theoretical validity of this later). Here, the evidence is concrete: The quantities to be sensed are in many instances literally absorbed by the sensing mechanism, and the absorbed portions are acted upon by subordinate regulating mechanisms to determine the set points around which the homeostats then operate (for review, see, e.g., Pribram, 1977b). Thus these are true representations in a most precise meaning of the term.

The more "psychological" needs, such as curiosity, also involve representational mechanisms. The term *need* is invoked when an organism varies its responses in the absence of observable covariation in the environment: A varying internal organization is inferred to account for varying behavior. Investigative behavior shows such variations and thus the conception of an information-hungry organism, an informavore whose appetitive fervor can be sated only to arise once more (Pribram, 1960). Information in its strict definition implies a set of alternatives about which the information is informative. When this set of alternatives describes the channel competency (or its inverse, the equivocation inherent in the channel) of the organism—its ability to process information—it constitutes its uncertainty. Information describing the set of alternatives (whether Shannonian [Shannon & Weaver, 1949] or Gibsonian) must address this uncertainty, as even

Gibson admits in his statement that information "is perceived *in relation* to the needs of the observer." The set that describes the uncertainty of the organism must, of course, constitute some representation. Perception, whether within a special sensory mode or beyond it, cannot take place without that specified *relation* between organism and environment. Consider an analogy: Humans do not perceive most of porpoise communication because we have no mechanism attuned to the information carried at 20 KHz and above. Thus no uncertainties were set, nor did we become curious, nor did investigatory behavior begin until John Lilly played a recording of porpoise communication at half speed, making it audible to us. Only then did the wealth of information (strict definition) that is now perceived in their communication make us uncertain as to the meaning of the information (Gibson's sense).

Further, the set of alternatives that describes the uncertainty of the organism is often referred to as "attention," and whether focused or skilled, Gibson admits to the existence of attention. My laboratory has devoted considerable attention to attention, demonstrating three major neural control systems that operate on the "focusing" of attention (Pribram & McGuinness, 1975) and showing by making electrical brain recordings that the association cortex is definitively involved in organizing attentional skills (Nuwer & Pribram, 1979; Pribram, Day, & Johnston, 1976; Rothblat & Pribram, 1972).Figure 17.2 diagrams the control systems, and Fig. 17.3 gives an example of the brain electrical activity involved in attentional skill. How could attention be controlled or attentional skill become developed if the attentional mechanisms were not apprised of what (information) was to be attended to? How could attention operate without some representational brain process upon which to operate?

Gibson creates a conundrum with his use of phrases such as "resonating, optimizing, symmetricalizing" with respect to perceiving, and "orienting, exploring, investigating or adjusting" with respect to acting. It appears that the brain that Gibson envisions can do none of these, yet current neurophysiology is concerned almost exclusively with just such mechanisms. Figure 17.4 illustrates the tuning curves of cells in the visual cortex to spatial frequencies. The cells are the same cells that respond selectively to lines presented in specific orientations. The sensitivities appear to be influenced as well by the number of lines and their relative widths and spacings. Thus the cells can be shown to "resonate" to one or another octave of the spatial frequency spectrum—the spectrum of light and dark that patterns the visual world. Optical engineers and computer scientists describe the result of such resonances as "image" or optical information processing to distinguish it from the processing of alternatives as performed by digital computers. Terms such as "optimizing" and recourse to symmetry analyses are commonplace, and I have repeatedly drawn the parallel between holograms that encode spatial frequency and certain aspects of brain function in perception and memory (Pribram, 1966; 1971; Pribram, Nuwer, & Baron, 1974). Is the notion of a brain process so irrelevant that even when the processes are shown to do

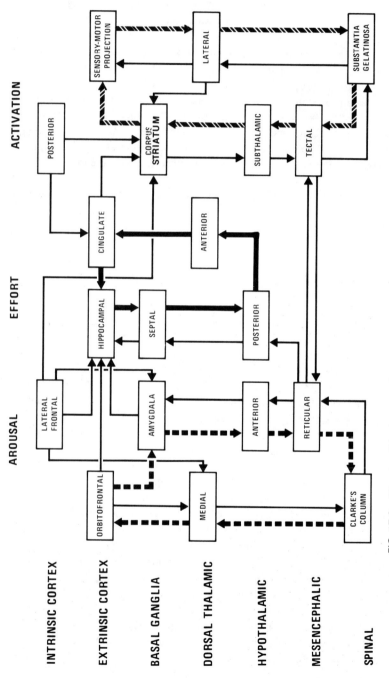

FIG. 17.2. Diagram of the three neural systems involved in the control of attention. These systems can be discerned neuroanatomically, neurochemically, and by the results of psychophysiological, neurophysiological, and neurobehavioral experiment. For complete review of the evidence, see Pribram and McGuinness (1975).

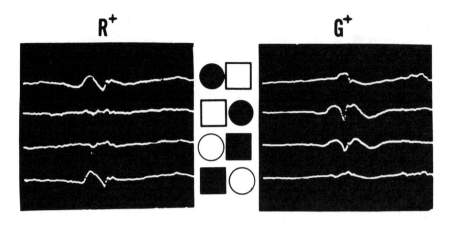

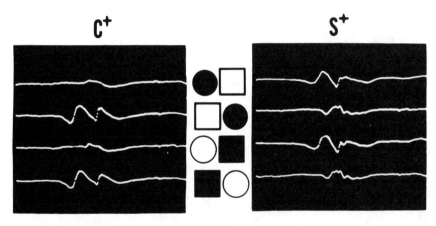

FIG. 17.3. Records of averaged electrical responses obtained from the inferotemporal cortex in the fully awake monkey. The averages are run both backward and forward from the midpoint of the record. The geometric figures represent slides that were briefly back-projected in random sequence, one at a time onto a vertically split panel. The monkey responded (i.e., paid attention) on the basis of the reinforcing contingencies that rewarded either one of the colors (red or green—represented here by black and white). Note that when, as in the upper panels, colors are being reinforced, the brain waves look alike when the colors appear on the same side irrespective of shape. When shape is being reinforced (lower panels), the brain waves look alike when the same shape appears in the same place irrespective of which color the shapes are.

exactly what is needed, they must be denied lest they do violence to the presumed virginal purity of psychological inquiry? Or does Gibson avoid discussion of neural processes because he has some objection to available theory and data? If so, why does he not at least mention it to argue against it?

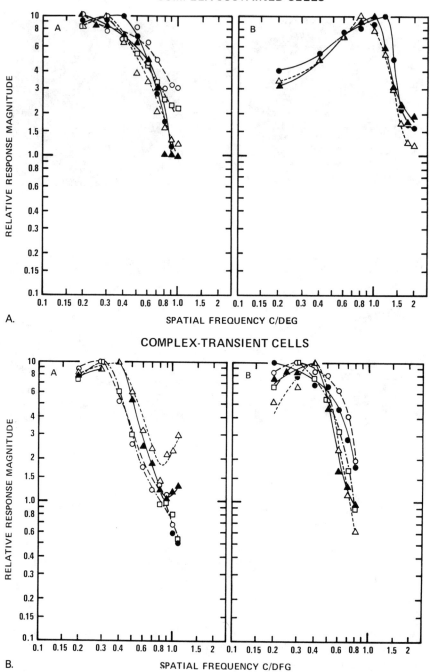

COMPLEX-SUSTAINED CELLS

COMPLEX-TRANSIENT CELLS

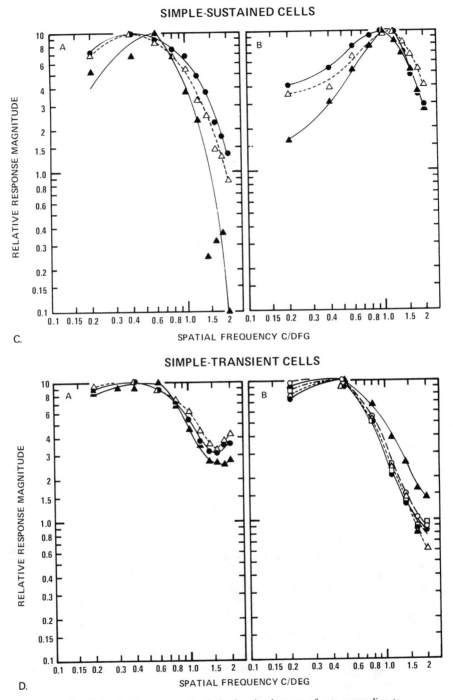

FIG. 17.4. Tuning curves of cells in the visual cortex of cats responding to suprathreshold drifting gratings of a variety of spatial frequencies presented in random sequence. Note the stability of the curves over time and a variety of conditions (represented by the different curves plotted in each graph).

I have already discussed "exploring" and "investigating," two of the action terms Gibson invokes. Ten years of research on the brain mechanisms involved in the orienting reaction (Bagshaw & Benzies, 1968; Bagshaw, Kimble, & Pribram, 1965; Kimble, Bagshaw, & Pribram, 1965; Pribram & McGuinness, 1975; Pribram, Reitz, McNeil, & Spevack, 1979) should be relevant to anyone interested in orienting, as should the earlier work on the neural processes allowing orienting to occur (see, e.g., the reviews by Horn & Hinde, 1970; and by Groves & Thompson, 1970). And certainly the exquisite work on the neural feedback and feedforward mechanisms operating to adjust to changes of load in both sensory and motor systems is relevant (for a review, see Pribram, 1971, Chaps. 12, 13).

One objection that the Gibsonian might raise to the relevance of such data must be dismissed in advance. Neurological data might be dismissed because they are at too fine grained a level of analysis to be relevant to some levels of analysis but this does not hold for an ecological approach. Further, Gibson's emphasis upon perception as the pickup of (ecologically relevant) information *over time* cannot be used to dismiss neurological data because such data are assumed to refer only to momentary, "frozen image," or static analyses, (as e.g. proposed by "snippeting" theorists such as Richard Gregory, 1966). Current neurophysiology deals with processes such as "orienting, exploring, investigating or adjusting" over time exactly as Gibson's account requires. Sooner or later his account must either incorporate such data or state specifically how it is incompatible with his ecological analysis.

COMPLEMENTATION

The subject of action brings us to the excellent contributions of Turvey and his colleagues. These investigators show less reluctance to mention the nervous system. For example, "spinal interneuronal pools" are invoked to handle Gelfand, Gurfinkel, Tsetlin, and Shik's (1971) observations. Statements such as "This approach yields *some* of the organizing problem to the environment" indicates that other aspects are left to the organism to handle. Thus Turvey's approach is more compatible with mine in that his ecology includes *specifications* of organism (especially neural) variables and constraints, whereas Gibson tends to leave the organism, if not empty, apparently stuffed with foam rubber. Moreover, Turvey's discussions in terms of free variables (information in the strict sense), constraints (redundancy and control; see, e.g., Pribram & Gill, 1976, Chap. 1), and coordinate structures are completely compatible with my own approach. To view muscles (especially the vocal muscles) as vibratory systems, to take one specific example, as did Carol Fowler in her presentation, made me nostalgic (Pribram, 1971):

"I love you." It was spring in Paris, and the words held the delightful flavor of a Scandinavian accent. The occasion was a UNESCO meeting on the problems of research on Brain and Human Behavior. The fateful words were not spoken by a curvaceous blonde beauty, however, but generated by a small shiny metal device in the hands of a famous psycholinguist.

The device impressed all of us with the simplicity of its design. The loudspeaker was controlled by only two knobs. One altered the state of an electronic circuit that represented the tension of the vocal cords; the other regulated the pulses generated by a circuit that simulated the plosions of air puffs striking the cords.

Could this simple device be relevant to man's study of himself? Might not all behavior be generated and controlled by a neural mechanism equally simple? Is the nervous system a "two knob" dual process mechanism in which one process is expressed in terms of neuroelectric states, the other in terms of distinct pulsatile operators on those states? That the nervous system does, in fact, operate by impulses has been well documented. The existence of neuroelectric states in the brain has also been established, but this evidence and its significance to the study of psychology has been slow to gain acceptance even in neurophysiology. This first chapter therefore examines the evidence which makes a two-process model of brain function plausible [pp. 3–5].

This compatibility of viewpoint and approach also provides a rich field for an appraisal of differences. For the main, these differences are in the detail with which each conceptualization is thus far developed. As an example of an important detail which has moved my thinking forward, take the following: An *overall* structure of the mechanism of control is already presented in *Plans and the Structure of Behavior* (Miller et al., 1960), *Languages of the Brain* (Pribram, 1971, Chap. 5), and *Freud's "Project" Re-assessed* (Pribram & Gill, 1976). Thus the organization of behavior, its serial ordering, is due not to the chaining of movements but to the differentiation, the decoding, of an already formed *spatial* configuration. The neural specification of such spatial configuration (see Fig. 17.5) is described more fully in Chapter 12 of *Languages of the Brain* (Pribram, 1971). The conception of hierarchical relationship among coordinate structures (although they are called "predictive representations") is detailed in Chapter 16 and is summarized:

Given (1) that the neural mechanism "because of its selective control over its own modification, allows a change in representation to occur over successions of trials," and (2) that whenever "complete match between representation and input is not achieved the representation is modified to include this information and trials continue . . . until corrective change of the representation no longer occurs," then any succession of *predictive* representations in essence constitutes a program or Plan producing an intent.

In review, achievements are organized performances and steps toward an achievement theory of performance have been taken. These steps account for the

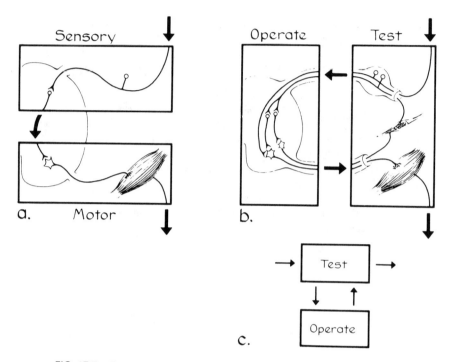

FIG. 17.5. Representation of the organization of control in a low-level (reflex) coordinate structure according to the Test–Operate–Test–Exit (TOTE) system. (a) The old reflex arc; (b) the TOTE feedback loop based on the γ efferents; (c) the TOTE representation. Note in b how the two types of γ efferents interact to produce an adaptive response. For complete details, see Pribram (1971), Chap., 13).

differences in function of reinforcers during learning (when they provide information) and during performance (when they value, bias behavior). At least one class of variables, response rate, has been shown to play a major part in determining the contingencies under which an organism no longer learns yet continues to perform—the means–end reversal. Performances achieve because of the hierarchical nature of the reinforcing (in stimulus language, the discriminative) process: Meanings are derived when information is hierarchically processed in sensory systems, and Plans, intentions, are constructed by hierarchical processing in the predictive motor mechanism [pp. 299–300].

Missing is a detailed statement as to the nature of the predictive representation. Carol Fowler's view of muscles as vibratory systems makes explicit the nature of the state variables which are noted in the foregoing quotation. By treating the muscular system as basically vibratory, Bekesy's classical experiments on the auditory and somatosensory mechanism become relevant to motor function and the conception of a holographically (i.e., *n*-dimensional frequency coded) constituted Image of Achievement (Pribram, 1971, Chap. 13) more plausible. Neurophysiological evidence for vibratory activity or control of the entire motor system (other than in vocalization, eye movement, scratch reflex, and locomotion where it is obvious) now needs to be sought experimentally.

Despite this compatability of approaches a fundamental difference between Turvey's views and mine was voiced at the meetings. Turvey suggested that the relationship between the neural mechanism and the environment that is involved in guiding motor behavior should be regarded as a complementation rather than a representation. My reply was that complementation is a form of representation. This point is both difficult and important. Complementation suggests something akin to a *mirror* image, whereas representation suggests an image that is more of a duplicate of what is imaged. The essential point is that in complementation, both organism and environment mutually imply each other. Thus the acquisition of a motor skill (or, for Gibson, a perceptual skill) is an attunement, in which the organism becomes tuned to the environment. With all this, I agree totally. But I would add that a skill results just as often from the attunement of the environment to the organism: the development of skis, skates, skateboards, bicycles, tennis racquets, balls, bats, violins, cellos, trumpets, saxophones, drums, pianos, harps, automobiles, and steam shovels (to name only a few common artifacts that are involved in skilled performances). Thus complementation is not limited to the form proposed by Turvey. Further, the figure–ground relationship was used as a model of complementation, and we know from studies using reversible figures that many figure–ground reversals can take place. In accord with Shaw's suggestion (see later), these circumstances are most likely described by symmetry relationships.

The question may therefore be posed: Does complementation entail representation? In *Languages of the Brain* (1971, Chap. 13), evidence is presented in support of the hypothesis that acts, not movements, are *represented* in the cerebral motor cortex. Acts are defined as the environmental consequences of movements—specifically, the forces engendered by and acting upon the muscular system. Turvey and his group define the coordinations involved in coordinate structures as follows: "It is neither muscles nor joints that are coordinated in the performance of skills, but forces, those supplied by the actor and those supplied by the environment." Experiments on the functions of the motor cortex (Malis, Pribram, & Kruger, 1953; Pribram, Kruger, Robinson, & Berman, 1955) demonstrated that "neither muscle contractions nor movements (defined as sequences of muscle contractions coordinated around joints) were impaired" by extensive resections. However, *specific skills were impaired,* thus the inference was made that this cortex was involved in actions, defined as the environmental consequences of the movement. The cerebral motor cortex is therefore a critical party to the formation and maintenance of coordinate structures as defined both by Gelfand, Gurfinkle, Tsetlin, and Shik (1971) and by Turvey (this vol.). Could not one conclude, on the basis of this evidence, that *a representation of coordi-*

nate structures is formed by virtue of the functions of the motor cortex? A representation encodes the invariances, the constraints, the parameters that describe the function. Such a representation makes possible environment-organism complementation instantiated in the skill. Note that I did not suggest that the representation of the coordinate structure was to be totally localized "in" the cerebral motor cortex—although this is not yet ruled out by the evidence. It is a more likely option that a number of other brain structures (such as the basal ganglia and cerebellum) are involved, and of course, they, in turn, control more peripheral motor organizations.

An important clarification needs to be made here. Whenever we talk of the localization of a function, there are two sides to the coin—and the two sides differ. The lungs are clearly involved in respiration. When, however, we begin to investigate respiratory functions, oxygen, carbon dioxide, lungs, red blood cells, membrane properties, hemoglobin, the brain stem respiratory control mechanism, and even temperature and gastric acidity (among other factors) become involved. What is localized in the lungs is the exchange of oxygen and carbon dioxide, and this property is critical to respiration. In biology we do not throw up our hands in despair and abandon the search for localized mechanisms because respiration is complex and involves the function of many structures. We do not in biological ecology eschew a search for the mechanisms by which organisms become attuned to their environments. Psychological ecology—the ecology of mind—need be no different. Precise mechanisms are localized in the cerebral motor cortex. They are critical to coordinate structures and may in fact be the embodiment of the most superordinate of these in that they encode the complex of relationships among the forces that describe an act.

How can the consequences of movements—the forces engendered in an existing field of forces—be encoded? Consider once again that the motor system functions as a vibratory system. The forces describing the action would fluctuate, and the fluctuations would occur with specifiable frequencies. This is essentially what Bernstein (1967) found in his elegant experiments. Bernstein was able to make predictions of the course of actions by performing Fourier analyses on the records he obtained. I suggested (Pribram, 1971) that what Bernstein could do, perhaps his *brain* might do; and if his, then ours as well. We have recently completed experiments that provide evidence in support of the hypothesis that the motor system behaves as a frequency analyzer of the forces involved in actions (Ahmad Sharafat 1981.) Thus the motor system can be seen to function much as the auditory system, the somatosensory system (Bekesy, 1967), and the visual system (Pribram, 1971, Chap. 8).

There remains the question of whether this complementation effected by the functions of the cerebral motor cortex provides evidence for a representation. In my contribution (Pribram, 1977c) to the previous conference and volume of this series, I detail evidence for isomorphism between environment and cortex in perceptual systems. Surprisingly, this evidence points to an order in the physical world that theoretical physicist David Bohm (1973) calls the implicate order and that is not the perceived world of appearance. The question is therefore raised as to whether complementation exists between the organism and an implicate order in the environment or between the organism and the explicate order of appearance. Or should the question be rephrased to ask whether complementation describes the relationship between implicate and explicate orders, whether in the environment or in the organism? I opt for this latter view because both Bohm and I were led to prehending the implicate order through the hologram. Holograms encode the frequency domain, yet because of symmetry relations (complementation) they can be readily decoded. Such decoding into the perceived world of images and objects can be effected by the operation of the feedbacks and feed-forwards that constitute coordinate structures. But I would add that what is complemented between organism and environment might be the frequency domain in one and the image–object domain in the other.

My conclusion, therefore, is that representations do exist in the brain; that they are instrumental in complementation, and that some representations encode, in the frequency domain, coordinate structures and thus complement the image-object domain. Complementation therefore describes the symmetry relationships (reversibility of transformations) between these domains and perhaps between one domain in the organism and the other in the environment. There may, of course, be other domains over which such relationships hold, but at present these have not been studied.

DUALITY OF IMAGE AND PLAN

Shaw's penetrating analysis of complementation suggests that dualities of this sort are the rule rather than the exception. I have been intrigued for years with the commonalities of description that make up the body of general systems theory, but have deplored the overly simplistic assumption that when two processes can be described by the same equation, they can be equated structurally. Something very important is missed when the interfaces between "levels" are ignored. So often the transformations from one level to another seemed to result in "mirror images" rather than similarities. The transformation from the image/object domain to the frequency (holographic) domain and back again by way of the inverse transform is a case in point. Even the term *mirror image* does not really convey the near identity yet vast difference between the two domains. I have used the term "stereo-isomer" (Pribram, 1965) because the functional properties of each isomer are often so different, but a more general conceptual language is needed. In his discussion of the variety of "dualities," Shaw has provided such a language.

One duality that is not recognized as such is the duality between what Pattee (1971) has called the dynamical and the linguistic (or structural) modes of organization, which in *Plans and the Structure of Behavior* (Miller et al 1960) were called Image and Plan. We pointed out then that Image and Plan mutually imply each other. But it is one thing to provide an intuition that a duality is involved and another to show how the duality might come about. David Bohm suggested once that perhaps two holographic (dynamical, Image) organizations orthogonal to each other might, at their intersection, produce the nonlinearities that give rise to structure (linguistic, Plan). Rene Thom (1975) has developed the theme that continuous topological representations can, under certain conditions (constraints), give rise to "catastrophes"—the discontinuities that form non-linear structures. Anderson (e.g., Anderson, Silverstein, Ritz, & Jones, 1977) has made the most precise suggestion as to how such a process might work. His model of the dynamical Image domain is based on Walsh transforms, which are finite, discrete, two-valued analogues of Fourier transforms. His model therefore also results in a holographic, dynamically distributed organization. Since its variables are discrete, however, he can represent this organization by a lattice. He defines "features," the elements of structure, as the eigenvectors of this lattice. A similar approach might be taken by using Lie groups (see, e.g., Hoffman, 1947) in which continuous variables can be represented. Whether these continuous variables are to be thought of as Fourier components of wave forms remains to be shown empirically in each specific situation.

SENTIENCE, SAPIENCE, AND SELFHOOD

The foregoing considerations were derived for most of us from experimental results that we could not explain in any more ordinary fashion. But of course, the novelty of this general approach has both philosophical roots and implications. Weimer has admirably drawn out both. He addresses the ultimate duality (the mind-brain problems) under the rubrics sentience, sapience, and selfhood. Once again I "resonate" to the views expressed since they "complement" my own. In *"Proposal for a Structural Pragmatism"* (1965), I suggested that a systems approach (but not general systems theory) to the mind-brain duality leads to a view in which mind and brain may be conceived as optical isomers of one another—brain being the product of a descriptive reductionist, whereas mind is the result of a relativistic conventional approach. Brain talk results from looking downward in a hierarchy of conceptualizations; mind talk, from looking upward.

The empirical problems of the organization of sentience yield definite answers once the dynamical holographic model is taken seriously. In a profession of reviews of pertinent neurophysiological data, I first proposed holography as a metaphor in "Some Dimensions of Remembering" (1966) and developed it into an analogy in *Languages of the Brain* (1971) and finally into a full-fledged model in the *Holographic Hypothesis of Brain Function in Perception and Memory* (Pribram, Nuwer & Baron 1974). The place of the model in sentience is detailed in "Problems Concerning the Structure of Consciousness" (1976b) and in "Some Comments on the Nature of the Perceived Universe" (1977c). Weimer amplifies considerably the nonneurological aspects of the theory presented in these reviews. Of special interest to me was the reference to Leibniz' *Monadology* (Lettvin et al. 1959, 1961, 1968). My attention to monads was first drawn by an article entitled "A Code in the Nose" by Lettvin, Gesteland, Pitts, and Chung (1968). Having pioneered the feature detector theory in "What the Frog's Eye Tells the Brain" (1959), Lettvin proceeded to use the same microelectrode techniques to explore the olfactory bulb. Contrary to what he had found in the frog's tectum, the olfactory system did not seem to detect any specific features. Rather, sets of neurons appeared to respond to a large range of olfactants. Lettvin used these data to argue that his earlier feature detection views had limited applications in explaining perception, an argument that went largely unheeded by the neuroscience community. He was puzzled by his results, which he said appeared to suggest a code similar in organization to the monads in the Monadology. The work of Rall (e.g., 1970) and of Gordon Shepherd, reviewed in his *Synaptic Organization of the Brain* (1974), has detailed the similarities in the organization of the olfactory bulb with those of the retina and brain structures such as the thalamus and cortex. The studies of Freeman (1975), of Bekesy (1967), of Hartline and Ratliff (see, e.g., Ratliff, *Mach Bands,* 1965), and of Campbell and Robson (1968) have provided the quantitative data and mathematical descriptions that support Lettvin's intuition. It is of course Leibniz' mathematics, his invention of the integral calculus, that led him to his views; and it is the same mathematics that describes the functions of the synaptic networks of receptors and brain—the very same mathematics that Gabor (1969) used to invent the hologram.

I discuss the neuropsychology of sapience in "Neurological Notes on Knowing" (1972), "The Comparative Psychology of Communication: The Issue of Grammar and Meaning" (1973), *Language in a Sociobiological Frame* (1976a), and "In Search of the Elusive Semiotic (1977a). It is interesting that with respect to knowing, Gibson's position is very similar to the one I derived from neurobehavioral experiments. Gibson speaks of mediated "secondhand information" acting back on the mediate "firsthand pickup"; my experiments show that the intrinsic (association) cortex functions by way of an output that preprocesses the information flow in the primary sensory projection systems before that flow reaches the cortex. My conclusion, because of the preprocessing nature of this interaction between mediated "secondhand" and mediate "firsthand" information, is more Kantian than Gibson's. I believe the evidence points to a much tighter interweaving of noumena and sensation within perception than Gibson allows, although one might have thought that the thrust of *The Senses Considered as Perceptual Systems* (Gibson, 1966) would have taken Gibson in this direction. When Gibson says that knowledge does not come from anywhere within, but from looking, listening, feeling, smelling, and tasting, he assumes that these activities by the organism are innately unstructured and only become structured as a result of experience. I have already presented here some of the evidence that makes me suspect that Gibson's assumption is wrong, although I would not go as far as Lashley, who once told me that he believed there was no organization ("information," Gibson's definition) at all in the environment and that it is the organism's brain that organizes the buzzing, blooming confusion of the universe. I think the evidence that is subsumed under the theory of evolution strongly suggests that the extreme views of Gibson and Lashley are wrong and that both organism and environment contribute to that organization we perceive as information and image/object.

I think we can, as Weimer details so clearly, go considerably further. His systems approach to duality and symmetry draws out the distinction between causes and reasons. He suggests that within a system, *causes* operate; between systems, *reasons* (which he defines as invariance relationships, harmonies) operate. Though close, I don't believe this is exactly correct (e.g., though we might claim that atomic number makes the periodic table of elements reasonable, we also ascribe the cause of the periodic table to atomic number). Rather, I would propose that in a hierarchy of systems, when the scientific analysis procedure is downward (thus reductive and descriptive), causal mechanisms are sought. On the other hand, whenever our investigations are directed upward (synthesis) in the hierarchy (as they are in thermodynamics, relativity theory, and some aspects of nuclear and quantum theory), then—as in the ecological approach to perception—it is reasons and invariances, not causes, that are the appropriate relationship terms.

It is this looking upward that also marks the presence of selfhood. In "Self-Consciousness and Intentionality" (1976c), I present neuropsychological evidence that bears on the problems posed by Brentano (1960) and William James (1950). Brentano defined "intentional inexistence" as the criterion for selfhood. Whenever we can separate our intentions from accomplished acts and our intensions and images from objects, we become self-conscious beings, Parenthetically, Brentano stated that explorations of consciousness were the province of psychology that would not yield to physiological analysis while nonconscious processes were physiologically determined. In a prescient footnote, however, he added the caveat that even conscious processes would yield to physiology if Leibniz' Monadology provided to be correct!

The model I have derived for self-consciousness is based on the feedforward, open-loop helical mechanism. Feedforwards are created whenever the tests of TOTE units become connected in parallel (Pribram, 1971) so that each test biases the others in the network. Parallel information and image processing results in willed, voluntary, intentional behavior. Biofeedback is an example where, by providing an appropriate external monitor (the biofeedback), the internal autonomic, unconscious feedback loop is brought under bias control (i.e., voluntary control, much as a thermostat's set point can be controlled by changing its bias, the little wheel on top). Whenever attention can be deployed in such open loops, intentionality and thus selfhood result. Evidence is presented (in Pribram, 1971) that demonstrates some of the neural mechanisms involved (cerebellar systems, hippocampal system). Whether the model is adequate to the profound difficulties that selfhood poses with respect to the uniqueness of humanity remains to be seen.

CONCLUSION

It is also this looking upward that unites us all in the ecological approach to mental function. Whether it is Dirac discussing matter swimming in a sea of densely packed antimatter (monads?) or Gibson, Pattee, Shaw, Weimer, Pribram, and Hayek in this conference, we all share this way of investigating our subject matter. When listening to Hayek, for instance, I was struck with the importance he placed on the distribution of information in the marketplace that allows each individual to act with respect to the whole. Are we economic monads perhaps? Is the supply of money the hologram of the marketplace, and is the neural hologram the marketplace of the brain? Some quantitative studies using Gabor's mathematics (Fourier transforms and the like) might uncover some of the reasons why *Small Is Beautiful* (Schumacher, 1973).

I have said enough to indicate the reach of this new view of scientific endeavor. I have stopped short of theology, but Weimer is bolder and quotes Weyl with respect to the deification of symmetry. But certainly within the more ordinary compass of scientific endeavor, a paradigm shift in Kuhn's (1962) sense is heralded by what we have all been inspired to accomplish by James Gibson's provocative approach to understanding phenomenal reality. The new frontiers created by looking upward are not all in outer space. At every level of inquiry, exciting vistas, heretofore ignored and invisible, seem to stretch before us, tantalizingly awaiting further exploration.

REFERENCES

Anderson, J. A., Silverstein, J. W., Ritz, S. A., & Jones, R. S. Distinctive features, categorical perception, and probability learning: Some applications of a neural model. *Psychyological Review*, 1977, *84*, 413–447.

Bagshaw, M. H., & Benzies, S. Multiple measures of the orienting reaction and their dissociation after amygdalectomy in monkeys. *Experimental Neurology*, 1968, *20*, 175–187.

Bagshaw, M. H., Kimble, D. P., & Pribram, K. H. The GSR of monkeys during orienting and habituation and after ablation of the amygdala, hippocampus and inferotemporal cortex. *Neuropsychologia*, 1965, *3*, 111–119.

Bekesy, G. von *Sensory inhibition*. Princeton, N.J.: Princeton University Press, 1967.

Bernstein, N. *The co-ordination and regulation of movements*. New York: Pergamon Press, 1967.

Brentano, F. The distinction between mental and physical phenomena. In R. M. Chisholm (Ed.), *Realism and the background of phenomenology*. New York: Free Press, 1960.

Campbell, F. W., & Robson, J. G. Application of Fourier analysis to the visibility of gratings. *Journal of Physiology*, 1968, *197*, 551–566.

Freeman, W. *Mass action in the nervous system*. New York: Academic Press, 1975.

Gabor, D. Information processing with coherent light. *Optica Acta*, 1969, *16*, 519–533.

Gel'fand, I. M., Gurfinkel, V. S., Tsetlin, H. L., & Shik, M. L. Some problems in the analysis of movements. In I. M. Gel'fand, V. S. Fomin, & T. T. Tsetlin (Eds.), *Models of the structural-functional organization of certain biological systems*. Cambridge, Mass.: MIT Press, 1971.

Gregory, R. *Eye and brain: The psychology of seeing*. New York: McGraw-Hill, 1966.

Groves, P. M., & Thompson, R. F. Habituation: A dual-process theory. *Psychological Review*, 1970, *77*, 419–450.

Hoffman, B. *The strange story of the quantum*. New York: Dover, 1947.

Horn, G., & Hinde, R. A. (Eds.). *Short term changes in neural activity and behavior*. Cambridge, Mass.: Cambridge University Press, 1970.

James, W. *Principles of psychology* (Vols. I and II). New York: Dover, 1950.

Kimble, D. P., Bagshaw, M. H., & Pribram, K. H. The GSR of monkeys during orienting and habituation after selective partial ablations of the cingulate and frontal cortex. *Neuropsychologia*, 1965, *3*, 121–128.

Kuhn, T. *The structure of scientific revolutions*. Chicago: University of Chicago Press, 1962.

Lettvin, J. Y., Gesteland, R. C., Pitts, W. H., & Chung, S. H. A code in the nose. In H. L. Oestreicher & D. R. Moore (Eds.), *Cybernetic problems in bionics*. New York: Gordon and Breach, 1968.

Lettvin, J. Y., Maturana, H. R., McCulloch, W. S. Pitts, W. H. What the frog's eye tells the frog's brain. *Proceedings of the Institute of Radio Engineers*, 1959, *47*, 1940–1951.

Lettvin, J. Y., Maturana, H. R., Pitts, W. H., & McCulloch, W. S. Two remarks on the visual system of the frog. In W. A. Rosenblith (Ed.), *Sensory Communication*. New York: Wiley, 1961.

Malis, L. I., Pribram, K. H., & Kruger, L. Action potentials in "motor" cortex evoked by peripheral nerve stimulation. *J. Neurophysiology*, 1953, *16*, 161–167.

Miller, G. A., Galanter, E. H., & Pribram, K. H. *Plans and the structure of behavior*. New York: Holt, 1960.

Nuwer, M., & Pribram, K. H. Role of the inferotemporal cortex in visual selective attention. *Electroencephalography and Clinical Neurophysiology*, 1979, *46*, 389–400.

Pattee, H. H. Can life explain quantum mechanics? In T. Bastin (Ed.), *Quantum theory and beyond*. Cambridge: Cambridge University Press, 1971.

Pribram, K. H. The intrinsic systems of the forebrain. In J. Field, H. W. Magoun & V. E. Hall (Eds.), *Handbook of physiology, neurophysiology II*. Washington, D.C.: American Physiological Society, 1960.

Pribram, K. H. Proposal for a structural pragmatism: Some neuropsychological considerations of problems in philosophy. In B. Wolman & E. Nagle (eds.), *Scientific psychology: Principles and approaches*. New York: Basic Books, 1965.

Pribram, K. H. Some dimensions of remembering: Steps toward a neuropsychological model of memory. In J. Gaito (Ed.), *Macromolecules and behavior*. New York: Academic Press, 1966.

Pribram, K. H. *Languages of the brain: Experimental paradoxes and principles in neuropsychology*. Englewood Cliffs, N.J.: Prentice-Hall, 1971.

Pribram, K. H. Neurological notes on knowing. In J. R. Royce & W. W. Rozeboom (Eds.), *The Second Banff Conference on Theoretical Psychology*. New York: Gordon and Breach, 1972.

Pribram, K. H. The comparative psychology of communication: The issue of grammar and meaning. In E. Tobach, H. E. Adler, & L. L. Adler (Eds.), *Comparative psychology at issue*. Annals of the New York Academy of Sciences, Vol. 223. New York: New York Academy of Sciences, 1973.

Pribram, K. H. Language in a sociobiological frame. *Proceedings of the New York Academy of Sciences Meeting on the Origins of Language and Speech,* 1976. (a)

Pribram, K. H. Problems concerning the structure of consciousness. In G. Globus, G. Maxwell & I. Savodnik (Eds.), *Consciousness and brain: A scientific and philosophical inquiry.* New York: Plenum Press, 1976. (b)

Pribram, K. H. Self-consciousness and intentionality. In G. E. Schwartz & D. Shapiro (Eds.), *Consciousness and self-regulation: Advances in research.* New York: Plenum, 1976.

Pribram, K. H. In search of the elusive semiotic. In G. H. Bourne (Ed.), *Progress in ape research.* New York: Academic Press, 1977. (a)

Pribram, K. H. Some comments on the nature of the perceived universe. In R. E. Shaw & J. Bransford (Eds.), *Perceiving, acting, and knowing: Toward an ecological psychology* (Proceedings and Development of University of Minnesota Conference on Cognition, Perception, and Adaptation). Hillsdale, N.J.: Lawrence Erlbaum Associates, 1977. (c)

Pribram, K. H., Day, R. U., & Johnston, V. S. Selective attention: Distinctive brain electrical patterns produced by differential reinforcement in monkey and man. In D. I. Wostofsky (Ed.), *Behavior control and modification of physiological activity.* Englewood Cliffs, New Jersey: Prentice-Hall, 1976.

Pribram, K. H., & Gill, M. M. *Freud's "Project" re-assessed.* London: Hutchinson; and New York: Basic Books, 1976.

Pribram, K. H., Kruger, L., Robinson, R., & Berman, A. The effects of precentral lesions on the behavior of monkeys. *Yale Journal, Biology & Medicine,* 1955, *28,* 428-443.

Pribram, K. H., & McGuinness, D. Arousal, activation and effort in the control of attention. *Psychological Review,* 1975, *82*(2); 116-149.

Pribram, K. H., Nuwer, M., & Baron, R. The holographic hypothesis of memory structure in brain function and perception. In R. C. Atkinson, D. H. Krantz, R. C. Luce, & P. Suppes (Eds.), *Contemporary developments in mathematical psychology.* San Francisco: Freeman, 1974.

Pribram, K. H., Reitz, S., McNeil, M., & Spevack, A. A. The effect of amygdalectomy on orienting and classical conditioning. In Pavlovian Journal Biological Science, 1979, *14*(4), 203-217.

Rall, W. Dendritic neuron theory and dendodentritic synapses in a simple cortical system. In F. O. Schmitt (Ed.), *The neurosciences: Second study program.* New York: Rockefeller, 1970.

Rall, T., & Gilman, A. G. The role of cyclic AMP in the nervous system. *Neurosciences Research Program Bulletin,* 1970, *8,* 221-323.

Ratliff, F. *Mach bands: Quantitative studies in neural networks in the retina.* San Francisco: Holden-Day, 1965.

Rothblat, L., & Pribram, K. H. Selective attention: Input filter or response selection? *Brain Research,* 1972, *39,* 427-436.

Schumacher, E. F. *Small is beautiful: Economics as if people mattered.* New York: Harper & Row, 1973.

Shannon, C. E., & Weaver, W. *The mathematical theory of communications.* Urbana: University of Illinois Press, 1949.

Sharafat, A. R. Sensory motor information processing. (Unpublished Ph.D. dissertation, Stanford University, 1981).

Shepherd, G. M. *The synaptic organization of the brain—An introduction.* New York: Oxford University Press, 1949.

Sutter, E. A revised conception of visual receptive fields based on pseudorandom spatio-temporal pattern stimuli. *Proceedings of the Conference on Testing and Identification of Nonlinear Systems,* 1975. Pasadena, Calif. Cal. Inst. Tech.

Thom, Rene *Structural stability and morphogenesis.* Reading, Mass.: W. A. Benjamin, Inc., 1975. Inc., 1975.

Author Index

Numbers in *italics* denote pages with complete bibliographic information.

Subject Index